Family and Gender in Renaissance Italy, 1300–1600

This book studies family life and gender broadly within Italy, not just one region or city, from the fourteenth through the seventeenth centuries. Paternal control of the household was paramount in Italian life at this time, with control of property and even marital choices and career paths laid out for children and carried out from beyond the grave by means of written testaments. However, the reality was always more complex than a simple reading of local laws and legal doctrines would seem to permit, especially when there were no sons to step forward as heirs. Family disputes provided an opening for legal ambiguities to redirect property and endow women with property and means of control. This book uses the decisions of lawyers and judges to examine family dynamics through the lens of law and legal disputes.

THOMAS KUEHN is Professor of History at Clemson University, South Carolina.

Family and Gender in
Renaissance Italy, 1300–1600

THOMAS KUEHN

Clemson University

CAMBRIDGE
UNIVERSITY PRESS

CAMBRIDGE
UNIVERSITY PRESS

University Printing House, Cambridge CB2 8BS, United Kingdom
One Liberty Plaza, 20th Floor, New York, NY 10006, USA
477 Williamstown Road, Port Melbourne, VIC 3207, Australia
4843/24, 2nd Floor, Ansari Road, Daryaganj, Delhi - 110002, India
79 Anson Road, #06-04/06, Singapore 079906

Cambridge University Press is part of the University of Cambridge.

It furthers the University's mission by disseminating knowledge in the pursuit of
education, learning, and research at the highest international levels of excellence.

www.cambridge.org
Information on this title: www.cambridge.org/9781107008779
10.1017/9781139047692

© Thomas Kuehn 2017

First published 2017

Printed in the United States of America by Sheridan Books, Inc.

A catalogue record for this publication is available from the British Library.

Library of Congress Cataloging-in-Publication Data
NAMES: Kuehn, Thomas, 1950- author.
TITLE: Family and gender in renaissance Italy, 1300-1600 / Thomas Kuehn.
DESCRIPTION: CAMBRIDGE, United Kingdom ; New York, NY , USA :
Cambridge University Press, 2017. | Includes bibliographical references and index.
IDENTIFIERS: LCCN 2016040140 | ISBN 9781107008779 (hardback)
SUBJECTS: LCSH: Domestic relations–Italy–History–To 1500. |
Domestic relations–Italy–History–16th century. | BISAC: HISTORY /
Europe / General.
CLASSIFICATION: LCC KKH540 .K84 2017 | DDC 346.4501/50902–dc23 LC record
available at https://lccn.loc.gov/2016040140

ISBN 978-1-107-00877-9 Hardback
ISBN 978-1-107-40132-7 Paperback

Contents

Acknowledgments

It takes something like a family, and even an actual family, to make a book. Certainly I have profited from a wealth of relationships formed over the years in completing this endeavor. I hope all these people do not find the bequest I am able to leave them too paltry an exchange for the rich endowments of aid and advice that I have received from them.

This project truly began with conversations with my Cambridge University Press editor, Eric Crahan. His enthusiasm for it and the consummate professionalism of his successor, Debbie Gershenowitz, have made this possible. Librarians and archivists have been kind and patient beyond words – at Clemson University (especially the Office of Interlibrary Loan), the University of California Berkeley Law Library and the Robbins Collection, at the Archivio di Stato and the Biblioteca Nazionale Centrale of Florence. My colleagues at Clemson University have been a source of intellectual stimulus and support over the years, notably during my fourteen years as department chair. They also graciously accorded me a sabbatical semester in which I was able to complete the writing.

Others have stepped forward and generously read different chapters in much rougher versions than they appear here. Daniel Smail, Anne Jacobson Schutte, and Caroline Castiglione have been enlightening critics. Julius Kirshner offered trenchant and penetrating comments on my work, as he has ever since I showed up in his class in graduate school at the University of Chicago. This book is much better for those contributions, while its shortcomings, needless to say, rest at my feet. In the midst of work on this book we lost John Marino, friend and colleague, who reviewed the initial proposal submitted to the press but did not get to see the results and provide his always incisive views. He is sorely missed.

Real family is what ultimately moves me to write books about other families from another time and place. Children and grandchildren bring smiles and a deep awareness of what lies in and outside of books. My wife, Teresa, has lived with this book as much as I have, notably taking thousands of photos of printed *consilia* for my use. She is the foundation on which our family is built.

Jurists

Anagni, Giovanni da (d.1457) Canonist who taught at Bologna and active in politics there, until left a widower and entered the clergy, becoming eventually archdeacon of Bologna.

Bartolo da Sassoferrato (1313–57) Most famous jurist of the period. From a small village in the Marche, studied at Padua and Bologna. Took his doctorate in 1334 and taught at Pisa and Perugia, where he taught the Ubaldi brothers. Stunning legacy of commentaries and opinions that all after him had to take into account.

Benedetti da Capra, Benedetto (1390?–1470) Born in Perugia. Studied at Bologna with Giovanni da Imola. Politically active in his native city, where he began to teach around 1422, mainly canon law.

Butrio, Antonio da (1338–1408) Lay canonist, taught at Bologna after taking his doctorate relatively late in 1387. Taught in Florence 1393–99.

Castro, Paolo di ser Angelo di (1360–1441) Doctorate and first teaching post at Avignon. Also taught at Siena, Florence (from 1412), and Padua.

Cavallo, Pietro (d. 1616) From the Lunigiana. Worked in grand ducal courts in Tuscany.

Cipolla, Bartolomeo (1420–75) From Verona. Studied at Bologna with Paolo di Castro and obtained his doctorate in 1446. Taught at Padua from 1458.

Corgna, Pierfilippo della (1420–92) From a prominent Perugian family, doctorate around 1444. Political posts there during his teaching career. Taught for a while in 1470s in Pisa.

Corti, Francesco (1432–95) Born at Pavia where he taught from 1453, also acting as counselor to the dukes of Milan.

Decio, Filippo (1454–1535) Of a Milanese noble family. Obtained doctorate at Pisa in 1475. Taught in Pisa until 1502 and again 1516–28. Also taught at Siena, Padua, and Pavia.

Imola, Giovanni Niccoletti da (1367–1436) Degree in both laws in 1397. Taught mainly canon law at Bologna, Padua, and Ferrara.

Maino, Giasone del (1435–1519) Milanese noble birth, possibly illegitimate. Taught at Pavia, 1471–85, then Padua, and back to Pavia. Famed humanist jurist Andrea Alciato (1492–1550) came to study with him.

Mugello, Dino del (d. 1303?) Tuscan by birth. Taught in Pistoia and Bologna. Involved with Boniface VIII in the compilation of the *Liber Sextus* of canon law.

Pellegrini, Marcantonio (1530–1616) Venetian attorney and counsel. Born Vicenza, doctorate in both laws in 1558 at Padua. Became avvocato fiscale for Venice in 1576.

Ponte, Lodovico da (1409–39) Brief but spectacular career. Doctorate from Bologna, taught in Florence for a few years (1428–31). The auditor of the Rota in Rome before going to Siena in 1433. Later Alfonso V's representative at council of Basel, where he died.

Ponte, Oldrado da (d. 1335) Born in Lodi, studied at Bologna, taught for a while at Padua, practiced at Avignon.

Sandei, Felino (1444–1503) From Ferrara, where he later taught canon law (also at Pisa). Held various posts in Rome and was bishop of Atri and Lucca.

Sozzini, Bartolomeo (1436–1506) Son of Mariano the elder, began study of law in Siena around 1452. Taught in Siena and Pisa.

Sozzini, Mariano (elder) (1397–1467) Took his doctorate around 1425.

Sozzini, Mariano (junior) (1482–1556) Sienese, known for the *cautela socciniana* in fideicommissary substitutions.

Tartagni, Alessandro (1424–77) From Imola. Degree in both laws. Taught at Pavia, Bologna, Ferrara, and Padua.

Ubaldi, Angelo (1325–1400) Perugia. Taught at Perugia, Bologna, Padua, and Florence.

Ubaldi, Baldo (1327–1400) Born in Perugia where he was taught by Bartolo and took his degree. Taught at all the leading universities at one point: Bologna, Perugia, Pisa, Florence, Padua, and Pavia.

Zabarella, Francesco (1360–1417) Canonist and cardinal. Doctorate from Florence in 1385, where he taught until 1390, then at Padua until 1410. Made bishop of Florence and cardinal by the antipope John XXIII.

Consilia

Angelo degli Ubaldi, *Consilia* (Lyon, 1551)

Baldo degli Ubaldi, *Consilia* (Venice, 1575; facsimile ed., Turin: Bottega d'Erasmo, 1970) Baldo degli Ubaldi, *Consilia*, 5 vols. (Venice, 1575)

Bartolo da Sassoferrato, *Consilia, quaestiones, et tractatus* (Venice, 1589)

Benedetti da Capra, Benedetto, *Consilia* (Venice, 1576)

Bolognetti, Giovanni, *Consilia* (Venice, 1575)

Calderini, Giovanni, Antonio da Butrio, Girolamo da Torti, Felino Sandei, *Consilia* (Venice, 1582)

Cavallo, Pietro, *Consilia* (Venice, 1607)

Cipolla, Bartolomeo, *Consilia libri tres* (Frankfurt, 1599) Pierfilippo da Corgna, *Consilia*, 5 vols. (Venice, 1534–35)

Costa, Francesco d'Antonio, *Consiliorum seu Responsorum liber*, vol. 1 (Messina, 1629)

Decio, Filippo, *Consilia,* 2 vols. (Venice, 1570)

Dino del Mugello, *Consilia* (Lyon, 1551)

Giason del Maino, *Consilia*, 4 vols. (Frankfurt, 1609)

Giovanni d'Anagni, *Consilia* (1540)

Giovanni da Imola, *Consilia* (Venice, 1581)

Oldrado da Ponte, *Consilia* (Lyon, 1550)

Paolo di Castro, *Consilia*, 3 vols. (Venice, 1571) and *Consilia*, 3 vols. (Venice, 1580)

Pellegrini, Marcantonio, *Consilia* (Venice, 1600)

Pontano, Lodovico, *Consilia* (Frankfurt, 1577)

Sandei, Filippo, *Consilia, quaestiones, et tractatus* (Venice, 1581)
Socini junior, Mariano, *Consilia*, 5 vols. (Venice 1594)
Tartagni, Alessandro, *Consilia*, 5 vols. (Venice, 1536)
Zabarella, Francesco, *Consilia* (Venice, 1581)

Statutes

Aquileia

Statuta civitatis Aquile, ed. Alessandro Clementi (Rome: Istituto Storico Italiano per il Medio Evo, 1977)

Arezzo

Statuto d'Arezzo (1327), ed. Giulia Maria Camerani (Florence: Deputazione per la Storia Patria per la Toscana, 1946)

Belluno

Statuti di Belluno del 1392, ed. Enrico Bacchetti (Rome: Viella, 2002)

Bergamo

Lo statuto di Bergamo del 1331, ed. Claudia Storti Storchi (Milan: Giuffrè, 1986)

Bologna

Gli statuti del Comune di Bologna degli anni 1352, 1357, 1376, 1389 (Libri I-III), ed. Valeria Braidi, 2 vols. (Bologna: Deputazione di Storia Patria per le Province di Romagna, 2002)
Lo Statuto del Comune di Bologna dell'anno 1335, ed. Anna Laura Trombetti Budriesi, 2 vols. (Rome: Istituto Storico Italiano per il Medio Evo, 2008)

Colle Val D'Elsa

Statuta antiqua communis Collis Vallis Else (1307–1407), ed. Renzo Minca, 2 vols. (Rome: Istituto Storico Italiano per il Medio Evo, 1999)

Cortona

Statuto del comune di Cortona (1325–1380), ed. Simone Allegria and Valevia Capelli (Florence: Olschki, 2014)

Ferrara

Statuta Ferrariae anno mcclxxxvii (Ferrara: Cassa di Risparmio di Ferrara, 1955)
Statuta urbis Ferrariae nuper reformata anno domini mdlxvii (Ferrara, 1567)

Florence

Statuta populi et communis Florentiae, anno salutis mccccxv, 3 vols. (Freiburg [Florence], 1778–83)
Statuti della Repubblica fiorentina, ed. Romolo Caggese, vol. 2: *Statuto del Podestà dell'anno 1325* (Florence: Adriani, 1921)

Foligno

Statuta communis Fulginei, ed. Angelo Messini and Feliciano Baldaccini, 2 vols. (Perugia: Deputazione di Storia Patria per l'Umbria, 1969)

Forlì

Statuto di Forlì dell'anno mccclix con le modificazioni del mccclxxiii, ed. Evelina Rinaldi (Rome: Erulanno Loescher, 1913)

Milan

Liber consuetudinum mediolani anni mccxvi, ed. Enrico Besta and Gian Luigi Barni (Milan: Giuffrè, 1949)
Mediolanensium statuta [1498] (Bergamo, 1594)

Montepulciano

Statuto del comune di Montepulciano (1337), ed. Ubaldo Morandi (Florence: LeMonnier, 1966)

Padua

Statuti del Comune di Padova dal secolo xi all'anno 1285 (Padua: Sacchetto, 1873)

Saona

Statuta antiquissima Saone (1345), ed. Laura Balletto (Genoa: Istituto Internazionale di Studi Liguri, 1971)

Siena

L'ultimo statuto della Repubblica di Siena (1545), ed. Mario Ascheri (Siena: Accademia Senese degli Intronati, 1993)

Treviso

Gli statuti del comune di Treviso (secc. xiii-xiv), ed. Nianca Betto, 2 vols. (Rome: Istituto Storico Italiano per il Medio Evo, 1986)

Umbria

La legislazione suntuaria secoli xiii-xvi: Umbria, ed. M. Grazia Nico Ottaviani (Rome: Ministero per i beni e le attività culturali, 2005)

Venice

Statutorum, legum, ac iurium d. Venetorum (Venice, 1564)

Viterbo

Lo Statuto del comune di Viterbo del 1469, ed. Corrado Buzzi (Rome: Istituto Storico Italiano per il Medio Evo, 2007)

Volterra

Statuti di Volterra (1210–1224), ed. Enrico Fiumi (Florence: Deputazione di Storia Patria per la Toscana, 1951)

Introduction

Law and Families,
1300–1600

The period covered by this book was one of astounding developments and events – in art, culture, intellectual life, and the economy. The realities of family life were shaken by the great plagues, the constant spread of warfare, and the ups and downs of economic affairs. Family provided much of the social context in which Italians met these developments and attempted to cope with them. This was a period, as well, in which awareness of family and gender became more prominent, in and out of law. The "quarrel about women" became a literary genre, as did tracts about family, aimed especially at fathers. Images of the Holy Family and even scenes of domestic life came into art. Spurred by plagues and other swift messengers of death, the art of dying too became a trope and came to include making provisions for one's property, both for the good of one's soul and for the sake of one's heirs. Coats of arms, family surnames, and more elaborate domestic architecture came to frame elite families apart from others. Governments used households as tax units and generated bodies to tend to orphans and destitute, to widows and abandoned wives and children, to poor girls unable to marry, and even to the policing of sexuality and morals.

It was also a period of transformation in law. Law, while not changing at anything like the pace of economic change (not to mention the sometimes dizzying political changes), did evolve over the three centuries under consideration. Family law especially was not static. The varying local laws, overlaid as they were upon a shared, complex, learned legal heritage, were formative of domestic life and generated possibilities for legal action and thereby conflict. There were both local legislative initiatives, especially with respect to women's legal capacity, and, if at yet slower pace, academic doctrinal developments. Laws responded to the exigencies of plagues and depressions, wars and political upheavals. Leading this legal response and addressing the complexities and gaps in the various laws were the university-trained experts who took an active role in court cases, attempting resolutions to problems that they brought into view. Laws regulating marriage, dowry, property ownership, and inheritance underwent developments, whether from external factors (e.g., demographic collapse) or from internal (e.g., jurisprudential elaboration of doctrinal texts), that facilitated certain developments and precluded or hindered others. Continuity and change in family law, and the factors that militated for or against change are an important focus of this study.

There is no claim here that law is *the* key to understanding family life in the past, but it is one of several keys, and it has been more neglected than respected. It set parameters for much of daily life and it was integral to shifting those parameters. It defined the status and agency of the family's members. In that regard law served to distinguish family from household, which had and retains distinct functional as well as symbolic qualities. And family itself had varying extensions, horizontal and vertical, metaphorical and legal.

It is also necessary to remain aware of the different possibilities of law by class and region, although it is difficult to plot them in any exact way. Poorer people had less use for law, but they too used it, especially when land and other real assets were at stake. But any simple distinction in legal roles between wealthy and poor has to yield to the reality that a debtor in one situation was quite likely a creditor in another. City dwellers whose wealth lay to a greater extent in commercial capital and bank assets availed themselves of contracts and other legal devices in manners that varied from those of nobles with large rural estates and firm claims to political offices. Women, of course, had different legal potentials and experiences from men, but also from women in other communities. The truly poor had little to adjudicate (and could not afford the costs). For the rest, some tenuous indicators may allow us to peg social and economic circumstances from time to time.

GENDER AND LAW

There are studies of families for many Italian communities for parts of the period 1300 to 1600. There are some, as well, that are comparative and range across the peninsula. These are enormously useful. Their utility is recognized throughout the notes and bibliographical entries. What the present work does that they generally have not is incorporate an attention to gender and the exploitation of legal sources. Too often legal historical studies neglect the dimension of gender or simply accept the biases encoded in law on the assumption that they worked out that way in life. We will find instead that women were capable of circumventing legal limitations and of using the law to their advantage and that of their male relatives on occasion. Social historical studies of family have necessarily confronted law, at least to trace the outlines of vital legal institutions, such as dowry and testament, but generally without awareness of the gaps, ambiguities, and complexities that riddled the laws. The premise here is that law was not backdrop; it was formative, an array of possibilities for those looking to marry, establish households, and pass property to others.

This book thus approaches the historical features of family, kinship, and domestic life from two perspectives. It stresses gender, a "useful category" for historical analysis, as Joan Scott put it thirty years ago.[1] Gender (as a set of culturally constructed meanings loosely related to but distinct from sexual biology) was enacted first and foremost in the home in the roles of fathers and mothers, sons and daughters. As Cesarina Casanova says, in an immensely useful study of Italian families in our period, "in the interior of the house, in which the encounters and affections of everyday are lived, the real position of each member is configured as the result of a continual negotiation, in which male and female confront each other and there are put into question the values and models of comportment socially imposed on the sexes and the different age groups."[2] Every aspect of family life struck men and women differently. It is impossible to understand family and kinship in different areas of Italy without considering the variant roles of men and women in the different communities.

While sociological, anthropological, and economic perspectives on family play a role – as they necessarily must, having been at the heart of so much existing research – it is the more neglected realm of law as a second perspective that holds a privileged position in this analysis. That neglect needs to be addressed. As Lloyd Bonfield has said,

Law governing family relations seems to be regarded as a product of family history, and not a participant in shaping either its biological or cultural elements.

---

[1] Scott, "Gender: A Useful Category of Historical Analysis."
[2] Casanova, *La famiglia italiana in età moderna*, 148.

In short, family law surfaces in historical studies of the family only occasionally, indirectly, and tangentially, as a collection of rules to be obeyed or circumvented as the case may be; its origins and nature, and its role as an integral part of the family and its structure are not discussed in any great detail.[3]

Lack of attention to law as a formative element of family life is all the more disturbing as so many of the processes of family life that historians have explored, and the documents they have used to explore them, are legal in form, purpose, and language. This is not to say that the sources for investigation of domestic life in the Italian past are all legal, or even predominantly so. For Florence, perhaps the most prolific site of family history research in Italy, effective use of letters, diaries, domestic account books, and civic fiscal records has been vital. But study of processes of marriage and dowry, inheritance, guardianship, domestic enterprise, kin membership, and more is not possible without utilizing records drawn up in legal terms, mainly in the papers of notaries.

Yet it is not so much the records of notaries recording the legal business of families, of men and women, in dowries, testaments, emancipations, and more that is the focus of our attention. It is the very different judicial records that are of concern here. Neglect of judicial materials and of prevailing and changing norms can tend to overplay regular patterns of family life and overlook or downplay consistent moments of intrafamilial conflict and dispute resolution. Conflicts and disputes were a regular feature of family life, especially at pivotal moments when the membership and fortunes of a domestic group were in play. François-Joseph Ruggiu, in one of the few studies directed at inheritance disputes, was moved to speak of the "banality of intrafamilial conflicts."[4] Above all, inheritance seems to have been regularly disputed. Marriage was another legal area where disputes were common. Yet only recently has systematic use been made of ecclesiastical court records to see how some marriages were less than peaceful.

Conflicts involved emotions and interests and could take form outside the legal, but they had to work themselves out in legal terms and to some degree in legal institutions. The law is a separate domain, a "distinct social form," a distinct form of thought even that, especially in early modern Italian societies, was sufficiently ambiguous to give rise to recurring issues in dispute. Social life is and was messy, and so is and was the law. Law does not just regulate; it constitutes society with whole sets of

---

[3] Bonfield, "Developments in European Family Law," 88.
[4] Ruggiu, "Pour préserver la paix des familles," 139.

categories and relationships. It is a way of understanding as well as manipulating one's world. And in early modern Italy there was not one law, but several. In that mess of materials were various ways of comprehending individuals and families, gender, property, generations, and much more.

The legal dimensions of gender and the experiences of women in law have also been relatively neglected, in contrast to the attention that has been shown to other matters, such as sexuality and marriage, motherhood, education, religion, and work. A seminal essay on women in the Renaissance entirely neglects the law in favor of examining images of women in literature.[5] Three decades later a collection of 29 essays on women in the Italian Renaissance placed five of them under a heading about "legal constraints," yet one was in fact about marital love and two were about sumptuary laws. Only one essay truly examined the legal contradictions revolving about gender in a particular city.[6] Even a fine overview of women in medieval Europe devotes only six pages to law, despite the fact that it notes that access to property gave women access to power and that changes in women's rights of inheritance and property holding are the "principal key" to understanding their shifting social position.[7]

The general disregard of law in relation to gender can be attributed to two things. For one, there is an assumption that law was not good to women. In an account of women in the Renaissance, Romeo De Maio devoted a chapter to women's "legal inferiority" (in fact largely relying on literary texts), and depicted marriage as the passage of a woman from the prison of her father's *patria potestas* (legal paternal authority) to her husband's control. He bemoaned the "harsh illegality, contrary to nature" of parentally dictated marriage choices that included directing women to convents rather than married life.[8] His is far from a solitary position.

Closely related is the sense that law itself was and is just not that important in life (not to say boring, perhaps). History has taken a linguistic and cultural turn. It has embraced narrative again. It is poststructural and postcolonial. It is about metaphor and representation. And, after all, the realities of daily life and love do not proceed through legalities, except

---

[5] Kelly, "Did Women Have a Renaissance?"
[6] Meek, "Women between the Law and Social Reality in Early Renaissance Lucca."
[7] Ward, *Women in Medieval Europe 1200–1500*, 4–11.
[8] De Maio, *Donna e Rinascimento*, esp. 95–96.

of course at pivotal moments like marriage or buying a house. And neglect of law is also to a degree the fault of legal history, of legal historians, whose neglect of more general history and pursuit of arcane details and stilted language can leave their perspectives as an outlier in historical practice, rather than in the mainstream. And it is undeniable, in our context, that looking at women and family through a largely legal lens means that we will see only hazy aspects of them as wives and widows, and nothing at all of them as thinkers, as midwives, servants, or even as nuns or prostitutes. We will be concerned with property and power.

Equally it can be said that early modern Italian families were about property and power. They were certainly different from the families of the contemporary West. Studying them puts us in a world where marriages were arranged and their economic bases carefully negotiated. Parental control over career choices was paramount. And yet parents were not themselves uncontrolled. Testaments had to recognize children and leave them an appropriate share. Testators were not entirely free to do what they wanted with their belongings after death. Kin relationships, across geography and across time, provided an individual with both options and constraints, places to seek help but from which help might also be sought. In all of this, then, law was a central element.

Law seems to have a certain autonomy in western European societies, including early modern Italy, with its numerous law courts relying on written documents and procedures, in dense, difficult, and arcane legal Latin. But law cannot be reduced to simple application of a rule. Law, as the French sociologist Pierre Bourdieu saw it (and he was not alone), obscured relations of power and contests over it. That does not mean that law is then only epiphenomenal. Law operates in the social and judicializes it. Or, in terms of Bourdieu's seminal contribution, the notion of *habitus*, people know how to act and succeed in the particular historical situation that is the law. There is a certain plasticity and motion in a field like law.[9] The relationship of law to power is not to be assumed but precisely what needs to be studied.[10]

To take a cue instead from a historian, Renata Ago, who notes that early modern Italian litigiousness was the result of more than a failure to banish all ambiguity from contracts: "Recourse to the court cannot indeed immediately be considered as the sign of the failure of an

---

[9] Bourdieu, "The Force of Law: Toward a Sociology of the Juridical Field."
[10] Engel, "How Does Law Matter in the Constitution of Legal Consciousness?"

agreement. It rather is seen as a means to integrate or remediate a defective situation."[11] Which is not to ignore the prevailing ambiguities in law regarding ownership, agency, person, and family. In families in which law was so pivotal, such ambiguities broke out in conflict with frequency.

With regard to women and gender, law is doubly important, for while law took a lead in defining and disadvantaging women, it is also true that within law women were able to do important things for themselves and others.[12] Women could turn notions of their supposed frailty and irrationality, notions also enshrined in the law, to their advantage to gain protection of their rights and persons. Above all, while law defined gender in part by agencies and abilities conceded to men but not to women, women still had important roles in transmitting and preserving family wealth. Women and men, as various studies have shown, used testaments differently. Those differences had to do with what laws allowed them to do. To understand such matters, in turn, requires that we look at what law was like in Italy between 1300 and 1600.

THE LAW IN ITALY

The law at work in Italy drew on two types of sources, issuing in two types of law. There was what was known as *ius commune* ("common" law). This common legal heritage itself derived from several sources. At its simplest, *ius commune* was the body of law given sophistication and coherence and expounded in the law schools to be found in several Italian towns (first of all Bologna, but also importantly in Padua, Perugia, and elsewhere). Its major components were the texts of Roman civil law, excised and assembled at the behest of the emperor Justinian in the sixth century, and collectively referred to as the *Corpus iuris civilis*. There were also the texts of canon law of the Church, of more recent creation, assembled and released in different forms from the early twelfth century, and known in parallel as the *Corpus iuris canonici*. To these were added a few fragments, imperial decrees, and a collection of traditions covering what is widely referred to as feudal law. Even more, *ius commune* included the glosses and opinions of jurists who read the texts into a coherent system, or tried to. *Ius commune* itself was no simple matter of distillation from Roman and canon law texts. The *ius commune*

[11] Ago, *Economia barocca*, xi–xii.
[12] Wiesner, *Gender, Church and State in Early Modern Germany*, 82.

constituted a bedrock of institutions and generally valid norms (Venice was a notable exception to its reach).

Alongside *ius commune*, presupposing it, relying on it, but also consciously modifying or rejecting it in line with local cultural models and customs (some deriving from Lombard or other traditions), lay the *ius proprium*, or more properly *iura propria* (plural). These were local statutes and customs, compiled sporadically in each community legislating for itself, as well as intervening provisions and exemptions. Here is where a great deal of variety crept into the legal situation on the Italian peninsula. Though many similarities can be found among the laws of very different localities (and notably so in regard to women's dowry and inheritance rights, as we will see), no two places were precisely the same (even when, as with Milan, a dominant city's statutes were the basis of those in nearby subordinate communities). One necessary dimension of the present project is thus comparison of statutes from different communities, large and small. These are not always easy to locate, and it is very difficult to track changes in them for communities that did not redact new versions with any regularity (as Venice did not after 1244, or Florence after 1415). I have pursued these in a large sampling of those Italian community statutes that are in print.

The pluralistic quality of the law necessarily made for uncertainties, which in turn made the law into a field of doubt and argument. As a noted scholar of Italian family history has recognized, "the incongruities between common law and particular laws opened a space of uncertain definition at the heart of which arose conflicts that were resolved in a disparate manner, depending on the court and the judge."[13] Those called on to adjudicate these conflicts thus stood at a privileged point where meaning and enforcement, law and culture, were in flux. It is their work, and those moments and types of fluctuating meanings, that are our focus.

In the juristic culture that came to maturity in the medieval universities, what mattered was mastery of grammar, rhetoric, and logic, and understanding of the fundamental elements of civil, canon, and feudal law. Proficiency in local law was left to practitioners to pick up as they went. Students in the law schools encountered the authoritative glosses, commentaries, manuals, *consilia*, and all else that contributed to the *communis opinio* (common position) on a multitude of issues, questions, and points of law. They learned rules and forms of interpretation, such as

[13] Casanova, *La famiglia italiana*, 88.

analogical reasoning. But their professional treatment of local laws, even at moments when they restricted or argued to void those laws, served to enlarge their weight and that of the institutions linked to them.

The learned law was a written law (especially in contrast to the Germanic procedures widely used in northern Europe), with little in the way of oral proceedings, aside from the taking of witness testimony where appropriate, and little of the drama of an actual trial. Just about every Italian city was teeming with notaries, who for a fee would record in Latin the legal (at times also illegal) doings of the city's residents, or, perhaps better, clothe their doings in legal garb. In a real way it was the notaries who embodied law, at the junction of *ius commune* with local statutes. But there were other legally relevant records as well. Merchants' accounts, for example, were part of the legal record in debt cases, one reason accounting methods and private accounts were so relatively advanced and sophisticated in Italy.

Though the law often being applied consisted of texts decades and frequently even centuries old, that does not mean that the law was an unchanging backdrop to the lives of individuals and their families. It is true that statutory legislating (or the official amending of a commune's statutes as a whole) was sporadic. But tinkering with statutory language and crafting exemptions was a continual process in some communities. Statutes and other forms of legislation clearly changed, annoyingly so, to judge by frequent complaints on that score, which reached a more sophisticated level at the hands of Francesco Petrarca (1304–74) and later humanists, who were regular critics of law and legal professionals. But the interpretations and uses of even the older canonical texts of the *ius commune* also changed.

We begin our examination around 1300 because of the state of the learned law by that point. The great gloss to the civil law and the parts (most of it) of canon law, also glossed, were completed around that point. The canonical texts had been seemingly integrated into a comprehensive *corpus*. The era of post-glossators or *moderni* saw new and more systematic approaches to areas of law. Rolandino de' Passaggieri (d. 1300) of Bologna constructed a *summa* of the notarial art; Alberto da Gandino (1278–1310) penned a treatise on statute interpretation; Guglielmo Durante (d. 1295) composed what amounted to a procedural treatise, *Speculum judiciale*; Dino del Mugello (d. 1303) supposedly talked Pope Boniface VIII into adding a section on rules of law (*regulae iuris*) as the final title in his compilation of new decretals to be added to the body of canon law in 1298.

The so-called *moderni* of the late thirteenth and early fourteenth centuries began to look as well beyond the canonical texts to the chaotic and often ill-written statutes of various city-states. The more legal objections were raised in courts as to the meaning of local laws and their relation to the "common law" as a font of logic and justice, the more judges who fielded those questions turned to learned jurists for help. Such jurists thus acquired real power to decide, or at least influence, the decision of actual cases. The means they used was the formal legal opinion, the *consilium*, which examined arguments advanced in litigation and, relying on canonical texts, texts of local laws, opinions of great academic jurists, and *consilia* of others, offered a resolution. From around 1300, then, it can truly be said that "to draft *consilia* became the most relevant judicial activity performed by professors, *doctores legum*, and simple judges."[14] The phenomenon would grow throughout the period and reach its apogee between 1400 and 1550.

The transition ran to the generations of commentators who followed, beginning perhaps with Cino da Pistoia (1270–1336), but encompassing figures like Riccardo Malombra (d. 1334), Jacopo Bottrigari (ca. 1274–1347), Oldrado da Ponte (d. 1335), Alberico da Rosate (d. 1354) – but most famously Bartolo of Sassoferrato (1313–57), his students Baldo (1327–1400) and Angelo degli Ubaldi (1323–1400), the canonist Giovanni d'Andrea (ca. 1270–1348), and later Paolo di Castro (1360–1441) and others, some of whom we will encounter. In their academic lectures and in their *consilia*, they made attempts at harmonizing diverse texts, including those of their predecessors, who determined the *casus* of each text and sought the underlying rule (*regula*). It is no accident that the writings of these men were cited and treated as authoritative. They were systematic, comprehensive in many cases, and learned. As practitioners themselves they shared the same problems so many other doctors of law faced.

Also arising early in the fourteenth century, after the full elaboration of judicially driven inquisitory procedures, was a new summary procedure. Problems of procedural delay, which had become apparent, were thus addressed to a degree. Litigation did not have to be so lengthy and expensive. Statutes quickly adapted it from canon law. Indeed, one of the other legally relevant developments in place by around 1300 was the fact that it was about then that civic statutes began to be assembled in a

---

[14] Vallerani, "The Generation of the *Moderni* at Work," 153.

widespread fashion. Statutes included rules of procedure for use in local courts. They made formal litigation possible and gave shape to local norms and customs, making their comparison to *ius commune* feasible. Indeed, one good reason for them was to set out rules that diverged from the common legal heritage and to cover areas not in *ius commune* (including political offices, guilds, and regulation of public spaces). Jurists themselves had an active role in the composition, compilation, and revision of civic statutes and in the elaboration of judicial procedures. And all these developments arose in the aftermath of the popular movements, successful at least momentarily in many communities, in wresting power from old oligarchic nobilities, in the course of the thirteenth century. Jurists, notaries, and the rule of law in general thrived on the assertion of popular perspectives on city-states and citizenship.

The major exception to such developments lay in the Mezzogiorno, the Italian south of the kingdoms of Naples and Sicily. There educated jurists concentrated on questions of practice, including those more germane to the south, such as feudal law. *Consilia* and other practical writings drew their attention, but little of that was eventually published. Law there evolved on the basis of models developed to the north (and important questions were at times referred to northern jurists for their input), but local norms and practices were different for such essential matters as inheritance and marital property. It is difficult, as a result, to integrate the legal situation of families and gender into an Italy-wide picture.

The learned law and the legal profession continued to evolve after the great fourteenth-century commentators had erected their imposing and authoritative bodies of work. Problems still arose in practice and were discussed in academic and judicial fora. The appearance of the printing press raised new opportunities to spread and preserve important works. *Consilia* could be gathered for circulation, and major jurists had one eye to accumulation of their opinions into volumes, even as they wrote them for the different courts and litigants. Courts themselves began to compile their decisions, especially as some courts, like the Ruota in Florence, were staffed with professional jurists serving for long or even open-ended terms. Such judges became their own source of precedents, eclipsing the judgments and authority of those who wrote *consilia* for them. This process would provoke what has been labeled a "crisis" for law in the sixteenth century. Judges and courts had opened up more avenues to argue for the weight of legislation, especially that of the great European monarchs, but also that of many lesser princes and cities, against the common law and its interpreters.

The use of law in practice and growing litigation also spurred the exploration of different areas of law in monographic treatises that became even more widespread and useful. The publication in 1584–86 of an enormous collection of treatises in eighteen volumes (26 bound books), known as the *Tractatus universi iuris*, was an important moment. It marked the maturity of a system of law that arose with the professor and the jurist, with the interpreters of law, even as their influence was waning in favor of the legislator. The future would belong to the latter and ultimately to codes of legislation.

THE INTERVENTIONS OF LEGAL EXPERTS

Our study of families and law coincides with the heyday of *consilia*, when jurists were the pivotal figures in formulating judgments. They are our main source to understand the complexities of property, gender, and family. These texts are dense, difficult, and important. They are where the *ius commune*, local laws, and social practices all met.

The academically trained attorneys relied heavily on the texts and premises of *ius commune* that they learned in school, but they were no longer in an academic setting when acting as a *consultor*. They were not free to ignore local positive law, much as they might be inclined to modify and restrict it. They were operating and practicing in and among courts run by governments or jurisdictional institutions such as guilds. Their interventions in cases made and kept *ius commune* as a living force in society, but it was not the only living force. Litigants could craft their own compromise resolutions that did not conform to, though they might be shaped by, any judicial resolution handed to them by a court. Judges could be influenced by *consilia* and at times bound by law to follow them, but they could also reach their own conclusions. It is just about impossible to determine what the outcome was in any one case, especially if a *consilium* is our sole source. But *consilia* are particularly useful and fruitful sources for study of family and gender because they can allow us to see how much law both constrained and enabled peoples' actions. We can see what possibilities law opened up. Laws made it possible to preserve families and their patrimonies over generations. Laws made it possible to exploit differences of gender and also to elide or circumvent them. Laws defined who was married to whom and who was not. Laws defined who were heirs. They provided procedures to examine and resolve disputed questions. How exactly they did all that was what jurists had to figure out.

To make all the forgoing clear, it is perhaps useful once to see a *consilium* in some detail. Here in translation from the ponderous legal Latin (making unfortunately for some ponderous English prose, which serves here simply to impart some flavor of the original) is a portion of the Paduan jurists' argument in a case we will see in Chapter 1. The problem is the legal presumption of consent of a father to a son's business contracts:

I judge [*arbitror*] that it should be ruled to the contrary because the statute demands knowledge, consent, and will. And knowledge alone without contradicting an act, according to its proper meaning, is not consent and will, but a sort of middle between wanting and not wanting something, <as in> *lex* 1, in the paragraph *si tamen* and said *lex* 1, the paragraph *si is qui navem* <in the Digest title> *De exercitoria actione* [D. 14.1.1,22 and 19], and in the rule *is qui tacet* of the rules of law in the Liber Sextus [VI. 5.13.44] and plainly by Bartolo <in the Digest title> *Soluto matrimonio*, the *lex Que dotis* [D. 24.3.33]. Therefore in a municipal law departing from common law this case is not covered, given that consent would appear by means of a fiction, as is well alleged above by the *lex* 3, paragraph *hec verba* <of the Digest title> *De negotiis gestis* [D. 3.5.3,1]. For which argues that the statute speaks by a [rhetorical] linkage, which links seem to join things <as in the Digest title> *De legatis iii*, the *lex ea tamen adiectio* [D. 32.1.46] and its nature must fall between diverse things, as is noted <in the Digest title> *De iuris et facti ignorantia* in its rubric [D. 22.6]. Fittingly therefore the statute was not content with knowledge alone but demanded true consent and express will, and as it clearly appears, this was the intent of the statute, because in the first part, when a son stands as master or partner, it was content with knowledge, without contradiction, <but> where he stands as factor or apprentice it demanded more.[15]

As can be seen, the jurist came to this resolution in a roundabout and technical way, but also in a thorough and authoritative way. He had recourse repeatedly to legal texts, once to a jurisprudential commentary, and to rules of grammar (copulative expressions), as he played one portion of a statute against another. The texts latched onto for analogies concern activities different from (though at times close to) those in the case. In this way he comprehended the statute within the terms of *ius commune* while conceding it, as he had to, some weight. He was building part of an argument to the effect that a father's knowledge that his son was in a business did not mean that he consented to every contract and obligation the boy entered into.

Generally there were two types of *consilia*. *Consilia sapientis* could be rendered for hypothetical cases, in which case they were extensions of

---

[15] Biblioteca Nazionale, Florence, Landau Finaly 98, fols. 309r–20v, at 313v.

academic exercises. But by and large they were produced at the request of a judge or other official, on his own initiative or at the request of the litigants, who usually bound themselves to abide by the jurists' sentence. Judges, even those of learned background, had limited knowledge of local laws and could feel the need for advice. Citizen judges, as legal laymen, might have some degree of knowledge of local laws or not – but little of the overarching framework of *ius commune* or its interpretive mechanisms – and similarly could feel impelled to seek guidance. Dossiers with copies of pertinent statutes and documents, a narration of legal facts, and questions of law and/or fact that needed answering, were sent to one or more jurists. As one expert in dealing with these texts has nicely put it,

> equipped with analogy-serving passages drawn from Roman and canon law and supported by references to ius commune authorities, all held together by syllogistic inevitability, jurist-consultors nimbly traversed the minefield of statutory indeterminacy to fashion determinate case outcomes that enabled judges and public officials to apply the city's laws expeditiously.[16]

The result, if requested by or through the court, was typically considered binding on the parties. The *consilium* could thus provide a solution that had weight and might end disputes and litigation in a surer and quicker way. It is important to realize that local governing authorities, including those of guilds and other corporations, created and staffed courts and issued procedural statutes that streamlined and modified the fulsome procedures outlined in academic jurisprudence and embodied to a degree in ecclesiastical courts. These bodies welcomed *consilia* for their procedural impact, although they also had to face the fact that the legal consultants might contest the legitimacy and justice of the rules and claims of such governing bodies and corporations. Legislation to reject jurisprudential voiding of local statutes (as Florence did in 1388) was one result.[17]

Consilia were gathered and ultimately those of the most authoritative jurists were printed. Others, faced with similar cases, could mine them for ideas, terms, citations, and arguments. But it is important to keep in mind that *consilia* possessed only "normative authority." There was no system of precedent by which previous judicial decisions were binding in subsequent similar cases. It could always be argued that a better opinion might come along, and authors of *consilia* often signed their works with a

---

[16] Kirshner, "A Critical Appreciation," 20.
[17] Kirshner, "*Consilia* as Authority in Late Medieval Italy: The Case of Florence."

disclaimer should a better argument arise.[18] Legal theory remained intact, moreover, as practical exceptions remained on the local level and did not need to be "normalized."

In fact, most of the *consilia* thus gathered were probably composed not at the behest of the court but for one of the parties involved in or anticipating litigation. The aim of these *consilia pro parte* was not juristic truth, but advancement of one party's claims. Such legal arguments were delivered to judges who, however, were not obligated to follow their findings (and how could one if there were *consilia* for both sides in a dispute?), but clearly were open to being influenced by them and having at hand legal arguments to back the subsequent judicial decision. Such advocacy of clients' interests provoked denunciations of *consilia pro parte* and consulting in general for obfuscating and delaying justice, even by jurists themselves, let alone humanists and other vociferous critics.

If anything, *consilia pro parte* had to be more thorough, rehearse both sides of a question, cover all the relevant authorities, and systematically argue both pro and contra. They had to be persuasive and legally authoritative in appearance. Such arguments had to be fully "motivated" (explained and textually backed), whereas decisory *consilia sapientis* could be quite sparing and were well advised to be so, so as to be beyond challenge in any particular. Clothed in the dignity of the legal profession and solemn forms, the *consilium*, with its invocation of the holy and its subscription and wax seals in the original, can thus seem rather oracular. As a practical matter, especially as surviving *consilia*, more so in print, excised factual material in favor of the jurisprudential arguments and references, it is often impossible to determine if a particular *consilium* was *sapientis* or *pro parte*, as they were otherwise so similar. *Consilia* were cited as authorities and examples, "arsenals of possibilities," as Mario Ascheri put it. From the point of view of a historian whose interest is social, not legal per se, such *consilia* retain a stubborn anonymity and resist contextualization. We will be able to say little about most litigants in the cases we will come across.

Still, the texts fashioned resolutions to the patchy relations between statutes and *ius commune*. The jurists who interpreted the texts, doctrinal and statutory, were providing law where there was none (at least in terms of a statutory rule). Where the relations among texts were uncertain, where the actions of people threw further doubt at the meaning of texts,

---

[18] Ascheri, "Il *consilium* dei giuristi medievali," 255.

the jurists stepped in. Their vital accommodations made them cultural arbiters in a wider sense, as in the Trecento and Quattrocento *consilia* became a widely diffused mechanism. By then even the southern kingdoms began to see more use of *consilia* and their collection for the use of later practitioners, even though the courts there had judges whose verdicts carried some precedential weight.[19]

Consilia furnished what the weak political formations and their infrequent legislation could not. The plurality of sources of law made for uncertainty. The *consilia* seemingly made for certainty and consistency.[20] Jurisconsults thus filled a cultural and political gap. *Consilia* generated, by the second half of the fifteenth century, a more systematic *communis opinio doctorum* to cover the lacunae between the different sources of law and behavior. The common opinion became itself a source of law, embodied in the growing collections of *consilia* in print. Deviation from the common learned opinion was not tolerated in practice. Francesco Guicciardini (1483–1540), a doctor of laws and statesman from Florence, commented on the state of law in his day. While he insisted that the facts of the different cases made it impossible to apply rules simply and led to the accumulation of contrary juristic opinions, he also lamented that

the science of law has come to such a pass that if one side of a case presents a cogent argument and the other presents the authority of a scholar who has written on the subject, more attention will be paid to the authority. And so practicing lawyers are forced to read everyone who has written, with the result that time which should be devoted to reasoning is consumed in reading books.[21]

The results of such reading are evident in the sixteenth-century opinions of a man like Mariano Sozzini the younger, who will appear in subsequent pages.

In fact limitations and exceptions were conceivable on a variety of grounds. Opinions termed common, in fact, began to mount up in opposition to each other across the sixteenth century. Judges again had to exercise discretion, but by then many more of them were themselves trained jurists. Judges of prestigious tribunals were more highly regarded than the teachers of law in the universities. In sum,

---

[19] Ascheri, "Il *consilium* dei giuristi medievali," 257; idem, "Il 'dottore' e lo statuto: una difesa interessata," *Rivista di storia del diritto italiano* 69 (1996): 95-113.

[20] Rossi, "La forza del diritto," 38.

[21] Francesco Guicciardini, *Maxims and Reflections of a Renaissance Statesman*, trans. Mario Domandi (New York: Harper, 1965), 94–95.

juridical science in Seicento Italy, chloroformed by the uncontested rule of common opinions, lacking concerns to reform it on the part of political power, locked in repetition of a method without alternatives, stands inexorably exhausting itself in the shrewd but sterile administration of the doctrinal patrimony accumulated in past centuries, even if the ultimate effects can only be perceived over a long period, to total ruin by now apparent.[22]

Still, the common opinion prevailed because it provided, in the words of another legal scholar, an "endojurisprudential instrument" of certainty.[23]

It is certainly not the case, as one prominent Italian legal historian has it, that studies of *consilia* (including my own) "all deny the *ius commune* any important role as a law capable of a real effect on local legal practice or doctrine, and their historiographical evaluations underestimate the multiple valences and capacities of the *ius commune*."[24] *Consilia* were not only about practice; they were about jurisprudence too. They were where law could be both formative of practices and confirmatory of them. That is why they will figure prominently and consistently in our examination. But we also have to remain alert to the fact that there was not a seamless connection between legal theories propounded in schools (and undoubtedly taken to heart by students who entered professional practice) and legal practices in actual courts (and there were many with competing and overlapping jurisdictions). We can see how inventive practices and doctrinal solutions to them were. We can see how law constrained and at times failed to constrain behavior.

PLAN OF THE BOOK

It is possible to use the surviving *consilia* of jurists to understand legal issues in dispute and, to an extent, the behaviors and interests of the litigating families or parties behind a dispute. The core of this study then is the use of *consilia*, largely in the sixteenth-century printed editions of major figures, such as Bartolo of Sassoferrato, Angelo and Baldo degli Ubaldi, Paolo di Castro, Alessandro Tartagni of Imola (1424–77), Filippo Decio (1454–1535), Giason del Maino (1435–1519), Bartolomeo Sozzini (1436–1507), Pierfilippo da Corgna (1420–92), Francesco Corti (d. 1495), Oldrado da Ponte, Lodovico Pontano (c. 1409–39), Benedetto de' Benedetti (Capra) (d. 1470), and Bartolomeo Cipolla

---

[22] Rossi, "La forza del diritto," 57–58.
[23] Di Renzo Villata, "Tra *consilia, decisiones* e *tractatus*," 54.
[24] Bellomo, *Common Legal Past*, 81.

(1420–75), as well as later figures like Mariano Sozzini junior (1482–1556), Pietro Cavallo (d. 1615), and Marcantonio Pellegrini (1530–1616). Coverage for southern Italy and Sicily is more problematic for lack of printed editions, but the work of scholars such as Andrea Romano and Igor Mineo makes possible some points of comparison.

Chapter 1 considers the legal meanings of *familia,* house, lineage, *parentado, casato* (and other terms), and the distinction between them and household. The perspective there is more anthropological and historiographical. At the center of law for all these forms of belonging lay the *patria potestas* contained in *ius commune.* The boundaries of this *potestas* with regard to children, in the common law and in statutes, lay at the heart of Chapter 3 (in such subjects as emancipation, adoption and fostering, and illegitimacy). But before that, Chapter 2 looks at the legal dimensions of gender and its historical treatment. Here too the approach is more anthropological, but we will also inquire into the legal depiction of women as the weaker sex, in need of protection, subject to husbands and fathers, and yet also supposedly the greedier sex, quite capable of acting in pursuit of their own interests. Perhaps unsurprisingly, it will emerge that there was no single consistent and coherent image of women in law.

The later chapters allow us to see gender in action in the cases of daughters, sisters, wives, and mothers and widows, and brothers, cousins, uncles, and so forth. Chapter 4 considers marriage, mainly its formation but also issues of its dissolution, and many dimensions of dowry. There we consider the extensions and limitations of paternal power in relation to daughters marrying out and the legal relations of husbands to their wives.

Much has been done on the law of marriage, which was largely a matter of canon law and church courts. Where church rules of marriage concentrated on marital consent, and thus the marriage as a natural and spiritual partnership, and on its effects on the offspring, local law looked to the economic partnership, to its limits and liabilities, its formation and dissolution. Included in rules on both levels were gender expectations regarding roles as fathers and mothers, husbands and wives. Here some developments of dowry law may help explain in part the inflation of dowry values that many historians have pointed to. The costs (not just monetary) of arranging marriages, in turn, can explain the increasing recourse to clerical alternatives to lay married life among the wealthier families throughout Italy by 1600.

One of the areas of change in dowry law concerns the fate of dowry when marriage ends, typically by death of a spouse. Children's rights to inherit their mothers' dowries varied by cities and regions, but the fate of that property was too important for law or social actors to ignore. This is part of the wider issue of property devolution and inheritance, arguably the most important area of law regarding family. It certainly was the most complex. Legal and social inclinations to treat property as a quasi-corporate family possession had to deal with the combination, conflation, and conflict of individually ascribed property rights. Owners could be both singular and multiple on the same piece of property, depending on one's legal angle of vision (a woman's dowry was just one example, as both she and her husband had rights on it simultaneously). A father both owned and controlled family property and yet was a steward of it for coming generations, hardly free to do whatever he wished with the wealth in his possession. Fathers could act as more conscious managers of an ongoing enterprise of people and things, but under the heavy moral, if not always legal, guidance of humanists and other moralists, who devised dialogues and other inquiries into child raising, property management, marriage, and fatherhood (one thinks here especially of Leon Battista Alberti).

Chapters 5 and 6 thus delve into the many and intriguing problems of inheritance, the fifth in some general terms and in instances of intestacy, and the sixth in the more variable and complicated instances of last wills and testaments. The changes in inheritance practices, and their allowance in law, that marked what many see as a growing aristocratization of the leading families of many communities, is a particular focus of the sixth chapter. Some notable changes in inheritance practices, made possible in both local laws and in *ius commune*, most importantly the *fideicommissum*, permitted those who wanted to take advantage to limit inheritance (e.g., primogeniture) or at least preclude division and alienation of property. Heirs, however, had both legal options (such as the rejection of an estate) and legal duties, toward their ancestors as well as their descendants. Young heirs found themselves under legal guardianship, and governments took oversight of guardians to assure the inheritance against their incompetence or malfeasance. Among the guardians were mothers, whose presumed legal incompetence in other areas here gave way to legal faith in their disinterested pursuit of their children's well-being.

In Chapter 7, other dimensions of the legal relation between governments, frequently depicted in paternalistic metaphors, and families, come into play. State paternalism is one area most clearly traceable in measures such as sumptuary laws and other morality legislation (e.g., sodomy, prostitution), bankruptcy, and even criminal laws. States also provided the courts in which people could pursue their family-based rights or complaints, so paternalism was effective, or not, in those arenas. It is in this context then that we will consider more peculiar regional variations of southern Italian law and cultural variation with Jewish laws and practices.

The conclusion aims at more than being a summary of findings. There are important themes that need to be brought together. There is a long-standing theme within Italian history and in governmental policies regarding the failure of economic and political developments in the Mezzogiorno, which has been linked (mainly or most evidently by American scholars) to an enduring and comprehensive familism, with a consequent lack of civic institutions and values. If anything, such familism would seem to be more vibrant in the early modern period. Beyond any such "amoral familism," and more peculiar to our period, there are the observations of historians who see a crisis in the early modern family and its marital and inheritance patterns. To this theme we have to add the role of the law and its own amorality, if such it can be called. Above all, inheritance practices were enabled and condoned in the law. The stances taken by jurists show an openness at times to the desires of individuals, in contrast to the family, but equally tendencies in the other direction. What became a "crisis" of continuity and preservation for one family may only have been a successfully seized opportunity for another. One problem with following a legal source like *consilia* is that we do not see the successes. We see the trouble cases.

It is important to note, finally, that the approach taken here, from the perspective of law and further privileging conflicts, cases, and jurists' opinions and resolutions, leaves out much that is also important about family and gender. We do not consider women outside the family – as nuns, for example, whose fate followed family dictates and became more strictly cloistered after Trent. There are excellent works on this area and more good work under way. We will not look at them as midwives, servants, spinners, or in other crafts. We will not look at them as prostitutes, witches, or criminals. Our attention is on women's lives in a familial context, where gender stereotypes were lived and disregarded at times, where women were deeply engaged in roles seen as theirs and not, supposedly, threatening existing order, but rather embodying it. That means also that we will be viewing men in their roles in relation to women in the family. Further, we do not take into account criminal law in general or areas of public law and citizenship that involved men and their family roles.

I

Family in Law and Culture

At some point in the early fifteenth century (before 1415), a Florentine merchant went to court and initiated a lawsuit to collect a debt. It seems he had employed a young man, named Guglielmo, as a sort of junior clerk (*factor seu discipulus*) and had sent him off to Genoa for some time, during which Guglielmo's father, Raimondino, died. Raimondino had been well aware of his son's nascent career and had not indicated any objections to it. He did not live long enough, however, to learn that his son owed his employer the handsome (but not huge) sum of 390 florins. That was the debt the merchant sought to recover from Guglielmo's three surviving brothers when he finally went to court – Guglielmo himself unfortunately having died, though not until after a stint in Rome in the employ of a different Florentine merchant.

Why start a book on families and family law with a seemingly pedestrian suit over a business debt? Because this merchant brought suit against the brothers, we have to concede that this case involved family. They were heirs to their father and brother; they held the assets from which the debt could be paid. The case involved family then because law (being in this instance the statutes of Florence) said it did.

And there may be no more likely problem for a family to face than a controversy over debt. Debt was everywhere. Most regular economic activities were marked by delays in payment, by extensions of credit in other words. These credits themselves entailed further expenses to be recovered, and beyond the directly implicated parties there was another category of indirect relations, to those who acted as guarantors or sureties. By law and default, these too were often kin. Suits themselves were often less a matter of gaining repayment than about establishing the fact and amount of an obligation (very pressing if one feared a debtor's bankruptcy and possible flight). It might then be convertible, albeit at a discount. Credits established in law were more than a discrete economic value; "they concerned also a social value, represented by the relation with the debtor, by the restraint thus imposed on his future actions, by the implicit weight of the trust underwritten by him." Still, bankruptcies were all too frequent, and individuals in the end, no matter the final judgments of courts, had to work out what accommodations they could.[1]

A partial record of the suit survives in the form of a *consilium*, in which there is a statement of facts (the basis of the little story above), a copy of the relevant Florentine statute, and an attorney's argument in favor of the brothers.[2] When one examines a text such as this, a number of curious features spring forth.

One is that Florence had a law that held fathers liable for their sons who openly practiced a trade or conducted business. It presumed that fathers knew of such public activities and consented to them. Other activities by sons for which there was open and overt paternal consent and willingness also, quite obviously, incurred paternal liability. Fathers could deny that liability, if they wanted to, by one of two public gestures that the statute recognized. A father could go to the relevant guild that oversaw whatever type of economic activity his sons practiced and declare that he did not want to be held liable for his offspring. Alternatively, he could go to a notary and enact a legal emancipation of his son from his paternal legal control (*patria potestas*), which dissolved all legal liabilities at that point and gave his son the legal status of a fully competent legal person (*paterfamilias*). In either case, written record of the act was required and, with regard to emancipation, the act even had to be reported to and recorded by the major merchants' tribunal of Florence, known as the Mercanzia (later also to be reported to the city's governing body, the Signoria). And it was not just the father who faced liability; the grandfather or even (however unlikely in fact) the great-grandfather was also liable, as *patria potestas* extended from and through them.

In other words, Florentine law – and Florence was not alone in this, though it may have taken more extreme steps than other places did – protected markets and economic activities with the express assurance that families and their property were on the hook for the actions of individual

[1] Ago, *Economia barocca*, 58, 104, 148–50.
[2] Biblioteca Nazionale, Florence, Landau Finaly 98, fols. 309r–20v.

members. The family, through its head, was the responsible legal and economic unit.

In the case of the hapless Guglielmo and his brothers, the Florentine statute's applicability hardly seemed in doubt. Raimondino had not emancipated his son, nor had he denounced him to his guild. He knew of and seemingly condoned his son's activities. And it only seemed natural and right that his liability pass to his sons as his heirs (and there were other statutes and more general legal rules that proclaimed heirs' liabilities for debts on the estates they inherited). Moreover, there was another Florentine statute that quite explicitly bound brothers living together in mutual liability (though in our case Guglielmo had been out of town most of the time). Yet the most interesting feature of this case is the fact that the brothers found a legal basis to avoid liability and seemed generally to have been successful. The solidarity and oneness of the family, at least as projected in statutes such as this one from Florence, apparently had limits in practice.

This is where a second feature of law comes into play. Alongside and behind the statutes was *ius commune*. In the statute that applied in the case of Guglielmo's debt, *ius commune* was present in the reference to emancipation and the presumption of *patria potestas* that lay behind it, while local practice was evident in the alternative of denunciation to a guild.

From the *consilium* emerges the fact that the statutory rules of Florence were at odds with *ius commune* on some points, notably on paternal liability. An entire title in that part of the *Corpus* known as the *Codex* (C. 4.13) established that there was no mutual liability between a father and an emancipated son. The Florentine statute recognized that effect of emancipation, while trying to regulate it with record keeping. But the Florentine law was said to be beyond the rules of civil law (*exorbitans*) and therefore subject by general juristic rules to whatever restrictive reading the legal experts would fence it in with. Indeed, the presence of *ius commune* in the society, in the court, and in the minds of the legal experts is most obvious in the numerous citations to texts of the two main bodies of common law, civil and canon. As soon as the attorneys appear, so do the citations. But they do not simply reference the basic texts, they also reference the systematic gloss of the civil law, known generally as the *Glossa ordinaria*, which was the carefully collected harmonizations of different, at times very contradictory texts, devised by previous generations of teachers. And the attorneys also referred to more recent jurists, renowned teachers of law. In this instance, they cited Jacopo de Belviso

(1270–1335), Baldo degli Ubaldi (1325–1400), Cino da Pistoia (1270–1336), and mainly Bartolo of Sassoferrato (1313–57). One element of these citations, explicitly invoked in this case, was that there was a divergence of views (*varietas opinionum*) among the experts, to the point of admitting that the authority of learned experts was only "probable" and not necessary.

The *ius commune* was also evident in the persons of the three legal experts who crafted the intricate argument to limit Guglielmo's brothers' exposure. Raffaele Raimondi da Como (1387–1427), Prosdocimo Conti (ca. 1370–1427), and Benedetto dei Dottori (ca. 1385–1448/54) were professors of law from Padua. They were not Florentines. Their presence (at least on paper, because it all may have been handled from a distance) is testimony both to the cosmopolitan qualities of the legal profession and to reliance on outsiders as a guarantee of their impartiality.[3] Italian cities since the thirteenth century had relied on outsiders in the office of Podestà and later that of Capitano del Popolo to act as neutral arbiters of citizens' disputes. Simple mediation or arbitration by third parties was a common means of dispute resolution. Finally, that such distant figures could be brought into play in a case such as this was in no small way the product of the legal procedure being used, by the fact that it was a written procedure.

How then did Guglielmo's brothers escape liability for his debts? There was no implication that this debt was anything but real and justifiably owed to the merchant employer, who had been granted a quick and summary judgment against Guglielmo. The problem lay in extending that claim to either Guglielmo's father or his brothers.

From the facts of the case and the statute arose two legal questions. Could the merchant-employer seek redress from the estate of Guglielmo's father, Raimondino, as a debt against Raimondino, in view of the statute holding fathers accountable for sons openly in business? Secondly, were the three remaining sons, who accepted their father's patrimony in equal thirds, making no mention of their predeceased brother, liable as their brother's heirs? The attorney who entered preliminary arguments for the brothers offered a resounding no to the first question. The father was dead. That circumstance was not expressly covered by the statute. To treat the father as if he were still alive was to perpetrate a fiction, not a truth. The statute was not to be construed fictively.

---

[3] Kirshner, "A Critical Appreciation," 18–19.

The second question was trickier. It hardly seemed possible that the three surviving brothers could each hold a third of the paternal estate without subsuming that fourth left by their brother when he died intestate, without children of his own, and never having formally accepted his quarter of the patrimony. But, just as he had introduced the distinction between fiction and truth in treating the first question of the father's liability, this attorney brought in the issue of intent (*animus*). The three brothers could well want to acquire their father's property without in any way intending to have the estate of their brother (which had never been formally carved out of the estate by the legal act of *aditio*). There was a legal rule that an estate not formally accepted was not transmitted (*hereditas non adita non transmittatur*) to the next in line as that of (and by right of) the putative heir. Here the authority of Jacopo de Belviso was invoked on what was admitted to be an area of law where there were many disputes (*fuerunt multe contentiones*). The brothers were not Guglielmo's heirs and so not subject to the claims of his creditors, at least not beyond a fourth of what they had claimed on inheritance.

One has no way of telling if that quarter was sufficient to settle the 390 florin claim. That was not an attorney's province, even if it was foremost in the minds of his clients. It did not matter either to the three Paduan jurists who wrote the co-signed *consilium* on the issues. They conceded that the language of the Florentine statute had the father dead to rights for his son's debts at first glance. They introduced another fine legal distinction – that the fact that the father had not contradicted his son's economic activities was not the same as consenting to or wanting them (as per the quotation in the introduction). Rather it was a "medium point between wanting and not wanting" (*medium quoddam inter velle et nolle*). A municipal statute departing from *ius commune* should not be accorded a fictive reading here either. Not just the father's knowledge of his son's acts but "true consent" and "expressed willingness" were required, when a son acted in a capacity other than as a recognized merchant or tradesman. The jurists argued that that standard had to be met to make the father's obligation in his person, as father, become an obligation on his property (*in rem*). So the three Paduans determined that the intent of the statutes (*mens statuti*) was that fathers' heirs not be liable, as it did not say that they were. As the brothers had not lived with Guglielmo, there was no question of them being liable by association with him.

As Guglielmo had not formally taken possession of his quarter of the patrimony, it simply remained to enrich the shares of his brothers. Still it could be argued they could not take the whole of their father's estate without effectively taking their brother's, even if by an error of legal reasoning or even as a result of flawed legal advice they thought that they were simply their father's heirs. The three Paduan jurists said it was perfectly possible for the brothers to see themselves only as their father's heirs; their failure to mention their brother made all the more sense as his estate was no bargain (*damnosa*), and it made much more sense to think the brothers acted in error than to think that they would voluntarily take on a burdensome estate and throw away their property in covering its debts. In keeping with what they declared was sensible, the jurists were limiting the damages to the brothers, though they were not doing the creditors any favors. If a fourth of the estate did not amount to the 390 florins owed, the creditors were out some portion, possibly most, of what was due them.

Three things stand out. First, when one reads the statutes of Italian communities, one finds they are replete with terms and institutions of *ius commune* (e.g., dowry, matrimony, *patria potestas*, testaments, emancipation). In some regard the medieval common law had parallels to the common law of England and the United States, in that it was not legislated or codified but accepted and customary, though modified or even abrogated by specific statute. The glaring (but in fact only partial) exception was Venice, for the Serenissima explicitly rejected the play of *ius commune* in its courts, opting instead for wide judicial discretion by its native patrician judges. Still, Venice accepted *ius commune* as customary and inherited law in its mainland possessions, once it began acquiring its Terraferma empire in the fifteenth century. Of course, what Venice rejected was not so much the Roman law (part of its Byzantine heritage, after all) as the medieval systematizing of that law, which employed various devices of legal reasoning.

In any case, the law at work in this case was not a centralized system of rules imposed from above by some higher political power. The law, rather, was a panoply of negotiable rules at work in a variety of discursive fields, such as that of the case of Raimondino's sons. The way was open to legal reasoning to make sense of the rules.

Second, legal reasoning introduced fine distinctions that were not in the minds of legal subjects or the legislating bodies that drew up statutes, often poorly worded or thoroughly thought out. In our case, notions of fiction and intent came into play through the legal experts. But it is also the case that the plaintiff had to build a case, and in this instance had not built well. Other Florentine statutes directly dealing with inheritance may have been invoked to good effect.

The third element is how the law, or those who applied it, protected the family. The brothers inherited and presumably carried on their lives and their households despite the failures of Guglielmo. The solidarity of the family, while presumed in the statute, was not going to be the device that would be its undoing. Distinct individual rights of ownership and agency were not subsumed, here at least, in the wider corporate household. Guglielmo's debts were first of all his own, and the jurists limited liability for them to him and his property in the end. And from the case it would seem that women were so subordinate in that unit as not to matter. Daughters, unlike sons, were not assumed to be liable for paternal debts, nor were their economic actions projected to raise problems for fathers in the way that sons' economic activities could. It is true that some historians have concluded that Florence, at least in its legal structures, if not in actual fact, was a more misogynistic city than others in Italy. That is certainly a subject to which we need to return, but for the case at hand the legal disadvantages heaped on women in *ius commune* and even more so in local laws were not in play.

So, let us briefly consider a case in which a woman, or her legal claim, was involved. Here we turn to a *consilium* of Baldo degli Ubaldi (1327–1400), one of the most incisive legal minds of the fourteenth century. The case arose at Borgo Santo Stepolo; when it arose is uncertain. The facts recorded give it a degree of specificity.[4] Three brothers obligated themselves for return of the dowry of the wife of one of them. The dowry was to be paid by the bride's two uncles, who made a legal promise to do so. These were everyday contracts surrounding what was women's more important and consistent legal property right throughout Italy, the dowry. And when the couple wed, the woman's uncles dutifully delivered the promised sum of 380 florins to the husband with no mention in that legal instrument of the two brothers who had previously bound themselves for return of that same dowry upon the end of the marriage. When the husband died later, his widow sued his brothers for return of her dowry, notwithstanding the fact that it had been paid to her husband and not to them. Baldo was asked to determine if she could do so. He rehearsed a couple of arguments for the brothers, but he then reversed course and gave the truer (*verius*) contrary opinion that they were obligated. The payment fulfilled the condition for their obligation to take effect, even though it had been paid to the husband alone. The fact was

---

[4] Baldo, 5 *cons.* 417, fol. 111v.

that in the instrument of dotal promise each brother had obligated himself for the entire sum (*in solidum*) and not simply for a share (*pro parte*).

Here the obligation of brothers was direct and voluntary, not inscribed in a statute, but in a notarial contract. And here the dowry right of the widow was clearly beyond question. The operative effect of this decision was perhaps the most vital feature of it. While the brothers were probably also her husband's heirs, and thus liable for return of the dowry on that score as well, there was no assurance that there was sufficient value in his estate to constitute 380 florins' worth. By Baldo's reckoning the brothers' patrimonies were on the hook for it all. Further, their obligation was immediate; it did not have to wait on formal acceptance of the estate or an inventory of its assets or any number of other delays, in theory at least. As a creditor in the estate, the widow came off better than the creditor in the previous case. Finally, we have to note that the husband's death, followed by legal (actual might be something else) retrieval of the wife's dowry, meant that a putative household was dissolved. The fact of living together, for brothers or for spouses, had limited resonance. Household and family (in a wider sense) were distinct, if inextricably intertwined.

FAMILY

To ask about family in the Renaissance and early modern era, throughout Europe and not just in Italy, is to pose a frequently pursued question to which there have been numerous answers. Whatever was going on in families then has been consistently seen as historically significant.

Jakob Burckhardt's conception of the Renaissance as modern meant to him the weakening of extended kinship ties, as seen in the large clans or *consorterie* that were active in the factional turmoil that marked life in many northern and central Italian towns in the thirteenth century. Thereafter he postulated a progressive narrowing toward the nuclear family household and the development of the individual in consequence. His view was contested almost immediately, and especially so for Italy and other Mediterranean lands. A century later the landmark work of Philippe Ariès powerfully revived the notion of a large, disciplined patriarchal family as characteristic of the early modern period, even as demographic studies, notably at Cambridge, produced a contrasting sense of the prevalence of the nuclear household as the typical family residential experience.

Coresidential patterns have since receded as the primary element of family life in historians' estimation, although important economic and demographic studies continue to point to the importance of household.

We must maintain the caution that "the notion of family as a coresident group does not suffice to define it: without a precise awareness of its ties one runs the risk in fact of assimilating a truly isolated nucleus with a family in fact enlarged as a part of a lineage."[5]

The average size of households and their relations with others so as to form a larger kindred cannot be divorced from demographic factors. And it remains the case, it seems, that the distinction advanced by John Hajnal a half-century ago retains currency. The northern European family, he said, was marked by delayed marriage for men and women and a high proportion of celibates, while a southern European pattern was marked by earlier age at first marriage, at least for women, with fewer lifelong celibates and larger households. David Herlihy and Christiane Klapisch-Zuber relied on Hajnal, while modifying his concepts and thus cementing in place a notion of the Mediterranean difference, in their landmark study of Tuscan families based on the Florentine fiscal census of 1427. In another, more recent formulation, northern European households are said to have been weak, southern strong, including the so-called stem family, where the heir remained with the parents to take over the home and economic functions.

These studies have been nuanced by the notion of the lifecycle – by the realization that family changes over time with the natural processes of birth, growth, migration, and death. A household that at one point can appear to have a simple nuclear form (i.e., a married couple and their children) can at a later point be larger and generationally extended (e.g., as by marriage of a grown child, adding a spouse and their children in turn) and later yet reduced to one parent and offspring or even the offspring on their own (e.g., brothers continuing to live together). The possible permutations are endless. A source such as a census, for whatever purpose it was taken, can only fix in a snapshot what was an ongoing process. One of the great virtues of the study of Tuscany by Herlihy and Klapisch-Zuber is their awareness of that limitation and the steps they took with other sources to overcome it.

Too much research has proceeded under the delusion of a linear progression of forms and ideas. With regard to family these include a movement from a patriarchal to an egalitarian form, from the logic of lineage to that of individualism. In fact, families should be of historical interest not for their putative contributions to modernity (however that is

---

[5] Casanova, *La famiglia italiana*, 45.

conceived) but for the fact that they were absolutely central to life – public and private, urban and rural, economic and cultural – in the Renaissance and early modern era.

Other approaches to family have broadened our understanding of what family was and did. Its functions in regard to biological, social, and economic reproduction have been illuminated in various contexts, including Italian. The relationship between families and political power, the markets, and simply to other families have moved to the fore. Families as sites of socialization, including morality and gender ideology, have become well known. Marital strategies and inheritance strategies have been entrées to study of sexuality and birth control, education, material life, and domesticity. Running through many of these is a theme most powerfully stressed by Lawrence Stone, that European families became less patriarchal, and more affective, more a partnership than a hierarchy, as expressed in the raising of children (Ariès's theme as well) and in the arrangement of marriages by the spouses themselves, fired by mutual attraction (that certainly did not preclude social endogamy). This theme too has been contested, as the affectionate family, nurturing and protective, has emerged as more a myth and an image than a reality. Marriages and careers were dictated; schooling and apprenticeship, and forms of service happened in others' homes. Closeness was not fostered in a prominent way in family relations, although there were those who talked about it.[6]

Yet it is also the case that forms of intimacy and affection grew and flourished in early modern Italian families. We just have to think of these matters differently. Affection did not arise from a parity of gender roles, because there was none. Still, the protective role of the head of the family toward wife and children did not mean relations were cold. Stilted, hardly intimate forms of address conveyed respect for authority and the fact of social asymmetries of gender, age, and more; but the relations of interdependence could still have an emotional quality.[7]

Beyond its undoubted domestic functions, and in keeping with other trends in historical studies, family has been posed as a matter of meaning and symbolism. Tellingly, in his fine book, *The History of the Family*, James Casey opens with a chapter entitled "The Meaning of Family," which is in fact an account of pioneering work by scholars such as Frédéric Le Play, Henry Sumner Maine, Lewis Henry Morgan, John

---

[6] Gillis, *A World of Their Own Making*, xv, 17–18.
[7] Casanova, *La famiglia italiana*, 152–53.

Ferguson McLennan, and Fustel de Coulanges in the nineteenth century, leading up to modern anthropological treatments of household and kinship. It was their work that led to "the discovery of the family as a problem" and to the determination "that family is best understood as a moral system rather than as an institution."[8] And as a moral system it is surely also a legal one as well. And the moral and legal dimensions point to the world outside the family as well as to the interactions of those within it. As John R. Gillis has pointed out, in the face of the fact that only a handful of families had the resources to manage their own reproduction and sustain a household, families were dependent on others. This dependence in turn rested "on the ability of everyone to imagine family as something other than that constituted by birth or marriage." An imaginary capacity allowed people to extend familial roles to strangers and move into the homes of others.[9] Part of this imaginary was the law and its fictions of blood, adoption, parenthood, fostering, and more.

Specifically for Italy, it has become apparent how complex the realities of family were. Roman and Germanic, mainly Lombard, patterns and meanings mingled and merged in the Middle Ages. The revival of Roman law in the twelfth century, coinciding with the aggressive push of canon law into matters of sex and marriage, of guardianship of the young, and of the provisions of inheritance for the benefit of the souls of the dying and the living, further complicated developments. Feudal nobles and urban patricians devised strategies to preserve and enhance their economic and political power. Patterns began to vary between the communal north and center and the monarchic south and Sicily. In the north, a numerically reduced but structurally complex household, agnatic yet also open to collateral branches, emerged.[10] In the south, the narrow agnatic focus of families in possession of fiefs varied from the more diffuse kinship of merchants.

The centrality of legal marriage in the formation of families and the status of their members can be easily measured by the enormous quantity of studies devoted to problems of marital alliance, accumulation of dowries, and the dissolution of marital unions (by death but also by other means). Also prominent in studies of Italian family life is the attention given to the role of the father as nominal *capo di famiglia* and increasingly now to the processes of inheritance. This latter dimension of historical studies has led to the widespread sense, best and succinctly captured in an

[8] Casey, *History of the Family*, 11, 14.   [9] Gillis, 10.
[10] Leverotti, *Famiglie e istituzioni*, 137–42.

essay by Gianna Pomata, that patriliny (as a vertical linkage of fathers and sons, over generations) became triumphant in Italy, especially between 1560 and 1700, in contrast to a more horizontal sense of kinship that included ties through women (cognatic) and marriage (affinal). This triumph of the agnatic *casato* over the affinal *parentado* deeply disadvantaged women and younger sons who lost out to the heir in primogeniture, who took on the role of the progenitor of the main branch of the family. This patriliny finally lapsed into crisis in the eighteenth century, when more individualistic ideas began to strike at this corporate form and conception of family. Cadet sons and women began to revolt, even in the form of lawsuits, against patriarchy and gender orthodoxy of the dominant family model.

Such patriarchy, at the expense of the aspirations of women and younger sons, fits ill with modern conceptions of individual rights. It is hard for us to conceive how such a system could arise and last for centuries. Yet, as Robert Ellickson, a law professor, has argued, what he calls a *paterfamilias* type of household that controls its members has lower transaction costs in organizing its affairs and passing along its resources, while "ambient social norms" set some restrictions and temper abuses. Law, in other words, will tend to regulate the establishment and ending of relationships, as there is social interest at stake, and in continuing relationships when the stakes are sufficient against costs such as abuse. The modern liberal state, on the other hand, is little involved in household formation, and such arrangements have greater impermanence and informality.

So we must note the social limits of patriarchal household forms in a preliminary way for Italy in the period under discussion. Sandra Cavallo, in a series of studies based mainly on Torinese artisans, has insisted on the variability and multiformity of families. Not only is there an evident "plasticity of the domestic group," but the horizontal ties between households continued to matter. Among artisan families one can see sons having much more control of their futures and even of their simple comings and goings than a rigid model of patriarchy would suggest. Demographic factors and economic problems could render families unstable and insecure, and beyond those "the frequent redefinition of the domestic unit owes very much in fact to conflict, an often forgotten element in the too mechanical and impersonal image of family strategies that has often prevailed in the historiography."[11] Artisan families and houses were less stable, less

---

[11] Cavallo, *Artisans of the Body*, 112–35, 202–8.

agnatic, and less patriarchal than those of elites. Business ventures, debts, and risks were more likely to involve others outside one's *casa*. Above all, as Cavallo rightly insists, it is wrong to identify family with the coresidential group.[12] But what then was family?

FAMILIA: THE CULTURE OF FAMILY

Anthropologists have long grappled with such questions, although their interests are not posed so much in terms of family as of kinship. In a succinct treatment, Marshall Sahlins finds that kinship is "a network of mutualities of being." More explicitly, "kinsmen are persons who belong to one another, who are parts of one another, who are co-present in each other, whose lives are joined and interdependent."[13] He goes on to argue for the disentangling of person and kinship, for seeing "person as the composite site of multiple others," with whom the sharing of a common substance (such as blood) is neither universal nor essential but is expressive of common being.[14] His is thus a formulation that seeks to deny the naturalness of conceiving kinship in terms of a tree-like chart gravitating around an Ego. In this regard his work is importantly enhanced for our period by the recent works of Klapisch-Zuber on the use and dissemination of family trees in western history. These traced descent with an active metaphor of the streaming of some substance down the line through the years: "the tree expresses both the continuity of a line and the community of a lineage." If nothing else, her studies confirm the made-up character and chronological context of genealogical renditions of kinship.

Critiques of the genealogical model of kinship are not hard to find among anthropologists. James Leach has noted about them that they have built in "the assumption that the essence of a person is received, by transmission, at the point of conception." Each line in the diagram depicts a channel for the transmission of this essence. It follows from that assumption that a person's essence is given ahead of his or her growth. That is not the case in other cultures, where "land and other factors feed a growth that is hardly conceived as determined at birth."[15] Tim Ingold has contrasted the rigidity of classificatory schemes like the genealogy, with the process and open-endedness of stories, whose meaning is not pre-

---

[12] Cavallo, "L'importanza della famiglia," 87.
[13] Sahlins, *What Kinship Is and Is Not*, 20–21.   [14] Ibid., 28.
[15] Leach, "Knowledge as Kinship," 187.

given but must be discovered in context. Genealogical diagrams posit descent from a common ancestor that, in fact, could not and was not known to all putative members of a lineage. To outsiders a common name might suffice to allow them to identify a lineage, but that did not sort out its internal dynamic.

The vocabulary of family and kinship in Renaissance and early modern Italy was rich and open to various meanings. Resulting ambiguities could lead to confusion, but they could also be serviceable. Just looking at Florence, William Kent uncovered *consorteria, casa, parentado, lignaggio, brigata, schiatta, stirpe, casato, progenie*, and of course *famiglia*, in only the vernacular. To these could be added Latin terms: *domus, parentela, agnatio* and *cognatio*. Some of these terms point to awareness of the residential group. The Florentine Leon Battista Alberti famously referred to it as a group united under a single roof, or as a *famigliola*, a little family led by "a good and just manager (buoni e giusti massai")."[16] This was a residential group that could also be captured metaphorically as a *casa (domus)* or more simply by a roof (*tetto*), or by the image of shared meals (*stare ad uno pane e uno vino*). Yet there were no firm boundaries about this group, and the indeterminateness of the terms used for it shows that its size and complexity were variable. David Herlihy did advance an argument that the residential unit, possibly beginning in Florence, came to be seen as more affectionate, cohesive, as a refuge from an external world, including the government, that was increasingly seen as hostile.[17] His is a sense of family life that seems greatly at odds with the prevalent view of the harshness of patriarchy.

In contrast stood those terms pointing to kin relations outside and beyond the household, whether contemporary or in the past. *Schiatta* (stock), *stirpe* (clan), *lignaggio, consorteria, agnatio, cognatio* – these all pointed to a larger and more diffuse array of relationships. These are what Alberti had in mind when one of his interlocutors in *Della famiglia* bemoans the dividing of families, the coming and going through separate entrances, advocating instead that all at least fall under a single will.[18] But this family could also be imagined in metaphoric extension as the *casa* or *domus*, or the *casata* (the large house). The residence of one could thus seemingly stand for all; and indeed family residences figured, at least for the elite, as treasured properties to be held for their symbolic as much as their economic value. Indeed, it may well be, as Gillis has it, that whereas

---

[16] Kent, *Household and Lineage*, 44–45; Herlihy, "Family," 132.
[17] Herlihy, "Family," 132–33.   [18] Kent, *Household and Lineage*, 53.

"we think a family requires a house," back then "it was the house that required a family" to undertake the necessary tasks of production and reproduction.[19] If we keep in mind that the house was simply the key component of a patrimony, we can extend his idea to say that a patrimony demanded a family.

The pivotal term *famiglia* (*familia*) ran across this spectrum. Its use in different sources could mean household, small family group, or large family. Its very indefiniteness made it ever useful. A Florentine, Luca di Matteo da Panzano, recorded land transactions by his uncle regarding castles in the ancestral region near the village of Panzano outside Florence as proof that "our family used to have more castles and dignity" ("più castelle e dengnità avea nostra famiglia").[20] There he posed family in a rather grand and backward-looking manner, though also clearly including his own household.

The economic dimension of his *ricordi* is not a succession of business transactions, but the enlargement and preservation of a patrimony, and that, in turn, is more than economic. It includes the symbolic capital of family identity and honor.[21] Later in the fifteenth century, another Florentine patrician, Giovanni Rucellai, constructed an enlarged sense of *famiglia* for his sons as he set down the "descent of our family of the Rucellai and other pertinent matters to the honor of the house worthy of memory."[22] And what did Lapo di Giovanni Niccolini, yet another Florentine, have in mind when he wrote about his marriage and prayed that his wife "be peace and repose of my house and of my family"?[23]

Another pole running across the different terms for family distinguished agnates from cognates, and blood kin from marital. Christiane Klapisch-Zuber found an exceptional genealogy of a fourteenth-century Florentine notary that constructed his family's past in 1366 through an array of women, relying largely on his mother's memory, it should be noted. In the aftermath of plagues, such a memory might well be bilateral. Later, and for wealthier folks, it was not. A wealthy and prominent

---

[19] Gillis, 38.

[20] *"Brighe, Affanni, Volgimenti di Stato": Le ricordanze quatrocentesche di Luca di Matteo di messer Luca dei Firidolfi da Panzano*, ed. Anthony Molho and Franek Sznura (Florence: SISMEL-Edizioni del Galluzzo, 2010), 34.

[21] Valori, "Famiglia e memoria," 268.

[22] *Giovanni Rucellai ed il suo Zibaldone*, 2 vols., vol. 1: *Zibaldone quaresimale*, ed. Alessandro Perosa (London: Warburg Institute, 1960), 1.

[23] *Il libro degli affari proprii di casa de Lapo di Giovanni Niccolini de' Sirigatti*, ed. Christian Bec (Paris: SEVPEN, 1969), 92.

merchant, such as Rucellai in the fifteenth century, utilized two key terms, *consorteria* and *parentado*, to sort out his genealogy and describe it for his sons. His *consorteria* was detailed in terms of successive generations of men, privileging father–son linkages, traceable in most simple fashion by the cognomen, the family name, which was a delimiter of sorts for social standing (a feature of elites that only later drifted down the social scale). He generally left out the *parentado*, the linkage created by marital alliances with others. From that perspective it was important to remember what women had married into the *consorteria* (and who their kin, especially male, were) and what *consorterie* had been married into by one's own women. The links of *parentado* Rucellai memorialized in his genealogy were not extensive; they included only women who married into his branch of the lineage and only one out-marrying female, his father's sister. These were potentially useful kin for him and his sons as his economic circumstances were weakening. His was a narrow perspective from the later fifteenth century, fixed on a bloodline unilaterally running from his grandfather to his grandsons. The *parenti* represented a possible range of kinship. Though there would necessarily be much overlap, it would then seem that *parentado* and *consorteria* would be a somewhat different collection of people for one's brother or cousin.

Genealogy was indeed not a passive document; it made one's ancestors; it postulated a social narrative, which was greatly simplified when it took a unilineal form, while presupposing temporal continuity. In the vicissitudes of nature and of political-economic power, marriages, and thus women, served to make and renew blood links that, along with the wealth secured in the forms of dowries, redistributed blood, money, and power within an elite.

Historians have arrived at the general view that in the sixteenth century the family and its place in society shifted, for elites at least, to a more aristocratic model. Cognatic kin receded in memory and social utility. Marriage for women and heirship for men became more restricted (Pomata's triumph of patriliny). Continuity in time outweighed diffusion of kinship ties in the present. Preservation of family holdings, family name, and honor were rooted in a single line of inheritance, most so when and where primogeniture became the norm.

Much of this sense has been worked out on Florentine materials, where the rise to power and prominence of the Medici and the ultimate consolidation of that power in the aristocratic state of the Grand Duchy of Tuscany plays to that sense. Still, the situation that arose in Florence was not so different from elsewhere. Veronese families also had a bifurcated sense of kinship, agnatic and cognatic, vertical and horizontal. They too took pride in their homes and adorned them with shields and other symbols of family identity. Milanese, Venetians, and others perpetuated their holdings and carefully calculated their marital alliances.

Families of lower social status and rural families were not able to fuse themselves so singularly around one line of descent or were even in a position to worry about such a thing. The struggle to survive, if not thrive to a modest degree, made it difficult to hold onto any person or asset past its utility. The cult of family memory participated in by a man like Giovanni Rucellai did not fix a family structure; it legitimated his branch of the Rucellai. As Sergio Tognetti reminds us, "kinship cohesion was a very weak notion and quickly lost meaning when patrimonies and business investments were no longer united; extended solidarity beyond the simple family nucleus was characteristic of the traditional great house of the cities."[24]

Cesarina Casanova has captured the process of the crystallization of patrilineages for such "grandi casate."

The definition of oligarchic groups, more or less precocious, accentuated instead the importance of patrilineal descent: ... verticalized the map of kingship in reference to an honorability derived from the memory of ancestors. The conception of the prestige of the influence of a family group changed from the criterion of numerical force, of the branching of lineages, to that of the antiquity of the origins of its concentration and immobilization of wealth.[25]

This does not mean that there were not indeed tensions between the need to preserve a line and the other relations it had (tensions productive of lawsuits, as we will see continuously). But it does mean that

the bond among genealogy, power, and patrimony is the pivot of the social transformation in an elitist direction: the tendency to restriction of the lineages corresponded to the definition of an identity of class and the formulation of an ideology of honor that would organize social relations according to vertical modules which would change the meaning of marriage, the value of dowry, the system of transmission of property.[26]

It was in the course of the fifteenth century especially that theorizing families in a humanistic vein, drawing parallels and examples from classical history, became something of a growth enterprise, notably so in Florence, though not there solely, by any means. It is merely that in

[24] Tognetti, *Da Figline a Firenze*, 97.   [25] Casanova, *La famiglia italiana*, 48.
[26] Ibid., 56–57.

Florence, there was the implication of family in a still fluid, even turbulent, political and economic situation, which furnished a highly creative context. The Florentine Alberti was certainly not beyond embedding critical stances on patriarchy and patriliny in his works, but he also managed to idealize family as a social element and fathers as vital to it.[27] Alberti's viewpoints (or those of his interlocutors) became influential through a partial version circulated as the work of a Pandolfini and came to influence the introspective musings of Giovanni Rucellai, as death approached and his fortune dwindled. In these visions, the formative moment for a family was marriage. Matteo Palmieri, yet another Florentine, envisioned the city as an amalgam of lineages interconnected by marriages in his *Vita civile*.[28] But these were also obviously families under paternal control, whose sons were to follow unquestioningly paternal dictates not just on marriage but on residence, dress, travel – matters not of moral concern, but family patterns that bespoke an enlarged notion of paternal authority in the moral education of children. "It was in the family that one learned to submit to the authority of governments."[29]

The most widely circulated portion of Alberti's *Della famiglia* was its third book, given the separate title *Economicus* and its own dedicatory preface. It presented the good *paterfamilias*, the key to whose proper management was a moralistic middle path between avarice and prodigality, termed *masserizia*. The dialogue considers thrift and the use of time, honor, public offices, and much more an astute *paterfamilias* had to take into account. In the same vein, Marsilio Ficino said it was necessary that the *casa* be "sufficiently provided with money and possessions for a good and honest life."[30] The image of the provident *capo di famiglia* directing wife and children, servants and property, would become a staple of a growing body of treatises published and circulated in the course of the sixteenth and seventeenth centuries. These treatises gave shape to a notional "ragion di famiglia" – a dedication of the family head and all its members to the overriding imperative to preserve family continuity, including status, honor, and wealth. That dedication, in turn, required the adoption of strategies, assuming the cooperation of those within the family and the hostility, or at least indifference, of those outside. Failure to manage property, tendencies to prodigality, to neglect family honor

---

[27] Leon Battista Alberti, *The Family in Renaissance Florence*, trans. Renée Neu Watkins (Columbia: University of South Carolina Press, 1969), esp. 30.

[28] Matteo Palmieri, *Vita civile*, ed. Gino Belloni (Florence: Sansoni, 1982), 159–62.

[29] Cavallo, "Family Relationships," 17. [30] Kent, 47.

and utility, became the hallmarks of insanity (a sort of "irragion di famiglia"). Here too is the broader cultural presumption of family solidarity that lay behind legislators' extension of liabilities among fathers and sons and brothers with which we began this chapter.

Hence we arrive at the dominant historical image of families in Italy in the early modern era:

We know that the image of the family in the modern era and among the aristocratic classes was that constituted by the corporate family, of clear Aristotelian influence, founded on the 'natural' principle of submission of the wife to the husband and of children to the father, and accompanied by measures like *fedecommessi* and primogeniture, intended to create dynasties, preserving the unity between a name, a line of descent, and an undivided patrimony. Fine language of theologians and jurists of the time, the superior goal of 'safeguarding agnation,' justified the fact of sacrifice of the rights of women and cadets; the prerogatives of the corporation in its entirety 'naturally' had precedence on those of its single members. However, even in the epoch and in the surroundings that had seen its greatest splendor, the agnatic system never arrived at perfection: too many are the contradictions that crossed it, be it on the practical level or the theoretical.[31]

It may not, in fact, be quite accurate to think of families and lineages as corporate (*famiglia-corpo* is Ago's term). Though there were plenty of occasions when a kindred might indeed seem to be corporate, to be "one person," events such as the legal case with which we began this chapter caution us that on the matter of property ownership the nature of the family is ambiguous. There were plenty of areas of interactions in the offices and markets, in the streets and piazzas, in the churches and courtrooms, where at best families emerge to our eyes as more nebulous kindreds, as federations of related persons and households that could become quite loose at times. It is the fact that the convergence of agnatic ideology and patrimonial practices was never complete that opens up to analysis so much of family life. The individualistic tendencies in law, to project the legal person as in possession of himself and his acts (*dominium sui*), ran up against the model of society founded on families that precluded much of any legal autonomy.

Choosing a wife, carefully raising one's children, managing property and relations with others (kin, neighbors, friends, and partners) – all that lay at the heart of the family as elaborated by such thinkers. From such a basis it was not a simple matter to delineate the boundaries of family. The

[31] Ago, "Ruoli familiari," 112–13.

array of terms in use – *casa*, *domus*, *familia*, *agnatio*, *casato*, *parentado*, and more – were used often synonymously, though not taken as exactly congruent. Total precision was unnecessary, as families changed constantly with each birth, marriage, and death, as well as every economic change. But it is striking that the expressions of family found in the culture do not generally take off from the same starting point as legal definitions of family.

SOME EXAMPLES

The experiences of actual families, as one might expect, lay somewhere between cultural norms, legal rules, demographic realities, and ever-changing markets. A few examples are in order. The Florentine family of the Ciurianni (six men, in fact) kept a succession of account books and family memorials across more than a century, 1326 to 1429. This rare collection allows tracking across generations. Families that kept accounts had something to keep track of. The Ciurianni books begin, however, by recording the repudiation of an inheritance by two young sons, who effectively found themselves heirs to over 1,300 florins of debt. Hardly an auspicious beginning; by 1339, with property now in the hands of a younger brother, there was a division of property, definitively separating the branch of Lapo di Valore from the cadet branch of Rinieri di Valore. The head of the first branch, Barna di Valorino, relied on marital kin for start-up capital. In the aftermath of the great plague of 1348, Barna saw the liquidation of assets to retire the considerable debts owed to one member of the powerful Strozzi lineage that had occupied family accounts for years.

At the heart of the family patrimony was a rural estate, called Il Monte del Salvatico, acquired in fact in 1311 from the assets of a formerly great family that had gone bankrupt. Terms like *castello* or *palagio* were used to convey a sense of pride in this holding. In fact marital kin had helped obtain this property, which had not been inherited but became the center piece of family strategies, especially inheritance. The rural estate fell to Barna's branch in the division of 1339, which appears to have been a rancorous occasion following on a decade of bickering since his grandfather's bankruptcy, which opened the family accounts.

So by 1351 Barna had lost most of what he had inherited in paying off debts, and he continued to face losses into 1360. Thereafter he embarked on a remarkable "refoundation" of the patrimony, which hinged on reclaiming the ancestral Torri del Leone in Florence, starting from an arbitration settlement in 1362. Barna restored material and symbolic coherence to his branch of the Ciurianni. One step in that was marrying a daughter from the Frescobaldi, another old lineage in financial distress, and taking a farm as a modest dowry and investing in it. Again and again he relied on his marital kin, not agnatic kin, in his dealings. To the family fortune, "which owed not a little to the wealth of the women entered into the family with their dowries," were added the dowries of grandmothers and mother, which were never "returned," as Barna was heir to them. More than half the value of the family's holdings in 1385 came from three dowries.

Barna's son, Valorino, oversaw the estate with different strategies. His daughters died before he could invest in marriages with them. Of his four sons, he only arranged marriage for the oldest, Lapozzo, and then only at the relatively late age of 35. Conflict with the younger sons was a probably inevitable part of this. Valorino died in 1429, and his children all succumbed in the next months. Despite careful efforts, the patrimony ended up dispersed in legacies and probably repayment of debts. Enduring patrimonial survival was a failed goal.

In the fifteenth century, we can follow the fate of a family begun by a Cypriot immigrant to Florence, Giorgio di Baliano di Flatro (c.1440–97). He came with an occupation as a medical doctor and with ambition. He quickly accumulated a fortune, married a woman from the important and extensive Bardi lineage, and built the basis for a line of descent to continue. Here again we see the importance of marital alignments that brought one allies in another family. Beyond his own marriage with a Bardi, it was pivotal that he married his eldest daughter to a member of the wealthy Aldobrandini, a lawyer, who was able to use his legal expertise in aiding Giorgio's widow in managing the patrimony after his untimely death. Giorgio also moved to acquire landed properties in the city and to invest in them, to dress them out as more imposing structures. Then he turned to purchasing rural properties.

His widow was the one who held it all together for the children, in difficult and tumultuous times. She stood out for "her capacity to interpret to best effect her traditional role but also to descend, if necessary, into that totally new and different role of 'padrone' of the house, to take care of the interests of the heir without giving the impression of being a passive instrument." The children, however, would quickly dissipate the built-up fortune, in part perhaps because they had no practical experience in accumulating it.

A similar trajectory struck the family and patrimony left by Jacopo Peri (1561–1633), the man credited with devising the first opera, in the seventeenth century. Here too marital kin played an important role. As was the case with the Ciurianni and Flatri, careful testamentary provisions were used to direct the estate to children. In Peri's case, his will specified the exact division of assets among his six sons, each equal. There was also a trust device, a *fedecommesso*, ordering his property be held as inalienable, which was not yet something seen much in earlier wills (not in the Ciurianni's, for sure), although they were familiar with one element of the trust, the naming of substitute heirs should the first heirs die or not have children of their own. Careful accounting of credits and debts was part of the daily reality of families. As happened with the Ciurianni, however, demography was not kind to the Peri, so only one son remained in 1640 and he fell afoul of the law. Jacopo Peri's widow carried on and willed her property to her brother.

These three examples all hail from Florence, it is true, but theirs are stories replicated again and again elsewhere. Lines of descent failed, and others arose. Management of property, both in terms of day-to-day transactions and in terms of careful legal strategies proceeded with an eye to preserving holdings and passing them along, while also using them to the honor and reputation of the family. Landed possessions were symbolic as well as real. Marriages were vital moments. Daughters received what fell to them (or their husbands did) around the time of marriage. Sons, while possibly using family assets in business (as it was assumed Guglielmo had), had to wait for inheritance to see the largest single transference of wealth in their direction. Legal devices, such as arbitrations or even litigation, served to define rights, affect divisions of assets, resolve debts. These were the moments when aspects of law related to family came to the fore.

FAMILIA IN LAW

"A monolithic legal system, let alone a discrete and internally coherent body of family law, did not exist in the Renaissance," Julius Kirshner has reminded us.[32] Along those lines, the esteemed Italian legal historian Giulio Vismara, in an extensive essay over fifty years ago, noted that there was no legal definition of family. In its essence as a social fact, as the

---

[32] Kirshner, "Family and Marriage," 84.

basic unit of society ("celula di base") with political and legal functions and affective intimacy, family was a metajuridical concept. Vismara went on to postulate that for fifteen centuries following the fall of Rome the historical reality of family changed little from a patriarchal social group. Against this "staticità" he did see some minor movements, the resting of family "unity" not only on being subject to the power of the head of family (as in Roman law) but to being resident under one roof. It was in the Renaissance, he says, that family solidarity was felt and practiced from a preoccupation "to save the unity of the family patrimony, to conserve for the family the goods in their unity. But the family identified itself then with descent, and thus with the name, with the ancestral symbol of the immortality of the house." This led to practices such as primogeniture and fideicommissary trusts and produced a family that was a little monarchy, whose unity was effectively sacrificed to continuity in wealth and power.

There is much from Vismara's essay that remains common among historians – the sense of the rigidity and unity of the family, its patriarchy, its marriages as negotiated alliances of two families, the subordination of individuals to family prerogatives. This vision, however, is too rigid. There was more flexibility within families and in the elements of law touching on them. There were opportunities for the expression of individual interests and goals, by children and by women. Social agents, notably jurists, were able to temper patriarchy's harsh edges. Law, beyond being a powerful engine for patriarchy, was also a means around it, especially in the multilayered law at work between 1300 and 1600.

The process began with the legal heritage of Rome. As Laurent Waelkens explains, in Roman law a person (*persona*, literally mask) was one who appeared in court on his own behalf or on that of others dependent on and subordinate to him. One who appeared to defend others, who had liability for them and their goods, was a *pater*, and they were his *familia*. If one lived alone, that person was still a *familia*, and that included women who managed a business and thus had a *familia* of their own. "The family did not originate in marriage, but in civil liability."

Moreover, there was no single subjective right vested in the head of a family. Different terms, different limits, were set on different objects of domestic control. Power over sons was not the same as over daughters, not the same as that relating to a wife, let alone power over one's slaves and other possessions. There were limits to these powers. Perhaps the least limited, in theory, were the rights of ownership (*dominium*), which vitally included the power to alienate one's property by sale, gift, will, or

other device. One of the few areas where real limitations were in place
was that of wills. Wills that were irresponsible to the family could be
overturned. Wills that consumed the estate in legacies had to be adjusted
to leave at least a quarter to the heirs. And any dynastic urge to keep
property in a family was limited in law (to four generations by Justinian),
until the period we are considering. It was in the Middle Ages, through
the Church's emphasis on the sacramentality of marriage (in which two
became one flesh) that canonists reinterpreted Roman law, conflating
different types of cohabitation with different liabilities and property
implications. Notions of "blood" as a substantial essence of kinship
entered the discourse. Then there arose a single legal persona, as opposed
to different transactional personae. Those trained in the civil law, while
they could comprehend the ecclesiastical emphasis on consent and sacramentality of marriage, still dealt with texts that treated *familia* as a matter
of liabilities. They still faced the legal consequence that when a
paterfamilias died his *familia* ceased and his property was dispersed on
intestacy to his "legitimate" heirs, each son now *paterfamilias* in his
own right.

In Rome *familia* was linked to durable assets that belonged to a person,
which included slaves (*famuli*). In that sense it was the economic where-
withal of a *pater*, who also held his property and slaves in subordination.
But *familia* was also tied to place, so a *pater* with dispersed holdings could
have several *familiae*. In that sense *familia* encompassed a house and
those in it, free or slave: *familiares* sharing *familiaritas*. Another sense of
familia was that of a group of relatives. Blood relationship in Roman law
was bilineal, described in terms of *agnati* and *cognati*; *agnati* traced a line
of *potestates*, the power of the *paterfamilias*. Roman society and its law
revolved around agnation. Cognation was the wider category and by the
time of Justinian, cognates were accorded rights of inheritance over more
distant agnates. Cognation included by definition all relations traced
through women or otherwise falling outside the realm of *potestas*.
Consanguinei came to refer to all sorts of relatives, although by the
fourteenth century renewed emphasis on blood deflected attention from
the marital relationship to generational transmission of belonging.

The authoritarian and patrimonial dimensions of *familia* continued to
mark the term in law. The definition taken from the jurist Ulpian (d. 228)
incorporated in the *Digest* says that *familia* refers both to things and
persons. It also has both a meaning *iure proprio* and a meaning *iure
communi*. The meaning *proprio* refers to those under a single *potestas*,
and as a *pater* had *dominium* "in domo," he was properly termed a father

even if he had no children. At his death, or on emancipation, children subject to him became *sui iuris* and heads of their own families, except that, as the last clause of the passage makes clear, "the mother is the head and end of her family" (*mater autem familiae suae et caput et finis est*). The meaning *communi* refers to all agnates, as each child proceeded "from the same house." It was recognized that *familia* might also be employed in a wider sense, to cover all who "spring from the last blood of the same parent" (D. 50.16.195, 2).

When the great civilian Bartolo of Sassoferrato approached Ulpian's text, he used it to determine if a bastard was included in the term *familia*. He tellingly drew the line at agnation; a bastard was not included when agnation was at issue, because he did not issue from a legitimate marriage. In other regards, however, bastards were part of their father's family (provided paternity was acknowledged, of course). Bastards might be termed "de domo" of their father (at least if, in fact, raised in his house). Though a term like *domus* seemed to refer to agnation, it meant much more in common speech (*communem usum loquendi*). Bastards were descended *ex eodem sanguine*, which meant they were covered in the most expansive sense of the term *familia*.[33] Bartolo's was so persuasive and authoritative a reading of the term that later figures were more or less content to repeat him.[34] In extending family membership, if not agnation, to bastards, Bartolo was playing down the issue of *patria potestas*, for bastard children were not subject to it unless they were legitimated, in which case there was also a fictional attribution of agnation.

In parallel was Bartolo's discussion of nobility in his treatise *De dignitatibus*, in which he rejected an emphasis on virtue (such as found in Dante) in favor of attributions of blood and wealth as defining of nobility. By this calculus a bastard could pretend to nobility that no peasant, however virtuous, morally upright, or wealthy, could ever lay claim. Perhaps a peasant's son or grandson might successfully lay claim to nobility, but only if wealth were to last that long.

Jurists at times rendered genealogies to make sense of relationships in complicated inheritance cases, and they were not free then to omit females. Paolo di Castro offered one genealogy that linked family groups, in which he included women as sisters. A monna Filippa was agnatic to

---

[33] Bartolo to D. 50.16.195, 2 *Provincia* § *familiae, In secundam ff. Novi partem* (Venice, 1570), fols. 247vb–48ra.

[34] As Lodovico a Sardi, *Tractatus de naturalibus liberis*, in *Tractatus universi iuris*, vol. 8, part 2, (Venice, 1584), fols. 29vb–45va, at 32rb.

the deceased, while Cicco di Tommaso was a male cognatic cousin who had sons, and Cione was a son of a female cousin. All the people in di Castro's figure were designated as living or dead. In an intestate inheritance case, his main task was to determine who was more closely related. In this case he had to conclude that all three, Filippa, Cicco, and Cione, were equally close (third degree).[35]

Family had more to do with genealogical relationships than with residence. Servants, apprentices, fostered children, or others who were often part of a residential group did not count in the law. They might be inserted into a person's will, to be sure, but they had no claims unless such a concession were made. Apposite here is the description offered by the Florentine Ufficio dei Pupilli of the range of kin who had six months in which to opt to take on guardianship of minors: "grandfather on the father's side, or the mother's, or aunt, or uncle on the father's side, or brother, or a paternal cousin."[36] Other than the two older women who had married into the agnate lineage, expectation of guardianship vested only in a narrow range of agnates. After that group only the supposedly neutral civic officials were to be trusted with the person and *substantia* of the young heir on intestacy. In neither case does the provision recognize that, as a result of the later age at first marriage of men, in many communities at points in the life cycle affinal kin could be more practically important for starting a young ward on a career.[37]

Family was also inseparably linked with ownership, but that, in turn, was rendered in individualistic terms. Bartolo made very clear the importance of ownership with his aphoristic statement that "he who enters an estate by reason of friendship or familiarity [amicitiae vel familiaritatis] is said not to possess it."[38] His paradigmatic cases were a son living with his mother on her property, and a brother and sister cohabiting on a *patrimonium indivisum*. On the first, the son could not claim ownership until his mother died and the property came to him. On the second, the brother alone dealt with rents and proceeds, though he was commonly perceived to be acting *ex causa familiaritatis*. Bartolo ended his discussion on a third

---

[35] Di Castro, 2 *cons.* 376, fols. 174vb–75ra.

[36] "Statuti o ordinamenti dell'Ufficio dei Pupilli et Adulti nel periodo della Repubblica Fiorentina (1388–1534)," ed. Francesca Morandini, *Archivio storico italiano* 114 (1956): 92–117, at 97.

[37] Rheubottom, *Age, Marriage, and Politics*, 118–22.

[38] Bartolo to D. 41.2.41, *Qui iure familiaritatis, Opera omnia*, 10 vols. (Venice, 1615), vol. 5, fol. 88rb.

case, namely that of a wife possessed of her property "although she never asserted her title and possessed through her husband."

Even the term "house" (*domus*) was confusingly multivalent in the law. In a *consilium* for a case in which inheritance of a shop was in question, because there were two floors to the structure, but no access between them, Paolo di Castro found it necessary to provide six different meanings of *domus*. It meant habitation, domicile, family, a group of agnates or *consortes*, patrimony, or edifice. As "all doctors" agreed that the municipal statute governing inheritance in this case preferred agnates to a mother, and this intent was served with regard to any "urban" building, whether dedicated to habitation or not, the shop went to the agnate heirs, by di Castro's reckoning. The *consilium* indicated that rural agricultural properties might not have been so treated, but if it were "principally on its own account and on account of the amenities more than on account of the rural land," it would be treated like urban holdings. It is clear di Castro was expanding the definition of *domus* beyond "that edifice which is arranged for habitation."[39]

The legal terms had to carry some of the other, nonlegal meanings, so further room for ambiguity crept in. We can sense some of this from the *consilia* authored by Filippo Decio (1454–1535), a Milanese who taught in Pisa, Siena, Padua, and Pavia in the course of his long and distinguished career. Among other things, in a testate succession, as opposed to succession on intestacy, one had to attend to the greater affection of the testator for those closest to him (in degree of relationship). For Decio the term *familia* did not preclude individual preference of a testator, as opposed to encompassing a wider kin and splitting property among them.[40]

In another of his cases, where civic statute controlled the events, other senses of family came to the fore. It is not certain what municipality was in question, but its statutory rule prohibiting alienation of *bona patrimonialia* "extra familiam" was similar to Milan's, with which Decio was familiar. The statute allowed that agnates could buy back alienated properties. But what if the property had changed hands several times and been "extra familiam" for quite some time? By the statute, agnates within four degrees (by canon law's computation) had to be approached before alienation of patrimonial holdings, or they had a year to buy it back if the sale occurred without their input. In this case, a sale by a man named Bartolomeo was contested by second cousins. The property could

---

[39] Di Castro, 1 *cons.* 92, fol. 50va–b (Venice 1580).   [40] Decio, 1 *cons.* 1, fols. 2ra–3rb.

be termed patrimonial by any one of three tests: "by paternal ascendant line" (*per lineam paternam ascendentium*), "by reputation that the item used to be of that agnation" (*per famam quod res consueverit esse ipsius agnationis*), or "by reputation that such item was conceded as patrimo-nial" (*per famam quod talis res fuerit pro patrimoniali concessa*). Pro-longed holding outside the family, however, though the property had been recovered by terms of an agreement of perpetual right, left open whether the property's quality had changed and it was no longer patri-monial but newly acquired by purchase. Such "new" property was much more fully under the legal control of the one who acquired it. Decio opted that the recovery by pact was necessary to retain, and thus had retained, the patrimonial character of the property. Even if at present the property were still outside family hands, the kin would still have right of recovery against the first purchaser or the current holder. The statute allowed recovery against any holder of alienated patrimony. Recovery by family and then realienation certainly did not change its character; the reason for recovery was to reintegrate the property into the patrimony.

The other conundrum in the case was, given a division of property between the grandfathers, as brothers, was division a form of alienation that then precluded the prohibition on alienation and left property freely alienable to outsiders? No. The statute expressly allowed division among agnates who were not presumed to have renounced their rights of recov-ery by participating in the division. While some distinction might exist in law concerning property acquired aside from inheritance, the statute in question spoke in general terms and made no such distinction. So Decio concluded "the role of the lord having to judge is to pronounce in favor of the plaintiff, condemning the possessors to restitution of property."[41] His opinion in this case probably stood as the sentence of the judge who seems to have solicited it. Left aside, curiously, in his discussion is any sense of just how long the holdings had been outside the control of anyone in the family. Decio's opinion seemed to give sweeping power and almost indel-ible character to agnation to permeate and imbue things. Clearly family and property were closely intertwined. But just as clearly the patrimony of one set of cousins was distinct from another, while they still had rights to reclaim property from an earlier patrimonial whole.

It was Bartolo of Sassoferrato in the fourteenth century who formu-lated a vital legal accommodation to the new realities of family formed by

---

[41] Decio, 1 *cons.* 88, fols. 99va–100rb.

marriage and held together by property. He hit on the equation of *familia* with *substantia* in law. Specifically, in an extended commentary on the Digest text *In suis*, in the title *De liberis et posthumis* (D. 28.2.11), which concerns the intestate passage of property from father to sons (as his heirs *legitimi et necessarii*), Bartolo said that "family is taken in law for substance" (*familia accipitur in iure pro substantia*). His notion caught on quickly, being echoed by his contemporary, Alberico da Rosciate (d. 1357), with the words "familia, id est substantia."[42] A century later the Milanese jurist Giason del Maino (1435–1519) subsumed the theme of *substantia* into a more expansive sense of *familia*: "The term family is taken in three ways: for a family of kin [*pro familia coniunctorum*] and thus for the same stock or kindred. For a family of freedmen or slaves [*pro familia liberorum seu servorum*]. Third as the substance of goods."[43] Added to that came the standard legal conclusion that *substantia* was preserved and transmitted through legitimate male children, and that was said by Rosciate to be the intent behind statutes laying out intestacy rules and of countless testaments.[44]

The text with which Bartolo was grappling as he came up with the equation of family and substance was one that considered the intestate passage of property from father to son. The transmission of inheritance between father and son, as Bartolo saw it, was so instantaneous, the son was so implicated in his father's ownership and management of the property, that a son could be termed *quodammodo dominus* of his father's property *vivente patre* (this despite the general rule that two could not be owner in entirety on the same property). Although this formulation, it had to be conceded, was *improprie*, it was as close as *ius commune* would get to a corporate sense of family property. Property was an ingredient in identity. The owner (*dominus*) exercised his will on this property, insofar as he could.

Substance also carried some sense of immutability to it, as something shared by kin, unchanged over the generations. What exactly Bartolo meant by the term *substantia* is not clear in his commentary to *In suis*. If we seek clarification in his treatise on witnesses and procedure, *De testibus*, we find little more, as there he said that *substantia* had three

[42] Alberico da Rosciate, *Dictionarium iuris tam civilis quam canonici* (Venice, 1581), s.v. *familia*.
[43] Giason del Maino to l. *Suggestioni* C. De verborum significatione (C. 6.38.5), *In secundam codicis partem commentaria* (1573), fols. 160vb–61ra.
[44] Alberico da Rosciate, *De statutis*, in *Tractatus universi iuris* (Venice, 1584), vol. 2, fol. 41rb.

qualities: "either they are in the soul or in the body or in both." Only a few paragraphs later, explaining how witnesses can contribute knowledge, Bartolo gave definition to *economica prudentia*: "that is, a dispensative prudence pertaining to rule of the family, and we call one having it a diligent family father."[45] There was a hard, yet still slippery, reality to *substantia* that made this knowable to most and capable of being labeled by them prudent management, except perhaps by minors and mentally handicapped.

Substance came to Bartolo's mind around the same time metaphors for sex shifted from the conjunction of flesh (*cognatio carnalis*) to the mingling of (blood) substance. Paradoxically anthropologists have used the term substance in relation to kinship in the opposite sense, as the mutable and transformable element in kinship. Putting the two perspectives together, in Bartolo's terms, even as substance endured the passage from father to son, it was changed to a new owner and put to new uses and further changed the family it supposedly defined.

In Bartolo's hands, law accommodated the more diffuse *vulgaris veritas* that saw the legal power and ownership of the father as also a trust for the son. More than inheritance of property was assumed to pass immediately and automatically – eligibility for public office, honors, status, relationships outside the home – all these too went to the son who was "almost the same person as his father." Jurists conceded to these conceits, however imaginary they found them to be from the point of view of the law. They too allowed that in the process of procreation something of the substance of the father entered the son and through him would pass to grandsons, and so on.

Legal definitions of family, then, privileged agnation and were also gendered to the core. Immediately after posing the definition of family as *substantia*, Bartolo proceeded to show that the same seamless transition existing between father and sons did not happen with daughters. The statutes of his day, as we will see, indeed tended to remove women from succession (except to their dowries). Still, his was a sense of family with a corporate dimension – marked by devices such as a cognomen or a coat of arms, built around a sense of honor as a precious corporate possession. Here was where law and culture met to devise means to preserve family and what it stood for, for men and women. Yet it importantly remains that the law made no provision for corporate/group ownership of

---

[45] Bartolo, *De testibus, Tractatus universi iuris*, vol. 4, fols. 63rb–71ra, at 65ra, 67ra, 68ra.

property or inheritance. At best in the law the family was only quasi-corporate, a kindred of descent, and that was to have important effects also.

SUMMATION

What Vismara termed the metajuridical quality of family for our period is nicely captured, in part, in a recent description by Massimo della Misericordia, speaking specifically about Milan.

To be and to have, which modern rationality contrasts, were instead, in the values and behaviours of these centuries, reciprocally linked. All this is valid for individuals: the patrimony was spoken of as a person's very blood, a true projection of the self. In turn, the family, especially the aristocratic lineage, identified itself with the property: to defend it was a matter of honour, to pass it on a question of identity. Succession to ancestral patrimony, at the end of the Middle Ages normally divided among all male descendants, then concentrated for preference in the hands of a few, if not of a sole heir, served to select, within the splintered group linked by blood, those who were recognized as relatives, and to reinforce the role of the men. The bonds of inalienability (*fedecommesso*), which from the sixteenth century more often burdened heirs, rendered fixed property the meta-temporal legacy of past generations. . . . The fulcrum of family property was the residence: distinguished by coats of arms placed on the portals and the windows, to show the identity of the inhabitants and to protect them with their symbolic force, it was safeguarded by particular juridical immunities, so that a physical threat brought up to the threshold by an outsider could be repulsed by any means. For this reason, family and house were terms used as synonyms, and enemies were those who, metaphorically, wished to destroy the family to its foundations and, concretely, manifested their wish in material destruction (of castles, for instance).[46]

His is an eloquent and powerful evocation of the idealized, but also real, dimensions of family as the basis of identity and material support.

While it might be that kinship was somewhat overdetermined, family in law was somewhat ill-defined. Kinship, for its part, was captured in genealogies and in a host of metaphors: house, land, blood, trees, coats of arms. Family was a term that encompassed both the wider sense of kinship and the experience of it in living arrangements and day-to-day interactions. It was about people, relationships (of descent and of marriage, but weighted differently in different contexts), and material and symbolic possessions. It was about individual and group rights and expectations. It was subsumed in the dominant father figure, yet its future

---

[46] Della Misericordia, "Founding a Social Cosmos," 372.

was dependent on the subordinate wife and children. Its extent as a group was hard to measure along agnatic lines; and cognatic connections, while downgraded, were not without consequence. Further complicating this picture was the fact that there was no single, hierarchical body of law to give shape and definition to family. *Ius commune* and statutes operated on different bases and with different ends in view. Even within *ius commune*, canon law had its own senses of paternal power, legitimate marriage, and the utility of testaments. All of these factors, as we will see, produced uncertainty and conflict. The legal realities of family life, leave alone the domestic, economic, and other realities that are not so much in focus here, belied the idealized images of unity and utility.

Even the patrimony was not a singular entity. Within legal holdings of any *familia*, as Manlio Bellomo has emphasized, there were different types of property. There was what belonged to the father, and supposedly what sons brought in fell under his ownership. But there were also forms of property (*peculia*) that were nominally the property of the son, acquired by him. Then there was what the wife/mother brought to the group, mainly dowry. This again was supposedly under the control of the household head and yet distinct and restricted. The pretended cohesion of family and patrimony ran up against these distinctions and the wills and actions of those who might express and exercise them.

Along the same lines, Casanova has remarked that individual power to choose and the affective ties among family members cannot be ignored. "The variable of individual choice is a constitutive element of the history of the family that is not an abstract institution but precisely a gathering of individuals."[47] The historical reality, or at least the legal historical reality, lay somewhere between the descriptions of della Misericordia and Casanova. But the context in which ideology, identity, desire, or emotion could play out, that gave shape and meaning to them, was precisely that of the law. The first place to explore is the relations between fathers and children.

[47] Casanova, *La famiglia italiana*, 25.

2

Gender in Law and Culture

Bartolomeo Cipolla (1420–75) was a doctor of law with an impressive reputation in his profession and in the city of Verona, where he was born, and in Padua, where he later lived and taught (both cities subject to Venice). Early in his career he was involved with other legists in an extensive revision of Verona's statutes in 1451, and the following year he confronted a case (along with another Veronese attorney) that concerned one of those statutes and the legal actions of a Veronese woman. Monna Agneta, whose husband, Piero d'Antonio da Santo Martino Bonalbergo, was in jail for a debt, tried to free him by paying the required amount. She had followed the local legal rule that a wife obligating herself had to have the consent of three relatives or, where they were lacking, as in her case, of three men chosen by the Podestà as judicial magistrate. Her actions also had to be formally drawn up in a legal instrument. The creditor who had clapped Piero in jail for his failure to pay his share of the local civic levy (*datio unius colonelli*) demanded that Agneta deliver an asset, as a pawn, into his keeping against, one presumes, future levies. Agneta, or her attorney (*procurator*), objected that a "a woman cannot obligate herself for her husband" (*mulier non potest se pro viro obligare*) according to the s.c. Velleianum of civil law; but the creditor, Aleardo, responded that his demand was valid, as it was a fiscal obligation that was in question, not a private debt.[1]

That was where the matter stood when it came to Cipolla. His decision was that the civil law provision that a woman could not obligate herself

---

[1] Bartolomeo Cipolla, *Consilia* (Frankfurt, 1599), 1 *cons.* 27, 82b–84b, at 82b–83a.

overrode even the formal agreement Agneta made with the aid of three consenting appointees. A wife could not obligate herself for her husband, even for a public debt, not even for the sake of freeing him from incarceration. Here the legal reasoning got slippery, as only legal reasoning can. A wife could pay, even from her dowry, to free her husband, but she could not obligate herself (seemingly to some future payment or condition): "And the reason for this difference would be because a woman is more easily persuaded to obligate herself than to pay, especially as the gender of women is most avaricious [*maxime cum mulierum sit genus avarissimum*] ... because men are more ready to make a promise than to pay up, as we see."[2]

Thus Cipolla larded a gender stereotype on top of the most evident disability of women in Roman private law (as opposed to disabilities of public law and citizenship). The senatus consultum Velleianum hailed from the first century. It prohibited women from acting as guarantors for someone else's debt-obligating themselves for another person. This clearly then distinguished a woman from a *paterfamilias*, whose power lay precisely in guaranteeing the acts of others and being obligated thereby. The Velleianum itself referred to obligating oneself for another as a male function (*virilibus officiis*).

Women, of course, in ancient Rome or early modern Italy participated in the economic and social life of their communities and in the markets. Nothing in this law prohibited women from buying and selling, owning and transacting, on, for, and with their own. The purpose of the s.c. Velleianum was to keep women at the margins of economic life, as their collateral liability might fail (if challenged) and thus leave them as lesser alternatives for credit. Yet it still allowed women to use their assets, to make loans directly, or even to enter collateral liability, which held if they or someone else did not invoke the *exceptio* of the Velleianum. In Cipolla's case just such a woman used her funds (perhaps at some discomfort or even shame to her husband), but this *exceptio* was moved (and upheld by Cipolla in no uncertain terms), and she was removed from future involvement with her husband's debts.

Cipolla noted that the law was very tough on gifts between spouses, "lest they despoil themselves in mutual love." Keeping estates of spouses separate was a key element of the Roman family, along with the male monopoly on *patria potestas*.[3] Mutual love of spouses might make them

---

[2] Ibid., 83b.   [3] Benke, "Why Should the Law Protect Roman Women?" 43–44.

act irrationally in regard to their needs. Cipolla found a parallel instance in law, in that children had a real obligation to feed and support their father, if needed, even if the father was not a good father (*impius*), but they had no corresponding obligation to cover his debts. Though there were provisions in *ius commune* allowing use of property under legal obligation to free someone from jail, they did not hold for wives and husbands.

> Moreover for this conclusion is the fact that if a woman could obligate herself for a husband jailed for debts, a fraud might easily be made ... because when a woman wants to obligate herself for her husband, it might be that the husband is jailed for an ascribed debt that is not to be pardoned ... because the evils of men are not to be indulged [*quia malitiis hominum indulgendum non est*].[4]

Aleardo did not get his pawn, but he was absolved of all expenses of Piero's confinement, except for half the cost of the two legists' opinion, which was read out on March 22, 1452, in the loggia of the magistrates of Verona in the presence of many witnesses.

Agneta, it seems, was just being a good wife, rescuing her strapped husband from his creditors and prison. And Cipolla allowed that it was possible for her to do so. But he had a hard time allowing her to enmesh herself in an obligation, especially for a husband. At two points he turned to arguments that were more ideological or cultural than strictly legal. One was invoking the possibility of fraud. A feigned arrest could pry away dotal assets, or so it seems that was Cipolla's fear. The other was the gendered stereotype that women were the greedy gender and would more easily obligate themselves than pay or give things away. Cipolla did not make up that association of women with avarice. He cited a civil law text in support of the assertion, and he could have added references to more recent jurists who repeated the same refrain. The law and its practitioners were not gender-blind by any means. They shared the stereotypes laden in their culture, and they relied on them at times in their determinations. One of the things we will go on to find is how strikingly infrequent overt appeals to gender were in legal cases. But it is also the case, one suspects, that even if not overt, gender stereotypes were barely below the surface.

Where they popped up most often in cases, as in Cipolla's, was where women's ability to act legally was circumscribed by law, including local statutes like Verona's. Such statutes were the point at which gender became law. Angelo degli Ubaldi (1323–1400), for example, faced a case

---

[4] Cipolla, *Consilia*, 84a.

with a statute such as found in Arezzo, Treviso, and Ferrara, whereby a
wife could only act with the consent of her husband or near relatives.[5]
Angelo's problem was whether a woman's acceptance of an inheritance
left to her also entailed obligating herself, and therefore required her
husband's consent. In fact, an heir was liable for debts and any other
obligations on an estate, so it was easy to see acceptance of an estate as
acceptance of debt. But Angelo saw no proof that there were indeed any
outstanding obligations on the property the woman in this case had
accepted without spousal consent. In fact, "it was articulated for the
plaintiff and confessed by this woman that said inheritance remains
substantial [*opulenta*]."[6] Moving from the specific state of the inheritance
to the general intent of the statute, Angelo argued that it wanted to
prevent a woman from entering into obligations when that was the
principal purpose of her act, not when it was a secondary consequence
of acquiring something. If a woman accepted a gift, she had an obligation
for *antidora* (acknowledgment in the form of a countergift), but that did
not mean she should not take the gift: "For this is totally false, because the
statute was drawn up in favor of women, wanting to provide for their
weaknesses, whence it must not be turned to their disadvantage." It was
gender that justified the statute that made it *favor* for women.

Where and how did these notions of gender find expression and how
did they change in the period of the Renaissance? In fact this question has
been asked frequently, at least since Joan Kelly refuted Burckhardt's rosy
claims for women in the Renaissance. There is now a large literature on
the topic and there is no need for a lengthy treatment here. We can
summarize the salient elements for our purposes and then look more
closely at gender notions in the law, both the *ius commune* and the *ius
proprium*.

GENDER IN VERNACULAR AND HUMANIST THOUGHT

From the pens of theologians, poets, and physicians, women were characterized not by worldly roles, as were men, but by sexual roles, as virgin
or virago, Eve or Mary.[7] A generally negative vision of women's vor-
acious sexuality underlay the constantly repeated male attacks on women
and the institution of marriage. Men and women were posed at opposite

---

[5] Kuehn, "Person and Gender in the Laws," 99–101.
[6] Angelo degli Ubaldi, *Consilia* (Lyon, 1551), *cons.* 317, fol. 175ra–b.
[7] King, *Women of the Renaissance*, 23.

ends of numerous dichotomies: men as active, strong, hot; women as lethargic, weak, cold. One of the intellectual products of Renaissance-era thought was the coupling of women with the devil and witchcraft. Another was the image of the armed and dangerous Amazon, the very vision of an inverted socio-sexual order. Men seemingly had to be persuaded to marry such creatures.[8]

The cultural misogyny was not only a matter of elevated thinking where lofty goals or institutional interests might be at stake. It was in the homes and streets. Paolo da Certaldo, a fourteenth-century purveyor of proverbial wisdom living in Florence, advised that one had to be careful with women, especially wives, "because all the great dishonors, shames, sins and expenses are acquired through women; and they acquire great enmities and lose great friendships."[9] Similarly, he employed an image of female weakness to urge husbands to keep their women under control, in fear, and always busy:

Woman is a very vain thing and easily moved, and so when she is without a husband she is in great danger. And so if you have women at home, keep them as near as you can and return home often and provide for your affairs and keep them in fear and trembling. And make it always that they have something to do at home and never stand around, because woman and man are in great danger from idleness, but it is more dangerous for the woman.[10]

His Lucchese contemporary, Giovanni Sercambi, echoed this sense in a story about the "beautiful and very vain" widow, who becomes lover of a friar, and both of whom are tricked and shamed by a young merchant who had lost his father's money gambling.[11] Here the friar had lost control of his life and love, and the empty-headedness of his lover exposed him (and her) to exploitation and ridicule. In another tale, when a new husband thinks his bride is not a virgin because she seemed to know what to do on their wedding night, a wise old woman tells him his wife was simply following her nature, just as a duck takes to water.[12]

Not all women in Sercambi's tales were vain and libidinous. Some were chaste and sage. The same can be said of the better-known literary products of the much more illustrious Giovanni Boccaccio. While the

[8] Maclean, *The Renaissance Notion of Women*, 76.
[9] Paolo da Certaldo, *Libro di buoni costumi*, in *Mercanti scrittori*, ed. Vittore Branca (Milan: Rusconi, 1986), 1–99, at 29.
[10] Ibid., 26.
[11] Giovanni Sercambi, *Novelle*, 2 vols., ed. Giovanni Sinicropi (Bari: Laterza, 1972), 1: 158–64.
[12] Ibid., 1: 253–55.

randy nuns and vain women in his *Decameron* are probably more mem-
orable, certainly humorous, they are matched by women who are constant and even clever, like Gilette of Narbonne, or the incredibly constant
Griselda. Boccaccio also initiated a genre of exaltation of famous women
(not all of them virtuous, however,) with his *Concerning Famous Women*
(*De mulieribus claris*). Those who were good shone forth by virtue of
chastity, obedience, even silence – properly patriarchal virtues for daughters and wives. Yet this same Boccaccio, not long after completing the
Decameron, penned the misogynistic dream vision, *The Corbaccio*, his
last work of fiction. While it can and has been maintained that this is a
complex tale to be read allegorically, it is nonetheless the case that the text
abuses women. Rather than humble and obedient, they spring eagerly to
be masters, and love is the device by which such reversal of order can
happen. New fashions and expenses arise for the male lover. Women

like swift and starving she-wolves come to occupy the patrimonies, property, and
wealth of their husbands, hurrying now here, now there, they are in continual
quarrels with servants, maids, factors, and with their own husbands' brothers and
children.[13]

Lustful, suspicious, ill-tempered, brutish, extremely greedy, fickle and
inconstant, loud, incessantly chatty, envious, deceitful, empty-headed
and yet cunning – a long list of negative attributes is rattled off by the
narrator, some of them contradictory.

As many scholars have remarked, the cultural preoccupation that lay
behind gender stereotypes was the notion of honor and its negative
correlate, shame. As honor rested more on the domination of persons
than things (although things could certainly be controlled through the
dominance of persons), and as the physically and mentally weak
members – women and children – of a family were necessarily threats to
the honor of the whole, dominance of their persons was doubly called for.
Sexual misadventures – loss of virginity, adultery, even rape – incurred
loss of honor, and many women caught in some sexual doings saw
withdrawal of family support. Negotiations of marriages were touchy
moments for many families, as they so implicated family honor in the
person of the (ideally) virgin daughter. The woman successfully married,
become a mother and a competent household manager, brought honor to
her husband's family and to her natal family (if less directly), or at least

[13] Giovanni Boccaccio, *The Corbaccio*, trans. Anthony K. Cassell (Urbana: University of
Illinois Press, 1975), 26.

helped preserve what honor there was. Honor was also a force that generated violence in its defense. But in that regard, sons and male kin more generally were one's allies in the agonistic display of honor, not women. In any case, honor was almost tangible, as a family belonging, a form of symbolic capital that could be "cashed in" if need be.

It is the very contradictory nature of the gender stereotype, among other influences, that led to the assertion of a counter-vision of women beginning in the Renaissance, what came to be known across the fifteenth century through the seventeenth as the *querelle des femmes*. While this process began with a female voice, that of the Italian-born, but raised in France, Christine de Pizan, a widow with experience of the French royal court, it was carried on mainly by men, until later figures like the Venetian Moderata Fonte (Modesta da Pozzo) emerged. Issues of authority and subordination dominate in the many texts, inspired in most cases by Renaissance humanism's worship of classical style and content. Those texts that offer defenses of women (and thus contest in some degree the negative stereotypes we have seen) point to their real power and agency in the home and outside it, in contrast to their lack of official, institutional and public authority. Constance Jordan finds remarkable in these texts, which she terms "feminist," the claims for equality of the sexes.[14] Insofar as feminine was defined as not masculine, defenses of women could also take the form of denigrating men's supposed superiority of reason, strength, constancy, and more.

Humanism argued for the intrinsic value of secular life, exalting family, communal government, and princely courts. It is from this direction that there arose some of the Renaissance's most famous texts, such as Leon Battista Alberti's *Libri della famiglia* and Baldassare Castiglione's *Il cortegiano*. The former, and texts like it or inspired by it, relied on the authority of Aristotle, who notably subordinated women to men in his examinations of civic life. Alberti, a Florentine writing from the perspective of his diminished and exiled family, and his status within it as an illegitimate son, had a sense of the role women had to play in helping conserve family wealth and thus the stability of the state. As Jordan says,

Rather than define her value as that of an object exchanged between men ... Alberti sees a woman as one who by conserving property limits the number of (real) objects to be exchanged among men, and thereby prevents rapid shifts in the fortunes of her family and, by extension, of those of others.[15]

---

[14] Jordan, *Renaissance Feminism*, 5.   [15] Ibid., 47.

His dialogue contains passages in which an Alberti patriarch patiently shows his young wife his wealth and entrusts her with its safekeeping in her role as keeper of the house, remaining within it, watching over it, and keeping its secrets, while he went into the streets and piazzas with other men to do business and governance. Alberti maintained a critical distance from some elements of the patriarchy that marked especially patrician and noble families (even as that patriarchy kept him at a distance), but he seems to have had no such qualms about the stereotype of women or their need to be subordinate to patriarchy. As Lionardo Alberti responds to Giannozzo in Book Two,

The character of men is stronger than that of women and can bear the attacks of enemies better, can stand strain longer, is more constant under stress. Therefore men have the freedom to travel with honor in foreign lands, acquiring and gathering the goods of fortune. Women, on the other hand, are almost all timid by nature, soft, slow, and therefore more useful when they sit still and watch over our things. It is as though nature thus provided for our well-being, arranging for me to bring things home and for women to guard them. The woman, as she remains locked up at home, should watch over things by staying at her post, with diligent care and watchfulness. The man should guard the woman, the house, and his family and country, but not by sitting still.[16]

It was natural law, in this account, that kept women in the home, constant, vigilant, and (though not mentioned) chaste.

Daily realities clashed with Alberti's domestic image in some regards. "Women's commercial transactions played vital roles in maintaining the economic well-being of their household," even perhaps yielding "a degree of financial independence."[17] Beyond the obvious foodstuffs and other consumables, objects of all sorts moved between households and markets, and women were involved in those transactions, directly or through intermediaries. Such involvement, of course, deepened when husbands were gone – away on business, in political exile, or just plain dead. The Florentine widow Alessandra Macinghi negli Strozzi is one well-known example of a capable household manager; Margarita Datini another. The wills and contracts executed by such women in a variety of northern and central Italian communities have been the basis of much important work on women's lives. Cultural expressions of misogyny seem almost a language of protest against realities of the markets and streets. Southern Italy

---

[16] Leon Battista Alberti, *The Family in Renaissance Florence*, trans. Renée Neu Watkins (Columbia: University of South Carolina Press, 1969), 2, 7–8.

[17] Matchette, "Women, Objects, and Exchange in Early Modern Florence," 246.

too witnessed the economic activities of women. Neapolitan women, faced with a tradition of treatises urging their obedience and submission to their husbands, nonetheless exercised real power. Noble families using parallel cousin marriages to reconstitute patrimonies gave prominence thereby to inheritance through women. Widows played pivotal roles there as they did elsewhere.

While Alberti spoke to the household and through it to the city (as his contemporary Florentine, Matteo Palmieri),[18] Baldassare Castiglione spoke later to the princely court, as both noble household and seat of government. His *Il cortegiano* dedicated one of its four books to discussion of the ideal court woman. It is a dialogue carried by males, though ostensibly in the presence of the duchess Elisabetta Gonzaga, of loftier status than any of the men present. The idealized lady has her virtues, worked out largely on classical examples (who are exceptions to misogynistic stereotyping). The ideal court lady was feminine, not like a man, but soft, delicate, beautiful, circumspect, affable, and modest. While ostensibly defending women at times, arguments effectively bring in all the stereotypes and make assertions that, for example, women should enter politics only as the guarantors of the legitimacy of a prince's progeny, in which case chastity was their highest virtue. At the end of the discussion, the representative of the misogynistic voice denounces the cruelty of women toward their lovers and their ambition in using men to advance themselves.[19]

There were idealized images of women, as wives of princes or merchants, and managers of households. These images did not reject negative features of gender. Indeed, they depended on them to define the limits within which women were deemed potentially competent (not to say necessary). Part of Castiglione's presentation involved arguments that denied (however equivocally) the gendered presumptions, but those arguments were always countered in the dialogue. Above all, in Castiglione's pages, other than the admonition about chastity and the resulting legitimacy of the blood line, women were not presented in their familial roles. Women did not figure as daughters or mothers, certainly not as widows.

Of a different quality is a text like Galeazzo Flavio Capella's *Della eccellenza et dignità delle donne*, published in 1545, which sustained arguments against women's supposed natural inferiority to men. His is still a curious approach. He does not so much deny negative views of

---

[18] Matteo Palmieri, *Vita civile*, ed. Gino Belloni (Florence: Sansoni, 1982), 161.
[19] Baldassare Castiglione, *The Book of the Courtier*, trans. Charles S. Singleton (Garden City: Anchor Books, 1959), 206–19, 240, 280–81.

women's abilities and intelligence as claim that male attitudes and actions made them that way. There is the possibility of changing things, but how likely is that? Issues of power were rendered more evident by such an approach, but it did not change the terms of debate. The "virile" qualities of Amazons or singular classical figures only served to confirm the correctness and utility of those qualities, while condemning those lacking them as effeminate. The feminine is never positive. Jordan thus points to a progressive rigidification of prescriptive roles for women as the sixteenth century proceeded.[20] Patriarchy became more adamant as the figures of father and prince were more continuously compared. It was possible for some to think of women in a different register, but by and large those who did were not legal professionals.

GENDER IN LAW

The cases with which we began this chapter showed us some gender terms in the law – that women were greedy and weak were two conceits referenced to justify juristic conclusions. As the privileged social location in which cultural presumptions met actions, law and its personnel could hardly escape the broad social construction of gender. Lawyers were not free, as poets and moral philosophers might be, to rethink gender. Or if they did, in the context of a case and specific actions and interests, they were best advised to leave some matters unsaid.

Courtroom and classroom were different environments. The second begged for exposition and the illumination of underlying rationales, in keeping with the professional approach to the canonical texts. With regard to gender, however, the *ius commune* of the schools was in fact equivocal on many points. The assertion of gendered weakness was not consistently possible or even optimal, despite broad assertions of the greater stature of males. The issues were somewhat different when it was a question of women possibly acting in more public realms, as rulers in some capacity. There the gendered exclusion of women was much more consistent. However, we are interested only in their roles in the more private confines of household and family, not that those did not also become public at times.

With all the trappings of the obligations and burdens that fell on the wife/mother, but with all the rights, privileges, and protections that also

---

[20] Jordan, *Renaissance Feminism*, 143–44.

derived from her position in the household, a woman "took up a role of first rank among the subjects that animated controversies that, in an equitable manner, tribunals found themselves having to resolve when they confronted the theme of family."[21] Alongside women's supposed weakness, common law and statutes recognized women's natural ability to take part in the running of the house. Such capacities were downplayed, if not obscured, in the prescriptive literature and in jurisprudence, but they emerge to view in cases and lurk behind many aspects of law relating to women.

There were no more consistent themes relating to women than those of submission and protection. In law submission of wives was expressed in conjoined concepts of *obsequium* and *servitium*. A wife owed her husband deference and respect that was captured in the first term, which was also employed in law to describe the relationship between a freed slave and his former owner, who had generously elevated his status. The second term stood for all the chores and household duties a wife owed. We could add to this the marital debt that canon law said spouses owed each other.

Alongside women's *obsequium* to the husband and her *servitium* to the house, there was protection accorded her and her interests in a number of ways. *Ius commune* furnished rights and protection regarding food and maintenance, guarantees for return of dowry (Chapter 4), and provisions for guardians, if needed. Local statutes also chipped in their forms of protection, further enforcing guarantees on dowry while setting limits or safeguards on women's legal capacities. In places like Milan, for example, a woman could not be jailed for her debts, unlike the men of the household, although not all places were so kind to female debtors. Protection of women, however, was always much more about male protectionism than women's concerns.

The underlying gender difference in learned law ran right through the heart of family. Women could not have *patria potestas* and thus pass on agnatic connections. By a well-known and oft-repeated legal aphorism (found in the *Digest* [D. 50.16.195,5]), "a woman is both the head and the end of her family" (*mulier familiae suae et caput et finis est*). Further, according to another well-known text of the *Digest* (D. 50.17.2), "women are excluded from all civic and public offices; thus they may not be judges, nor magistrates, nor advocates; nor may they intervene on another's behalf, nor act as procurators." And, as we have

---

[21] Zorzoli, "Una incursione," 620.

seen, by the Roman senatus consultum Velleianium, women were not permitted to obligate themselves for others or be obligated by others. As Yan Thomas has observed, in Roman law, in which division of the sexes was a fundamental tenet, "women were legally incapacitated not in their own right but only when it came to representing others."[22]

When early modern jurists came to these texts and these areas of legal rights and capacities, it was not difficult for them to insert the language of gender. *Infirmitas sexus* was a term they could find to hand in the Justinianic texts, as well as *imbecillitas sexus, ignorantia, levitas, fragilitas*. Thus Bartolo, commenting on the lex *Quae dotis* (D. 24.3.33), a law he termed beautiful (*pulchra*), containing "everyday material and subtle and badly examined" (*materiam quotidianam et subtilem et pessime examinatam*), began with the assertion that women were a most greedy gender.[23] In the same vein, Baldo degli Ubaldi listed five reasons for the fact that women could not inherit fiefs: they were too weak to bear arms, were modest, were weak in counsel, were deceitful, and could not keep secrets. Elsewhere Baldo openly equated the *imbecillitas* of women and minors as he confronted their parallel disabilities to act in law.[24] Women and minors needed protection in the law, even to the point of annulling their legal acts as insufficiently informed and potentially harmful to themselves and others. Under the aegis of statutes protecting females, families could invoke such incapacity as grounds to invalidate acts they came to regret.

Paradoxically *ius commune* was in some other regards generous to women. Even as Baldo ticked off his five reasons against women inheriting fiefs, he conceded that they could still inherit fiefs in the absence of men, either by successory pact with the lord or by local custom. Bartolo too said women could exercise powers of jurisdiction and public offices, otherwise forbidden them by law, if custom allowed. Other jurists followed his lead here, and the effects of these sorts of opinions were far reaching in the highly feudalized south.

While, as a rule, they could not obligate themselves in *ius commune* for others, women were quite capable of obligating themselves and conducting a range of business. The very assertion of their supposed greed rested on the fact that they exercised that vice. The Bolognese jurist Rolandino

---

[22] Thomas, "The Division of the Sexes in Roman Law," 88.
[23] Bartolo to D. 24.3.33, *Commentaria in primam infortiati partem* (Lyon, 1555), fol. 25rb–va.
[24] Baldo to D. 29.1.7, *Opera omnia*, 10 vols. (Venice, 1577), vol. 3, fol. 105rb.

Passaggieri (d. 1300), who wrote the most influential manual of notarial instruments in the late Middle Ages, made it clear that adult women *sui iuris* could by *ius commune* enter into all sorts of contracts and did not need the approval of husband or kin. Centuries later Cardinal de Luca (1614–83) similarly stated that in civil law there were no differences between men and women.[25] He noted the limitations on women from the Velleianum and the Lex Julia that protected dowries, and the prohibitions or discounting of women's testimony in most types of legal cases, but declared that any other limitations of female legal capacity resided with statutes.

It was local law that was aggressive in circumscribing women's legal actions, if not their economic activities. The picture, however, was not always uniform. Patrizia Mainoni, for one, has found that women in the southern region of Puglia "enjoyed juridical-patrimonial conditions more favorable than the women of north central Italy," at least until the fifteenth century, when new laws were enacted to limit women's legal capacities.[26] Part of women's legal abilities in such a southern society related to the persistence of Lombard legal institutions that vested them with portions of their husbands' property. Another factor was the Lombard *mundium*, which was a right of guardianship over women that fell to men of her family of birth, which meant that they retained a very active interest in women and their property after marriage.

Where women's legal capacities were more carefully circumscribed in law, there was a certain similarity in legal language. Women were treated similarly to minors, except that they had greater ease of disposition of dowry than minors and could intervene to aid their husbands or children. As Cardinal De Luca recognized, women and minors were not in fact the same:

if a woman without suspicion of deceit or force says she wants to donate some of her belongings and rights, and in consequence to do an act harmful and prejudicial to her interests (there must be provision every time that in some manner she cannot be said to remain undowered), it cannot be forbidden to her; neither by a judge nor a relative, nor by the guardian given her if he tries to deny her his consent, after they have well warned and instructed her; she may do what she wants, as long as she is owner of her property and solemnities are brought in to ward off deceits and seductions, but not when her will is sincere and determined. Because in contrast to a minor who can be denied, saying that it may be done

---

[25] Giambattista de Luca, *Il dottor volgare*, 4 vols. (Florence: Battelli, 1840), vol. 3, 355.
[26] Mainoni, "Il potere di decidere," 212–16.

when you are older, and so later he donates; because a youngster in that age does not know what he is doing, and is not used to value property, in a way that it can be said that there is some natural imperfection of understanding.[27]

So De Luca allowed that women could alienate property as long as they had been instructed in the possible consequences.

Bartolo opined that women could act as mutually agreed-on arbitrators in disputes between friends or relatives who had such trust in them. They could act as agents for relatives, including father and husband (this seemingly in contradiction to the s.c. Velleianum). No jurist doubted that women could own and inherit property. Indeed, in civil law women's inheritance rights were equal with their brothers'. But rights to own property, as Simona Feci has vitally pointed out, coincided with family roles (as daughter, mother, wife, widow), whereas legal capacities to act on such ownership rested on personhood and identity as female.[28] Statutes that then addressed female capacities did so, says Marie Kelleher, from the perspective of female "absorption" into patriarchal households and consequent limitation of personhood.[29] A good example is among the rules of the Florentine magistracy for orphans and wards, the Pupilli. An enactment of early 1478 reiterated an earlier one and affirmed that wards were released from care at age eighteen, but changed that for unmarried women, as it seemed "absurd" that they not continue to be protected. As it was, they and their *substantia* after guardianship ended fell into the hands of their kin, "who many times let the girl grow old so as not to have to disburse and extract [the dowry] from their hands." Such unmarried women were to remain then in tutelage to age twenty-five, if necessary, and the magistrates were urged to find them mates as soon as possible.[30] Here a civic magistracy usurped a familial function, a paternal prerogative (such as it had been exercising in any case as guardian for a minor), to arrange a girl's marriage.

In regard to day-to-day matters, including payment for services or products in local markets, women were commonly able to dispose of cash or be extended credit without having their husbands, sons, or brothers at their elbows. Yet when wives ventured into the markets, or sent servants there, they were perceived as agents of their households, acting for their

---

[27] De Luca, *Il dottor volgare*, 356–57.   [28] Feci, *Pesci fuor d'acqua*, 13–14.
[29] Kelleher, *The Measure of Woman*, 5.
[30] "Statuti o ordinamenti dell'Ufficio dei Pupilli et Adulti nel periodo della Repubblica Fiorentina (1388–1534)," ed. Francesca Morandini, *Archivio storico tialiano* 114 (1956): 92–117, at 103.

husbands, "as if he himself made the contract" (*ac si ipsemet contra-xisset*), even as they were going about the kinds of tasks that Alberti, for one, projected as their appropriate sphere of activity.[31] It was in broader areas of activity, especially those that might involve large sums or immovable property, that legal disabilities on women, especially married women, were more likely to arise. These were generally matters of local laws, as we will see when we examine some of them in later chapters; although the gendered language found in Roman law and repeated by practicing jurists was always available to justify and even amplify statutory disabilities. Women's ability to dispose of property was limited or subject to guardianship; their ability to testify in court or witness legal documents might be denied or limited. And yet the necessities of daily life and the realities of the markets also meant that various exceptions entered law or were left tacit and informal.

The relative generosity of *ius commune* with regard to women's ownership and inheritance of property and their abilities to dispose of it flew in the face of the cultural presumptions about gender and the incipient patriarchy of family. It fell then to local statutes to rein in these rights and abilities. Most every jurisdiction had a statute regulating intestate succession, and these invariably postponed women's rights in favor of close, agnatically related male kin (but also sometimes sisters, as agnates, in preference to other women or men related through them). These were fathers, brothers, sons, paternal uncles, and cousins, for the most part. A number of communities also enacted laws that restricted women's legal agency by demanding that male relatives or at least some male (as with Florence's *mundualdus*) express consent to their acts. These were perhaps less consistent, as the presence and power of men might well be assumed without legal expression. But Simona Feci has determined that in the course of the fourteenth and fifteenth centuries more communities felt compelled to erect limitations on female legal capacity.[32] Some cities, like Ferrara, did so with explicit invocation of gender characteristics; others, like Milan, simply inserted a new rule for consent of men to women's obligations and alienations without remarking on gender.

Behind the laws more closely governing women lay the desire for the preservation of family and property and growing worries as to what women could do to that, as the leading families of the nobility and patriciate tended to consolidate in extended lineages of descent. The

---

[31] Zorzoli, "Una incursione," 630.   [32] Feci, *Pesci fuor d'acqua*, 53–64.

growing concerns about family also provoked some jurists, again paradoxically, to express doubts about gender-related disabilities. Paolo di
Castro (ca. 1360–1441), perhaps influenced by cases he had seen in
Florence or Padua, argued that women, who knowingly circumvented
laws requiring male consent to their contracts (as evidenced by their
special oath not to contravene their actions), should be held to their
contracts. Such laws had a sound basis in *boni mores* and *publica utilitas*,
and they presumed that acts that violated procedure were fraudulent and
deceptive.[33] He was aiming at the problem, explored by Feci, that
women's acts constituted an instability in the markets and for families,
as they could be rescinded later, when and if they proved disadvanta-
geous, on the grounds of a failure of gender-based guardianship, coercion,
or lack of the proper oath.[34] As deceit was one supposed attribute of
women, Paolo di Castro considered that such laws were only regulating
that and protecting society, particularly husbands and children, from it. It
was also the case that the others who had negotiated and contracted with
women presumably acted in good faith and did not deserve to see their
plans later put in abeyance and cast into confusion by a reversal on
grounds of womanly weakness.

Di Castro might well, then, have disagreed with Cipolla's conclusions
in the case of monna Agneta. In fact, in a case he faced while teaching in
Padua, di Castro said that a daughter, who at the time of her marriage
renounced her paternal and maternal inheritance claims in favor of her
brothers, was bound by that act, despite the fact that a local statute
required the consent of two near male relatives – a requirement seemingly
not met.[35] For one thing, she had not really given anything away, as
nothing changed hands at the moment she renounced an inheritance. She
had simply repudiated an (anticipated) estate. For another, it was not true
that there were no close relatives present, as her father and mother were,
and they had not consented to their own advantage (which would have
been disallowed) but to that of the sons who gained what their sister
renounced. The case was complicated by the fact that the woman was no
longer alive. It was her son, with his father (her husband), who was
making a bid to overturn the renunciation and inherit what the mother
could have realized from her mother (her brother would have excluded
her from her father's estate in any case). The final point di Castro made

---

[33] Paolo di Castro to *Si quis pro eo* (D. 46.1.56), *Super secundo Digesto novo* (Lyons,
1548), fol. 80va–vb.
[34] Feci, *Pesci fuor d'acqua*, 170–75.   [35] Paolo di Castro, 2 *cons.* 419, fols. 192vb–93rb.

was that the woman, while renouncing parental estates, also acknowledged that she had been "sufficiently dowered," and so she had no claim
to a legitimate portion (*legitima*) on her parents' deaths, as she had
already acknowledged receiving its equivalent.

Di Castro made no overt gender distinctions in his opinion. He did not
even stress agnatic descent. He simply upheld a valid legal act from a
number of years before. It may have been that the daughter succumbed to
parental prodding and pressures as she renounced her inheritance rights
at her wedding. But that was not *contra bonos mores*, as di Castro
pointed out. It was, if anything, in keeping with a patriarch's desire and
imperative to direct family patrimony to his son. A typical statutory
exclusion for dowry would have precluded her inheriting from her father.
It would seem that, had she not repudiated it in advance, she would have
received an equal share of her mother's property along with her brother.
That was not the case by statute in Florence and many other communities.
He kept his exposition technical, close to the texts. Many other attorneys,
whose work we will soon see, did the same.

Di Castro's opinion upheld a legal act and did not fall for the stratagem
of invoking female weakness and means of protection to overturn it. But
his arguments also turned on the rationality and utility of such a renunciation of inheritance in exchange for dowry as a means to preserve family.
And that was often the point. Certainly statutes accorded validity to
women's legal acts insofar as they conserved family and the society that
rested on the stability of its families and perpetuation of their patrimonies.
And they voided or disallowed women's acts by the same measure.
Women's position in law, while clearly not equivalent to men's, was far
from uniformly negative. They occupied an incredibly murky legal region
with multiple sources of murk.

3

Family Life and the Laws

In theory fathers had sole control of family property while they lived. At times, rare perhaps, present control and future inheritance by the sons could be at odds. Paolo di Castro came to a one such case on appeal, after another jurist had rendered what di Castro termed a bad opinion. In fairness, it was a complicated case. It seems a ser Giovanni had been named heir by a ser Ettore (not his father, it appears), who had also named Giovanni's sons as his heirs in turn (substitution). Giovanni and his sons were termed relations (*attinentes*) of Ettore, such that there was some form of affection (*ordo affectionis*) between them. In any case, Giovanni had entered an agreement with his brother, messer Francesco, giving him half this estate on condition that Francesco return to and live in their *patria* of Fréjus in Provence. The sons sued against this conditional gift, saying that their father had no right to make a contract in prejudice of their rights. The first jurist had agreed with them. Di Castro argued instead that, although a father in this situation had to return property to his sons on his death, "in the meantime however, for as long as he lives, he is plainly and in the whole owner, and his sons have no right in these [properties] during his life." The sons' rights were in the future (no matter that Bartolo had posed that a son was *quodammodo dominus* with his father), and meanwhile the father as sole owner could act to the prejudice of his own rights and alienate property, especially as he was not expressly prohibited from doing so. Only if there was not enough in the estate to constitute the half Giovanni kept for himself could the sons hope to act against his grant. Had the sons been directly vested in half by Ettore, the matter would have been different, for then they would own that half and their father would have only rights of usufruct on it, being unable to alienate it.[1] In this case there was no restriction on alienation.

To the opposite effect in a way was the decision of Bartolomeo Sozzini in a case near the end of the fifteenth century. There he upheld the gift by Francesco of a mill to his son, Niccolò, against the claims of an outsider (Gerardo Levante da Tunicella). Niccolò had been *in potestate* at the time of the gift, thus he was incapable of holding title to property in his own name, especially from his father, so there seemed a powerful legal argument against the gift's validity. Sozzini thus referred to the "natural obligation" between father and son. In fact, the father had assigned the mill to his son, who bought out the share of his brother, Baldassare. Gerardo had use of the mill, and apparently believed that gave him some form of ownership. So he had also alleged a statute (that Sozzini admitted he had not seen) that forbade alienation of commonly held properties. Sozzini denied that Gerardo's right to use the mill without payment constituted a share of ownership; it was only a *ius familiaritatis*.[2] It would seem that behind the suit was Niccolò's interference in some way with Gerardo's right of use, which, reduced to *familiaritas*, was ended by the true owner and possessor of the mill. Here the singularity of ownership, Francesco's or Niccolò's, was also important.

These cases say a lot. They say fathers had full ownership of family property, that sons had every expectation of inheriting. They point to an affection between brothers, even to the point of offering substantial inducement to return home and live nearby, if not together. They reveal that there might be a pattern of use and familiarity that still did not rise to the level of a legally protected right. They say, as if it needed repeating, that there was always the potential for conflict in the family and that legal conflict usually concerned the *substantia* and one's interests in it. These and more all begin with the experience of living together and the legal powers of the father in that circumstance.

IUS COMMUNE: THE PATRIA POTESTAS

The key to family life in terms of law was the *patria potestas* – the legally delineated power of the father over his children. Closely related to it was his power over his property (*dominium*, or ownership) and his control of his wife (a looser legal situation to be examined later). *Patria potestas* was

---

[1] Di Castro, 2 *cons.* 370, fols. 172va–73ra.   [2] Sozzini 1594, 3 *cons.* 107, fol. 140ra–b.

a peculiar institution of Roman law, accepted but also modified in canon law, and accepted and assumed in civic statutes, though at times further reshaped by them.

Ordinarily *potestas* arose at the birth of "legitimate and natural" children by one's legally recognized wife. However, there were broadly two other ways in which *potestas* might be acquired in Roman law. One was adoption. A formal legal adoption rendered a child subject to the *potestas* of the adopting father. In that case one was looking at a legitimate but not natural child. Adoption was in fact very rare legally. Fostering, which was mainly informal legally, was common. Fostering, while it might lead to a private (as opposed to judicial) act of adoption and to some expectation, even in written form, of inheritance, did not generate *patria potestas*. Only formal adoption generated *patria potestas* and an at least fictive agnation, as well as an absolute expectation of succession to the *pater adoptans* or *adrogans*. There is some basis for attributing paternal power to the priors of foundling hospitals, who arguably had power over infants and children in the extensive *familia* of the institution. The priors saw to the feeding, care, education, and even career and marital choices of those (tragically, a low percentage) who survived the institutional care, which for many began with being put to wet nurse. Such priors then had an effective sort of *potestas*, especially when they oversaw an act of legal adoption by a fostering parent.[3]

The other mode of acquisition of *potestas* was legitimation of a bastard, who was, to start with, a natural but not legitimate child. In fact, the legal situation was a bit more complicated with illegitimate children. Technically the "natural" child was fathered on a concubine, someone with whom a man had a long-term and generally monogamous relationship. Both parents were unmarried, including to each other. Children resulting from adulterous relationships (i.e., one or both married to others), incest, or just transient encounters were termed spurious or bastard, not even natural. Spurious children had fewer claims, especially in regard to inheritance, than natural children. The key feature, for our purposes, of any form of bastardy, is that there was no *patria potestas* over the child. Lacking *potestas*, there was not even legal agnation, which was central to inheritance rights in Roman law. Bartolo of Sassoferrato had thus entertained arguments that bastards were not "de domo" because the *domus* or family name were about agnation; but he also

[3] Gavitt, *Charity and Children*, 244–58 and *Gender, Honor, and Charity*, 18, 64; Terpstra, *Abandoned Children*, 12–14, 249–50.

conceded that it was a difficult matter in which one should take account of the common meanings (*communis usus loquendi*). If a law was concerned more with those of the same blood, then bastards were included, as "nature rather than law is in question." Otherwise "no right is said to fall to a bastard" (*ius non dicitur cadere in bastardum*).[4] His treatment was echoed by others decades later.[5]

The parallel to adoption for illegitimate children was legitimation. Formal legitimation, available in a variety of forms, typically placed the bastard under paternal power as "legitimated." Arguably then, in the law the *legitimatus* acquired agnation and consequent inheritance rights, although jurists kept alive various distinctions between *legitimus* and *legitimatus*, such that the latter's agnation was not retroactive.

Legitimation was much more frequently used than adoption by someone who was otherwise childless but intent on having an heir. Although in law the term "natural" was only applied to those born of a concubinage relationship, there was still a sense in which there was a natural attachment – blood, if you will – between a legitimating father and the son (very occasionally a daughter). There was no such in adoption necessarily, though adoption of kin (nephews, for example) was possible. Adoption bore a certain stigma and was effectively outlawed in some areas of Europe. To its opponents, the adoptive child was a thief, stealing what he inherited from others in the family line, property inherited over generations through strategic employment of marriages, wills, and other legal acts. As Nicholas Terpstra puts it, "adoption that brought an outsider into the family undermined proper patriarchal authority and family solidarity, encouraged illegitimacy, could lead to unintentional incest, and challenged the fundamental belief that blood alone bound families together."[6] Of course these issues mattered much more to elite families than others.

Legitimation necessarily required a prior acknowledgment of paternity and the parental care of the child being legitimated. Despite implications of sin and dishonor in the procreation of bastards, numbers of fathers did recognize paternity and raise their illegitimate children. Only a fraction of them saw formal legitimation and few of those, in turn, were able to inherit without contest from other (legitimate, if more distant) kin.

[4] Bartolo to D. 50.16.195 *Provincia § familiae, In secundam ff novi partem* (Venice, 1570), fol. 247vb–248ra.
[5] Lodovico a Sardi, *Tractatus de naturalibus liberis, Tractatus universi iuris*, 28 vols. (Venice, 1584), vol. 8, part 2, fols. 29vb–45va, at 32rb.
[6] Terpstra, *Abandoned Children*, 13.

From the foregoing it is clear that with the *patria potestas* Roman law drew an important distinction between legal and social paternity on one hand and genetic paternity on the other. Effectively paternity had a volitional element to it – in marrying, in recognizing an illegitimate child as one's own, in adoption or legitimation. By the adoption of *ius commune* as a legal basis to life in cities and regions of Italy, those elements became part of early modern life as well. Some other dimensions of fatherhood, however, were not so flexible. Rights of even bastards to material support were also encoded in law. As we will see, fathers were not free at all times and places to leave their sons unequal shares of inheritance and certainly not to disinherit them on some whim. The importance of the social forms of filiation that came with *patria potestas* meant that blood alone was not enough to establish filiation; yet filiation also carried some important rights and could not be blithely overridden.

However *patria potestas* arose or was acquired, in Roman law one of its most distinctive features was that it lasted as long as its holder did. That is, children did not become full legal persons in their own right simply by reaching a certain age of legally presumed maturity. They remained under the control of their father until he died. If he died when the child was young, then the offspring might be provided a guardian (*tutor*) to manage his affairs until reaching an age of majority (twenty-five in Roman law, often adjusted downward in local statutes). But it was only for the fatherless, those who were under no one's legal control (*sui iuris*), that an age of majority mattered. As long as one was subject to the *potestas* of one's father, he or she was not a full legal person and thus unable to undertake legal business on his or her own. The *filiusfamilias* could not own property and thus not transact it (acquire, alienate, obligate). He could not enter into contracts with others or write a will. In fact, within Roman law there arose a concept of property belonging to a child in *potestas*, known as *peculium*, which was further differentiated by what came to him from father, mother or other kin, and by his own efforts (initially in the form of military pay). A *filiusfamilias* at least had claim to such property, if little real control, but it became his and subject to his control following emancipation or the father's death.

Normally, within Roman civil law, the powers of the father were extensive, demanding obedience and submission from one's sons and daughters. The sixteenth-century jurist Ascanio Clemente Amerini published a treatise in 1571 that attempted to grapple systematically with the *patria potestas*. The reasons behind such *potestas*, he said, were two: it was a reward to the parent and useful for the child. While mothers could be said to love their children more, after the whole laborious process of pregnancy and parturition, the father's care was more useful and law had more faith in him than the mother, which is why she did not get *potestas* over her children (*ad multa non est apta mulier*).[7] In his similar treatise the Vicentine Sebastiano Moniculo simply asserted that mothers, the head and end of their family, were not accorded *patria potestas* and did not transmit agnation.[8] In any case, a father loved his son more than himself, it was claimed, and in consequence there was reason behind such legal provisions as punishing a son for his father's crimes. So immense was paternal love that the law considered the two one and the same (*una et eadem persona*), such that a father could not truly give his son property, as it was still his (in part the basis of Gerardo's argument in Sozzini's case). In response, the son *in potestate* owed his father reverence (*pietas*) and even greater love in return, up to the example of Christ's obedience to His Father.

Failure of a child to display suitable reverence to his or her father, or worse, was the sort of behavior that justified use of the ultimate paternal sanction, disinheritance. In fact recourse to disinheritance was rare, because standards for it were rigorous. In and outside the law there was a reluctance to penalize children with total disinheritance, which for boys especially flew in the face of ideals of father-son relations. Those ideals provoked the instantaneous passage of substance from father to son on inheritance that Bartolo emphasized, and in the course of his commentary he had to wrestle with the contrary possibility of disinheritance, and not comfortably. Only serious offenses could justify so drastic a step, and testamentary disinheritance had to be explicit, naming the child and alleging the grounds. Mere failure to mention him in a testament was, in fact, sufficient grounds to get a testament nullified as "unduteous." Successful challenge to a testament on those grounds would nullify it in its entirety and leave the inheritance to the terms of intestacy.

The existence of disinheritance also calls to mind the fact that the realities of family life could and at times did stray far from ideals. Intergenerational conflicts were endemic, if not always spectacular enough to lead to disinheritance. Youth was seen as a period of dissipation and license; a good father was to rein in his sons, help them get to the point where such *giovani* were fully integrated, responsible adults in the

---

[7] Ascanio Clemente Amerini, *Tractatus de patria potestate*, in *Tractatus universi iuris*, vol. 8, part 2, fols. 98ra–127rb, at 99va, 100ra.

[8] Sebastiano Monticulo, *Tractatus seu commentarius de patria potestate*, fols. 127rb–38ra.

community. The counterpoint lay in notes of fear of what the young might do, to their families and their communities. Towns issued statutes giving fathers greater powers of correction over wayward sons, even to the point of incarcerating them. But fathers were equally often called to account for their sons' crimes. Fathers were advised not to become overly fond of their children. Obedience was a quality they wanted to instill in sons and daughters. Ideally then children would "interiorize their family's interests" and come to follow "spontaneously" the path set out for them. On the other side, in the normal course of events grown sons could come to doubt their fathers' competence as managers of the property and prestige they hoped to inherit. We know, of course, that some did rebel, but many more seemingly did not. After all, the father too, as a link in the chain of family continuity, was constrained and burdened with responsibility.

In reality, a father faced more than generational resistance to his *potestas*. Others – neighbors and kin – had interests also in what he did and how well he did. His sons might find support, help, and comfort among such others, as with maternal uncles, who frequently provided an alternative gender role model. Other kin might step in when decisions on choice of spouse, say, arose. Certainly they would try to step in at moments of overt conflict and try to mediate or arbitrate a mutually agreeable solution; and at times again local statutes would encourage or even mandate such intervention.

There was a creative tension in the raising of children. The image of the father in control, provident and perceptive, could give way in the face of the realities of change, lost opportunities and assets. The seamless continuity between father and son in transmission of patrimony was not a foregone conclusion. As Casanova puts it, "the preservation of decorum and of a tenor of life adequate to one's rank, the so-called normality that inspired maxims and strategies of any good father, depended on a constellation of favorable circumstances – a number of children as restricted as possible in each generation, equilibrium between resources and consumption, success in one's career, shrewd choices of spouses – in reality so difficult as to prove to have been exceptional."[9]

There was a way out of *potestas* short of the father's death. A father could choose to emancipate a child from his paternal power. This voluntary renunciation of paternal legal control would render a child *sui iuris*,

[9] Casanova, *La famiglia italiana*, 198.

even though the father was still alive. As the child was no longer so thoroughly subsumed in the father's legal persona, it was now possible to establish contractual relations between parent and child, which was often given substance by the bestowing of a gift, usually termed a *prae-mium*, on the emancipated child, in addition to any preexisting *peculium* that now came into the child's control as well as nominal ownership. It was also conceded in law that if a son lived apart from his father, with consent or at least noninterference, making his own living, for a sufficient period (ten years), he was rendered tacitly emancipated. In that way the legal household and actual co-residential units came more closely into line.

The emancipated child could enter into legal agreements, buy and sell things, make a testament, and so forth. He could take on obligations in his own name. He also was no longer necessarily in his person (as opposed to in property he had not yet inherited) obligated for his father's debts and liabilities. Indeed, broadly emancipation did two things, either one of which could be uppermost in mind at the moment. On the one hand, as Sandra Cavallo found for artisans in early modern Turin, emancipation could function as an enabling device for sons coming of age and starting on a business or craft.[10] On the other hand, emancipation could serve to limit liabilities and even shelter assets in one set of hands rather than another. In civil law a father had liability for acts of a son, not so after emancipation. The son too escaped liability for his father's acts and obligations.

This was also where statutes might step in. The assumption of liability built into the civil law's identification of child with father was overturned by an emancipation. Insofar as every community in Italy accepted *patria potestas* and its related assumptions into the legal life of the community, that overturning by emancipation needed to be addressed, as we will see shortly.

The other, and numerically dominant, mode by which *patria potestas* ended was the father's death. That was a critical moment, no matter his effective or ineffective exercise of paternal control in fact (though probably more so when ineffective). It was not just that ownership of property was now parceled out to others, although that too was supremely important. The household had to subsist or be peaceably dismantled. But if there were heirs of sufficient age to begin to act on their own (if they had not

---

[10] Cavallo, *Artisans of the Body*, 202–8.

already), then it fell to them either to keep the (legal) household functional and intact or to divide the holdings into their own legal households. The common law said that, following a *paterfamilias*'s death, each son became *sui iuris* and *pater* of his own *familia*; but by reason of habit, blood connections, and economic interests (which might be no deeper than a sense that a partial patrimony was just not sufficient), brothers might choose to stay together – *indiviso, simul habitantes, ad unum panem et vinum*. These living arrangements were also patrimonial and, in consequence, raised legal problems. At what point did a communion of blood, name, and affection (*fraternitas*) become a functional legal and economic unit, with liabilities and assets? When did individual rights of ownership of each brother consequent on paternal inheritance become collective? Brothers, even their sons and uncles, might live and work together, and commingling of business capital and patrimonial holdings became all the more difficult to disentangle. We saw one such case at the beginning of Chapter 1.

Within jurisprudence these issues fell under the heading of "materia de fratribus insimul habitantibus." The central problem was determining at what point, following the father's death, brothers who continued to live together entered into a tacit business partnership (*societas*). The first jurist to offer a thorough treatment of this was Bartolo, who near the end of his life penned a *Tractatus de duobus fratribus*.[11] In fact, he did not live to finish it, so he only completed his consideration of division between brothers while their father was still alive. Bartolo looked at different situations and decided that only when brothers were both engaged in trade and placed their earnings in common could one presume a *societas* had been contracted. A communion of households of itself did not rise to the level of a business venture.

Baldo degli Ubaldi brought a certain synthesis to the matter in his commentaries on a number of doctrinal texts and completed the treatise Bartolo began. Baldo also applied his ideas in a number of cases, as we will see. He conceded that a *societas* between brothers existed not only when both were engaged in commerce and pooled their profits and losses (Bartolo's situation) but also when by simple affection brothers put together their earnings from any and all endeavors, effectively treating all their property as common holdings (*societas omnium bonorum*). Baldo agreed that merely living together was not enough to infer *societas*.

---

[11] Bartolo, *Consilia, quaestiones, et tractatus* (Venice, 1589), fols. 139va–41rb, followed by Baldo's, fols. 141rb–43vb.

One had to see if profits or acquisitions were shared. This did not mean that all expenses had to be shared; there were always personal expenses aside from common.

To Baldo a *societas* existed when common were such things as the payment of debts, ransoming a captive, or providing medical treatment. Payment of a penal fine or of a daughter's dowry was personal, and evidence of fraternal help in meeting such expenses was not evidence of *societas*. The labor contribution of each member of the house – brother, son, uncle – to any enterprise, commercial or agricultural, was to be compensated per capita, as each was equally a partner, so that even a son who had reached adulthood had to be considered at least as *quasi socius*, equal to his father and due his fair share of the fruits of the enterprise. In all this, the manifest will of the parties was what mattered. The main problem was that "while cooperation served the interests of all heirs, and in that sense enhanced their ties to the lineage and its patrimony, it was pursued to further the interests of each heir's household, rather than secure the integrity of the patrimony and the future of the lineage."[12] Even despite living together, the reckoning of households could remain separate.

Prevailing senses of collective family responsibility, whatever the legal situations of property ownership and control of persons, put a premium on proper education of children to accept their lot, obey their fathers, and look to family as a whole. Youth was a potentially dangerous period, and coming into responsibilities of family did not coincide with coming into the age of majority (however it was defined in any given community). A father had to keep careful watch over his sons, and his relatives were expected to step in were he to die with young sons. The *giovani* had to be controlled, while also accorded opportunities to express themselves and learn by experience. Some of this activity and attendant concerns gained expression in civic statutes and burst forth in legal cases.

STATUTES AND CASES

Regulating *Potestas*

There are a number of elements of *ius commune* that received no or little explicit treatment in statutes. *Patria potestas* is not generally defined in statutes, nor is *familia*, *casato*, or any analogous term. These are fenced in

---

[12] Hardwick, *Practice of Patriarchy*, 156.

with some restrictions or elaborations that were thought to make them fit with local customs and presumptions. Ages of majority, for example, varied by community, but none seemed to treat any age as emancipatory. Only a few statutes drew a distinction between *acquisti* and inherited property, and most did not address the different types of *peculia* a son might have.[13] Southern jurisdictions – Naples, Sorrento, Syracuse, Catania – recognized the difference so as to affirm that a person had more latitude to dispose of *acquisti* by will than inherited property.[14] These issues were all left in the realm of the common law. Generally the same could be said for adoption and filiation.

While the legal family defined by *patria potestas* need not have much resemblance to actual living arrangements, statutes concentrated on commonly observable phenomena. The house and its occupants were a common point of concern and of departure. It was something neighbors and relatives would see and know. So Venice did not recognize the efficacy of an emancipation if the son continued to live with his father.[15] The statutes of Forlì gave expression to the weight of household when they forbade arresting anyone in his home: "As the house is a most safe refuge and a vessel of repose" (*cum domum sit tutissimum refugium et repausationis tabernaculum*).[16] This protection did not apply, however, to those who were in debt to the Church or the commune of Forlì, nor, in reality, did it apply to prying eyes and sharp tongues.

The integrity of the household under the father was expressed statutorily in a variety of measures. Padua, for example, declared that a father could not be compelled to give his son his share of the property, but he had an obligation to provide for indigent offspring.[17] Treviso laid stress on the opposite obligation of children in possession of sufficient resources to care for indigent parents, while also noting the correlative duty of parents to their children.[18] The provision of *alimenta* and general living expenses seems the very epitome of family. Still, there were occasions when rights and obligations regarding *alimenta* had to be spelled out. Even as late as the early seventeenth century (1605), Pietro Cavallo had to elaborate on the undoubted obligation of a father to feed his illegitimate children in order to insist it also held for the illegitimate's children, or to illegitimate children of legitimate children. One's death passed such an obligation to one's heirs. Only if the child or grandchild had means of his

---

[13] Marongiu, *Beni paterni e acquisti*, 90–94, 209–10.   [14] Ibid., 145.   [15] Ibid., 95.
[16] Forlì, 176.   [17] Padua, 191.   [18] Treviso, 337–38.

own to support himself and his family did the obligation end. A parallel obligation went for dowering daughters or granddaughters, who, if they had their own means, did not have to be dowered by father or grandfather. The problem put to Cavallo by Alberico Cibo, prince of Massa, was whether a grandfather was on the hook for *alimenta* of a young man capable of serving a prince and thereby gaining a stipend. Cavallo kept such earning potential distinct from actually possessing the means to get by, and noted that because someone could be a courtier or condottiere, or a merchant for that matter, did not mean the obligation necessarily ceased, but "in fact there are few who could not purchase food and clothing either in the military, in commerce, in service of some prince or of a great noble."[19]

The absolute opposite to the right to *alimenta* was disinheritance. It was a rare occurrence and drew little statutory attention, but some cases did arise. Baldo began one with the observation that a father was fully in his rights to disinherit a daughter who had chosen "luxuriosam vitam." Such conduct had to be proven according to local repute. Were it proven, the daughter lost the legitimate portion owed her by natural law (effectively her dowry by statutory law). Still, Baldo said, it was more humane if she were left something.[20] In another instance he defended the disinheritance of a Bartolomeo by his father, Juciarello, who justified it by saying his son had struck him and injured him. The disgruntled son had contested his father's will on the grounds that the charges were unproven, as there were no specifics as to when and where, how often, with whom, and by what means he had supposedly injured him. Baldo in fact defended the will, saying the father needed only invoke a "causa ingratitudinis." But he also burdened the consequent heir (identity unknown from what we have) with the need to substantiate the charges as true, including when and where the son supposedly struck his father.[21] The filial disrespect had to become as evident as residence and filiation undoubtedly were in order to overturn what the latter circumstances entitled a son to.

So many other statutes, however, betray a reality of conflict and resolutions not so easily reached. If a son's indigence arose from dissolute behavior, statutes in some cities gave fathers the right to ask that their miscreant offspring be cast in jail by civic officials. In Forlì fathers could do such to sons who drank too much or gambled or otherwise dissipated

---

[19] Cavallo, *cons.* 154, fols. 188rb–90vb.
[20] Baldo, 2 *cons.* 253, fol. 72rb–va; edited in Kirshner, "Baldus on Disinheritance," 201–02.
[21] Kirshner, 209–11.

the household's wealth.[22] Siena and Florence likewise provided for incarceration of sons of *mala vita*.[23] Other communities provided instead that
a father or another could step into court and seek to have such dissipatory
behavior quashed. Viterbo allowed that anyone who "badly used his
property" (*male utatur re sua*), on the petition of anyone, not just a family
member, following judicial determination, could be assigned a guardian
and legal acts undertaken before that point could be annulled. It took the
father to do that to a *filiusfamilias*.[24] Bologna gave its podestà the power
to step in to stop the acts of prodigal persons on the petition of the
propinqui (an imprecise term that could mean neighbors or near kin).[25]
In these communities the failure of the *pater* to constrain a son thus
occasioned the bringing to bear of more considerable resources to maintain a strong family unit.

The expectations regarding fathers and sons that lay behind such
statutes are well illustrated by Paolo di Castro, one of the most prolific
and influential *consultores*. He argued that a son should be held liable,
even held in jail, in place of his father, who had fled Ferrara to avoid his
insistent creditors. The son's main defense was that he was not yet twenty-
five (thus not adult by *ius commune*). Among other things di Castro
determined that the son was at least seventeen and old enough to be held
for his father; further by *ius commune* he could be disinherited if he did
not act to get his father out of jail.[26] The son had been involved in
attempts to settle his father's debts, which seem to have been considerable
and called forth the attention of the courts, so his father's incarceration
was something he might well have predicted.

The right to *alimenta* rested on ties of filiation (hence the right applied
to illegitimate children). Filiation was not necessarily easy to prove.
Mostly the matter fell to ecclesiastical courts, but some communes' statutes are indicative of attempts to assert or deny relationships, generally to
gain a piece of an inheritance or to avoid one burdened with debts. Colle
Val d'Elsa, a Tuscan community, recognized that the main mode of proof
of filiation was *publica fama* and fined anyone who denied a relationship
and was disproven about it.[27] Likewise Forlì leaned on *publica fama*,
though specifying that *fama* equated to three trustworthy witnesses.[28]
Bergamo probably relied on a similar mode of proof, although its statute
on the matter did not say so, neither did Milan's.[29]

---

[22] Forlì, 264–65.   [23] Siena, 239; Florence 1325, 103; Florence *Statuta* 1415, 1:191–92.
[24] Viterbo, 129, 135.   [25] Bologna, 537.   [26] Di Castro, 2 *cons*. 52, fol. 25rb–vb.
[27] Colle Val d'Elsa, 307.   [28] Forlì, 181.   [29] Bergamo, 112; Milan 1498, fol. 26v.

The need to demonstrate filiation typically arose if an inheritance was in doubt and someone hoped to gain something by establishing filiation. Giasoṅ del Maino (1435–1519), a Milanese jurist of wide reputation, responded to a query from a judge about the case of Agostino de Fornari, to whom had passed the estate of Jacopo di Bertone. Jacopo had called the plaintiff, Antonbattista, his son in an instrument of ratification and in a contract of power of attorney. Was assertion in two legal instruments sufficient to prove filiation so that Antonbattista could claim a share with Agostino? The statutes specified the need for proof and penalties for false assertion, but they said little about procedures and modes of proof. Jurists like Maino wrestled with those issues. As the assertions of filiation were offered in the course of other acts (*incidenter*) and were not the main reasons for them (*principaliter*), Maino said they carried no weight. Any such "quasi-possession" of filiation would only affect the father who had made it, not third parties, and certainly not with regard to the assertion that Antonbattista was also legitimate. Antonbattista thus had not produced enough evidence to prove his case, so Agostino de Fornari did not have to provide for him from Jacopo's estate.[30] It seems hard to see how someone could step forward at the point of inheritance and claim to be a son and heir and yet seem otherwise unknown and unable to do more than allege two legal documents.

Fostering a child, even one otherwise unrelated, brought up another confusion between actual residence and legal family rights of filiation. Benedetto da Morano of Modena left an odd will in favor of any legitimate or even just natural child, or even to a child neither natural nor legitimate he might someday have. If there were no descendants, his property was to go to the convent of Sant'Agostino. On his death there was only a three year-old whom he had taken in and took care of for two years. Was this child the heir, or was the convent? The whole matter hinged on the filiation of the child, who was at best some sort of illegitimate child and certainly had not been adopted. But the testator had called him son on occasion, and obviously had taken care of him, which generated a strong presumption of filiation. Giason del Maino sided with the convent (his client, no doubt) that calling him son and feeding him did not make him the deceased's offspring. The fact that in life the testator may have been overheard saying "my son, come here" or "my son, go there" was merely incidental. To put the child in "quasi possessione

---

[30] Del Maino, 1 *cons.* 106, fol. 309ra–va.

filiationis" required something more solemn than such "perfunctory" declarations, especially when the apportioning of an estate was in play. Being fed and housed did not imply filiation but could be a simple pious act of charity. One wonders who was available to speak up for the child and who took over his care and maintenance once the convent obtained the property. But the fact that Maino's arguments were plausible, if not compelling, speaks to the distinction between legal rights and physical residence.[31]

Another reason to assert filiation was to claim property alienated to others, and here an occasional statute expressed concern to limit such assertions. In Padua Bartolomeo Cipolla faced a case in which messer Andrea de' Borromei claimed to be agnate in close enough degree to reclaim a possession sold to messer Giovanni da Orsato. To Cipolla's mind Andrea failed to prove the "legitimacy of his person." He could show he was agnate and "de familia Borromei" but not what degree of relationship he was to Filippo di Carlo, who had alienated the property he was seeking to recover. The relevant statute offered broad latitude – ten degrees of agnation by civil law computation. The statute should not be construed beyond ten degrees, as if agnation ended at that point. Despite two witnesses who placed Andrea in seventh degree from Filippo and Carlo, Cipolla found their assertions lacking. Further, although the Paduan statute gave an agnate a period of thirty years to contest a sale (creating, it would seem, some underlying uncertainty for purchasers), Padua's overlord, the doge of Venice, had decreed a limit of one year to act, except in cases of absence from Padua or otherwise demonstrable lack of knowledge of the sale, neither of which held for Borromei. Indeed an agnate would be presumed to know of a sale, so Borromei could not try both to assert his agnation and deny knowledge. A fine irony Cipolla stressed.[32]

Did a bastard have sufficient agnatic standing to retrieve alienated property? A man named Antonio di Cristoforo left his son Bartolomeo as heir with a substitution if he had no children "that his house in which the testator lived may revert in posterity to his house and family." The son in fact sold the house to a Benvenuto, who then put money into repairs and upgrades. When Bartolomeo died, his bastard son Graziano (born of a married woman) came forward to claim the house under terms of the will. Did he have that right and if he did, what about the expenses

---

[31] Maino, 4 *cons.* 102, 379a–81b.   [32] Cipolla, 1 *cons.* 43, 144–47.

Benvenuto had put into it? Benedetto de' Benedetti da Capra (d. 1470), a Perugian, argued that Graziano had no such right. "The house is taken to mean agnation," (*domus accipitur pro agnatione*) he declared (an echo of Bartolo's *familia accipitur in iure pro substantia*). A bastard had no agnation in civil law. It was conceded that the testator and even the *communis usus loquendi* might mean something different by the terms *domus* and *familia*, but an adulterous bastard was not of the house or family by any stretch of the terms.[33] Graziano got whatever else there was in his father's estate, but he could not gain back the pivotal patrimonial property that was the house Benvenuto had just as clearly made his own.

Filippo Decio (1454–1535), a Milanese contemporary and sometime antagonist of Maino, faced another filiation issue. In his case there were witnesses and a much different conclusion was reached. The Florentine Antonio Guidetti seemingly had to prove he was a legitimate son to gain his inheritance, which he was not otherwise in possession of. It appears Antonio had the misfortune to be away on business, and presumably had been for years, when his father passed away. Decio was quite aware of arguments pushing for a hard form of proof of filiation, something more than local *fama* and testimony about how his father treated him. Decio cited Bartolo in support to say that full proof required demonstration of the parents' marriage, cohabitation, and marital lifestyle, that the son was born in the house, had quasi-possession of filiation, and was treated as a son and reputed to be such by those who knew him. Decio then determined that Antonio had met his burden of proof, citing the testimony of individual witnesses by name, who substantiated his treatment by his parents and reputation as son to Giovanni and brother to Bernardo, Leonardo, and Pietropaolo. As one witness said, "he kept him in his home along with his other legitimate and natural children and fed him, clothed him, and treated him like the others." Indeed alimentation, said Decio, was stronger proof of filiation than merely being called son, "as feeding is more linked to natural affection and is done for near relations more than are words" (*cum alimentatio est magis coniuncta naturali caritati et facta vero proximiora sunt quam verba*). Further, he claimed that the burden of proof had now shifted to whomever it was who was contesting Antonio's right to inherit (his brothers?). The witnesses gave substance to the *publica vox et fama*, and it was proven that "he was held and reputed by father and neighbors knowing him as a son and for a son" (*habitus*

---

[33] Benedetto da Capra, *cons.* 90, fols. 130va–31rb.

fuit et reputatus a patre et a vicinis cognoscentibus eum tanquam filio et pro filio).[34] Notably he was not reputed to be a brother in this summation. The fundamental issue behind proof of filiation was almost always a right to inherit, but it interestingly rested on memories of domestic life on the part of others. And here domestic life had been fluid.

Alimentation was owed to children. Gifts to one's sons *in potestate* or even emancipated were a different matter, not at all obligatory, though also not likely to be an issue while the father was alive to maintain or, if he chose, change them. Such gifts did not require legislative attention in and of themselves. They could become a forensic issue, however, after the father's death. A difficult case went before Oldrado da Ponte (d. 1335). A father consented to his dowered daughter's gift, *mortis causa*, which went to her brother, who was still in potestate. This could be taken as a way around the fact that a direct gift from father to son would not have made the property sufficiently separate for it to withstand a challenge from a paternal creditor. Oldrado argued to uphold the gift. Among other reasons, by *ius commune* the daughter's dowry was to return to the father, so by the gift he consented to its real loss to him.[35] In a parallel case Baldo degli Ubaldi faced a gift, a renunciation of all she might claim, in fact, by a monna Antonia of Cesena in favor of her two brothers. She was supposedly content with her dowry as her share of the estate and acted with her father's consent. This was a dotal agreement many women were held to at marriage. Subsequently the brothers died, then the parents. Her sisters became the heirs and moved to exclude her because she had renounced the estate. Baldo argued that she had a right to return her dowry to the common patrimony and then take a full share with her sisters. For one thing, the cause of the gift was the benefit of the brothers, but that was no longer possible in view of their deaths. More to the point, the renunciation was no longer valid

because by common law, which governs the publication of gifts, [the estate] cannot be renounced, and not therefore by municipal law, because the same reason moves municipal law, namely that it is not realistic that someone throw away his property. Likewise because it must not be permitted that someone badly use his substance, and especially women, who are easily deceived.[36]

He asserted both the superiority of *ius commune* and local statute, as well as the weakness of women to advantage this dutiful daughter.

[34] Decio, *cons.* 54, fols. 62va–63rb.   [35] Oldrado da Ponte, *cons.* 26, fols. 11vb–12ra.
[36] Baldo, 1 *cons.* 115, fols. 34vb–35ra.

If gifts to children *in potestate* raised problems, those to emancipated children were not questionable, but there could be concern about fraud to creditors or unfairness to other children. In a case involving the marchese Bonifacio de Careto, Baldo found that the marchese had admitted to owing his son Giorgio 6,490 florins, which Giorgio had paid to his father's creditors from his own pocket (*de propria bursa*). Giorgio obviously had his own considerable professional means. As a result, Bonifacio gave his son a fortress held in fief from the marchese of Monte Ferrari, worth "some thousands of florins," for the single sum of 500 florins. This gift was not publicly registered (*insinuatio*) for more than the 500 florins, which Baldo acknowledged, and that opened the door to arguments for its invalidity, as "registering is a certain great solemnity and introduced into the instrument such that no fraud can be thought of in gift instruments." Baldo, however, defended the gift as "valid without doubt between a father and emancipated son, because every obligation can exist between them" (*quia inter eos omnis obligatio consistit*). The gift, which occurred in the presence of the feudal lord, was sufficiently "insinuated" by that formal investiture; and a fief could be given entirely to one son to the exclusion of Bonifacio's other sons.[37]

Related to filiation cases and heavily tilted to consequences for inheritance were those involving acts that established *patria potestas* – legitimations and the much rarer formal adoptions. Here communes legislated, if at all, mainly to preclude or limit what an illegitimate could inherit. Generally, as at Arezzo, Perugia, and Pistoia, illegimates were allowed to inherit only in the absence of legitimate heirs. Often such rights were accorded only to *naturales* (Lucca, Genoa, Florence), and canonists were strongly opposed to inheritance by *spurii*. Means of legitimation in *ius commune* were recognized tacitly, although thorough equation of legitimated with legitimately born was not always conceded.

The strong prejudices, legal and moral, against bastards are apparent in cases. Filippo Decio proclaimed that the case of a man who named his legitimated son as heir was "valde dubitabilis," although he noted that the intent of the testator to have his son as heir was clear enough. But the testator's move was invalid and the estate should go to the nearest heirs (*venientes ab intestato*). The bastard was spurious, against whom the law held greater *odium*. Here was one instance in which the testator's intent (*voluntas testatoris*), otherwise the crux of the interpretation of

---

[37] Baldo, 1 *cons.* 451, fol. 144ra–b.

testaments, was overturned. Decio was inclined to err on the side of the claims of legitimate agnates.[38] In another case from Lucca, he dealt with the legitimation of infant girls, *spurias,* by means of a count palatine. Bartolomeo Sozzini had already given his opinion on the matter, so Decio was ostensibly confirming and expanding his arguments. He defended the count's power to legitimate infants. He also defended the legitimation against the fact that the agnates who would otherwise have inherited had not been summoned to be present at the event. The real problem was that the property the girls hoped to inherit from their father was subject to a *fideicommissary* substitution, which settled property on agnates if the heirs were childless (no legitimate children). That *fideicommissum* might override the inheritance rights of a *legitimatus.* Decio argued that the *fideicommissum* was in fact extinguished by the father's succession to it and by his having validly legitimate(d) heirs. Besides, the girls were in closer degree than the nephews who were contesting their rights.[39] The status of the girls as the products of an adulterous relationship by their married father had been laid out at the legitimation, so there was no deception as to their status. This second opinion seems at odds with the first, which had defended the claims of similar agnates, and together they are indicative of Decio's prominence as a hired gun in important cases. They are also proof that the law was uncertain enough in this area that cases would arise with regularity to challenge inheritance even by the legitimated.

Pierfilippo da Corgna (1420–92) faced a case that helps us understand the sentiments at work with illegitimate children. He was concerned with a testament in which a woman named as her heir the legitimate child of her spurious son. Corgna noted that a spurious son could not be made an heir, "for this affection is from a damned and evil means [*ex mala damnata media*] and the sin was not purged but continued." But he determined that the grandson was able to be instituted heir, as it was possible for a grandparent to love a grandson as much as a son. Even without an intervening legitimation, the legitimate grandson of an illegitimate son could gain an inheritance, which in this case was a shop.[40]

The validity of a legitimation itself was open to challenge on a variety of technical grounds. Did the count palatine who officiated have the requisite authority? Did the exact birth status and parentage of the bastard have to be set forth in the resulting charter? The rare adoptions

---

[38] Decio, *cons,* 176, fols. 189ra–90vb.   [39] Decio, *cons.* 65, fols. 63rb–65va.
[40] Da Corgna, 1 *cons.* 25, fols. 24vb–25va.

in law were also easily challenged on technicalities. Da Corgna defended an *adrogatio* (adoption of someone who was *sui iuris* at the time and thus had to consent to entering into another's *patria potestas*) from a set of challenges to the authority of the official, who was a cardinal acting on papal directive, to perform the act to the detriment of the inheritance rights of a mother, who should have been summoned to attend, it was claimed. One of his arguments was that sons had a "considerable" expectation of inheritance from their father. Even emancipated sons retained "remnants" of *patria potestas* and the expectation to inherit; but that hardly held for a mother, so her absence from the *adrogatio* was not a fault in the act. The mother had no grounds to contest her son's will in favor of adopted children.

An extension of the broad sense of family solidarity was the prevalent statutory provision that tried to minimize disputes among kin. Forlì and Bologna, as just two examples, enacted laws demanding that kin submit their disputes to binding arbitration and abide by the results.[41] At least in that way such disputes might remain extrajudicial, less formal and more simply settled. Tuscan communities – Arezzo, Siena, Volterra – seem to have been most concerned about this. Arezzo in the early fourteenth century (1327) worried about common holding and maintenance of towers or palaces, as opposed to division of other assets.[42] Two centuries later Siena (1545) was more concerned with elaborating a procedure to keep otherwise peaceful a moment of great potential for friction.[43] Sienese legislation did insist that a division worked out by a father, by testament or other means, had to be observed by children, in power or emancipated, and could not be challenged as long as the legitimate portion was assigned. Statutes such as these often ran into complications too subtle for arbitrators to decide.

So Baldo degli Ubaldi had to decide what to do when two brothers, not emancipated, had been given a sum of 400 florins by their father, while their third brother had been married and a dowry handed over to the father at that time. In order to affect a division of the estate among the three brothers, it had to be determined if the gift of the proceeds from the dowry used to support the burdens of married life (*onera matrimonii*) had to be calculated into the inheritance. Baldo decided that as the gift of 400 florins was given to unemancipated sons, it was simply part of their *peculium* and thus part of the father's estate, not an outright gift, as

[41] Forlì, 180; Bologna 1352, 2:924–27.   [42] Arezzo, 178–80.   [43] Siena, 180–82.

would have been the case if they had been emancipated. As for the dowry, the third son had to calculate its proceeds (but not its value) into the estate, because as *filiusfamilias* he was not beneficiary of a gift "but a simple commission of management is presumed" (*sed praesumatur nuda administrationis commissio*).[44]

Pierfilippo de Corgna decided that the portion of a farm bought by one son, Lorenzo, with the father's money had to be shared and divided on inheritance with the other son. This was *peculium profectitium*. Even returns or earnings from the farm since the purchase were to be shared, mainly as they were taken in bad faith and not by a legal error, "especially in view of the quality of Lorenzo, who is a doctor of law in whom ignorance of the law is intolerable." Corgna declared that his fellow jurist had effectively been given the farm, and that was a gift of no validity between father and son *in potestate*, though later confirmed by the father's death. Also arguing in Lorenzo's favor was that he had lived on and exploited the farm for a long period, while his father was alive, so his brother had to know their father effectively consented to that state of affairs.[45]

Where a father ascribed certain business proceeds to a son *in potestate* (clearly working with and for him), Baldo argued that transfer took the legal form of the *peculium profectitium* that came from one's father, rather than another form of *peculium*. *Profectitium* had to be computed into the estate's total value. If the son were emancipated, then it would be considered to have become a gift, a *praemium emancipationis*. So in this case he was considering, Baldo decided that one son got a portion from his two brothers.[46]

The option of division was mainly complicated by what brothers had accomplished prior to their father's death. When Baldo confronted a case in which one son had left home and sought his fortune "ex sua industria" and then returned but lived apart from his parents, he denied the brother who had remained at home any share in those earnings as somehow part of the father's estate. If paternal capital had been involved, then at least part of the gain would fall to the father and thus to his heirs. In this case, however, Baldo determined that all profits were the result of an industrious son's labors and all accrued to him alone.[47]

In a Florentine case a father divided property between two sons in his will, leaving less to the elder, Giovanni, but making up for that with a gift.

[44] Baldo, 4 *cons.* 394, fol. 111vb–12ra.
[45] Da Corgna, *cons.* 235, fol. 178ra–va.
[46] Baldo, 3 *cons.* 394, fols. 111vb–12ra.
[47] Baldo, 5 *cons*, 259, fols. 64vb–65ra.

The younger son demanded that the gift be conferred back into the estate or his brother be barred from taking under the will. The younger had won in the court of first instance. On appeal the case came before Filippo Decio, after two other Florentine attorneys (Domencio Bonsi [1430–1502] and Francesco Gualterotti [1456–1509]) had weighed in. Decio found that the undoubted common opinion was that a gift to an emancipated son had to be returned to the common pool for the sake of equality. Decio held, however, that the father had deliberately manufactured an inequality among his sons and clearly wanted things that way. Conversely, Giovanni could not be the only one to return his portion; all would have to do so if there were to be a division afresh.[48]

CIVIL LIABILITIES

Legislation concerning the obligations and capacities of fathers and sons provide an interesting vantage point into the way communities saw families and households. It is equally a vantage point on the interplay of domestic communities with the wider society, in this case in regard to markets and productive activities, the reality of which might be quite different from the assumptions behind the figure of the *paterfamilias*, and the consistency of a family's patrimony. The most common concern of statutes with regard to the relations within a household was undoubtedly the liabilities of those known to be co-resident, including those of sons for fathers and vice versa. Those behaviors, legal or not, that undercut the presumption of household integrity were the ones most in need of statutory correction. They were also most in need of judicial resolution.

Communities had an interest in clarifying property relations between fathers and sons in order to avoid fraudulent losses to third parties. In that regard, determining ownership of acquired (as opposed to inherited) property and the rights of control over it (not always the same as ownership when dealing with *patria potestas*) was not always simple. The relatively early statutes of Volterra (1224) proclaimed that any *filiusfamilias* was liable for his contracts, but that his father was liable for them if he was willing and did not speak out against his son's acts, especially if the son's contract somehow worked to the father's benefit.[49] This law seemed to give wide latitude to sons. Conversely Arezzo took the position that no son under age twenty-five, even emancipated, could obligate

---

[48] Decio, 1 *cons.* 59, fols. 67va–68va.   [49] Volterra, 134.

himself without paternal consent, and if he was over twenty-five, only if he "traded and conducted his affairs publicly" (*publice meraretur et bene ageret facta sua*).[50] That was quite a narrowing of filial prerogative in favor of a sense of household economic unity centered on the father. Cortona, for its part, decreed that those under twenty-five could not enter contracts without paternal consent or that of guardians, or of two or three male relatives. If emancipated and between fourteen and twenty-five, the minor's acts had to be conducted before the podestà unless he was a public merchant.[51] Florence had a similar allowance for sons practicing a trade openly, in which case paternal consent could be assumed, but in no way did she try to clip the wings of emancipated sons, as Arezzo had. Quite the opposite, in Florence emancipation served to free the father from any liabilities for such a son, while bestowing similar freedom from liability for the father on the son.[52] Siena specified that no *filiusfamilias*, "neither male nor female, neither minor nor adult," could in any way contract or transact without express consent of his father. But as in Florence, a child's public exercise of a craft or profession, without a declaration against it by the father, resulted in his liability for the child.[53]

Branching out from Tuscany, one finds the same concerns elsewhere. Belluno and Treviso determined that a *filiusfamilias* under twenty-five could not act or obligate himself without paternal consent, and over twenty-five could do so only as a "publicus mercator." Even then he could not simply obligate himself as a surety for someone else, recalling the general prohibition of such obligations by women in *ius commune*.[54] Treviso added the provision that the quashing of acts done without paternal consent did not hold "in sons or daughters *in potestate*, for themselves and living apart from their fathers, grandfathers, and great grandfathers, publicly and commonly conducting themselves like fathers, nor in menservants, women servants or cooks, nor in working another's lands, acting like fathers and owners in so far as they work for those obligating them." Visible residence elsewhere trumped *patria potestas*.[55] Montepulciano and Viterbo likewise demanded that *filiifamilias* have paternal consent, unless they acted publicly as merchants.[56] The unanswered question is whether the same apparent liability attached to acts undertaken by such a publicly known merchant that, however, had no bearing on business – acts such as purchasing a home or arranging a

---

[50] Arezzo, 174–75.   [51] Cortona, 218–24.   [52] *Statuta* 1415, 1: 201–03.
[53] Siena, 240.   [54] Belluno, 2:336–37.   [55] Treviso, 336–37.
[56] Montepulciano, 130; Viterbo, 120.

daughter's dowry. For those it was best to be emancipated, even tacitly by living apart for a long time, in order (for the son) to do them and not share liability.

Bologna, home to a major university, devised a long and complicated statute on these matters. *Filiifamilias* could not act or obligate themselves without paternal consent – in that Bologna was assuredly not unique, nor was the exception allowed for public pursuit of business, except for the addition that sons be "of good repute and conditions" (*bone fame et condicionibus*), and living with their father if between twenty and twenty-five years of age, or living apart from their father if over twenty-five. Exception was also given for one whose father was demonstrably mentally enfeebled and for the purposes of a dowry, for nobles in the countryside, and for "footmen, servants, school boys, and foreigners."[57] Age, status, and residence were thus all factors mitigating or defining fatherhood in Bologna.

Statutes that established no liability in the case of separate residence were working from what would seem to be the most easily established type of relationship, co-residence. Venice (1244) specified that a son living separately (*divisus*) from his father was not bound by any written agreements the father made, which could not be said for other potential heirs still residing in the family home.[58] Statutes of Aquileia seem most transparent on this score, as they made all sorts of liabilities – "father for son," "husband for wife and master for slave [famulo]" – depend on the fact of living together.[59] That sense of place found liability extended as well to payment of taxes levied on households. Arezzo provided that even emancipated sons who still lived with their father, or all brothers living together, were obligated for fiscal duties.[60]

Florence's laws laying out the liabilities of fathers for sons and vice versa were unexceptional in this regard, though perhaps a bit more overtly concerned with possible fraudulent practices in setting such liabilities on paper. But Siena and Viterbo, among others, were generally adamant that fathers faced liability for acts of unemancipated sons when they consented to such acts, even tacitly.[61] Fathers were not liable for criminal acts of their sons, but they might be made to hand over the son's share of the patrimony to cover fines and so forth. When crimes were the father's, some communities made sure that some portion of family property made it to his sons, so that they were not totally impoverished by

[57] Bologna 1335, 2:524–28.   [58] Venice, 19.   [59] Aquileia, 301.   [60] Arezzo, 185.
[61] Siena, 241–42; Viterbo, 129.

paternal misdeeds. Political crimes, such as open rebellion resulting in execution or exile, might be another matter entirely.

Statutes regarding liabilities among family members came into conflict with provisions of *ius commune* or at least raised grey areas with some frequency. Jurists were not generally in favor of such statutes extending liability to unemancipated sons. Filippo Decio deemed the Sienese statute that held sons liable for their bankrupt father harsh and hateful (*rigorosum* and *odiosum*), because holding sons for their father was unnatural (*contra naturalem equitatem*). The statute had to be strictly interpreted, and one way of doing that was to posit that it did not apply to contracts and transactions arising outside Sienese territory. The statute also spoke generally of sons or descendants in possession of any property of the bankrupt debtor, so, said Decio, the statute seemed to make the same assumption as did another about repudiation of inheritance that "a son living in his father's house seems to act as heir." But if the descendant was in possession not in a general way, by expectation of inheritance, but by another specific right, he was not open to claims any more than if he had repudiated the inheritance but remained on the property by some other right. So Decio exonerated sons who held property by right of an arbitration settlement and thus restricted the statute.[62]

A decision such as Decio's could leave a large opening to circumvent a law otherwise intended to be favorable to creditors. So it is not surprising that other jurists found occasions to uphold statutes and enforce liabilities. Dino del Mugello argued to enforce those on a twenty-six-year-old *filiusfamilias* who had transacted just like a *pater* when he stood surety for someone.[63] Giovanni da Imola (d. 1436) had before him a statute of Tizano, located near Parma, that held a father liable for a co-resident son's business debts, even if entered into without his knowledge and consent. The law spoke in general terms, made no distinction about location of a contract, and did not seem contrary to *ius commune*, which also held *filiifamilias* liable. The jurist, however, like Decio later, saw the statute as in conflict with *ius commune* in holding the father liable, and so claimed it had to be restricted to acts within Tizano's little territory.[64] Probably he would not have had a problem with enforcing the son's obligations.

Because much relied on the equation of liability with co-residence, the civil law institution of emancipation posed real problems. Emancipation

---

[62] Decio, *cons*, 491, fol. 516va–b.   [63] Dino, *cons*. 33, fols. 43vb–44rb.
[64] Giovanni da Imola, *cons*. 80, fols. 43rb–44ra.

dissolved liabilities, but it did not necessarily change residence. Was the emancipation in fact a separation of sorts between son and father? Was the father not still in charge? And how were others to know there had been an emancipation when co-residence continued?

Some communities tried to take account of emancipation. None forbade it, but some did seek to regulate it in the interests of greater transparency in the markets and the avoidance of fraud. To begin with a late example, Siena's statutes of 1545 decreed that anyone wanting to emancipate a child had to have that intent proclaimed through the city by a public herald, and the ensuing legal act had to be duly drawn up by the hand of a public notary. Any property given to the then emancipated child would not be exempt from the potential settlement of preexisting paternal debts.[65] It is interesting that the very next statute speaks directly to fraudulent practices, such as disguising ownership of assets in a third party. Bergamo two centuries earlier had also looked to public proclamation of emancipation, though after the fact, not before. Bergamo added to that the keeping of a registry of emancipations (giving the names of father and child, of the officiating notary, and the date).[66] Two decades later Florence followed suit.[67] Verona remained content with public proclamation to establish the fact of an emancipation, while Colle Val d'Elsa required as well that the act of emancipation itself occur only before the podestà or other communal judge.[68] Bologna's statute was the most extensive treatment of emancipations, utilizing all the measures detailed above – full notarization, public proclamation, registration, and officiating by a communal judicial figure – with a further expectation that the father and child both formally swear before the official that their act was in good faith and not to defraud Bologna, any of its dependencies, or any single person.[69] Milan, in its early statute of 1216, had an entirely different approach to emancipation, it seems. Nothing was said about heralds or registries. Instead, a father who emancipated a son was required to give him his share of the patrimony.[70] By that measure the emancipation would function as premortem inheritance and possibly be an incentive to physical separation, making the emancipation real in terms of liabilities and households.

Bologna took a further peculiar step regarding emancipation. There it was decreed that if a son dissipated his father's *substantia* or mistreated

[65] Siena, 229.   [66] Bergamo, 202–3.   [67] Kuehn, *Emancipation*, 36–38.
[68] Verona, 1:351; Colle Val d'Elsa, 308.   [69] Bologna, 1352, 532–33.
[70] Milan 1216, 91.

his father, the podestà, on request of the father, could compel the son to accept emancipation and his share of the estate, in usufruct only, to serve as his due *alimenta*.[71] Again, Bolognese legislators looked to as total an coincidence of residence, ownership, and liability as they could fashion. This particular measure, arising in a city most prominent for its law school, was hard for jurists trained there to swallow. Emancipation was supposed to be voluntary. It was also considered a favor and privilege for the son, not a punishment. Forcing a son to accept it ran counter to what the institution was for.

Because they affected liabilities and because statutes complicated the legal situation, unsurprisingly emancipations were the subject of lawsuits. Emancipations could be challenged on technicalities, which local statutes at times interfered in with demands for publication and registration. Alessandro Tartagni had voided the emancipation of Simone and Andriolo di Pietro Batisterii of Bologna for failure to register the act, as well as for improper verbiage employed by the notary. Still, he said, the emancipation gift (*praemium*) remained valid, or was at least confirmed by the father's death as a gift to his sons. The gift was clearly an act of generosity on the part of the father, "because when he emancipates a son it is the father who deserves a gift from the son because the son, where he was placed under the ties of paternal power, is freed by emancipation." So in the end the fact the gift was part of an emancipation, even an invalid one, still mattered.[72] But in this case there was no immediate implication of fraudulent activity.

Giovanni d'Anagni, who practiced mainly in Bologna, argued for the nullification of an emancipation as an act of intentional fraud. A father had emancipated a daughter from his second marriage and then had a testament drawn up naming her as heir, thus defrauding his sons of his first marriage of the share due them by law. Both the effect of the testament and its following immediately on the emancipation argued for its fraudulent intent. These acts could not be upheld to let the father enjoy the benefit of his malice (*militia*). His intent also ran contrary to that of local statutes governing succession.[73]

The main issue raised by emancipation was the mutual liability of fathers and sons. There was an expectation, elaborated in statutes, that fathers and sons supported and stood up for each other. There was an expectation of similar form for brothers, but it was not as easy to spell

[71] Bologna, 1352, 533–34.   [72] Tartagni, 3 *cons.* 112, fol. 91ra–b.
[73] D'Anagni, *cons.* 23, fol. 13ra–b.

that out, either for them or for those with whom they dealt. If brothers chose to divide the patrimony, there were inevitably problems in achieving some sort of equity. If they chose to live together, there were the added difficulties of determining if they were in a *societas* or a mere *fraterna*, and thus deciding who was liable to outsiders.

The problems raised by a *societas* among brothers were a bit trickier. When faced with a Pisan case of brothers living together in a *societas omnium bonorum*, Decio argued that the dowry of one brother's wife, whose predecease gained her husband half of her dowry (an issue we will examine later), had to be shared. He was quite forthcoming on the conditions that made for *societas* among brothers: "Whence a communion of property among brothers after the father's death, and continued cohabitation together, and always gathering of fruits from the possessions in common, and never an accounting among them of expenses and burdens on things or people – these make for presumption of a contracted association." On the other side, fashioning a dowry for the daughter of one brother equally came out of the common fund, at least as long as the other brother(s) did not protest.[74]

Decio also dealt with an appellate case regarding the statutory imposition of liability on brothers for one of their number gone bankrupt. The statute, Decio declared, was *odiosum* and due the strictest possible reading. He then proceeded in detail to claim that the conditions set forth in the statute were not met in his case. For example, its language specified that it meant *fratres carnales*, but witness testimony did not establish that. They had not established a relationship to a common ancestor, merely "that these lived together like brothers . . . they saw them leave the house and enter it like brothers." It also had not been proven that they lived together at the time the bad debts were contracted and that their father was not alive at that time. Witnesses merely believed as fact that the brothers lived *familiariter* and ate and drank together, though they had not in fact seen them *ad unum panem et unum vinum*. The fact that the brothers were in business together had likewise not been adequately proven. Decio's was a circus act of argumentation to an absurd level, doubtless to create some sort of doubt in the judges' minds and get his clients off.[75] In fact, there seems to have been a good deal of substantial witness testimony in the case.

As hard as Decio split hairs and questioned witness testimony to deny a *societas* among brothers, Lodovico Pontano worked to establish the fact

---

[74] Decio, I *cons.* 66, fols. 74vb–76rb.   [75] Decio, *cons.* 424, fols. 548vb–49va.

of one. Cohabitation and common actions certainly demonstrated a tacit *societas* with regard to business, but was this a *societas* of all property? The jurist noted the argument that even keeping the inherited patrimony in common did not necessarily imply an agreement to pool other forms of gain or revenue. The one brother, ser Niccolò, had bought things in his own name and presumably with his own money, so it might be argued there was a separation of goods. Pontano, however, rejected this argument. The property Niccolò had bought had been fiscally appraised in both brothers' names. Their mother had also given them a gift in common. And Niccolò, in Giovanni's absence, had declared they had all things in common. So despite counterarguments from fellow attorneys, he held that there was an association of all properties between the brothers. The *societas* had come to an end, and Niccolò had placed credits in the public debt in his son's and wife's names; but the jurist argued for an equal division of all assets.[76] In parallel Giason del Maino decided that the persistence of common living arrangements and expenses, the keeping of only common accounts, meant the children of two brothers who had died would split evenly with their uncle, the surviving brother.[77] They were heirs to their father's half, not two-thirds of the active members of the *societas*.

Of course, some divisions were easier than others. Paolo di Castro fielded questions from the sons of two brothers as to the status of dowries and clothing and some contracts that were not for the common good of their *societas*. Di Castro's Solomon-like division excluded daily wear but calculated expensive and festive garments into the common holdings. Dowries paid out fell to each separately, as did any contracts not made for the common well-being.[78] Giovanni d'Anagni had a case that involved two brothers who lived together for over 50 years, "cum eorum familiis ad unum panem." Bartolomeo never really had a trade and earned little in his life, whereas Jacopo was industrious and earned enough to make sizeable purchases of public debt shares that he kept separate. Bartolomeo and his heirs, perhaps unsurprisingly, claimed those were common property. Anagni argued that they were not because "no association appears to have been contracted among them, because living together and keeping the paternal estate together undivided is not enough to make an association unless profits are treated as common [*nisi lucra ponantur in communi*]." He cited numerous juristic commentators, including Baldo, to

---

[76] Lodovico Pontano, *cons.* 291, fols. 143rb–44rb.   [77] Del Maino, 3 *cons.* 3, 15a–18a.
[78] Di Castro, 2 *cons.* 358, fol. 168va–b.

back that position. He also alleged the presumption that purchases in one's own name were made with one's own money.[79]

In one *consilium* Baldo enumerated six tests the *societas* between brothers had to meet: living together (*coarctatio in una domo*), taking meals in common (*commensalitas*), common income and expenditures, common legal activity, property held *pro indiviso*, and local repute (*publica vox*) as to their association. The association of brothers before him, however, did not meet these tests. For one thing, shifting now to a definition of a fraternal *societas*, "it is nothing other than an agreement among two or many or of the community of the whole about what is sought in any way or are sought in the future by industry or fortune." The holding of some things or some activities in common did not necessarily imply that all was in common. The witnesses had not provided the sort of evidence needed; in fact, there had been implication that some goods were held in one name only and not at all in common. The *publica fama* was not of itself proof.[80] Baldo was equally tough in another instance, in which he noted that if brothers lived together, but one operated alone and earned money, as by travel, and used those business proceeds to acquire things like cattle or pastures, the acquisitions were evenly distributed among the brothers because they were all contributing to the common enterprise. But if one brother was not capable of contributing (*aptus ad operandum*), then what an active brother acquired remained his alone. There was also the possibility that one then had a greater share in the patrimony and thus gained more of subsequent acquisitions, as was the case when two unrelated business partners started a venture with unequal contributions to its initial capital. Losses were shared, even if incurred on behalf of one partner, if it was a fortuitous event (the example used was capture and ransom), but not if the loss had nothing to do with the *societas*.[81]

In Perugia, Pierfilippo da Corgna confronted the question of the continuation of a fraternal situation after one brother died, leaving minor children as heirs to his share. The uncles, who were also the guardians for their brother's children, seemed to go on as before, making agreements that also were binding on their nephews. The uncles also continued the same set of books, yet not in the same manner. The jurist acknowledged that it could be argued that different combinations of the three brothers' names for different transactions at the distinct times and in the different

---

[79] Anagni, *cons.* 65, fol. 37ra.   [80] Baldo, 5 *cons.* 482, fol. 129rb–va.
[81] Baldo, 5 *cons.* 172, fol. 46va–b.

places did not preclude that they were continuously carrying on the same business in common. The sons of the deceased brother were creditors and debtors in the different acts, as appropriate, in the same way their father had been, as would be the case, as "heirs are considered the same person with the deceased" (*heredes censentur eadem persona cum defuncto*). Despite the previous findings of other consultors in this case, Corgna argued that the *societas* ended at the death of the one brother and that the minor heirs could not contract a new one. The uncles as guardians could not also treat their wards as business partners. As tutors their role was to deal with the personal expenses of the minors, not their business. Such minors could not agree to the association on their own, as they were too young. Any *societas* would have to be new, not a continued or renovated version. The two remaining brothers were the contributors, not their young nephews, so any *societas* should have been with them only. Conversely, if they operated for their nephews, they were putting their share at risk of the dangers of seaborne traffic and other perils of the world of trade. Though there were transactions on the books that were said to be also for the sake of the nephews, there were many more that were described as implicating only the uncles.[82] It is interesting that in reaching this decision, Corgna at no point mentioned any of the other evident features of a *societas*, such as common household. He kept the focus on business and saw the *societas* in those terms alone. He also kept his eyes on individual ownership rights and shares, while, in contrast, it seems the uncles were keeping their eyes on the patrimony as an entirety and as something that continued through time. They hardly took account of the minority of their nephews and could not dictate a new arrangement with their wards.

Another case, finally, reminds us that not all domestic situations were peaceful. One man used his will to name a minor son heir and impose the charge to live with his uncles (the testator's brothers) and not to come to a division of property with them before turning twenty-five. The testator also wanted his widow there with usufruct for her dowry. So the boy and his mother lived there for fifteen years holding in common, perpetuating their domestic lives with the uncles. Then the boy sought division, which his uncles denied, as he was not yet twenty-five. Son and mother moved out and sought financial support. The podestà of Massa heard the charge that one uncle had tried to hit the boy and frequently threatened him, and

[82] Da Corgna, *cons.* 308, fols. 242va–43va.

that was why they had left. They wanted arbiters appointed to affect a settlement. The uncles argued that the son's acts were contrary to the will and provoked the whole situation, and they denied that they were quarrelsome. The marchioness of Massa sent the case to Mariano Sozzini on December 8, 1523. He decided that the son's case should be heard and that he clearly had rights to a portion of the property from which the *fructus* would serve to support him and his mother separately. Such an allowance was not the same as dividing title. It was clear that the son did not want to live with his uncles.[83] Sozzini acted to keep peace and order in the short term, as sooner or later the boy would reach twenty-five and be free by terms of the will to seek a division. One wonders how that went.

CONCLUSIONS

In the legal terms of family belonging, as distinct from those of residence, being subject to *patria potestas* was defining of membership for those in ascending and descending lines (marriage being a different issue). The father was also legal owner of family property (again, marital property being an exception), though legitimate sons had so automatic a claim on the property and came to contribute to it that their rights were a form of restriction on the father's free control and disposal of property.

Household integrity was a different matter and was highly problematic in early modern Italy. The biological basis of the home was weak under the unending assault of high mortality rates and fluctuating markets. Many of the residents were not blood related, as young people moved about for education, domestic service, or other business. Conflicts – between fathers and sons, between brothers – might all lead to changes in residence or to frequent comings and goings so as to confuse the most observant neighbors. Legal obligations did not neatly map residence. A son living with his father might be emancipated and thus legally severed from liability, while a son living elsewhere might be his father's agent and fully liable. These liabilities, or their lack, might be useful to those within a household or to those outside it, depending on circumstances. Law was the filter through which so much of such change and interaction ran. The bottom line was that legal acts always carried a double meaning, on the one hand expressing sentiments and desires, on the other touching in some way the structure of the family and its patrimonial viability.[84]

---

[83] Sozzini, 1 *cons.* 79, fols. 140rb–41rb.
[84] Bellomo, "Famiglia (diritto intermedio)," 748.

As the legal family did not necessarily coincide with the residential unit and the ownership of property was not truly collective, there was substantial room for discrepancies between expectations (of those inside and outside the family) and realities regarding rights and obligations. These could be further complicated by inserting under *patria potestas*, by means of legitimation or adoption, those not initially subject to it. Jurists confronted the resulting cases with juristic tools of interpretation, not always to similar results in every case (how could they, as they took on clients on different sides of parallel issues over their careers?) but along similar lines of argument. And the issues were astoundingly similar across a number of cities and jurisdictions thanks to the underlying consistency of *ius commune* and to a certain similarity even of statutes. Residence in common and ownership in common were circumstances all were familiar with. There could be and were mutual liabilities in such situations that statutes strove to enforce. But *societas* was about management of the fruits and revenues of an estate, it was about *industria* and *fortuna*, and only in those dimensions was individual ownership and agency coopted and, only by mutual (even if tacit) agreement. Even within the *societas*, then, a non-business-related expense, such as dowry, came from the putative share of the father whose duty it was to meet that expense. Others in the *societas* were not liable for it, except with their consent.

4

Household

Marriage and Married Life

Monna Leonarda, daughter of Count Silvio of San Bonifacio, was married by her father's arrangement to messer Antonio Nogarola of Verona with a promised dowry of 1,000 ducats. Her father's property, however, had been confiscated by the duke of Ferrara, and the public treasury (fisc) contested her claim for the dowry on the grounds that a father was not bound to dower a married daughter, and so much less so was the fisc bound to dower her with his confiscated wealth. If she was due a dowry, there was enough value in other of her father's holdings in and around Verona to take care of it. Bartolomeo Cipolla was thrust into the midst of this highly politicized dispute between the wife of a prominent citizen and the officials of Verona. He also found himself in the midst of a legal debate, as the *communis opinio* was that a father was not obliged to dower a daughter already married, but equally there was a common sense that fathers had an obligation to dower their daughters, even if they married without paternal consent.

Cipolla, acting with decisory capacity and not *pro parte* in this case, determined the father was in fact obliged to marry and dower his daughter, and Count Silvio had accomplished only one of those tasks. Leonarda's need for a dowry had not vanished once she was married, "since it is in a woman's interest to have a dowry so she may be better treated by her husband." Leonarda had been married with her father's consent to an extremely worthy man, so she was entitled to a suitable dowry. Cipolla also noted that typical inheritance statutes left a woman with only her dowry as inheritance from her father:

but if by statute a dowered daughter does not succeed, but must be dowered, there being son or agnate males, as is commonly the case in Italy, then it would be evident and most equitable that a married woman can seek to be dowered, lest she lack both the right to succeed and dowry.

Cipolla said a judge should step in and compose a fitting dowry in view of her father's wealth and the high rank of her husband. And the fisc was liable to provide from her father's property. The obligation did not fall on her brother Leonello, who had been given paternal property near Verona with the intent that the property remain in the hands of the counts of San Bonifacio in perpetuity.[1] Cipolla went with a noble family in preference to the fisc, notably so in keeping the son's stake, the true patrimony of the counts of San Bonifacio, out of account for the dowry.

Here we see two vital elements of a valid marriage in Italian societies: consent of the spouses (though arranged by the parents, or at least the wife's) and the provision of a dowry from the wife's family. The dowry, as Cipolla's *consilium* makes clear, was the woman's inheritance share (in the face of brothers or other male agnates) by local statute. So her right to dowry (and to its preservation, as we will soon see) was forcefully stated and defended. We also encounter one cause of frequent disputes about dowry, a serious delay in payment. Placing in the hands of arbitrators the judgment as to how much worth a suitable dowry should have was also fairly common, if there were dispute. To a professional like Cipolla, the amount of a dowry was not a matter of law but a matter of fact, and thus best left to others closer to the family. Delicate negotiations, typically between a girl's father and her future husband or his father, lay behind many dowries.

IUS COMMUNE

In medieval and early modern societies, and not just in Italy by any means, marriage was the main event in women's lives, socially and economically, of course, but also legally. In most all of Christian Western Europe the establishment and dissolution of marriage fell to the canon law and ecclesiastical courts. That fact placed a large part of a vital social moment outside the purview of lay laws and courts. Roman civil law had necessarily been concerned with marriage, though in surprisingly loose and even sparse terms, so there was a textual tradition there that could come under discussion in the universities and contributed to canon law's treatment of marriage. But canon law was also bound to the Church's

---

[1] Cipolla, 2 *cons.* 8, 30a–34a.

sacramental notion of marriage and therefore bound to diverge from the sense of marriage to be found in secular civil law.

There were two main points of divergence between canon and civil law regarding marriage. One was that canon law demanded marital consent from the spouses but not from their parents or other kin. In canon law *patria potestas* did not play into the establishment of a marriage, although it continued to play a vital role in the establishment of a functioning household in the gifts and property arrangements that accompanied marriage. The other point of divergence was the effective absence in canon law of divorce in anything like the form it had in Roman law. Judicial separations could be allowed under certain circumstances, but not even adultery could be alleged to end a marriage. In fact, given life expectancies and mortalities resulting from pregnancy and, for some social classes, difference in age of spouses at their wedding, it has been calculated that the average marriage lasted only fifteen years or so. Remarriage, especially for men, was fairly frequent and, as a result, so were what now are termed blended families of stepparents and stepchildren, uterine and agnate siblings.

Canon law, for all its insistence on spousal consent and sacramentality, also strangely had no prescribed ritual of marriage and no formal requirements establishing proof of marriage. What mattered was the expression of consent by each spouse to the other in words of the present tense (e.g., I take you as wife/husband). If consent were expressed in the future tense, the result was an engagement or betrothal, not yet a marriage. The betrothal (*sponsalitium*) was an enforceable contract that could carry significant penalties if it was not observed. A highly public engagement involved the honor and reputation of the families, so the breakdown of a betrothal could be an emotional and volatile moment. It is interesting that in Florence the legend persisted that the city's notorious Guelf and Ghibelline factions of the thirteenth century had their origin in the vendetta unleashed in consequence of a broken engagement.

In the absence of requiring witnesses or registration, or an officiating presence, the problem of "clandestine" marriages plagued Church courts. Were persons betrothed by the terms of canon law to have sexual intercourse later, even without ever exchanging words of consent in present tense, they were considered married in the eyes of the law. So, despite the emphasis on consent, consummation continued to play a role in defining marriage. But unless someone witnessed such intercourse or, more normally, the exchange of present consent, it was possible for one of the spouses, or even both, to deny they were married. Such denial could make for de facto divorce. It also left a great deal of uncertainty around a vital social institution, the stability of which and the offspring from which contributed to enduring social stability. But effective divorces or separations could take many forms, including legal separation. It was also possible for spouses to seek to end a marriage by alleging some impediment or disqualifying factor. The definition of marital incest within four degrees of consanguinity at the Lateran Council in 1215 provided a fair range of people one could not, in theory, marry. Dispensations were sought to get around such prohibitions – that of Henry VIII of England, so he could marry his brother's widow, Catherine of Aragon, was only the most famous. But consanguinity might be alleged to end a relationship, even after many years (as Henry VIII also tried to do). It was also possible to argue that one was too young at the time, although persistence in the relationship after reaching canonical age (which was in the early teens) could well undercut that argument. Another potential argument was that one entered a marriage (or a convent, monastery, or clerical life in general, which was the alternative to marriage) only under pressure and out of fear, of one's father, for example.

There was also the complication of acts of compulsion or seeming compulsion to affect a marriage against parental wishes. Acts of rape or abduction could also function as forms of elopement. As Giovanni Cazzetta has nicely noted, from ancient times law was inclined to protect not free will but honest choices. The result was a constant tension between the values covered by a term like "honest" (or honorable) and the acts of will that did not always correspond. Women could be "persuaded" to dishonest things in the eyes of the law. Categories of rape (*stuprum*) with force, without force, by persuasion – all carried different penalties.

The indeterminacy of the legal boundaries between women's consent and dissent belongs then to the logic of the system and is a faithful reflection of it: it is not born from the incapacity to individuate abstract reconstructive rules, but from the need to recall all the threads of the discourse on the model of honesty.

The woman whose choices were not in accord with *honestas* was not worthy of law's protection. There was no general discussion of freedom to make sense of consent.[2] Where compulsion was established, the case often resulted in the culprit being ordered to marry his victim, if he could, so as to salvage her honor and that of her family, or at least being ordered to give her a dowry. So the ravishment of a maiden could serve as a

---

[2] Cazzetta, *Praesumitur seducta*, 15–95.

convenient fiction to force a father's hand, at least as far as agreeing to the marriage, if not extending to generosity in the form of a dowry and other marital gifts. This was an area in which marriage problems touched on criminal law, as was also the case with bigamy and adultery. And there were always sexual unions, including those of clergy or religious, that were real but unofficial, of varying duration, and productive of illegitimate children.

Stricter patriliny, as in elite marriages in Bologna, required greater control of marriage choices as a vital family strategy. In this situation Mauro Carboni then finds that women were ready if passive tools: "Women's silent obedience conformed to the submissiveness prescribed by patriarchal ideology and was, in itself, a clear indication of the patriarch's ability to impose strict discipline. It signaled, also, the daughters' acceptance of their obligations to the family, and of the ancillary role assigned to their gender."[3] Yet Lucia Ferrante, looking at the same city, but utilizing ecclesiastical court records and not marriage contracts, found that women especially were quite willing, with a court system open to their pleas on the basis of lack of consent, to argue – albeit after the fact – against parental spousal selections. They sought separations or annulments. They alleged breach of promise and even bigamy by their husbands. These women were hardly docile, at least once opportunity offered, which might not be until after parents died. And it was not just Bologna that saw such behavior. Daniela Hacke and Joanne Ferraro have found parallels in Venice. And any fear alleged as precluding true consent had to be substantial. Mere fear of one's *pater* was not sufficient to breach a marriage or monastic vow. Such "reverential fear" did not rise to the level of the "grave" or "horrible" fear that was required to claim there was no valid consent to one's vows.

If anything, it was sons who were more docile before paternal wishes, as they had to fear disinheritance. Another part of the equation of male docility seems to have been a practice, general in many families, to see to the marriages of women first. That would both delay marriage for men (and even more so in larger families) and keep them working to contribute to their sisters' dowries. Contrarily, men whose marriages might be postponed until after their father's death were able to choose their bride more freely, while also coming into a dowry from her at the point the father was no longer around to try to control it.

---

[3] Carboni, "Marriage Strategies and Oligarchy in Early Modern Bologna," 246.

In his investigation of families and marriages in Veneto cities, James Grubb concludes that the lack of any uniform marriage ritual left observers uncertain as to what moment marriage actually occurred. Church authorities and ecclesiastical courts, unsurprisingly, were resistant to easy dissolution of marriage and took the stance of a bias toward marriage (*favor matrimonii*) when in doubt. Bigamy, concubinage, rape, while they all were transgressive moments, in fact also point to a degree of flexibility and adaptation. Roman law, unlike canon law, continued to recognize concubinage as a long term sexual and residential relationship that implied a sort of "marital affection" but that nonetheless did not rise to the level of formal marriage, although the partners were able to marry each other legally. Mainly in concubinage there was no dowry and thus no commitment equivalent to marriage. Children from such a union had a particular status as *naturales*, better than spurious bastards, but they were not legitimate. Still, they had some rights to inheritance, and thus statutes of some cities took cognizance of them and attempted to regulate those rights. In the end, as Cristellon remarks, "the boundary between betrothal, marriage, and concubinage is slippery" and so was the boundary on the other side, between a recognized marriage and its dissolution.[4]

In most laymen's eyes and those of most jurists, the one thing that unequivocally established the fact of marriage was the assignment of a dowry from the wife's family to the husband, with corresponding counter gifts from him to her. This was not only a set of material and symbolic transfers, it was the substance of a marital contract. "Endowment presupposed a certain social status and had the meaning of an important public manifestation insofar as it was an exchange between families."[5] Countervailing commitments of familial resources were in reality at the heart of marriages at least as much as any expressions of consent.

Not until 1563, near the end of the Council of Trent, dedicated to Church reform in the wake of Protestantism, did the Church devise a format for the celebration of marriage that would do away with the problem of clandestine marriage, something which Protestants ridiculed as they reformed marriage themselves. The Catholic Church continued to insist on the centrality of spousal consent, but after Trent it ordered that marriages take place in the woman's parish and only after the publication of bans (notice of intent to marry) over several preceding weeks. So while parental consent was still not an operative feature of marriage formalities,

---

[4] Cristellon, *Carità e l'eros*, 29.   [5] Mainoni, "Il potere di decidere," 218..

bans at least gave parents and kin a reasonable opportunity to learn of their offspring's intent and act on it. Bans also provided some discipline to the process of betrothal. The presence of an officiating priest ensured both a witness and some guarantee of the proper expression of intent. Marriage, which began, as always, with a private agreement, became legalized in a public ceremony, and took on a more religious tone, as the priest took on a centrality that used to be the woman's father's in most instances. In the conciliar debates on marriage, there was clear division between advocates of the requirement for parental (read, paternal) consent with a family-oriented sense of marriage and those in favor of no such requirement, wary of the shortcomings and self-interests of parents.

Marriage established the husband as head of the family, but it did not give him a power over his wife that was as consistent as the *patria potestas* he could hope to have over his children from her. Texts of the *ius commune* conceded that a wife was in submission (*obsequium*) to her husband and owed him various tasks and labor, covered under the term *servitia* (which also described the duties a slave owed her master). There was a vague allowance made for physical punishment of a noncompliant wife, but there were also limits to the husband's powers of coercion and correction that canon law courts were willing to explore. The realities of a woman's contributions to a household could always temper masculine impertinence.

One other important area of the influence of civil law was the wife's status after marriage. Though she changed households, she did not change families. That was at the heart of her ambiguous position in the marital home. If under her father's *potestas* at the time of marriage, she remained so; she also remained agnate to her natal family. Her property remained separate from her husband's. To keep her husband from tricking her out of her holdings, as she was free to make legal contracts, the Roman law came to carry a ban on inter vivos gifts between spouses that became part of the *ius commune* as well. The converse to this legal protection was the wife's exposure to prosecution, by husband or father, for adultery (with consequent loss of dowry on a successful prosecution).

The *ius commune* thus precluded the sort of legal situation married women in England faced, which was known as coverture. The ecclesiastical and sacramental conceit that husband and wife became one flesh (an expression also used in civil law regarding father and legitimate son) in England resulted in the sense that the one flesh was the husband. Though marriage could result in a quite effective partnership, social and economic, the wife's legal identity was subsumed into that of her husband (to reemerge in her widowhood). It was not possible to bring suit against one's spouse, aside from a few matters and some exceptions allowed in London. Conversely, a woman under *ius commune* retained some legal independence, if only because of her continuing legal ties to her family of origin. Her property remained separate, if not necessarily under her control. She could, in legal theory, transfer it or concoct a will to direct it to whom she wished. The realities might be something different, and the jurisdictions of Italy weighed in on women's status and legal capacity as they saw fit, opening up several interesting areas of contrast between local laws and *ius commune*.

Roman law furnished a base line on women's status to which statutes variously reacted. True, women were not equal to men; D. 1.5.9 admitted as much. In theory they could not obligate themselves for others and in that regard were supposedly barred from much contractual business. In fact, they were quite active as guarantors of others' contracts, though, as we will see, statutes often demanded that they be accompanied by consenting males when they did so. Their ability to do so rested otherwise on the fact that women had inheritance and other property rights and were able to act in law to exercise those rights. Of course it was easy for jurists to accommodate a level of misogyny and uphold women's disabilities, at least in theory. The jurist Lorenzo da Palazzoli, in a treatise on the very common statutes disadvantaging women in inheritance, certainly had no problem justifying statutory disadvantages: "nature gave the husband power over the wife. Likewise much greater sense and mind. If therefore nature honors males more in respect to the woman, why can it not honor them more in inheritance, which is, as I said, a matter of positive law, although it has a natural quality" [*instinctum naturae]?*[6] There was some provision of guardianship for women, while civil law precluded them from being guardians of others, even their own children, until some late reforms of Justinian. It was here that canon law had another effect, as it looked to maternal affection as a guarantee for children in the absence of a father and allowed mothers to act as their children's guardian. The separate status of her property was a positive factor. In contrast to guardians who were agnate and likely in the line to inherit from the minors under their tutelage, a mother was seemingly disinterested because she could not inherit from them, while her property was a benefit for the children in other regards.

---

[6] *Tractatus super statuto communiter per Italiam vigente quod extantibus masculis foeminae non succedant,* in *Tractatus universi iuris,* vol. 2, fols. 272ra–83rb, at 279ra.

A woman's right to dowry was one of the most strongly stated rights in the civil law. In his commentary to the most vital text regarding dowry (D. 24.3.22), Baldo degli Ubaldi explained that "the nature of the dowry and the father's obligation for dowering a daughter cannot be removed by a simple agreement, the nature of dowry is a sort of communion between father and daughter (*quadam communione inter patrem et filiam*) . . . and the father's obligation provides for the daughter even on dissolution of marriage."[7] That sense of communion between father and daughter mirrored the substantial union of father and son that Bartolo had projected with regard to inheritance. And the obligation of a husband's property for return of the dowry on the dissolution of the marriage was equally absolute. Her dowry gave a woman a lien on her husband's property (an implied mortgage), giving her priority (but certainly not exclusive claim) over all her husband's creditors.

Dowry was the main area of interest regarding marriage for secular courts and the point at which fathers had the most influence on marital formation. The father would determine when and how much the dowry would be. The husband then became steward but not owner of the property, most often an amount of cash or property given a monetary value. The dowry was to be "returned" at the dissolution of marriage, which, in the absence of divorce, mainly meant at the death of one of the spouses. Further restricting the husband was the rule that dowry property could be alienated only with the wife's consent. Adultery, however, could cost the wife her dowry.

Ius commune in the course of the fourteenth century went further and fully elaborated the right of a wife whose husband was going broke (*vergens ad inopiam*) to seek her dowry, to place it under her control, even during marriage (*constante matrimonio*). More pointedly, if her husband mistreated her, as by physical abuse or by taking a concubine and bringing her into the marital home, a wife could sue, mainly in ecclesiastical courts, for a separation of bed and board (*a mensa et thoro*). If that succeeded, she might get her dowry, but more likely separate maintenance while the dowry remained with her husband. She had an undoubted right to seek support (*alimenta*) from her husband. Dowry was said to exist for the sake of supporting the "burdens" of married life, so it could not be allowed to dissipate and leave a wife in penury, at possible peril to her soul, should she be driven to prostitution or other dishonest acts.

---

[7] Baldo to D. 24.3.22, *Opera omnia*, 10 vols. (Venice, 1577), vol. 3, fol. 10va.

A wife had a more direct right to other property she might have brought to the marital home that was not dowry. These goods were broadly labeled *paraphernalia*, and the husband had rights of control or use on these too, but in a weaker fashion than with dowry. Roman law also provided for a *donatio propter nuptias*, a gift from the bridegroom to his bride at marriage, which was a guarantee of support for her initially. Justinian's rule that the *donatio* was to be of equal value to the *dos*, however, was more or less a dead letter by the late Middle Ages. The practice persisted and was part of a cycle of prestations around the event of a marriage, but dowry became the key ingredient while the *donation* diminished in value. Still, there could also be considerable value in the gifts, especially of jewelry and clothing, that the groom would provide to attire his bride suitably for her ceremonial passage to his house (*ductio*). He would retain ownership of these items, but they could amount to a substantial investment. To secular courts proof of dowry was the best proof of marriage.

STATUTORY LAW AND CASES

Dowry

As dowry came into general use in the twelfth century, coinciding with the renewed interest in and study of Roman law and the expansion of canon law, the communes and principalities had to integrate it into a web of existing cultural and legal practices, including those revolving around gender and family. What almost every community decided was to proclaim that the dowry was the woman's share of the patrimony of her natal family. She could claim no more family assets if she had a dowry.

At first the exclusion of a dowered daughter was accomplished by having her formally renounce her rights to seek any more than the dowry, which was usually done at the time of the wedding. This practice would continue in sporadic use. But ultimately most everywhere cities enacted a statute, or several, governing intestacy and decreeing the exclusion of dowered women from becoming heirs to father, brother, or other agnate men when there were surviving legitimate male agnates. Mothers were similarly excluded from inheritance from their children or grandchildren; in some cases the excluding presence included not only children, brothers, or fathers, but even sisters, as agnatic relations (which a mother was not). Some statutes also limited what a dowered woman could inherit by testament. The exact shape of the exclusion of dowered women varied from place to place. We will examine these measures more fully in the next chapter.

Marriage was "the central event in a woman's life." Dowry was crucial to that moment and also, according to one historian, "an adaptive mechanism coinciding with peak fertility to ensure survival of offspring."[8] Jurists had it that dowry was a device to meet the material burdens of married life. From a more overtly economic position, it has been argued that dowries to daughters at marriage avoided the disincentive to sons that would result if bequests to daughters also came at inheritance, instead of at marriage, because the son would have remained in the paternal home, while his married sister would have moved away. This argument sees no real favoritism toward sons as opposed to daughters, and no disproportionately larger shares for sons. But it is also importantly the case that dowry was about more than material assets. It was also a cultural artifact whose primary association was with female and familial honor. Dowry was accompanied by other gifts and property transfers, in both directions, which spoke to the union of members of honorable families.

It is broadly assumed that a woman's dotal share was usually less than the inheritance share her brother realized, and thus dowry was a disadvantage in general to women. Scholars as diverse as James Grubb and Anna Bellavitis, working on Veneto and Venetian materials, and Christiane Klapisch-Zuber and Isabelle Chabot working on Florentine sources, have stated that daughters' dowries were less than their brothers' inheritance shares. The logic of the dotal system would seem to demand such a distinction in values between men and women. In a classic study examining the law on dowries, Manlio Bellomo noted that jurists came to see dowry as a daughter's inheritance share (*patrimonium filiae*) that, as Laurent Mayali also observed, was not the same as a legitimate portion of the inheritance. Above all, it was left to the father, or whoever else constituted the dowry, to determine what was a fair value for it. In any case, it is fair to say, as Kirshner has concluded, that "unlike sons, daughters, even with enviable dowries, occupied an anomalous legal space. Technically speaking, they were neither legally disinherited nor legally heirs."[9]

Yet, as Bellomo also points out, in order to justify the exclusion of dowered women from inheritance, there had to be real value in the dowry. Statutes, however vaguely, seemed to demand that. The reality of dotal values was echoed in the frequent complaints of fathers and

[8] Hanlon, *Human Nature in Rural Tuscany*, 111–14.
[9] Kirshner, "Family and Marriage," 100.

others about the difficulties of assembling dowries. Florence went so far as
to establish a civic dowry fund to help the city's fathers cope with the
problem. So there are those scholars (Botticini and Siow) who maintain
that what sons eventually inherited was not terribly disproportionate to
what their sisters took away as their dowries, especially as the sons
remained unmarried, contributing to those dowries and to the size of
the estate they hoped to receive.

The value of dowries clearly also escalated nominally in the period
1300–1600. Agreement on this score is just about universal among the
scholars who have studied dowry values. Such inflation may have
changed the relative dynamic between women's and men's shares of a
patrimony. Stanley Chojnacki has suggested that higher dowry values put
more wealth in the hands of women and amplified their power and roles
in the family. Others (Chabot, Bellavitis) are not so sure of that. Simple
logic might say that higher dowry values meant fewer dowries could be
assembled. The result was fewer women married, more of them remaining
celibate, with the fortunate ones finding space in a convent. Convents
undoubtedly spread in urban areas and saw increasing numbers of nuns.
The driver behind this inflation, according to Grubb and Klapisch-Zuber,
among others, was social competition for prestige by getting a more
desirable match. The boost to family honor was greater the higher the
dotal sum celebrated at marriage. In any case, those higher dowry values
may have made girls more dependent on parents to assemble the dowries,
and thus more compliant to parental choices. They certainly made it more
difficult for them to marry.

Poorer folks sometimes married with unspecified dotal values, but by
and large poorer girls received aid from testamentary bequests of local
notables or charitable institutions to assemble some sort of dowry, with
little parental help. Allan Tulchin has argued that in France such poor
girls were more liable to operate without parental permission or involvement in their marriages, but there seems little evidence that such was the
case in rural areas of Italy. Even the poorest had pretensions to honor and
thus to a marriage that involved parents and some small portion of
family goods.

For now, with regard to marriage and related topics, leaving aside
their effects on inheritance, the important point to make is that the
statutes excluding dowered women typically also gave solid guarantees
of the right to a dowry. How large the dowry should be was left
vague at best, buried behind terms like suitable, fitting, adequate, or
"competent." And it was certainly true that the dowry required for a

girl's entry to a convent need not be as large as that for a marriage. But the guarantee of a dowry was set forth in statutes more forcefully than even in *ius commune*.

Ius commune itself was quite forthright in protecting women's right to dowry. Bartolo noted that a father could be forced to provide a suitable dowry and that for purposes of assembling one, property could be pried out from other obligations. The right to dowry was concomitant with the right to be fed and supported: "For just as it is a paternal duty to dower, so it is a paternal duty to feed [one's offspring]."[10] Baldo degli Ubaldi followed his teacher's lead, adding that constituting dowries "is special in favor of marriage" (*est speciale favore matrimonii*) and that it was a matter of public good to promote marriage. Return of dowry to a woman on dissolution of marriage was similarly privileged and protected. Baldo also took note of the statutes that demanded dowered women remain content with the dowry as their portion of an inheritance and declared that if the dowry given by a father was not, as the statutes demanded, *congrua*, then goods otherwise obligated for some reason could be alienated to bring the dowry up to that standard.[11]

Statutes were very direct about women's right to dowry. Florence's statutes of 1325 said that a woman not yet dowered "convenienter" at the time of her father's death was to be dowered from his property "according to the father's status and faculty" (*secundum dignitatem et facultatem patris*). Until she was married she also had a clear right to *alimenta* from his estate. This language persisted in Florence's later statutes of 1355 and 1415, the latter making only the slight change from "convenienter" to "competenter."[12] Milan's statutes of 1498 carried the provision that women were excluded from ascendants in the male line in favor of men but that they had to be dowered "appropriately according to the quality of the persons and the strength of the patrimony" (*decenter secundum qualitatem personarum et vires patrimonii*) by the time they were eighteen, and furnished *alimenta* before that point. If they were not, then they had the right to petition the courts for up to a third of "what they would have received by *ius commune*."[13] That clause may betray an interesting presupposition as to what percentage of patrimony was meant by "competenter" or similar terms.

---

[10] Bartolo to Auth. Res quae, *Opera omnia*, 10 vols. (Venice, 1615), vol. 6, fol. 45ra–b.

[11] Baldo to Auth. Res quae, *Commentaria in vi codicis librum* (Venice, 1577), fols. 160vb–61va.

[12] Florence, *Statuta* 1415, 1: 223–25; Florence 1325, 139–41.   [13] Milan 1498, fol. 82v.

In Treviso a couple of different wrinkles were added, along with the usual guarantee of a dowry and *alimenta*. If no dowry was left in a will, a group of six close kin, three from the father's side and three from the mother's, were to decide on dowry. If they could not agree, the matter could then be taken to court, presumably by the girl or her prospective husband, though the statute itself does not specify a procedure. Another statute noted that girls whose fathers had died were at the mercy of brothers or others who by negligence or some other reason did not hasten to set up a dowry and marry them off. So it was allowed that once a woman reached twenty, two kin, one paternal and one maternal, could devise a dowry for her with the aid of the podestà.[14] Viterbo concocted a similar rule, aimed squarely at brothers as the culprits in delaying dowry and marriage, ordering the city's podestà to force the issue of dowry, "according to the value of the farm and the status of the person and the customs of our land" (*secundum facultatem poderis et conditionem personae et consuetudinem terre nostre*).[15] Another statute, in vaguer terms, spoke of the advice of near kin (*consanguinei*) to fatherless girls about marriage and having their marriages and dowries documented before Viterbo's priors.[16]

Communities like Treviso and Viterbo, needless to say, shared Baldo's view that marrying was in the public interest. Marrying outside the community, however, was not necessarily so good. Arezzo declared that if a foreigner married an Aretine girl and they lived elsewhere and did not return to Arezzo, after six years the wife could seek her dowry and possess it directly (*intrare tenutam*).[17] It is hard to see how a decree of an Aretine court would be upheld in whatever distant venue the couple then lived in, but the sense of loss of a person and, more importantly, taxable property was something most every city faced in marriage with citizens of other places.

Dowry was also a consistent feature of Jewish marriages. As with Christian marriages, dowries were recorded in written acts, often by Christian notaries, who operated on the assumption that Jews had their own law. Of course there was no official Jewish law code, and most cities or regions did not house a rabbinical court. Some Jewish dowry pacts sought the return of a deceased childless woman's dowry to her natal family, in contravention of what was seen as rabbinic law and even local statutes. Jews could thus take advantage of the willingness of local courts

---

[14] Treviso, 369–70, 380.   [15] Viterbo, 142.   [16] Viterbo, 156.   [17] Arezzo, 172.

and authorities to entertain a distinct law for them. As Jews tended to marry earlier than their neighbors and in greater proportion (as marriage was a universal ideal), retrieval of a dowry when there were no grandchildren could allow for marriage of another girl.

This chapter began with a case in which right to dowry figured. *Consilia* consistently show jurists strongly upholding women's rights to dowry. On January 24, 1461, Bartolomeo de Moreni promised Antonio de la Rosta a 250 *lire* dowry for his daughter Lucia, engaged to Antonio's son Marsilio, to be taken in the form of property Bartolomeo had near Carpi. Father and son bore the expenses of the household for several years before the dowry was in fact paid over. Their suit was about their claim to realize equivalent fruits from the property for those years and possibly even a penalty for late payment. Alessandro Tartagni posed that a dowry promise was a form of *ultro citroque* (back and forth) contract that was effective from the point the wedding and *ductio* (public transfer of the bride to her husband's home) occurred. The bride's father was indeed liable.[18] Legal practitioners such as Tartagni were avid to enforce payment of dowries, which otherwise generated suits such as this.

One case that came to Filippo Decio even raised the rare issue of how much a dowry had to be to be truly suitable or congruent, to use the language found in statutes. When the daughter of Jacopo dei Rubei married, her dowry was 500 *aurei*. Her father thereafter did quite nicely for himself, so at his death the daughter argued (or her husband did) that her dowry was no longer *competens* and she should be allotted more. Decio knew that she could not claim to have been dowered *incompetenter*, because her father had done the best he could with what he had at the time, considering his wealth (*facultates*) and the status of the prospective spouses. Certainly "the father better than others seems to take care for his daughter," Decio added, "because no love exceeds paternal love" (*quia nullus amor vincit paternum*). So the amount she had been given, he declared, was just and right. It was also consistent with the customs of Pistoia, where dowry did not rise to the level of a legitimate portion of the inheritance, especially as this daughter's dowry was not being constituted from the estate after her father's death, but had been arranged by him in life. To ask for an increase just because the father had gained more wealth did not seem equitable because certainly "if the father's assets had been diminished the daughter would not want the dowry given her to

---

[18] Tartagni, 5 *cons.* 147, fols. 107rb–8ra.

diminish." Decio, nonetheless, shifted ground and agreed with her argument, claiming that the *communis opinio* was that a dowry should approximate the legitimate portion. The main prop to his opinion was that at Pistoia by statute a daughter was excluded from inheritance in favor of males. In compensation for her exclusion the dowry should not be less than the legitimate portion, such that her exclusion was mitigated. Only if the statute further demanded that the dowered daughter remain content with the dowry – as, in fact, many such statutes did – could she not seek to supplement her dowry in light of the size of a legitimate portion.

Pistoia's statute made no such demands, and many times fathers did not either. Decio's decision thus emerged from a narrow reading of the statute, favoring the daughter. We do not know if his argument swayed the judge, but it is interesting that he could advance it. It was the case that some fathers supplemented daughters' dowry shares with bequests in their wills. Such testamentary gifts were one means of achieving more parity with the legitimate portion. Had there been another daughter, unmarried and undowered, her dowry would have been drawn up from the greater wealth Jacopo dei Rubei had at a later point, closer to his death, which would mean that the married daughter would be in worse position (*deterioris conditionis*) than her younger, undowered sibling. The exact dimension of *competenter*, said Decio, was to be weighed at the time of the father's death, because it was in that context (succession) that the term arose in the statute. The argument from equity, that there would not be a proportionate reduction of the dowry if the father's fortunes had instead been adverse, did not hold in view of the statute that excluded the dowered and married woman from inheritance, for then "in compensation for exclusion she must be more richly endowed" (*pinguius debet dotari*). There was in this case an additional wrinkle, in that the father was also owner of extensive properties in the territory of Naples, which could not be governed by a Pistoiese statute. Decio thus concluded that the additional assets to increase the dowry should come precisely from these Neapolitan holdings.[19]

His decision could not have been well received by her brothers or whomever was heir to her father, and Decio's decision was unique among those I have consulted. Other jurists in so many other cases had little trouble deciding that what a woman realized as dowry did not have to be

---

[19] Decio, *cons.* 276, fols. 301va–2rb.

a full, legitimate portion of the paternal estate. None of them insisted that the suitability of a dotal share was measured at the point of inheritance rather than at the point of marriage. Acting in a partisan manner, Decio found a loophole in the statute, or believed he had, that was unlikely to have precedential weight in many other jurisdictions.

It certainly did not in Tuscany later. Federico di Ruberto de' Ricci in 1572 wrote a will in favor of his son Ruberto, substituting his nephews Ruberto and Vincenzo to him in the absence of heirs in the male line. Dowries to female descendants were to be competent as calculated by good men, but to be at least 2,000 florins. Ruberto inherited and, in turn, left a son and two daughters, who were married. Their brother died childless. The married sisters sued Ruberto and Vincenzo, now heirs by substitution, for those "competent" dowries promised in their grandfather's will, though they had both received dowries of 800 scudi from their brother. The case came to Pietro Cavallo from both parties, so his view was to be decisory. It rested on the subtle reading of the testator's intent, because it was not so easy to see if "competent" dowry was the same as 2,000 florins. The women had in fact received very handsome, more than competent dowries of 800 scudi, and Cavallo's opinion hinged on that. The obligation to dower did not rest with the grandfather, but the father, who had fulfilled his role by providing dowries. The generous dotal bequests to an unknown (at the time of writing the will) number of female descendants might have irreparably harmed the Ricci by diminishing the patrimony. In this case there was no increase of the dowries.[20]

Marriage and Sexuality

Beyond the issue of a dowry, a few cities legislated regarding the forms wedding ceremonies took. As noted already, prior to Trent, the Church really had no single ceremonial and really only the requirement of the exchange of consent in the present tense. Who was present, where, what exact words were used, and what props were used (e.g., a ring, wine, or food) were all fairly fluid. In the previous chapter we saw what sorts of things were looked at in proving *societas* among brothers. Proof of marriage was similarly complicated, unless there were notarial instruments.

[20] Cavallo, *cons.* 69, fols. 73va–78va.

One mode of proof or demonstration of marriage was to make a spectacle of sorts of the move of the wife to the home of the husband (virilocal residence being the norm, at least in wealthier classes). Foligno addressed that matter, known there and many other places as *ductio*. The wife was to go to a church, where the husband was to find her. Accompanied by four men and four women, they were to proceed to his house. As subsequent statutes set out that six men and six women could then dine with the bride and groom, that two days later four of her kin could come to eat with her in her new home, and similar measures, it seems that the main concern in that statutory framework was sumptuary restraint on display and expenditure. The size and expense of the celebration were thus kept under control, as they were by other measures addressing jewelry and clothing. Still, the idea of thus establishing the fact of marriage was not lost on Foligno's legislators. They added directives that any notary involved in a marriage had to notify the podestà immediately about the marriage, and another ordering that the spouses, or one of them, report the marriage to the podestà at least one day before *ductio*, and that the podestà was not merely to accept their sworn word but to make his own inquiries.[21]

Padua sought to regulate marriage at an early point (before 1236) from concerns about parental consent. Anyone who married or betrothed without consent of the woman's parents (both father and mother are specified) would supposedly be fined. Betrothals were also to be recorded in a public instrument, so at some point a notary would be involved and engagement could be known beyond the two immediate families.[22] More than three centuries later, on the eve of the opening of the Council of Trent, Siena issued a law that anyone who betrothed a woman had one month from the day they ceremonially clasped hands (*impalmamento* in some places, described in vernacular expression in this statute as "toccargli la mano") to give her a ring. Young fiancés (minors) were to wait until they came of age. Failure to do so would cost the couple one-quarter of the dowry's value. The father of the husband, who otherwise might receive the dowry, was absolved from the statute's requirements only if his son lived apart or if the betrothal had been arranged without his permission.[23] Parental permission also figured in a Trevisan statute that fined someone 300 *lire* for marrying or betrothing without paternal or maternal consent. If there was doubt as to their consent (presumably

---

[21] Foligno, 334–37.   [22] Padua, 190.   [23] Siena, 243.

because they had since died), the husband had to provide five good and true witnesses. If the woman had no parents, the groom had to marry her before a dozen Trevisan men. The same penalties were said to fall to a woman who married without the permission of the husband's parents.[24]

Saona's laws were concerned only with the woman who acted without parental permission. At least that community had a law to the effect that any woman who left the parental home and stayed away two months, during which she was publicly held to commit adultery and be a whore, was to lose any property or right to it from her family.[25] This could cover what we might take to be elopement. The following law dealt with the case of a woman who left her husband's home, not to live with any close kin but seemingly either simply to separate or to take up with another man. It ordered confiscation of her dowry. The woman was also to be expelled from the city and its territory and could be killed with impunity by anyone who took up a vendetta against her. On the other hand, a husband who ceased to treat his wife as such would be judicially admonished to take her back and change his ways. Intransigence past fifteen days could result in a penalty of twice the value of the dowry.[26]

These measures show how issues of simple consent elided into matters of rape and adultery. At Forlì a law that began with penalties for sodomy moved on to those who raped virgins, wives, or widows of good reputation – penalty of death – while one who kept another's wife without his consent faced a hefty fine, with a lesser fine if the husband knew. A willing adulteress was to lose her dowry to her husband, which was consistent with *ius commune*. A raped virgin who agreed and whose parents consented was to be wed by her attacker.[27] This seems a classic instance of weighing the penalty by the supposed damage to the father, as the deflowered virgin may have had little option but to consent to marriage to salvage her honor.

The commune of Belluno aimed penalties at rapists in accord with the status of their victim. Rape of a loyal and chaste wife resulted in capital punishment, as would rape of a maiden or virgin unless marriage ensued, in which case the appropriate penalty was left to judicial discretion. The penalty was in all cases less if there were only abduction (*raptus*) without sexual contact. Adulteresses in that city also lost their dowries. *Stuprum* (broadly, illicit sexual intercourse) with a good widow led to a fine not only on her attacker but on her, if marriage did not result; and she was

---

[24] Treviso, 380–81.   [25] Saona, 31–32.   [26] Saona, 32–33.   [27] Forlì, 216–18.

also to be exiled from the city.[28] Finally, Florence had a statute that fined one for taking a woman from the family home. It also fined a man or woman who pressed a suit to have a relationship declared a marriage in ecclesiastical or secular court, unless the marriage was demonstrated by a public instrument.[29]

If, at times, statutes such as these contemplated misdeeds by women that reflected badly on their fathers or husbands, there were other moments when statutes confronted misdeeds by those same men, but mainly the husband, in relation to a woman. Arezzo set the line followed by nearby Montepulciano, allowing retrieval of dowry by the wife for mistreatment. If, however, the woman had not been a good wife, she could not then retrieve her dowry. If adultery on her part was established by the testimony of ten good men, then the husband no longer had to feed her. She did not lose her dowry, though she could not petition for its return to her *constante matrimonio*. If there were full judicial proof of adultery, then she would lose her dowry.[30]

Court cases concerning marriage and sexuality have been the object of concern for a number of historians, and in the past decade there has been a fine large-scale project to exploit ecclesiastical court records regarding marriage and related matters from all over Italy. The only comparative study of marriage cases in church courts is the important work of Charles Donahue drawing on records from England, France, and Belgium. Ending with a brief comparison to studies of Italian courts, Donahue offers his impression that Italian courts caught fewer cases than courts to the north. He suggests that the reason behind the statistical difference was that in Italy there was greater parental control of marital choices and more consistent recourse to notarized documentation of betrothals, marriage vows, and dowries (elements of what he characterizes as a "communal" marital property system in Italy).[31] Daniela Lombardi, who has studied marriage law and cases comparatively within Italy, adds the perspective that ecclesiastical judges (at least prior to the implementation of changes in marital law arising from the Council of Trent) tended to be passive rather than active, leaving the parties (under the pressure being applied by one of them by bringing suit) to work out an accommodation that they could live with. Only by the end of the sixteenth century were judges more active and directive, concerned more that parties conform to ecclesiastical

---

[28] Belluno, 289–91.   [29] Florence 1325, 207–08.
[30] Arezzo, 172, and Montepulciano, 139.
[31] Donahue, *Law, Marriage, and Society*, 625–31.

rules.[32] These studies and others have not generally concerned themselves with juristic *consilia*, but as we have seen, these are insightful in many ways, both of actual behavior and of legal issues that made that behavior problematic, or that themselves became problematic in the wake of behavior. Particularly with marital cases, juristic opinions reveal the uncertainties in law and the presumptions of *consulentes*, operating *pro parte* in most instances, thus aligning clients' interests with flexibilities of law. The problems raised by vows in present and in future tense, clandestine unions, marriages contracted through agents, problems of lack of free consent and the role of parents, and the ascertaining of impediments were all recurrent features of court cases concerning marriage.

Few *consilia* deal with exchange of vows and basic assertion of validity of a marriage, and in that seem to support Donahue's impression about Italian marriage courts. Alessandro Tartagni had a situation in which the woman's case for marriage rested on two witnesses. Neither, he claimed, truly showed there had been consent in present tense. The second witness had variously reported that the supposed groom said either "I will take you" or "I take you and I will not ever take another wife than you and I will never leave you until the earth covers my eyes." Such ambiguous evidence could not be construed to mean a marriage had happened, or an injustice would be done to one of the parties to the suit. The assertion that the husband said "I will not take another but you" did not mean he had taken her. Indeed, Tartagni argued that such a florid declaration was not an expression of consent, it was an act of deception, as was the testimony that a third witness had seen her bloody shirt and his bloody member as proof of intercourse following these "vows."[33]

Tartagni was probably acting as counsel for the putative husband in this case and thus argued against the marriage. Lodovico Pontano looked at arguments in favor of one, starting from the fact a court of first instance had decreed that it was valid and, unchallenged, that ruling had become definitive (*res iudicata*). He denied that the wife's arguments against marriage carried any weight on their own. Among other things, if her arguments were to win out, that meant that her deceased husband's son was spurius, had no inheritance rights, and certainly no claims on feudal properties, which then fell to *consanguinei*.[34] More interests than those of a married couple were at stake. Clearly, in his case there had been much more of a marital life and relationship than some brief fling.

---

[32] Lombardi, 156, 165.   [33] Tartagni, 5 *cons.* 152, fols. 112rb–13va.
[34] Pontano, *cons.* 367, fols. 191va–92ra.

A complicated case arose in Padua in 1532 in which Anna Belinger, daughter of the jurist Giovanni Belinger, said she had contracted marriage with the young noble, Jacobo Ollor, and she sought from a judge an order that Jacobo accept her and treat her as his wife. Her proof was a series of letters sent her through an intermediary in which he asked her to marry him. After showing this to her mother and sisters, she had responded affirmatively, "and so for some time they remained in this mutual agreement, though secretly, awaiting the appropriate occasion to proclaim it." Mother, sisters, and a go-between all confirmed the tenor of the letters, but the young suitor denied it all and said "those letters were amatory that he dictated to be written and they had been sent back to him, and he asserted she had torn them up." Sozzini from the start of a long opinion declared that the marriage was valid, and that was the conclusion that coincided with his inclination in such cases. He argued that exchange of consent by letter was perfectly acceptable and that, in any case, jurists commonly held that words were not necessary for marriage but that consent might be proved by many means. The fact that the witnesses in this case were all women did not matter; they could testify in matrimonial cases, unlike in many criminal matters. Sozzini had to spend a lot of ink defending all these witnesses against allegations of bias or lack of knowledge. It seems it was the groom's story he was not buying. What kind of marriage they would end up having in such circumstances is hard to tell. Sozzini's opinion offers no sense that the groom had family and interests and how they might clash with hers. One can doubt that the matter rested there in law, and certainly it did not rest there for the putative bride and groom.[35] But Sozzini's opinion seems to have been given for the judge, so his decision probably followed it.

In another case, also from Padua, Sozzini argued opposite his self-proclaimed inclination to favor marriage. The witnesses to establish the fact of marriage between Giovanfrancesco Ricci and Laura Moranzane were not trustworthy. Presumptions in favor of marriage did not work in this instance:

because great scandal would result that someone unwilling is joined in marriage, it is also by reason of avoiding scandal that one must judge for marriage, for the same reason in our case it is to be judged against marriage. But as from the aforesaid it is resolved from these [witnesses] who are not domestics, since all [allegations] that were brought out against monna Laura appear most clearly

[35] Sozzini, 2 *cons.* 29, fols. 35rb–37va.

false, and so with the reverend Advocate I conclude no marriage is proved and so monna Laura is to be absolved of it.[36]

We do not learn if there was ever a *ductio* of Laura to Ricci's house, though something like that may be what the maligned witnesses were supposed to prove. In any case, Sozzini agreed with Laura's attorney that there had been no marriage. Maligning the witnesses may also have been a consequence of distrust of Ricci's motives in the case.

One way for someone to try to find his or her way out of an unsatisfactory marriage was to allege that it was entered into under duress. Canon law allowed that coerced consent was not free consent, and its consequences could be voided in law. Bartolomeo Cipolla confronted a spectacular case. He began his opinion by noting that he was persuaded against his customary presumption to argue for marriage (*favor matrimonii*). This may just be a declaration of professional neutrality by someone who, in fact, took sides; but he also accorded the other side's arguments some respect, even as he maintained that Girolamo Delfino had been coerced into marrying monna Laura. There were two questions to be resolved in his mind: was Girolamo freely able to marry Laura, and was any fear he might have felt later "purged," such that the marriage could be said to have become valid later, if not immediately. The presence of fear at the marriage's inception could be evaluated in three ways: by threats, by captivity or physical assault, or by suspicion of violence. The problem was how a judge could determine that fear had indeed been a factor.

The arguments in favor of the wedding's validity were rather weak. Delfino should not have felt fear, it was said, "especially as he had often before had carnal relations with her and for that reason he had come back." A sexual affair between Girolamo and Laura had been open knowledge, including to the father. But that knowledge also gave him a motive to force a marriage. Testimony by the father revealed that Girolamo had been summoned to the bride's house so that he could be discovered there and made to marry her. Another man had also been called to the house, so he could act as a witness, but he was also another person Girolamo had to fear. Further, Girolamo's discovery at night in Laura's room gave him sufficient reason to fear, as fathers and husbands had legal leave to kill a man caught in the act of violating a daughter or wife. There seemed sufficient grounds to see fear at work in what we

---

[36] Sozzini, 2 *cons*, 88, fols. 118va–20ra.

might anachronistically term a shotgun wedding. Then there was the fact the father and his friend were armed when they came upon Girolamo in Laura's room, and they used their weapons to cut his thumb and strike him in the mouth and cut his beard in two places. Three witnesses and a barber attested to those wounds. And still Girolamo refused initially to marry Laura, which led to the verbal threat, with flourishing of a key, that Girolamo would not leave the house alive. Girolamo gave in. His alarm did not cease at or after that moment, as even though the arms had been laid aside, they were still close at hand and the father's friend still stood by the door.

For all these reasons, and because the father was "stronger and more daring" (*fortior et magis audax*) than Girolamo, Cipolla found sufficient reason to say that the marriage had resulted from fear and should be dissolved. It was even reported (by Laura's father!) that at the time of marriage Girolamo sighed, "which sigh signifies that he was not satisfied." Yet witnesses also reported that Girolamo went on to eat with the family, shake hands, and kiss the bride. All these circumstances seemed to indicate a lessening or "purging" of his fear. Cipolla argued that all those gestures occurred immediately and thus did not indicate an end to Girolamo's fears. If there was any doubt on that score, one had only to look at what Girolamo did when he finally was no longer a prisoner in his father-in-law's house:

because as soon as he left the house of messer Andrea he showed his finger and broken jaw to an associate of messer Andrea, and he told him what had happened, he was acting against his will and he did not want that Laura as his wife: so on account of this contradiction made immediately after, it appears that what he did he did not do voluntarily nor freely but by force [*nec libere sed coacte*].

Handshakes and kisses could also be acts done out of fear and did not tell against him.[37] Of course, in the end Cipolla was arguing to release a noble caught in flagrante by a possibly irate but also shrewd father. Was Girolamo's fear of weapons really greater than his fear of the resulting social misalliance that frequently sent sexual predators of the nobility and patriciate to court to deny a wedding? In any case, it is clear that all sorts of factors could be and were alleged to substantiate or deny *metus* or free consent.

The canonist Felino Sandei (1444–1503) dealt with a case in which a woman alleged fear. Stella had married Cristoforo Vecchi, a barber, but

[37] Cipolla, 2 *cons.* 16, 71b–75b.

Sandei found no genuine consent on her part. He had no witnesses. She did. And to Sandei's mind they confirmed that she had been afraid her father (dead by the time of the suit) would kill her. Mere *reverentia* for her father that might lead her to consent, lest she incur his anger (*indignatio*), was not necessarily equivalent to acting from fear; but because she was "weaker by reason of her sex," fear was more likely and excusable. In fact, Stella had voiced her disapproval of the match beforehand. The judge should also consider such bits of evidence as "flight from the house, tears, and the difficulty they had taking her back home, and an expressed threat of death" (*fugam de domo, lachrymae et difficultatem eorum qui reconduxerunt eam ad domum et expressam comminationem mortis*). Her father had a reputation of being severe, likely to strike her.[38] So though the indicators of *metus* in a woman were not as great as for a man, as Sandei implied, he still found plenty of them. What we do not know from the *consilium* is how long the coerced marriage went on or, perhaps more revealing, how long it persisted after her father passed away.

In contrast, in another case Alessandro Tartagni looked at witness testimony for both sides, clearly contradicting each other, as to whether Petro de Vandino acted from fear in marrying Appollonia di Giovanni di Paolo de' Prandi. The marriage had occurred between the third and fourth hours of the night in August 1464 in Appollonia's father's house, with a bristling of arms (*rumor armorum*) and several witnesses present, who testified that a choice along the lines of marry or die was put to Petro. Experience taught that a secret event in the middle of the night was a proof of justifiable fear. Tartagni concluded that the judge should absolve Petro and leave Appollonia to her conscience.[39] In this and the other cases, it was the testimony of witnesses and their general veracity that was at the crux of the matter. Marriages may have been posed in the law as a matter of mutual spousal consent and some sort of marital affection, but they were also social facts, with effects on kin and neighbors.

All these cases were also about the consent of the spouses. What about parents and kin? Tartagni faced one such case where a statute demanded that a virgin under twenty years of age had to have consent (of father or grandfather or brother). If she married without such consent, then the father or whoever else did not have to dower her. Was the statute valid, especially as it had the seemingly laudable motive of protecting a weak

[38] Sandei, *cons.* 14, fol. 18ra–va.   [39] Tartagni, 5 *cons.* 156, fols. 116ra–17ra.

and vulnerable young woman? The statute could be defended as tinkering not with the spiritual essence of marriage (and thus not altering divine law) but with accidents, such as procedure and dowry. But Tartagni invalidated the statute on the grounds that no *ius* gave a brother a right to consent, as had happened in this case, in which the brother had also withheld the dowry left his sister in their father's will. Her right freely to contract marriage (*libertas contrahendi matrimonium*) was not to be taken away by statute. She might be open to disinheritance for contracting marriage with an unworthy man, but even then the marriage stood. As the groom was not in fact said to be *infamis* or otherwise unworthy, there was no need to apply a statute whose presumed intent "was to provide that a girl not marry to the shame of house and family" (*cum ignominia domus et familie*).[40] This groom was not unworthy, but it is not certain that he ever saw a dowry for his bride.

In another case it was alleged that Lisabetta d'Antonio da Radulfo of Verona, left a handsome sum by her father as her dowry, but in ill health and cared for at great expense by her brothers, as her father's heirs, nonetheless married at age nineteen without their knowledge. She left the house and lived with her husband, despite her brother's disapproval. She had sworn supposedly she would not marry the man she did, and that if she did she was content to lose her dowry; or at least one relative stood as witness to such a promise. Lisabetta sought her dowry anyway. Cipolla weighed whether her marriage damaged her father and brothers and what was the penalty to be imposed, including loss of the dowry. He claimed the marriage to a man of inferior station was not only an *iniuria* to her dead father and her brothers but to her entire family. He admitted there was no law that required her to have brothers' consent to marry, but "by customs and good practices of a city she must do this and this is honorable" (*secundum consuetudinem et bonos mores civitatis debebat hoc facere et hoc honestum est*). It took little effort to determine she should be punished and that it could take the form of lessening the dowry. But how much it was to be reduced was left to arbitrators.[41]

Sexual relations outside marriage, as we have seen, were a matter of concern to civic legislators and, as a result, to courts. Such relations begged to be stopped or at least regularized, if possible. Consequences of such actions for property rights and family had to be addressed, as well as for any children who might result. Daniele di Marqualdo claimed that

---

[40] Tartagni, 1 *cons.* 97, fols. 75ra–76rb.   [41] Cipolla, 2 *cons.* 35, 144b–46b.

the patriarch of Aquileia should not have found him and his companions guilty of *raptus*, because the supposed victim, Appollonia, was his wife. While civil law forbade a *raptor* from escaping punishment by marrying his victim, canon law permitted it. Fourteen witnesses had been examined. They said Appollonia confessed she was Daniele's wife at Pentecost in 1471. But Bartolomeo Cipolla agreed with the ecclesiastical court of first instance, struck, it seems, by the publicly violent nature of the deed, and by the fact that following the abduction they had had sex (*copula carnalis*) when she was taken to Daniele's house. That Appollonia was supposedly married was belied by the fact that force was used; that she cried out for help; and that later she hung her head and refused to answer if she was married, all of which seemed to indicate lack of consent. Her later attestations to have been married were, by the testimony of some witnesses, given under duress. Certainly her "kin were despoiled of quasi-possession of their daughter." Appollonia and her father had taken the case to the patriarch's court and vigorously denied any marriage. Cipolla agreed with the punishment of the secular court, based on the patriarchal judgment, that Daniele had been justly condemned and banished and could face the penalty of decapitation for abduction of a virgin.[42] The fact that she and her father had not seen fit to salvage her reputation by allowing the marriage may have been the most telling bit of evidence. Cipolla too was not going to let the ravisher get away with simply marrying his victim.

In another of Cipolla's cases, in contrast, the noble Francesco de' Bissari had sexual relations over several months with Caterina, who for years had been servant to a local tailor. Her willing visits to his house were followed by an abduction, when Francesco left the countryside and moved to the city, Vicenza. Her father demanded her back through a court. Returned by an armed squad, Caterina soon ran off to resume her life as Francesco's concubine, and her father "sought abolition [of any marriage] conceding any injury, as he saw she was incorrigible." Vicenza had a statute about violent abduction and another about abolition of marriage. The statute spoke of one abducting a woman "of honest life, good station and reputation," qualities that the promiscuous Caterina did not have. Any presumptions of good character were out the window with her. On that basis Francesco could not be prosecuted under Vicenza's law.[43] Her father was washing his hands of her, although being

---

[42] Cipolla, 3 *cons.* 56, 175a–77b.   [43] Cipolla, 3 *cons.* 57, 177b–79b.

concubine to a noble may not have been such a bad deal for the daughter of a humble man. Her actions seem to say as much.

Paolo di Castro took a similar tack before a statute punishing *raptus* or *stuprum* with an "honest" woman. If she was taken by force, the penalty was capital; if no force was needed but the woman was not a prostitute, a fine of 100 *lire* was applied. Di Castro noted several juristic opinions that in instances involving married women, even living *inhoneste*, there was still adultery or *stuprum*, because of the harm caused to the husband, which was something that did not hold for single women living *inhoneste*. So in his case the fact that the woman had allowed herself to be *stuprata* meant she did not have *honestas* any more, and there was thus no crime of *raptus*.[44]

Adultery generated its own legal and evidentiary problems on the occasions that it came before the courts. Issues of honor were best dealt with outside judicial forums, where conflict could not be so overt and bloody, though the punishments courts had available could be attractive. But courts certainly were needed to give satisfaction regarding dowry. When a man named Muzio accused his wife Mita of adultery with a man named Matteo, he produced four witnesses, including his father and brother. On the basis of their testimony, which was not conclusive, a judge ordered Mita be tortured to extract a "voluntary confession," but that ruling was quickly appealed. The testimony had lodged suspicions about Mita's nocturnal doings, going to *loca suspecta* and consorting with *personas suspectas*, "as it is foul and shameful for men and women at night especially to be in secret and hidden places" (*secretis et abditis locis*). The testimony justified the application of torture, said Lodovico Pontano, because, even though two of the witnesses were kin, they had suffered defamation as "adultery denigrated and stained the entire line" (*adulterium totam cognationem denigrat et maculat*). If Mita withstood torture, then she had to be absolved.[45]

Finally, it should be noted that widows were not free of implications about their sexual dealings. One widow guilty of *stuprum* (presumably voluntary), thus harming her husband's brother (his heir), still sought return of her dowry. No longer married, she could not commit adultery, which was the offense that would cost her the dowry, but it could be maintained that *stuprum* was a violation of the "putative" marriage such as that of a widow still in her husband's home. On the other hand, the

---

[44] Di Castro, 2 *cons.* 272, fols. 130vb–31ra.   [45] Pontano, *cons.* 451, fol. 242rb–vb.

right of a husband to prosecute his adulterous wife and gain her dowry was not something that passed to his heir. But Paolo di Castro, with surprisingly little in the way of strictly legal argumentation, posed that the brother was offended by her acts and could move suit against her and claim her dowry.[46] His was an opinion handed to the judge as the basis to his finding in the case. His seems to have been moral, not so much legal indignation, to rise to equating her acts with adultery, though she was clearly guilty of sexual indiscretion. But there were widely shared presumptions of chastity on the part of widows and, just as clearly, strong responses when that chastity failed.

Marital Property

Protection of women's property during marriage was a common goal of communal statutes throughout Italy. That protection went hand in hand with the exclusion from inheritance that was premised on dowry. Padua, for example, had a device by which a woman could reclaim her dowry, but its justification was vague, "her husband being in the situation where dowry can and must be paid and demanded."[47] That could cover the case of physical mistreatment or, more likely, the sorts of contingencies addressed by legislation in Foligno that a woman who did not want to see her dowry lost to her husband's creditors had the ability to submit to the judgment of two close friends. If she thus secured real property, any surplus value beyond that of her dowry had to be available to the husband's creditors, and if creditors wanted to buy that property and simply leave her with the cash value, they could.[48]

Arezzo also allowed that "during marriage, if the husband was heading to bankruptcy or badly managing his property or not [managing]," a wife could act to defend her dowry from his creditors.[49] Florence, eventually, in 1415, also allowed such retrieval of dowry (*consignatio dotis*), making clear that it was the threat of insolvency on the part of the husband, and with that the loss of the dowry to his creditors, that permitted a wife's action to retrieve her dowry and make good her tacit hypothec as his foremost prior creditor, precisely for the dowry.

This was an area of law often simply left to *ius commune*, so here, as on so many matters, many civic statutes were silent. But places such as Pisa and Bologna, home to law schools, and Ravenna and Vicenza, enacted

---

[46] Di Castro, 2 *cons.* 147, fols. 62vb–63ra.   [47] Padua, 190.   [48] Foligno, 1: 89.
[49] Arezzo, 173.

statutes expressly allowing *consignatio dotis*, making apparent its availability as a legal remedy in the community. Florence simply added a
protection for other creditors – as, again, a wife controlling her dowry
but living with her husband ran counter to the expectations of others
concerning affairs in a household – by registering these acts in the same
volumes in which emancipations were registered. Siena's late statutes of
1545 on the same subject uniquely added a provision for proof of sorts of
the husband's deteriorating finances, either in the opinion of neighbors or
in the fact of being judicially banned or condemned as bankrupt. Recognizing that waiting for that level of proof might mean there was not
sufficient worth left to cover the dowry, the statute allowed the wife to
recover objects pawned to other creditors. Funds recovered by a wife were
to be reinvested in stable goods [*bonis stabilibus*] for security of her dowry.
Priority of claims between a wife and creditors was to be quickly determined by a judge as part of the same process, so that matters were not
constantly delayed.[50]

The possibility of *consignatio dotis* raises another issue about wives
that was frequently legislated in the statutes of the later Middle Ages.
There was recognition and even expectation that a wife, with her otherwise legally separate property, would act to aid her husband financially,
but quite possibly to her detriment. Behind this concern lay a general
presumption that women might have property distinct from dowry that
they could dispose of in that manner. Statutes, however, did not always
provide much room for women to acquire such property. Many civic
statutes stated that property acquired by a wife during marriage accrued
to her husband. So Bergamo simply decided that whatever a wife obtained
was presumed to be her husband's unless she gained it by inheritance,
bequest, or gift (all presumably from her family and intended for her).[51]
Milan's statutes of 1498 said that whatever a wife, mother, or grandmother gained went to the husband, sons, and grandsons respectively, if
they lived with them, and through them it was available to their creditors,
unless it came to the woman by way of inheritance or was part of her
paraphernalia.[52] A husband who alienated or converted paraphernalia to
his use exposed it to his debts.[53] In 1325, Florence declared that any
objects, houses, lands or vineyards a wife gained yielded a right of
usufruct for her husband, whether the wife wanted that or not. Ownership was the wife's, and she could defend her right against her husband's

[50] Siena, 245–47.   [51] Bergamo, 192.   [52] Milan 1498, fols. 79v–80r.
[53] Milan 1498, fol. 87r.

creditors, but he had all use and revenues. Still, what came from her family belonged only to her and was not subject to his debts. He did not even get usufruct if the property came to her with the specification (which was employed at times in testaments and deeds of gift) that he not have usufruct.[54] Another provision ordered that no wife could defend her husband's property against creditors (except those obligated to her for her dowry).[55] The converse to all these provisions was the rule that a Florentine wife could not cede any action on her dowry to another while her husband was alive.[56] Yet another Florentine statute said that a wife who contracted and obligated herself for or to others with her husband's consent by public instrument was bound and could not seek to revoke her act. Property subject to such a commitment had to be non-dotal.

Two years later, nearby Arezzo and Montepulciano allowed a wife to obligate herself for her husband and to his creditors, as long as she had her father's consent or, he being dead, of her brother over age twenty-five, or of two close *consanguinei*.[57] At about the same time, nearby Cortona allowed to stand contracts of wife and husband regarding her dowry or parapherna.[58] Treviso ordered that *bona immobilia* that were part of a dowry could not be alienated, except by decree of the podestà and consent of two close relatives of the woman.[59] Forlì, which decreed that goods acquired by a wife gave her husband usufruct similar to what he had over dotal property, declared any sale or other contract on a woman's property in concert with her husband was valid and not to be revoked. Husbands were admonished to designate other property equivalent to that alienated to take its place as surety for the dowry.[60] These statutes moved to keep women from taking advantage of the disability in *ius commune* from obligating themselves for third parties. They appreciated that it was too easy later to overturn women's acts and make all dealings with their (non-dotal) property seem provisional.

The relatively small community of Colle Val d'Elsa found it expedient to issue a set of statutes dealing with wives' use of dowry. It did not allow women to preclude the *fructus* of their dowries going to creditors *constante matrimonio*. They were to be allotted equivalents to their dowries once the husband died. Contracts women made with their husbands were enforceable, in contrast to *ius commune*. Wives could defend their husbands' property from the commune of Colle to the value of their dowries,

---

[54] Florence 1325, 103.   [55] Florence 1325, 93.   [56] Florence 1325, 107.
[57] Arezzo, 174; Montepulciano, 130.   [58] Cortona, 327.   [59] Treviso, 384–85.
[60] Forlì, 317–18.

but they could not be given any portion of the family home if the husband had been convicted of serious crimes, such as homicide, highway robbery, or arson.[61] Volterra, more than a century before, ruled that women who consented to their husbands' sales of property could not later move to revoke them (again, the awareness of uncertainty in the markets).[62] Volterra also allowed women to make gifts to their husbands (a provision quite at odds with *ius commune*), but no more than five *soldi* for each *lira* of their dowry (i.e., one-quarter).[63]

These restrictions in statutes were all attempting to keep something of the property separation of husbands and wives while coping with the actual mingling of their property in domestic life. Such separation of property was not a foregone conclusion in southern Italy, but it became more common in time. In Naples, by the mid-fourteenth century, expectations of wives inheriting from their husbands were overturned, at least for aristocratic families, while provisions for return of dowry were strengthened. In Sicily more marriages took place according to the *mos graecorum*, which was in line with the separation of spousal property in *ius commune*, than by the *mos latinorum*, which merged the wife's holdings into the common household property.

It is not surprising that large active commercial centers like Milan and Venice faced more complex situations regarding wives and husbands. Venice declared that all uxorial claims on the husband took effect not when charters of dowry, for example, were drawn up, but from the day the wife was taken to her husband's house. On a parallel, no charter made by a wife while "in potestate viri" was valid if it was against her dowry right; but she had every right to have charters drawn up to delineate and defend her rights, notably as to her dowry.[64] Viterbo had a different take. There it was possible for a wife with children to consent validly to any sale by her husband from his property. Alienations from her dowry she could act to retrieve, but arbiters would be assigned to make sure she got the equivalent to her dowry, but no more, so the husband's creditors could have some sort of settlement. Conversely, a woman could not alienate property from her dowry unless the one who established it for her (e.g., her father) consented. If she alienated without that consent, it did not hold, unless a valid reason (*necessaria causa*) was present and verified by two close kin, and then a judge was needed to complete the sale.[65]

---

[61] Colle, 1: 302–3.   [62] Volterra, 1: 8, 2: 124.   [63] Volterra, 2: 137–38.
[64] Venice, 18, 20, 57–58.   [65] Viterbo, 133 and 149.

Siena's sixteenth-century statute confronted issues and nuances not apparent to those statutes drawn up some two or three centuries earlier. Goods obligated or alienated to a wife on the pretext of dowry were to be returned, as the transfer was invalid if the husband was in debt, except for the obligation he made to his wife at the time of marriage (i.e., no increase of the marital dowry could be alleged). Siena too assumed that monies resulting from contracts in which a wife participated belonged to her husband. An exception was allowed if it could be shown that the money was in fact converted to her benefit, which consisted of clothing, food, or rent, as those were regularly the man's duty.[66]

Keeping the wife's property distinct from her husband's debts could extend in other directions. Women were not generally exiled for their husbands' financial or even political failures. Debtors were subject to incarceration or even exile, but jailing women was contemplated only with difficulty. Belluno's statutes of 1392 allowed jailing of a woman only for criminal offenses. She was not going to be held for her own debts and contracts or those of anyone else.[67] Milan, in effect, would not let women's property be seized for debts "public or private."[68] That property was in fact limited to her clothing, bed, chests, and other dotal goods or even paraphernalia, except to cover rent of a house for which the woman had contracted or for her alimentary support. On the other hand, Arezzo allowed women to escape being held only if they ceded their dowry rights to creditors.[69]

Households were typically formed (or reformed) by marriage. They also came apart when marriages ended on the death of one spouse. When that happened, the disposition of the different forms of property was of immediate concern, and those types of property became visible to the courts that received disputes.

Women brought to marriage property other than dowry, notably a trousseau of some sort and possibly other belongings. In an opinion dealing with property relations between spouses, Baldo degli Ubaldi began with a set of distinctions. Some property was in the *dominium* and under the administration of the husband. This was the dowry and its *fructus*, whether consumed or compiled (although this was clearly on overstatement of the husband's title to dowry, which was more properly equated with legal possession). Some property was in the *dominium* of the wife but under the husband's management. This was the *res*

---

[66] Siena, 257, 259.   [67] Belluno, 274.   [68] Milan 1498, fols. 75v–76r.
[69] Arezzo, 124.

paraphernales, on which the husband had to exercise care and for recovery of which his property was liable. Other property was in the *dominium* of the wife and under her control. This was the *res extra dotem* and its *fructus*. With this third form of property, either the wife used that to the benefit of children, in which case she was not due compensation, or she used it to her husband's benefit and, though there was some opinion that she could seek compensation, Baldo denied it. The wife had a duty to aid her husband in times of necessity. "For they are partners of a divine and human home and one flesh (*sunt enim socii divinae et humanae domus et una caro*), and one must bear the burdens of the other, but a husband for his wife because women are always in need . . . and a wife for her husband rarely and contrary to common happenings." A relatively rich wife of a struggling husband thus had the rare privilege of taking care of him, and the husband owed her compensation if he ever got back on his financial feet.[70] Statutes had issues with wives bailing out their husbands. The *ius commune*, it seems, expected it, as long as the wife's title claims were protected.

Married women's actions with their dowries were always full of problems. In one case a husband had sold a rent income (*census*) from his wife's dowry, and both had acknowledged receiving the 400 *lire* for it; but the husband had not declared that the property was hers or that she was due the money. Was it, therefore, given her silence, all his and thus to pass to his heirs? Paolo di Castro concluded that half the proceeds were presumed to have gone to her. She was unable to revoke what she had clearly been a party to, so she could not regain the other half.[71] That went to her husband's heirs.

Property gained by a wife aside from marriage was definitely not the husband's. In this regard Alessandro Tartagni upheld a separation of property ownership. But could the wife use and enjoy the property even against her husband's will? The husband had rights on paraphernalia. That third type of feminine patrimony, that Baldo had called *res extra dotem*, consisted of possessions that were not assigned to him and that he had no role as administrator of. Any of that he used had to be restored to the wife, unless there were clear permission from her. The husband could not be assumed to be consuming her property by her leave, if only because of the assumed greed of all women [*genus mulierum avarissimum est*], who were thus highly unlikely to be so generous. The *fructus* belonged to

[70] Baldo, 5 *cons.* 478, fol. 128va.   [71] Di Castro, 1 *cons.* 359, fol. 190rb–va.

her, "because in the wife is bound a reverence toward her husband, because of which results a presumption of disagreement or of consent." Especially in a second marriage, her goods could not be considered her husband's when she had children by the first husband and by statute they had rights to a portion of her dowry.[72] Tartagni thus inclined to concede the wife full agency on those goods not otherwise bound to her husband. His decision was in line with that of Antonio da Pratovecchio (1380–1468), his colleague, who also authored a *consilium* on the case.

Antonio da Pratovecchio was faced with an interesting problem. He began with the remark that a father-in-law was "cruel" to his daughter-in-law by preventing her from remarrying on the death of her husband (*vere crudelis videtur hic socer huic nurui sue que mortuo viro potuit nubere*). Years ago Christiane Klapisch-Zuber called attention to the "cruel" remarrying mother. Here it is the one who would prevent her remarriage who is labeled cruel. The father-in-law's "cruelty" rested on the fact that the widow had waited a year as an appropriate mourning period. During that year the widow, not having recovered her dowry, was due *alimenta* and clothing. Only after that year was restitution of dowry owed her. If her father were alive, she would still be under his *potestas* and he would be able to pursue the claim for the dowry, which would accrue to him. As he was not, she could still hope to regain the dowry, but with difficulty for not having his help, leaving her at the mercy of the "cruel" father-in-law.

Claims to return of the dowry, however, were not the issue in this case. The problem was her claims to what she was due beyond the dowry, for things she did and labored at in the year of marriage and in the year of widowhood. To clarify these matters Antonio da Pratovecchio had to consider the nature of wifely duties and activities. Thus this case puts us at the heart of households and spousal relations in legal terms. The jurist noted that "a husband has a double right of service in his wife: one for rendering the [marital] debt, the other for work in the home" (*vir habet duplex ius servitutis in uxorem: unum quo ad debitum reddendum aliud quo ad ministerium*). What a wife established with her husband was a form of *societas* (on analogy to the fraternal associations we saw in the previous chapter), but what she acquired in it was for herself, not necessarily for him:

Although the law says that she must be in the submission to her husband, that law speaks of servile obedience (*servitiis obsequialibus*), which must be understood

---

[72] Tartagni, 5 *cons.* 144, fols. 140vb–5va.

according to the quality of the person. . . . Certainly if a wife performs some craft or trade or is a bawd or midwife (*sirufica vel obstetrix*), which are not domestic and family activities, what she might acquire from these acts does not accrue to her husband, because she is not held to do business at the behest of the husband. And so she is not in obedience to her husband by his fault, she is held to [to give him] nothing.

By this jurist's reckoning the wife was not in the power of her husband but was his partner (*socia*), and thus shared income with him. He introduced a distinction between constructive activities (*operas fabriles*) and subservient ones (*operas obsequiales*), from which he turned to Bartolo and Baldo:

if she has sustenance and does not want to perform acts, so much the less will she have what is the price of the acts, and I understand the expected subservient acts [to be] those in the home, such as running the family and very much also if she was accustomed during her husband's life to do rustic acts, as cutting grain or harvesting, because to all things other than to the carnal debt she is said to be in the husband's home (*quia quo ad omnia preter quam quo ad debitum carnis dicere esse in domo viri*).

So her failure to be a good wife in terms of domestic chores might cost her outside earnings. In that case she was insufficiently obedient to her husband.

   Still, the wife remained in the legal power of the father, even though her husband's control over her was more immediate and greater on a daily basis, because there were still things she could not do without her father, like make a testament. Thus Antonio da Pratovecchio drew another distinction, that he found in Baldo's commentaries, between two types of power, *paterna* and *maritalis*: "paternal, because whatever my wife acquires she acquires for her father as far as usufruct, and not for me, unless she acted from marital subservience, just as all daily chores in which she is held to work for the husband."

   In effect this jurist gave women a large capacity to acquire for themselves, even within a domestic context, which would add to what this widow might be able to claim. What of the period of more or less enforced widowhood? It might be argued, on the basis of something Bartolo said, that "a widowed wife is in the service of the heirs" (*uxorem viduatam esse in servitio heredum*), and *alimenta* to her during widowhood was compensation for that. Baldo proclaimed that the *opera* she did

must be taken as subservient, such as making the bed and cooking and carrying water, if she was accustomed to do such things, for she must not stay in the house like a dead body (*corpus mortuum*), but she is not bound to render lucrative or craft activities and otherwise I used to say about profits, what a wife makes in weaving and darning and sewing clothes and from gilding and making jewelry [is hers], as long as subservient activities in the home are not impeded.

Obsequiales were different from *fabriles* (constructive) acts, such that nursing [another's child] was of the latter and not the former. Which then meant, as Antonio da Pratovecchio concluded his opinion, "that if the fee from nursing was paid to any father-in-law an account of that payment is to be rendered."[73]

There are few examples so vivid in making apparent the paradoxical position of the wife in the home. These paradoxes became evident, of course, at the point of widowhood and possible remarriage. The wife's father-in-law was intent on avoiding repayment of the dowry, but instead, in this instance, was seemingly also being tendered a bill for services rendered. We do not know what the final verdict was in this case (or in so many others, for that matter), but it is revealing that such a set of claims could be so plausibly laid out. And this woman emerges as hardly as compliant as the language of subservience would lead one to believe. She was able to press suit against her father-in-law and gain the powerful adherence of a jurist to formulate her case.

Women's Legal Agency

Whatever the nature of ownership and rights of usufruct on women's property in any given community, the capacity of women to act on their property rights was a distinct issue. In some places women might have full ownership of goods but be more or less unable to dispose of them. Their legal agency was limited. Historical studies of women's agency have thus flourished over the past four or five decades. Gender conceptions of female weakness have been located behind all sorts of disabilities nominally heaped on women in *ius commune* and in statutes. Restrictions on women's legal and economic agency (leaving aside political and religious restrictions) come off as a feature of the broader interplay of gender and power. There were undoubtedly severe limitations on what women could do in law. We have already encountered a number and more lurk ahead of us. But two things need saying. One is that these laws were in flux to some degree. As Simona Feci has noted, such laws were infrequent in earlier statute redactions, but by the end of the sixteenth century they had

---

[73] Tartagni, 4 *cons.* 303, fols. 97vb–98rb.

appeared in many cities of northern and central Italy.[74] The spread of these laws to places they had not been found earlier can be taken as a worsening of conditions for women through the period. These laws responded to a broadening notion of the distinctions between public and private worlds and to the realities of plagues, famines, wars, and all else that might remove interested males, whose guardianship of women might otherwise render such laws moot.

That brings up a second point – women were often active and not at all the subservient and humble objects of male control they were depicted ideally to be. They managed property, their own and others, and transacted it; and the law and courts had to take cognizance of their actions. To some, such actions seem subversive (in pursuit of individualistic female-centered interests); but to others these acts are in line with reigning social values and were incorporated, as by the reasoning of jurists in cases, into a mainstream order of family and agnation. What do the different statutes show us on this score?

The broader issue of agency for women was addressed by civic statutes in roughly the same manner as agency for minors and children *in potestate*. One of the earliest examples hails from Foligno. There, in recognition of the needs of widows to care for their children and the problems caused by their dotal assets being in the hands of relatives or others who might defraud them, it was allowed that they have their dowries and that they could convert the cash into real assets that they could use at their own discretion (*pro earum libito voluntatis*). Further, they could retain an attorney (*procurator*) to seek, manage, and defend their property. Similarly "lest paternal power impede the good that aforesaid women want to do for their souls," widowed women were allowed to have a will and bequeath for charitable purposes, notwithstanding paternal absence or lack of consent (as long as she was not a minor). Fathers, mothers, brothers or other kin were ordered to leave her and not exert force, fear, or terror on her person or her dowry.[75] There was no mention of women's supposed *fragilitas* here. They were assumed to know what was good for them and their children and how to get it. But there was also clearly at play a tacit sense of female weakness and susceptibility to pressure from kin, especially the father. And the abilities accorded to women by this statute were only for widows. Married women, in Foligno and most everywhere else, had fewer options for action in deference to their husbands.

---

[74] Feci, *Pesci fuor d'acqua*, 39–40, 46–49, 61–64.   [75] Foligno, 2: 93–94.

Florence fashioned a statute that took aim at all women and all private civil acts. Bookending a law otherwise setting out what a husband could inherit from his wife and specifying that in Florence the age of majority was eighteen were two pivotal sentences for Florentine women:

We establish and order that no woman can obligate herself without consent of a guardian [*mundualus*] or husband, if she has one. Likewise that any woman can [have] whomever she wants to choose as guardian, and he should be given to her, notwithstanding that she have another, or they may have or would have, another guardian.[76]

The term *mundualdus* reveals that this peculiar Florentine institution was an adaptation from Lombard law. It featured in all Florence's statutes. Here the *fragilitas* of women was overmatched by the male, and the "surplus" that male participation and authority provided to a woman meant that any male could authorize a woman's acts.[77] The assumption that a woman's husband acted as *mundualdus* meant that wives were taken care of. As Chabot and others have demonstrated, Florentine wives, as opposed to widows, were less active in the kinds of contracts and transactions that show up in the papers of notaries.[78] But it is important that Florence's *mundualdus* was not limited to a woman's male relatives. In that regard, despite its seeming universality, the *mundualdus* could be less restrictive for women than the sorts of guardianship erected in other cities, where the approving males had to be relatives. In contrast to Florence, Saona, for example, strove to keep the consent function in the hands of men who in some degree knew the woman and had some interest in her acts. Even then her sales of property were not valid unless also proclaimed by herald throughout the community.[79] Treviso simply limited the consent function for a married woman to her husband, leaving no provision for kin or neighbors.[80] Two *proximiores*, however, were required for a Trevisan woman to have a valid will or transact non-dotal property.[81]

Arezzo allowed an unmarried woman to operate with consent of two close but upstanding relatives (*bone conditionis et fame*).[82] Cortona restricted married women from contracting without their husbands' consent, except for seeking return of dowry from an insolvent spouse.[83] Milan set up a more complicated scenario. If a woman was unmarried

---

[76] Florence 1325, 130.   [77] The term surplus comes from Feci, 49.
[78] Chabot, *La dette des familles*, 51–67.   [79] Saona, 211–12.   [80] Treviso, 352.
[81] Treviso, 374–76, 384–85.   [82] Arezzo, 174.   [83] Cortona, 327.

or her husband was away, consent of an agnate was required for any contract. Lacking agnates present or willing to consent, she could proceed with a formal judicial oath from her husband or agnate that the contemplated legal act was in her interest. If she were defending her dotal property against her husband (presumably *consignatio*) or agnates, she could appoint an attorney and proceed with the approval of a judge.[84]

Some later statutes were more forthcoming as to their rationale and more complicated in the scenarios they envisioned. Ferrara prefaced its 1567 legislation allowing close relations, as well as the husband, to consent to a woman's acts, with the statement that women were weak and easily enticed by words or cowed by threats. One consequence was that obligations entered into for the benefit of a husband were considered the result of force or fear, even if later the woman swore to stand by her deed.[85] Siena specified that a wife have her husband's consent, if she had been taken to his house and lived with him. Even then she also needed consent of her *propinquior* – said to be first her father, lacking him paternal grandfather, if not him then maternal grandfather, or then her sons over twenty-five born of any marriage, then her brother, then her uncle, the half-brother, the brother's son, then uncle's son, then maternal uncle, then son of an agnate sister, then a maternal cousin, then an agnate within four degrees in order of precedence, then cognates within four degrees. All of these potential approvers in this stunningly thorough and graduated list had to be adults of good repute, capable of acting on their own. If all else failed, if there were no one in Siena or no one capable, the woman could seek the consent of the ordinary judge of civil cases. If any of these declined to consent because the act in question appeared to be harmful to the woman, a judge had to inquire and agree if there were grounds to worry. Consent to alienation from dotal property fell to her husband and one *propinquior*. While a woman's act, it was affirmed, was valid under these circumstances, it was also conceded that if she had lied about not having a husband or *propinquior*, "such an oath is presumed extorted by fraud and force," if later it proved untrue, and her act was nullified. So a loophole remained. Her word was not simply to be accepted about, say, spousal absence; there was to be some sort of inquiry *extra iudicialiter*.[86]

It is hard to imagine a more thorough attempt than Siena's to cover each and every possibility, all with the aim of keeping consent in the

---

[84] Milan 1498, fol. 94r–v.   [85] Ferrara, fols. 84r–85v.   [86] Siena, 259–62.

hands of kin, on either side. In contrast Florence's *mundualdus* may hardly have been restrictive at all, and the *mundualdus* may not be sufficient evidence to hold, as some have, that Florence was a bad place to be a woman. Without all the order of march and judicial intervention set up in Siena, a Florentine woman could have found the necessary consent from any man who happened by. Of course, the *mundualdus* also had no liability and no need to certify that a given act was in any way to a woman's benefit; it was left to her to figure that out. Statutes such as Siena's, or similar but less exhaustive ones like that of Arezzo, did not indicate if the kin bore any liability for bad acts to which they consented, but, insofar as they expressed concern about fraud, they were raising an issue that did not arise for a *mundualdus*, who was not related to the woman in question. Yet it is also clear that women in Siena were quite active legally for their families, especially for female kin.

These laws bring us back to the central paradox of woman's legal gender – they had to be able to act at times and had separate property and interests to be concerned about, but they were also supposed to submerge themselves in a household, both in youth and once married, and even in widowhood. How were the two facets of legal womanhood to be kept in balance? We are accustomed to seeing the fifteenth and sixteenth centuries as an era of tightening, rigidifying, even stifling patriarchy. But women could also look beyond their fathers and husbands, to their brothers, for example, who might find their sisters useful or burdensome, depending on circumstances. Women could negotiate between natal and marital families. There were things women could and did do, with but also at times without leave from men. As Megan Moran says, "the diversity of family relationships mediated by women, and by men, portrays a more flexible and dynamic set of kinship associations than one institutionalized patriarchal 'system,' defined by male authority and patrilineal interests."[87]

We should note that there were some communities, Venice and Bologna, for example, that did not impose statutory limitations on women's actions beyond those set out in *ius commune*. Indeed, in Venice women were not only active in courts and before notaries on their own behalf; they were accepted as representatives for others, in clear contravention even of the Velleianum of Roman law. All this does not mean that women in Venice and Bologna were not subject to the control of men in the household or that their acts were entirely of their own contrivance.

---

[87] Moran, "Brother-Sister Correspondence in the Spinelli Family," 71.

What a wife could do with her property, especially with or for her husband, also raised lots of issues and concerns with defrauding of creditors or of wives themselves. Women were quite capable of engaging in fraud, after all. So Ancona had a statute requiring a woman have her father or, lacking him, *consanguinei* present for any action or obligation she entered into, or else it was null and void. A woman of Ancona had legally accepted an inheritance (*aditio*), but another potential heir had asked if that action was covered by the statute. Angelo degli Ubaldi determined that it was not. *Aditio* was not a contract or obligation. True, acceptance of an inheritance meant acceptance of obligations incumbent on it, but Angelo maneuvered past that. Obligations to creditors of the estate, he said were secondary and indirect. They were merely byproducts of taking title to the estate. And in this case there was no proof there were any outstanding obligations on the estate, otherwise described as *opulenta*. True, given the usual debts "there cannot be an estate without problems (*non posset esse hereditas sine vexatione*), although it be sufficient yet not lavish," but this estate was still to her advantage. The statute was also concerned with a woman making herself the principal debtor in a transaction, and thus it was to the woman's advantage to provide for her *fragilitas*. It did not mean to prevent her from accepting an inheritance or gift.[88] Thus Angelo bored one loophole through such statutes, so at least acceptance of an estate did not require consent of males who, by the terms of the statute, might themselves be interested to gain the property, precisely by forbidding a woman to claim it.

Angelo's brother Baldo also revealed himself inclined to read statutes about female agency in fairly narrow terms. A woman, in the presence of her consenting father, but absent her non-consenting husband, made a gift *causa mortis* (becoming effective on her death). Baldo both distinguished that handing over something (*traditio*) was not the same as creating an obligation and that promising something was not the same as yielding it. Further, such a promise was not a contract, as it failed to generate the formally required elements to be a contract in law. So, unless there were some fraud being perpetrated, or she had children who would be harmed by the gift, it should stand and the statute (from where?) did not apply.[89]

Bartolomeo Cipolla decades later confronted the role of Verona's analogous statute. In 1444 Magdalena had given her *bona mobilia et*

---

[88] Angelo, *cons.* 317, fol. 175ra–b.   [89] Baldo, 2 *cons.* 455, fol. 121rb.

immobilia, all rights and actions – seemingly everything she had – to Jacopo and Margareta, a married couple, reserving usufruct to herself, with the agreement that they feed and support her, see to her burial, and have annual memorial masses said for her. One has to assume that Magdalena was childless, and seemingly without kin to care for her in old age. Margareta, however, wanted to renounce the gift in preference for payment of the 122 *lire* still outstanding on a debt Magdalena owed her for services. It was argued that Margareta's renunciation of the gift was invalid, because by statute she could not make a donation during marriage (in this instance, giving away something she could have had) without consent of three agnates or cognates, or if they refused or were involved in the transaction, three men appointed by the podestà, who would ascertain that no threat or fear was involved. In fact only three men from Leviacco, not Verona, had been present, appointed by the vicar of that village. Cipolla sided with a prior opinion by Andrea di Bartolomeo da Sicilia that the statute, which did not invest a right of consent in her husband, existed "in women's favor, lest by fear or deception of her husband a wife be forced to sell or give something away." That Margareta made her condition better by the renunciation was also apparent from the fact that Magdalena's stipulations regarding support for the rest of her life and for her burial amounted to "great expenses and a great burden." Though Magdalena was said to be over sixty, she could still live five years or more (by a calculation derived from a text of ius *commune*). In fact, Magdalena had survived more than four years from the time Margareta refused the deal. Cipolla estimated yearly expenses of 15 ducats, or 75 in total for the putative five years. It was possible to calculate what would have been expended for *alimenta* and for burial and obsequies, as well as the 122 *lire* and the value of usufruct over four years. The result was a burden on Margareta greater than the value of the gift, so she had improved her lot by turning it down, and the statute did not apply.[90] Women, that *genus avarissimum*, were seen to be quite capable of recognizing what was to their material advantage.

Paolo di Castro was more hard-nosed about women's legal capacities and their resulting liabilities. When a woman named Aurianda married, she swore to both parents that she was content with her dowry and would seek no more from the patrimony in deference to her brothers. Di Castro took the side of the parents, or their heirs, and upheld the terms of that

[90] Cipolla, 1 *cons.* 14, 49a–51b.

contract. He noted that "such agreement is not disgraceful nor is it contrary to good practices." What she had done, strictly speaking, was not to make a gift to her brothers (as there was no transfer of ownership at that moment) but merely effectively to repudiate an inheritance, which she was competent to do. That Aurianda was a minor (under twenty-five), who had seemingly acted contrary to local statute regulating the legal acts of minors and women, who could not give away property without the consent of two *propinqui*, did not matter. In fact her two parents had been present, "than whom no one is closer and who are not presumed to work any fraud or deception on their children." They did not directly gain from the act, so they were not disqualified from extending consent on grounds of being self-interested. That di Castro thus choked off Aurianda's recourse to challenge her own act, meant he also choked off any access by her son (Ciccolino) and his father (Crescenzo), her husband, to try to claim half of the property that had belonged to Aurianda. She had renounced her rights, so she did not have them to transmit to Ciccolino.[91]

Paolo di Castro was far less likely than others to let a woman enjoy the law's protection to revoke acts after the fact, even when undertaken on behalf of her husband. Again and again, di Castro ruled against revocation, seemingly more concerned with the image of the avaricious woman than that of the weak woman. To see women as avaricious, however, implied that their rights were real and substantive. For example, a case from Feltre, between Contessa, wife of Pasquale di ser Benedetto, and ser Vivaldo di ser Pietro, her husband's creditor, was about their house. Contessa alleged her rights to a portion of it as secured for her dowry, but Vivaldo claimed she had renounced them in a credit instrument. Di Castro found that Contessa had allowed Pasquale to obligate her property to Vivaldo. In so doing she had doubtlessly greatly harmed her interests. He understood one could consider all her actions of no moment, as *ius commune* forbade her to obligate herself for her husband and she could not renounce her dotal hypothec on his property. He did not even need to allege statutory protections. But di Castro opted, ever consistent on this score, to enforce what she had done. She harmed only herself and did not seem to be acting from fear or duress. If she wanted property for her dowry, she first had to seek legal relief (*consignatio*) from her husband, and only thereafter could she try to get his property back from creditors.[92]

---

[91] Di Castro, 2 *cons.* 419, fols. 192vb–93rb. [92] Di Castro, 2 *cons.* 8, fol. 5ra–b.

In another case Lapo di Giovanni acted as his own agent (*procurator*) for his mother (Bartolomea) and his wife (Appollonia), with the consent of close relatives, as required by statute of Pistoia, to fulfill an obligation to a hospital, retaining usufruct to himself and to his wife after his death on the goods whose title was passed to the hospital. He lived there with the two women until his death, and Appollonia kept the usufruct, as he desired. But she moved against the obligation to the hospital, arguing that it included her dowry incorrectly and that she could not have obligated herself with her husband. The hospital responded that it was not a gift but a ceding of rights, as she had usufruct. The presence of relatives also validated her action. Di Castro again upheld a woman's legal acts, even against her interests. True, as all her husband's goods were ceded to the hospital, there was nothing else on which to capitalize her dowry, but she had made a donation for the good of her body and soul and enjoyed usufruct on all her husband's goods and not just her dowry.[93] Di Castro would not overturn a transaction that had been honored for some amount of time.

If these decisions seem to have been hard on women, we still have to concede that women (possibly with the help of interested men) were able to use their rights and that jurists recognized them. In some cases the women won. A Roman named Bartolomeo had married his daughter Ricca to a noble named Giovanni. He provided a dowry and saw her off to her new home. After several years, there being no children from the union and no dotal instrument, Giovanni, facing heavy losses of his *substantia*, had a public instrument made with the help of an attorney, confessing to receipt of a 2,000 ducat dowry, explicitly hypothecating properties at Castro Canaro and elsewhere for the dowry, swearing to all this on the Gospels. He made himself his wife's agent on those properties. Giovanni's brothers, one a cleric, ratified their brother's move with similar assurances to Ricca's father. By this maneuver, Giovanni was sequestering 2,000 ducats away from his creditors under pretext of their hypothecation for the dowry.

After her husband's death Ricca sought her 2,000 ducats; but the brothers-in-law resisted. Di Castro found that if the dotal instrument had been drawn up at betrothal or the wedding or *ductio*, or before, "at a time love had not yet begun to be marital" (*tempore nundum incepit amor esse iugalis*), then there could be no presumption of fraud. Same if

---

[93] Di Castro, 1 *cons.* 41, fols. 22vb–23rb.

he were not noble and she were, in which case the value of the dowry would match her social worth. But in this case the prohibition on gifts between spouses justified the suspicion of fraud with this "dowry." Still, this had not been a simple gift, and it had not led to real transfer of belongings to another. So the *confessio* of dowry was said to stand, insofar as it gave the wife a right against her husband's heirs, but it was of no avail against his creditors. In doubt, said di Castro, the proper thing was to judge in favor of dowry "lest many wives remain unhappily undowered and lose their dowries, which they gave and for which had not had an instrument made, which we very frequently see happen."[94] It was thus not beyond the realm of possibility, in di Castro's experience, that there was some justification for a dowry after the fact.

Such issues of female legal capacity continued to plague jurists over the next centuries. Late in the sixteenth Pietro Cavallo faced several. In 1593 a wife named Flora had been surety with her husband for the dowry of her sister Lavinia. Cavallo said she was obligated, notwithstanding *ius commune's* prohibition on women being surety for others, because this was about a dowry. The statutes of Florence and Anghiari regulating women's legal capacity did not apply to a dowry obligation, or that was a broadly common opinion. Flora's goods, even *constante matrimonio*, were thus obligated and could be sold off or alienated for that dowry.[95]

A common limitation on such statutes regarding female agency was geopolitical. Cavallo followed a long line of similar interpretations when he confronted a complicated case spanning Fivizzano to Bologna in 1607. Cavallo began with the Tuscan (but not Florentine) statute that to protect a woman any alienation or contract had to be in the presence of father or husband, or relatives, or when all else failed, two neighbors, whichever of these swearing on Scripture that the act was to her benefit. Reggio and Modena had no such statute but deferred to the *dominante* that women needed two near relatives of good repute. In the little village of Comano there was no notary, so it had been necessary to go five miles to Fivizzano. There it was that Antonia di Niccolò di Giovanni Poli of Comano, with two relatives, gave all her property to her maternal uncle, Antonio di Giovanni Lazzari de' Bellagardi, receiving usufruct for life and authority to sell things for her needs up to the sum of forty scudi. Later she married Andrea Simonini and gave him those same goods, revoking the gift to her uncle, but she died within a few months with no children. Unsurprisingly the uncle and husband

[94] Di Castro, 2 *cons.* 383, fols. 176vb–77vb.   [95] Cavallo, *cons.* 69, fols. 62rb–63rb.

pursued their conflicting claims in court. Handed the case by the podestà of Comano, Cavallo found for the uncle. Although Antonia's gift to him did not follow the procedures of Comano, which was both her place of origin and residence, she had done it outside that territory not by reason of trying to commit a fraud by evading Comano's laws, but for the simple reason that there was no notary there. A foreigner had to follow the form of the place (in this case Varano), as her ability to contract was not removed by local statute, just some formalities added to the process. A statute demanding consent from male relatives was set aside, no matter its supposed laudable intent protective of women. The revocation of the gift to the uncle did not hold, because Antonia had not obtained absolution from her oath to abide by the gift. Cavallo noted as well that he knew nothing of her age, the quality of her person or property, or of her husband, and so on.[96]

Filippo Decio, in contrast, faced two cases in which there figured a statute forbidding a woman to make contracts involving dotal property. In one he was seconding another *consultor's* opinion that a woman who had sold property from her dowry had violated a statute forbidding such sales while the husband was alive. In her case it was a *donatio causa mortis*, which did harm her dowry and her children who expected to get it. She had in fact directed the gift to her stepmother with consent of her father, not to her husband. Decio held that the father's consent had been given in his own interest and as such was not licit. Decio had to concede, and list, the multitude of opinions on both sides of the issue of the gift's validity. But he suspected it deeply because it was made the same day the dowry was established. She was "seduced" into defrauding her children.[97] Decio was employed by the husband, intent on realizing the entire amount of the dowry he had been promised. In another case from Ferrara, where a statute regulated women's contracts and mentioned dowry, Decio confronted arguments excluding dowry from its terms as a special and privileged matter. But Decio said the statute applied even when a woman obligated herself for return of a dowry (thus at its establishment). The statute's terms were general precisely to catch all forms of contract. It deserved a broad reading:

because the statute presumes and has a constant [goal] that, without statutory formalities, women obligating themselves would be seduced because of the shame of the sex and reverential fear, thus, as the statute arose to remove fraud, such statute must be fully and freely interpreted.

[96] Cavallo, *cons.* 180, fols. 241va–44rb.   [97] Decio, *cons.* 279, fols. 304rb–5rb.

That rationale held with dowry because it was even easier to deceive a woman on that score.[98] Decio was almost alone among those we have seen who sought a broad reading of such a statute. He was not hung up on the fact that the statute was corrective of *ius commune* and thus supposedly deserving of a restrictive reading, as jurisprudential wisdom held. He was in all likelihood arguing for those who would gain by quashing the gift, but he also ended his text with the assertion that he was following a ruling from a case in Florence that arose when he was lecturing at Pisa.

The husband's involvement in dotal property was a constant source of problems. His normative command of the household seemed to give him control, including daily management; still, at best he had legal possession and was not nominal owner. Clearly men used their wives' property; they were encouraged to invest it in business and in domestic activities. Just as clearly there were likely to be creditors seeking to be satisfied. In an early case Dino del Mugello ruled that just as a husband could not give property to his wife *inter vivos*, an underage wife could not give property to her brothers, more so for not observing the formalities required in Parma for acts of a minor. She could not alienate dowry *constante matrimonio*, even with her husband's consent.[99] Baldo seconded a workmanlike opinion of Andrea Alfeo of Cortona, his student, who carefully distinguished a married woman's *patrimonium* into the three types Baldo had laid out. This wife's property in the case before Andrea and Baldo was described as *extra dotem*, because they could find no concession of control to her husband. His heirs were thus bound to return it to her, unless there were exigencies not the husband's fault, in which case a wife was bound to use her wealth to see to household necessities. One could not presume that she had given her property to her husband, both because the nature of both sexes was "such that no one in doubt is presumed to throw away his money" (*ut nemo in dubio presumatur pecunias suas iactare*) and because to give was to lose, which contravened the avaricious nature of the female sex. One could not presume this woman would diverge ("discreparet") from her gender. Further, "it is inconceivable and monstrous ("incongruens et monstruosum est") for a woman to give to her husband, rather the husband must give to the wife." That her husband in fact managed and used the property did not on face of it mean she had consented to cede him title: "because when I keep silent before one doing

---

[98] Decio, *cons.* 301, fols. 329vb–30vb.   [99] Dino, *cons.* 44, fol. 53ra–vb.

something with my property or my right, to whom I owe reverence, I am not seen to consent, and reverence removes such presumption." Baldo concurred, as his student had "alleged all that could be alleged," noting only that *fructus* that had been put to the common use of the household was not to be returned.[100]

One possible area of leeway, allowing wives to obligate themselves and their dowries for their husbands, was to get them out of jail. We saw one such case at the opening of the second chapter. The opposite of using one's dowry to rescue a financially burdened husband was seeking dowry from among his assets. Di Castro was generally unsympathetic – unsurprisingly – to women seeking *consignatio* to preserve their dowries. In one case Andriola di Bonaguita da Pesaro sought her dowry back from Francesco di Vito, her husband, for not financially sustaining the marriage for some time, as was his duty. But her petition seemed suspect. For one thing, her request for *consignatio* did not seem so much a matter of economic indigence as an act of spite, as he had been adulterous and kept a lover. Andriola had been given only the minimal allowance of food, been ejected from the house, and refused to follow her husband to his new home in another city. It was not sufficient for her to argue that Francesco had moved the dowry from Pesaro to Venice and that he traveled the seas to trade and was always in danger of losing his fortune in such endeavors. If he was a merchant before marrying, that could hardly be held against him afterward. He had to be shown to be mismanaging his property. It was his move to Venice that could not be anticipated, so her desire to stay with her kin in Pesaro was perhaps not so unreasonable. But it was also not proven that he used dotal assets in his business. He was ordered to feed her suitably but not to return everything. Again and again di Castro poked holes in Andriola's story (*narratio*). There was no real proof of the adultery or of any mismanagement (as opposed to engaging in high-risk trade).[101] This seems to have been a troubled marriage in which there had already been a suit in canon law for a formal separation, which was effectively the result of her resolve not to move to Venice. Di Castro argued there was no proof of adultery, but the whiff of it seems all around this case. We might take Andriola to be an abused spouse seeking to extricate herself from a bad marriage; di Castro did not.

Di Castro was similarly hard on Mattea whose husband, Andrea, was mismanaging his assets. Her mother-in-law and brother-in-law had

---

[100] Baldo, 2 *cons.* 366, fol. 100rb–vb.   [101] Di Castro, 1 *cons.* 65, fols. 31vb–32vb.

obligated themselves for return of the dowry, so Mattea was seeking her property mainly from her mother-in-law (another woman obligating herself despite the sc Velleianum), who apparently was now managing it all and had promised to restore the dowry in every instance, including separation, where restitution was called for. *Consignatio* was not restitution strictly speaking, at least not to di Castro, though it was to others. By his lights the dowry went to the husband and he was principally obligated for it. So Mattea could not sue her mother-in-law, though she clearly had right and need to do something to protect her dowry.[102]

Bartolomeo Sozzini was much more supportive of women's efforts to retrieve their dowries from mismanaging husbands. When Francesca and her daughter-in-law, Antonia, successfully obtained *consignatio dotis* from ser Ludovico, his creditors, who had prior claims, challenged to get the properties. Sozzini rehearsed the argument in support of their claim, including to the effect that, as *consignatio* was intended to make sure the wife could feed herself and her family, "it could easily be provided for this effect, putting the dowry with these merchants for honest profit." But he supported the women with a barrage of references to teachings and *consilia* of authoritative jurists. At one point he noted a contrary argument by Paolo di Castro, "who was contrary to himself" (*qui fuit sibi ipsi contrarius*). There was a line of reasoning that creditors could act to gain payment if the wife did not first assert her right of *consignatio*, and they certainly could act when the marriage had ended. Vital to this was an opinion of Bartolo that Sozzini himself said he had not seen but had to believe the many learned figures who had referenced it.

Mainly, *consignatio* was not the same as return of dowry at the end of marriage, and creditors could not allege their right against *consignatio*. *Consignatio* was about providing *alimenta* to support the wife and not about a simple assertion of a debt. The wife was not well served by an offer to substitute a sum of cash for the assets consigned her as equivalent of her dowry:

because rather it is in the wife's interest to have the hypothecated goods with her than money offered by the creditors; because it is safer for her, from the fact that it is not easy to find someone with whom money is safe, and from whom one can realize its fruits, as often these merchants are shown to be bankrupt, as experience teaches, which is an area for the judge ("rerum magistralis").

[102] Di Castro, 3 *cons.* 6, folws. 9va–10va.

The irony was that the husband's bankruptcy put the wife in this position. So Sozzini did see a danger in reducing her dowry to a cash deposit held by a merchant, whereas di Castro saw that as perfectly lucrative. Sozzini admitted that there were still some weighty opinions favoring such creditors, but he said the greater weight of opinion favored the wife: "whence the judge can be kept from rashness, who upholds the opinion of so many men . . . and especially in the case of dowry as it is to be judged for her in ambiguous circumstances . . . even if there are fewer opinions for her."[103]

LEGAL AGENCY OF WIDOWS

The balance between families and gendered behaviors may have seemed most precarious in widowhood. In that circumstance a woman might enjoy more latitude, especially if her father was out of the picture as well as her husband. Leaving aside the whole realm of male fears of widows' sexuality, let us look at two places where it enters law – mother's guardianship of minor children and the consequences of remarriage.

Widows, as we will see more fully in the next chapter, had rights in many cities to return to their family of birth and to be supported there, and to the return of their dowry on the dissolution of marriage. This was a vital and often contentious area of law and life. A widow's marital kin had distinct interests in seeing her remain among them and not actually (as opposed to legally) extract her dowry from household assets. But their interests and hers were not necessarily the only ones in play. Even if they were inclined to stay in their husbands' homes, especially to care for their common children, there were still the interests of the family of origin to consider, which might dictate a remarriage that also was quite contrary to the interests of marital kin, who were agnate to her children. Husbands' kin wanted widows as a rule to stay and care for the children, which had the added benefit of allowing them to keep the dowry and not have to scramble to reassemble or reconstitute it.

By and large, guardianship of minor children was another area of law that fell largely to *ius commune*. But cities would have good reason to restate and enforce the laws in that realm to protect their young citizens. It was not necessary for statutes explicitly to allow mothers to be guardians, because that was covered in *ius commune*, although some did. That renowned home to jurists, Bologna, felt compelled to recognize that

---

[103] Sozzini, 3 *cons.* 111, fols. 142va–43ra.

mothers or grandmothers could come to the role of *tutrix* by the terms of a testament or simply *a lege*. But if after four months the mother did not evidently act as such, then any other *tutor* (male) came to be primary and the woman was excluded. Further, if the mother proceeded to remarry, she could not name another as *tutor*; and if the new husband or any of his kin, agnate or cognate, was among the guardians, he was excused. The city would step in to name a *tutor*.[104] Saona also recognized the guardianship invested in mothers, but added that they had to be given a *contutor* from among the near kin from the male line, or if one was lacking, then from the maternal.[105] Florence went so far as in 1393 to construct a civic magistracy to manage wards' properties (of at least 200 florins in value), either as executors or as appointers and overseers of *tutores*. An entire array of rules was generated for the board. It was conceded at Florence and elsewhere that, as mothers generally could not inherit from their children, they were the perfect disinterested guardians, concerned only with care of their children and not with any potential gain to themselves, unlike relatives who might be next in line and thus, while having reason to see to the maintenance of property, had perhaps less incentive to see to the persons of these wards. Remarriage in Florence and elsewhere disqualified a woman from formal guardianship, though it did not necessarily end her effective involvement with children from her earlier marriage.

Again, the later statute of Siena was more thorough. It declared that if the mother or grandmother lived with the children, she was to have precedence among any other *tutores*, unless the local officials (*sapientes pupillorum*) determined otherwise, as these officials could override any rule in the best interest of the wards. If there were no surviving mother or if she refused the job or remarried or otherwise declined to live with her children, the magistrates could step in and select a guardian from among agnates in the third degree, or if none, cognates.[106] In all these cases, widows operated with whatever restrictions fell on them as such in their community, but as *tutrices* they operated for the good of others and in company with or supervised by some men. They acted, as well, as part of a household, as most evident in Siena's statutes.

Public officials overseeing wards were the bodies to which widows as guardians appealed for help and relief. They had prerogatives to care for their children, but they were also caught up in potential conflicts between

[104] Bologna, 568–69.   [105] Saona, 245.   [106] Siena, 95–96.

families. As widows, they gained prestige and power from their roles as mothers. Magistrates tended to favor mothers as guardians because they were disinterested while also loving. These magistrates would come, even in the course of the sixteenth century and later, to allow careful formal arrangements permitting widow guardians to remarry but continue as guardians to their children from earlier marriages and to bring them into their new home. Conflicts with the deceased husband's kin at such moments were predictable.

The dissolution of a marriage on the death of one of the spouses was always a disturbing moment. The household was in flux and succession was immediately in question. When the wife was the survivor, she faced new circumstances and tough questions, with the answers to some of them at times thrust upon her by her natal family. Where now should she live? Should she remarry? Could she retrieve her dowry? Had her husband left her anything? Were there children?

Unprotected by a husband, although male kin, his or hers, might be readily at hand and eager to get involved, a widow had to cope with these questions and more. The tendency on the part of those who have studied widows has been to see widowhood as both a precarious and yet a liberating status. Loss of the husband, settlement of the estate, expenses of raising children, and the severely limited capacity of an ever-older woman to realize an income on her own all substantiate the sense that widows faced tough financial circumstances. Yet many have described the commercial and legal activities of widows and marveled at their capacity to cope. Certainly it is as a widow that a woman was more likely to enter into the legal records that remain to us. Advice books tried to caution widows about being active in lawsuits, which is indicative of the fact that they were. Examination of surviving *consilia* and other judicial records more than confirms that impression.

The most thorough recent account of widows in an Italian society is that of Isabelle Chabot for Florence (part of a study of women and dowry). She concentrates on the pivotal role of the widow in the gener-ational and domestic transition inaugurated by her husband's death, including her possible remarriage. The debt that the widow's dowry constituted on the family ledgers was the source of her influence and also the constraint on her. Chabot's view of widows is fairly pessimistic. She does not see widowhood as a state of relative autonomy. It may be that autonomy is a misplaced term here, as it imposes a more contemporary set of values on women's activities. But it is nonetheless the case that widows had more to do and more space in which to do it. If not autonomous, they were still more active and powerful, maybe especially in the vital first months and years of their new, post marital status.

Francesca, of a noble Mantuan family, married messer Giovanni di Francesco degli Strigi with a 1,000 ducat dowry. After marriage, her husband, though a minor, had been enabled by ducal decree to sell a farm to members of the da Carpo family for 500 ducats and shortly thereafter bought a house and land from the da Labbate. Both sales had a delay feature, such that ownership stayed with the seller until the full purchase price had been delivered. When the da Carpo paid, Giovanni immediately turned over the cash to the da Labbate to complete his purchase. After her husband died, Francesca sought the farm sold to the da Carpo for her dowry (partial), and they in turn gained hold of the house purchased with the proceeds from the farm. But as Francesca was still owed half her dowry, she asserted her hypothecary right over both properties. Strong arguments militated against her claims: by the sale Giovanni had sworn to uphold the da Carpo title, which seemed prior to his widow's. The house would not be part of Giovanni's property if he had not first sold the farm, so it seemed "absurd and inconvenient" that his widow end up in possession of both. But Sozzini said that Francesca's claim was "better and more powerful," and the basis of his decision was that "such lien of monna Francesca for her dowry is said to be privileged as by the law *Prefertur* she is preferred to all other creditors even previous ones." Sozzini asserted as close to an absolute sense of the priority and privilege of a dotal hypothec as was conceivably possible. Even sales of property did not remove the "lien" from the property, at least when the hypothec was not simply tacit (as included in any dowry) but was also expressed in the pledge of all one's goods for return of the dowry at the time of its receipt. His was a long and needlessly subtle opinion, but his intent was clear and he served his client's interest with his arguments.[107] Still, in his determination, those who bought from her husband would have lost their money, with only a claim for the amount against his estate, which does not seem to have had other assets. The dispute may well not have ended there.

Retrieval of dowry was in all likelihood the first step a widow had to take, and thus the first expression of her newly gained capacity to act on her interests. The issues of inheritance and dowry retrieval will be taken up fully in the next chapters, as they are more properly about inheritance

---

[107] Sozzini, 3 *cons.* 10, fols. 16va–18vb.

and related property settlements. Guardianship of children, however, was an equally pressing matter with regard to continuing in some fashion the household one was in. Or there was the opposed possibility of remarriage. The husband, were he the marriage's survivor, it must be noted, faced analogous questions. He too had to contemplate the possibility of remarriage, though in good part because he also needed help in managing the household and raising children. We know that many widowers did remarry, and their remarriages are testimony to the importance of a wife in the household (beyond having children) and of the dowry she brought to it. But the children were his; the father was the legal guardian; the children remained *in potestate*. That was not the case on his death. Then *potestas* ended. A *tutela* had to be established. Shepherding the minors and their property through the transition to adulthood was a socially vital process. Men often left their wives something extra in their wills – cash, property, or simply right of use and dwelling in the house – to encourage them to stay with the children, even when their natal families might have an eye on an advantageous remarriage. By contrast, as Christiane Klapisch-Zuber has revealed, the widow who remarried and left her children in their father's home and in the care of others was denounced as a "cruel" mother (even if she was being a good daughter).

For jurists the questions that arose were about the eligibility of mothers to be guardians, about the validity of their acts as widows and guardians, and about the consequences of remarriage for a woman. The first two issues seem to have gained juristic resolution by the mid-fifteenth century. Fewer such cases needed learned intervention thereafter. Remarriage, however, seems to have been a perennial problem and perhaps became more pressing over time, at least for social elites who were putting fewer girls into the marriage market and more of them into convents.

As we have seen, Bologna had a statute that presumed a mother or grandmother had *tutela*, but removing her if she made no effort to exercise it for four months. When a man named Odo died, he left a young daughter and his wife's mother Lucretia, who took on *tutela* of her infant granddaughter. Odo also had some property in Apulia, where he died, and his uncle Egamo had himself declared the girl's guardian in order to recover those properties, about which Lucretia was unaware. When Lucretia moved to have all of Odo's property put in her hands as *tutrix*, Egamo resisted, arguing that Bologna's statute did not apply to the maternal grandmother and that he was thus the real guardian. Lucretia's counter was that the statute did not say paternal grandmother, leaving the term indistinct, and that no one had come forth to contest her role during the four months allotted. Alessandro Tartagni offered his reading of the statute as clearly preferring mother or grandmother to any other guardians, designated by law or by testament. The statute, he said, was issued precisely to obviate the variety of opinions among jurists (those teaching in Bologna foremost) whether other tutors were preferable. The statute gave the women preference, while setting a four month period for deliberation and mourning. And he saw no distinction between paternal and maternal grandmothers. Her exclusion from succession by another statute did not exclude her from *tutela*. Though *ius commune* had a preference that "he who is preferred in succession be preferred in guardianship" (*ille qui prefertur in successione preferatur in tutela*), the statute again changed that, as it preferred the mother as guardian not because she was heir but precisely because she was not.[108] As Giulia Calvi determined in examining guardianship in Florence, the mother was seen as disinterested and thus a better guardian because she could not inherit from her children as so many other likely guardians could.

When Andrea di messer Giovanni da Porto of Vicenza invested certain properties on Ugana di Jacopo di messer Lipo, widow of messer Giovangiorgio di messer Giovanni, who was acting on behalf of her four children, the question arose as to who was liable for the rent. Baldo degli Ubaldi, noting that nothing was said in the rental agreement about the use of the children's money or any ratification of the action by them, declared that the contract was the mother's and directly implicated her alone and her resources alone. If she acted for the children, then she was not liable, but any *fructus* consumed in the interim was due from the children's property because the rental was to their benefit.[109] In parallel, in another opinion, Baldo argued that a widow was a competent administrator for her children. The widow in that case had bought some property, which her children claimed was theirs, purchased with their money, but which she claimed came "from her own efforts and labor" (*de propria industria et labore*). Baldo rattled through some conjectures. Were the *pupilli* rich and the mother poor, the purchase presumably was theirs. An industrious mother and poor children generated the opposite presumption. But if neither, the law's presumption was for the mother, unless the children could demonstrate she had used their money. Whereas a wife's acquisitions in ordinary domestic affairs were by law her husband's (other acquisitions, such as *bona non dotalia* and earnings outside the house,

---

[108] Tartagni, 3 *cons.* 109, fol. 88rb–va.   [109] Baldo, 3 *cons.* 162, fol. 47rb–va.

as we have seen, were not), "there is not the same rationale with a widow, as she might acquire by her own acts, because she is not held to work for her husband's heirs as she is held to work for her husband" (*tenetur non operari heredibus viri sicut tenebatur operari vir*).[110]

By *ius commune* and under statutes in many places, second marriages disqualified mothers as *tutrices* of the children of their first marriage. On that basis a mother's remarriage upset familial and social order, although in reality a mother might still be involved in the lives and the economic support of her children by a previous marriage. A woman designated *tutrix* in her husband's will and given incentive to do so in the form of a testamentary bequest lost all that by remarrying. Husbands and local statutes wanted the sort of wife who would serve *maritalem honorem*, "and in doubt [the statute] seems to presume that a husband did not want to privilege her in his property because his memory would be offended by [her] proceeding to a second marriage" (*cum memoria eius per transitum ad secundas nuptias offendatur*).[111] So in the case in which Niccolina, having had two sons by Leporino, remarried to ser Donato, bringing a 300 *lire* dowry, but declaring that if she died before him her dowry would remain with Donato and his father, Orlando, Baldo struck down her seeming betrayal of her children. When Niccolina died, leaving a second set of children, the first children sued for half her dowry and *fructus* from the day she died. Baldo did not want to see the elder children defrauded. He determined that they should get half; but he did not give them *fructus* from the date of death, as their ownership really only began with this judgment.[112] This was the kind of case that several communes had in mind when (as we will see) they legislated that a remarried woman's dowry went to and stayed with her new husband and family. Such legislation was out to avoid the sort of judgment Baldo made. Whether he made that judgment at the behest of the judge or as advocate for the older children is not clear from the text.

Lodovico Pontano faced a case in which a husband, in a fairly rare step, encouraged his widow to remarry, leaving her 70 florins if she remarried. In stark contrast a local statute set penalties for remarriage, and *ius commune* at least denounced remarriage within the one-year mourning period expected of widows. But if the woman married after a year, though her second marriage might cause *iniuria* to her children (the reason the statute set a penalty), she could remarry; and obviously here

---

[110] Baldo, 5 *cons.* 137, fol. 35rb–va.   [111] Baldo, 3 *cons.* 51, fol. 14ra–b.
[112] Baldo, 5 *cons.* 22, fols. 7va–8ra.

she was not damaging a husband who had encouraged remarriage. Pontano absolved her of the statutory penalty. But a daughter from the first marriage had also asked for *auxilium* (for dowry) and cited the statute. Pontano noted that the statute forbade a remarrying woman from disadvantaging the children, lest "there would arise greed and unrestrained desire (*cupiditas ac ineffrenata voluntas*) of women who renounce not only the property but even the life of the children to new husbands, as many do." But this woman had remarried not by *voluntas* but by *necessitas* in order to gain the 70 florins. Pontano also noted that the Florentine statutes had gone to the extreme of leaving all of a remarried woman's dowry with her second husband, to the total detriment of her children by her first husband. These statutes thus provided a counter example, where a governing body chose to promote remarriage in some sense. Finally he got to the intriguing question. Would one not expect *paterna pietas* to provide a portion from the dowry for children of the first marriage? His answer was that "a woman wanting to do that [remarry] could find no husband, as it is not probable that someone would return a dowry right according to the Florentine statute.[113] Second marriage, in Florence at least, was encouraged by directing the entire dowry to the second husband and any children. To Pontano's way of thinking there was no dowry right for the daughter from the first marriage, at least not from her mother's dowry.

When Angela, widow of Rinaldo of Orvieto, remarried, she wanted guardianship to pass to her brother. But there were paternal relatives – the father's sister and a second cousin – and they were wealthier and of greater reputation. A local statute ordered that when a *tutrix* remarried the *tutela* had to pass to the most worthy of the near relatives (*consanguinei*). Benedetto Capra, a canonist, sided with her selection, as her brother was a close relative (indeed maternal uncles often played an active role in children's lives). He read the statute as not privileging only agnate or paternal relations. He also reminded the podestà, who had to appoint the guardian, that Angela's brother was sufficiently noble and wealthy himself.[114] Not said, but possibly part of the attraction of this solution, was that her brother, like Angela herself, was not in line to succeed to these children and thus disinterested, in contrast especially to the agnate sister.

---

[113] Pontano, *cons.* 219, fol. 112rb–vb.   [114] Capra, *cons.* 37, fol. 59rb–vb.

CONCLUSIONS

Investigations into court cases, says Cecilia Cristellon, result in "a very fluid picture of marriage, more so than that at times drawn in the historiography of marriage in Italy, which has privileged the use of normative sources and has assumed as the object of inquiry principally marriage of the ruling elites: a monolithic marriage, celebrated at a precise moment, fruit of an alliance between families, monogamous and indissoluble, 'exclusive site of the exercise of sexuality and legitimate procreation.'"[115] Our investigation of cases confirms this. At least for the marriages that came to court in one way or another, whether to establish their very legality or to sort out dowries under the duress of financial failure or death, there were shifting and dynamic relationships.

The different jurists, working on cases ranging from the early fourteenth to the late sixteenth century, drew on gender stereotypes to understand women's actions and the import of their titles to property, especially dowry. Women were described as weak. They were said to be irrational. But they were also described as avaricious and well able to understand and pursue their material interests. And they were depicted as loving mothers and daughters. The protective functions of law were activated when such gendered notions were invoked, and some women were in consequence able to keep or retrieve property. Just as the legal family and the domestic unit did not coincide, leading to legal problems, gender stereotypes and the real titles and abilities of women did not coincide and led to legal problems. The very fluidity of marital arrangements and ceremonies embedded ambiguity in the family at its inception. The exact import of any marriage could reveal itself only over time. Local statutes tried to provide some certainty in line with local needs and experiences, stressing documentary evidence, dowry, and transfer of a wife to her husband's house, and notably in seeking increasingly to limit or preclude women's legal acts without male oversight.

As another layer in an already complex legal situation, statutes at times only added to the confusion. Protection of women seemed to demand that they be subordinate to men or at least act with them (or their consent), but it also seemed to rest on keeping their property distinct from that of men and apart from their financial or even political misfortunes. A woman's

---

[115] Cristellon, *La carità e l'eros*, 81.

marriage was supposed to be arranged by her family and supported by property; but her free consent was also necessary and formative for marriage, hence fear could be alleged to justify overturning such arrangements. Even more direct transactions were subject to being overturned, nominally to protect women (except in the eyes of Paolo di Castro). Perhaps the most glaring contradiction was the provision for return of dowry, *constante matrimonio*, when a husband was in financial difficulty. Yet this too was part and parcel of the legal guarantees of a right to dowry that was also the compensating feature to the exclusion of dowered women from paternal and fraternal inheritance. That right was as firm as the right of any child to a legitimate portion of the inheritance by *ius commune*, such that Bellomo has posed the equation of *dos* and *legitima* and disclosed the arguments of jurists that dowry was *patrimonium filiae*.[116] But it was also "not considered a female share in inheritance," as Klapisch-Zuber has insisted. Dowry nonetheless was something; it was not absolute exclusion from inheritance. These was real value there in many instances. Value worth fighting for in court.

To put the matter in terms employed by Renata Ago.

the instruments with which the family corporation is furthered and protected are rather imprecise. Law presumes that the married woman is poor, but admits exceptions for nobles and merchant women. Feudal law and statutory law distance her from the estate – from the property – in favor of collateral males, but in practice it is impossible to guarantee their control totally against the risk that a wife may finish up as the sole heir and so have access to all the property. Moreover, just because they are excluded from the estate, women are generally recipients of testamentary bequests, which are hardly ever subject to dotal rules and thus give them access to property. Moreover, the same dotal system is adapted only to a certain point to the principle of full control on the part of the husband, because the wife can dispose of her dowry by testament, assigning it so sons and depriving the husband of the usufruct that would normally belong to him.[117]

We have yet to see some of the situations she cites, and not all these situations prevailed in every jurisdiction, but it is beyond question that patrimonial strategies could empower women in important ways, despite, and yet also because of, lineage and gender ideologies. Ago does not even mention one of the more important situations where women could have real capacity to affect family life and control of its property – guardianship of children.

---

[116] Bellomo, *Ricerche sui rapporti patrimoniali tra coniugi*, 169–78.
[117] Ago, "Ruoli familiari," 126.

One of the debated issues in the expanding literature on the history of families in Europe is the rise of companionate marriage. At what point, to put it simply, did marriage cease to be a matter of family strategies and arrangements and become a matter of personal identity and development – of love, in other words? One suggestion has been that companionate marriage had an easier time of it where marital property was communal and thus more egalitarian. Such arrangements were more often found in northern Europe. However, scholars have also pointed to evidence of intimacy and affection in southern regions, like Italy, and have noted that various arrangements and rules mitigated the total separation of property where it was not held commonly. Still another suggestion, therefore, is that more reliance on moveable forms of wealth to support the family (as opposed to land and real estate in general) was fertile terrain for companionate families. More time had to be devoted to managing such wealth, and households on such a basis had to cope more on their own without extended kinship networks.

The evidence we have utilized in this chapter hardly equips us to resolve such a large issue, even the handful of cases that dealt with *stuprum* and related sexual actions at the formation of marital or extra-marital relationships. The norms and cases arising in a system of separate marital estates do not afford much purchase on emotions. But they also do not rule them out. Spouses colluding to preserve property by legal means, widows struggling to maintain guardianship over their children and manage their resources for that purpose, could well have been acting equally on profound emotional attachments. Those emotions were just not legally relevant. Or they were assumed and buried in gender stereotypes, like that of the loving parent. Per Daniela Lombardi,

the image of the family in the past where relations between husbands and wives, between parents and children were based exclusively on the brutal authority of the *paterfamilias*, where there was room for interests but not for emotions, is no longer acceptable. Emotions, as we know, could be expressed even with the language of interests or, in another way, with expressive codes different from those to which we are accustomed today.[118]

Our sources immerse us in the language of interests, to be sure, but they cannot keep us from seeing some of the life behind them.

The main thing to keep in mind is that the women we have encountered in these cases, whose actions were anticipated in statutes and

[118] Lombardi, *Matrimoni di antico regime,*?304.

jurisprudential commentaries, were part of kin networks that included men. These networks were widened and yet complicated by marriage, perhaps best seen in the conundrum of the remarrying widow, caught, at that point, between three families. The law gave women and men tools to negotiate their social existence. Juristic accommodation of rules and stereotypes was perhaps the height of such negotiation, for then the instruments of the law itself, its practitioners too, became involved.

5

Inheritance

Intestacy

The two nodes around which family life turned, *patria potestas* and *patrimonium*, were both thrown into crisis and out of equilibrium when the *pater* died.[1] It is not that there were not critical problems on the deaths of other family members, especially of a wife and mother, but the major share of the property and its management were in question on the death of the head of household. The *ius commune*, drawing on the rich veins of Roman law, provided two main modes in which the critical moment of succession could play out – intestacy or testamentary succession. The first provided the default mechanism. It consisted largely of rules for the order of succession and established the base line for what succession should look like (e.g., equal division among children or others in the same degree of relationship to the deceased). The second allowed for individual initiative to adapt and modify the order of succession and, perhaps more importantly, the size and quality of the different shares to be carved from the deceased's effects. As we saw in some examples in the previous chapter, it was also possible to leave property to someone by a third mode (closer to testamentary) of a *donatio causa mortis*.

Intestacy was also governed by local statutes, and there was hardly a jurisdiction in Italy that did not legislate on intestacy, pointedly modifying the basic rules of *ius commune* in view of local customs and expectations as to how property should transit the moment of death and come to the hands of the next generation of owners. The centrality of intestate inheritance statutes is attested by the fact that the very first *consilium* in the

---

[1] Romano, *Famiglia, successioni e patrimonio familiare*, 19.

printed collection of Mariano Sozzini's opinions, and among his earliest, dating from 1517, and one of the longest (ten full folia), was about an intestacy case. In it, an unmarried daughter, Nicola, and a son, Tannelluccio, were survivors of their intestate father. Nicola subsequently accepted a dowry from paternal and maternal funds, giving a formal renunciation from seeking more from her mother's property, on condition that there were male heirs who stood to gain by that renunciation. So when her brother died leaving only a daughter, Agneta, Nicola made her claim for a portion of the maternal estate, which presumably would amount to more than her dowry alone. Two statutes figured in. One kept a dowered woman from claiming from her parents, if there were a son. The other said that a woman could not inherit from her brother, if there were legitimate heirs. Thus one statute affected Nicola's claims on her mother, the other on her brother (there was no question, in view of the statue, of her receiving more from her father). On first sight, as no male survived, her statutory exclusion disappeared, so her succession to her mother could be restored; but the existence of a daughter, her niece, kept her from her brother's estate, as the statute did not specify that only a male heir deprived a sister of succession to her brother.

The statutes relevant to Nicola did not expressly declare their purpose. The two statutes consistently distinguished men from women. Their rationale, said Sozzini, "is a certain public utility which results from conservation of family dignity and of the agnation or the symbol of the house ... the principal and basis of the aforesaid dignity is wealth [*divitiae*] without which the dignity and honor of the family diminish and decline." The desire to preserve property in the hands of agnate heirs on intestacy was a commonplace in juristic interpretation of such statutes (at times explicitly stated in some of them). So Sozzini found that, although it could be said that the purpose of the statute was "to preserve the honor of agnation" (*conservare honorem agnationis*), it was not served in the immediate case, as either way the property would go to a woman, and although both of these women were agnate to the deceased brother, neither could transmit agnation, by definition.

Still, Sozzini found that the exclusion of a dowered woman (the sister) could make sense by a different line of reasoning: "because dowered women, of whom [the statute] speaks, when they go to their husband's home, do not need as much substance for sustenance of them and theirs as men need." The argument about compensation for greater burdens on men meant that the provisions for "legitimate heirs" had to refer to men. Also, the statute was "exorbitant" in relation to common law and in need of strict interpretation. And on that basis, after considering a number of arguments about the role of sex in the statutes, Sozzini decided that "legitimate heirs" meant male only and did not include women, the paradoxical result being that the niece did not exclude the sister, who was then free to pursue her claim on her brother's estate by returning her dowry back into the estate and splitting the resulting value with her niece.[2] In other words, in the absence of a surviving male heir, the estate would be split evenly between women.

The role of this chapter is to examine the rules of intestacy such as those Sozzini confronted and elucidate the sorts of ambiguities and problems that emerged in practice for inheritances that passed in intestacy. In the absence of a testament, the "intent" that guided inheritance had to be sought, as Sozzini found it, in a rationale attributed to statutes. They therefore figure prominently here. In the absence of obvious direct male heirs (i.e., sons), that statutory intent was truly uncertain. The constant disruption of direct descent by failures of procreation and mortality kept courts and jurists busy. So did the interested claims of relatives seeking some portion of wealth at the moment when its title and destination were most in doubt.

INTESTACY IN *IUS COMMUNE*

There are those who maintain that inheritance with a will predominated in Italy (or even in classical Rome). There was plenty of advice literature, legal and moral, urging people to make wills and put their affairs in order as a good manager and family member. In the era of plagues, the advice to be prepared for death at any moment, spiritually and materially, was pressing and omnipresent. The Church urged use of testaments so as to direct bequests for the benefit of one's soul, for charitable distribution, and for atonement of one's sins in regard to wealth (as in the dispersal of the ill-gotten proceeds from usury). Yet people continued to die in intestacy (it is impossible to give a precise percentage, but sporadic evidence, as from Florence, would indicate that half or more of estates of some value were intestate) and in at least some cases that was by choice or at least by not getting around to it, and not just a matter of relative poverty (having little to leave to justify the bother of composing a testament).

It is also simply the case that wills attract attention (then and now). They are consummately intriguing (if at times boringly formulaic)

_____

[2] Mariano Sozzini, 1 *cons.* 1, fols. 2ra–11rb.

expressions of individual intent to direct property in ways and to persons
that provide historical insight into cultural values and personal relationships. They have, in the hands of scholars such as Jacques Chiffoleau and
Samuel Cohn, yielded insight into spiritual concerns of the testators and
reflections on family and gender. For study of poorer social groups, who
clearly did have recourse to wills at times, and for women, for some of
whom a testament was their sole surviving legal act, that in any case gave
the rare opportunity to express their values and needs, wills are a privileged and vital source.

Testaments also drew a great deal of attention in courts because they
changed the default rules of succession. More juristic attention, more
legislative effort, much forensic time, and a great deal of interpersonal
conflict arose over inheritance. Most of that fell around the peculiar issues
that each and every testament could raise, despite every effort by those
involved to keep their language precise. It is telling that almost one-
quarter of the *Digest* is devoted to aspects of inheritance, and most of
that concerns wills. But as testaments are modifications of the rules of
intestacy, if only to understand them correctly, we need to begin with
intestacy. There is plenty there to explore.

The Heir in Law

The heir in Roman law (by intestacy or testament) did more than take
ownership of lands and goods, he succeeded to the entire legal position of
the *de cuius* – rights and actions, debts and credits. A testament had to
designate an heir (*heres*); it was voided if it did not. The main concern of
the law of intestacy was to determine who was heir to the deceased whose
(*de cuius*) inheritance was at issue. A successor to the deceased's legal
personality was the first order of business.

The order of succession by the time of Justinian had come to be
cognatic, though remnants of the more agnatic scheme of earlier centuries
were still embedded in the excerpted texts gathered under the relevant
headings in the *Codex* and *Digest*. First in order of succession came
descendants – essentially children or their children – inheriting equally
by branch (*per stirpem*). Though earlier distinctions between legitimate
children and emancipated or adopted children had been largely elided by
Justinian's time, there was still the legal fact that children *in potestate* at
the death of their *pater* became *sui iuris* and also *sui heredes* (literally,
heirs to their own and "his" [the deceased's] heirs). All those who fell in
the category of descendants inherited, male and female, closer degree of

relationship to the *de cuius* being decisive. Next in Justinian's scheme were ascendants and full siblings (or their descendants), again sharing equally and without gender distinction (i.e., brothers inherit with sisters). Half-blood siblings came next. Lacking any in that category, the next to claim succession fell to other collaterals, nearer degree precluding more remote, all of the same degree sharing equally, both agnate and cognate. Low in the order was a surviving spouse, which is quite the opposite of many modern inheritance systems. But dowry had first charge on a deceased husband's estate, so a widow who had a dowry would sup- posedly be taken care of. If there were no persons in these categories, property passed to the fisc as *bona vacantia*. Essentially left out of the mix in intestate succession were illegitimate children. Only those who were *naturales* (born of a long-term relationship between two unmarried people) had some lesser rights to inherit.

There might be no heirs, not because such people were not alive, but because they chose to reject what fell to them. Even the *sui heredes*, who did not have to enact a formal acceptance (*aditio* or *cretio*), had the right to repudiate an estate as burdensome or of little worth (*hereditas damnosa*). Justinian fixed a term of three years to decide to exercise the right to abstain (*ius abstinendi*); heirs in the meantime could not meddle in the estate and thus act like heirs (*inmiscere* in the late medieval terminology). Refusal moved the option of inheriting to the next in line. The universal succession of the heir generally merged the inherited prop- erty with his own and left all of it liable for debts – hence the real legal risk of losing more than gaining in an inheritance. For creditors, an heir who had little or nothing was also a risk. There were a couple of legal devices to help with the settling of an estate's debts. The creditors could apply for a juridically decreed separation of the two estates until the inherited debts had been settled. For the heirs Justinian provided a *beneficium inventarii* that would confine liabilities to the assets of the estate, provided an inventory were made within three months. In the opposite direction, heirs otherwise had legal remedies to seek what was owed to the *de cuius*. These rules of repudiation or acceptance of inheritance, use of inventory, and pursuit of an estate's debts and credits were all a living part of the law, explained in the law schools and incorporated or understood in the laws of Italian communities.

Succession in Roman law was thus not only seemingly gender neutral and biased toward equal division among all heirs of the same class or degree; it was also largely individualistic and voluntary. Of course the most voluntary element was the testament (also known, after all, as a will [*voluntas*]), but even in intestacy the right of refusal to be heir was patent. The Lombard legal legacy regarding inheritance was different – a more communal sense of ownership, a distinction between genders and bias to agnation, and an eschewing of testaments. According to Andrea Romano, the first step back toward testaments on a more or less Roman model was the adoption of succession pacts by which the *de cuius*, at first for spiritual purposes, might influence the destination of some of his property by entering an agreement with an heir.[3] Such bilateral contracts gave way to the more unilateral testament as Roman law revived in the schools and in the streets. Canon law had long encouraged testaments, as they provided the mechanism of making a bequest (*legatum*) to ecclesiastical bodies or charitable institutions. Against the individualistic sense of ownership making its way back into practice through Roman law, agreements to hold property in *consortium* or as a *communio* (*fraterna*) or *societas omnium bonorum*, such as we saw in cases in Chapter 3, attempted to give some cohesion to a family and to a patrimony, at least for the life of those so joined in agreement. A *societas* could emerge from an estate passed to heirs in intestacy or by testament. A laterally extended group sharing patrimony and meals (*ad unum panem et vinum*) was thus possible. The house (often a defensible tower in the medieval cities, later a more elaborate dwelling, or *palazzo* among the wealthier) became a vital asset and symbol of domestic union. It was thus possible to use pacts among individuals to affect a sense of community and common ownership as against a sense of individuals holding apart.

Yet another form of family and inheritance was enshrined in feudal law, the textual basis for which came from a Milanese, Oberto dall'Orto, around 1155. The basic rule of succession for a fief was set by the act of concession by the feudal lord. Some fiefs were divisible, some were not. Illegitimates were largely excluded from inheriting fiefs. Women were too, most so in central and southern Italy, on the grounds of their unsuitability for the largely military *servitia* attached to the fief. Unless the act of concession of a fief allowed women to succeed, they were left out. So there was a substantial bias to men (*favor masculinitatis*) in feudal law. In fact, the most widely diffused type of fief in Italy was the so-called Lombard form, which called for division of ownership among multiple male heirs. But by the thirteenth century these too were largely held by only one heir and went by the rule of primogeniture. The jurist Cino da

[3] Romano, 28–32.

Pistoia saw primogeniture as an iniquitous practice imported from England, and it would take some effort and textual manipulations to get it accepted in some regions of Italy, where equality among heirs was so traditional and widespread. It nonetheless became more common during the fifteenth and sixteenth centuries (next chapter). Primogeniture, indivisibility, and virtual exclusion of women in succession to fiefs, in any case, contrasted strongly with Roman inheritance law. The fief also had a lord, and the consequent multiple, overlapping forms of ownership on a single property, while accommodated ultimately in *ius commune*, were also at odds with the Roman law of ownership.

In social, economic, and legal terms, inheritance was a big moment. Property changed hands. Sometimes, if not most times, households broke up and reformed. People realized gains or losses unrivaled at other life points (except for dowries for women). Inheritance was, of course, linked to death, though it was not always an immediate consequence. Sometimes the inheritance was delivered before death, as *donatio causa mortis*, and other times heirs delayed in taking an estate, using the interval to deliberate on their options. And frequent lawsuits further delayed effective passage and use of a *haereditas*. Anyone with a claim on an estate might be well advised to pursue legal remedies as the gains could be quite high, even on relatively modest holdings. And the law was so complex that sound arguments were possible from numerous angles.

Even the very nature of inheritance raised legal difficulties. No less a figure than Baldo degli Ubaldi had to wrestle with that. In a *consilium* for a Milanese case, it seems, he began by posing the question of the precise meaning of *haereditas* after it was accepted by an heir or simply entered into by a direct heir (*haeres suus et necessarius*). It could be argued that one had *haereditas* only after it had been accepted (*adita*), for only then could items be sold or alienated. In fact, Baldo found, there were two possible ways to see *haereditas*:

one mode is it is of the person of the heir and he represents the person of the deceased, and then it is not said to be accepted, because it represents the shadow of the deceased and not a real person. Second mode is the estate is said to be its goods, and then it is termed the estate of and in ownership of a living person, and ownership is of the living ... inheritance is the same as ownership, and ownership is of the living (*nam hereditas idem est quod dominium, et dominium est viventis*). For in truth death dissolves all ownership ... we speak of disposing of the estate in habit and act and that is understood to be acceptance.[4]

---

[4] Baldo, 5 *cons.* 393, fol. 102ra–b.

The second was the correct understanding. So to his mind the basic issue was the effective transfer of legal title and real *administratio*. Regarding Milan's statute, which held a woman's property by inheritance to consti- tute her dowry when married, Baldo said either she received it as dowry, or it was tacitly so, or she had had it even before her father's death (*peculiata*). Whatever the mode, the statute applied to a *haereditas adita*, not to one yet to be accepted. His decision seemed to leave room for the woman in question to repudiate the bequest for dowry and seek more.

Baldo also faced the general issue of who was part of the line of descent that was to inherit. It could be argued that father, mother, paternal uncle and aunt, maternal uncle and aunt, or other ascendants in direct or transverse line were not *de linea filii*. Thus fathers did not inherit fiefs from their sons. But Baldo argued to include the father, as no one was closer to the son than he. Baldo went further to claim more transverse ascendants were also part of the line: "and this is confirmed by a visual example, imagine a man on a cross with arms extended, there is the head on top and feet on the bottom, and arms [are] transverse parts and all from one trunk." So a restriction by which a testator forbade making a will beyond a certain type of persons did not work when no such person was available. This was a result, said Baldo, of the fact that "a son is of the substance and soil (*substantia et arena*) of the father; but the father is not of the substance and soil of the son, because nature and reason do not begin from later fact."[5] Metaphors aside, Baldo was arguing to maintain a wide range of possible heirs, at least where inheritance of fiefs was not in question.

Fiefs were often a source of inheritance problems, primarily from disadvantaging women. As more fiefs were established, and contested, over the course of the fifteenth and sixteenth centuries, more cases and complicated problems arose. Paolo di Castro looked at a fief held from the monastery of San Zeno that had passed from grandfather to his two sons, then to the son and three daughters of the son who lived longer. When the last of the invested fiefholders, one of the sisters, died in 1427, the son of the brother who had died first, Chichino, who had been an infant when his father passed away, finally learned of and pressed his claim to be invested in the fief (what remained of it, as his father and uncle had sold off a portion with the consent of the abbot who was its lord). Chichino alleged his ignorance for not acting earlier and asserted that the

---

[5] Baldo, 3 *cons*, 339, fol. 96ra–b.

fief, in his family for three generations, should pass by male line, and he was the sole male descendant. But the abbot's vicar had awarded the fief to another, in no way related to Chichino. Di Castro declared the vicar's decision unjust, arguing that Chichino's rights were not lost to prescription from the passage of thirty years due to his youth and ignorance, and the unjust vesting of the fief only in his cousins.[6] Chichino was an available agnatic male heir. In a much more politically complicated matter, Gianfrancesco Gonzaga, lord of Mantua, invested a fief on Guido di Francesco di Feltrino, nephew of the previous holder, Jacopo de Volutu, who with his father had been vested in the fief even in Jacopo's lifetime by the archbishop of Mantua. The three sons of Jacopo's son Filippo contested his claim. In fact, the original investiture had been in five sons of the original holder, Lodovico. Di Castro claimed there was no doubt that one of those portions belonged to the three sons of Filippo. The issue was the other four portions, which he determined also went to those three.[7]

Women could inherit fiefs if the clauses of investiture so allowed, and the duties attached to it were such that a woman could perform them as well as a man, and that was fairly rare. Pierfilippo da Corgna looked at the contrasting claims of Count Ugolino's daughter, Mariana, against her niece by her brother, Marsilia. So it was inheritance by women, but one clearly younger and probably marriageable. Neither ended up with it. At least Corgna dismissed any claim by Marsilia and said the fief lay in the hands of the city, Orvieto, because the holder died without male heirs.[8] It may well have been the city that asked the jurist to look into the case. The Bolognese jurist Giovanni Bolognetti (1506–75) probably hoped to have so easy a case. He did not. At its heart was whether a granddaughter descended from the firstborn son excluded her father's sister from the fief in the Kingdom of Naples. He decided that the aunt, Antonina, took it in preference to the granddaughter of Don Carlo de Baresio, Baron of Militelli. In the Regno there were four factors in inheritance: degree of relationship, sex, age, and line (*gradus, sexus, aetas,* and *capillus*). If the first was the same between two claimants, the other three came into play, by which simply, better man than woman, better older than younger, though better unmarried than married. Antonina was in first degree; Caterina was in second. If one accepted the argument that Caterina in fact took the first-degree spot of her father,

[6] Di Castro, 2 *cons.* 181, fols. 79va–80rb.   [7] Di Castro, 2 *cons.* 184, fols. 38vb–39va.

[8] Corgna, *cons.* 239, fols. 181ra–82ra.

and that she was not disadvantaged as to sex and age, then marital status was the deciding issue. Antonina was not married; Caterina was. Of course, the laws of the Regno that favored unmarrieds were clearly contrary to *ius commune*, and there were precedents arguing restrictively against them. Were Antonina dowered from her father's holdings, then she would be excluded from succeeding him, but not her mother. It was dowry, not a husband, that was the factor that would exclude her. Bolognetti, nonetheless, defended the constitutions of the Regno. An unmarried heir could have a husband chosen for her by the feudal overlord, after all.[9]

Another later jurist, Marcantonio Pellegrini in 1598, judged in favor of the claims of a father near Naples because, although he found feudal law gave little prerogative to paternal wishes (as to advantage one son over the other with a larger share), the fief he was considering was different. For one thing, it resulted not from a free act of lordly generosity but as compensation for 8000 ducats loaned to its lord. This was not inherited quite so obviously by feudal rules.[10] He confirmed the judgment of the royal council of Naples that the grant of the fief of Castro Pediluci to Matteo Poiano by Nicholas V included the possible succession of men related through women. The act of concession mentioned males but not agnation. This was not a typical fief, if only because it seemed to allow female succession.[11] Nor was that invested on Guasparre di Benedetto of Padua by the cardinal bishop of the city in 1568, after the death of the previous feudatory, Annibale a Ligname, whose mother and sister sued to have the fief. The different investitures of Annibale's father in 1482, 1488, and 1508 brought him a number of lands. Pellegrini found on that basis that the fiefs Annibale held in Villafranca, Ciconia, San Michele, and elsewhere could not go to these women; but the fief at Limina was perhaps different, invested back in 1438 on the original holder's wife, and not demanding military service but income from its produce (*fructus*). But Pellegrini struck down those arguments. It was a fief to which feudal law applied. The grant to a woman by the bishop was a special recognition of her good life (*vitae bonitas*). There was no Paduan custom of inheritance of fiefs by women, so the judgment of 1582 left the mother and sister high and dry.[12]

[9] Bolognetti, *cons.* 8, 155a–60a.   [10] Pellegrini, *cons.* 10, fols. 45ra–46ra.
[11] Pellegrini, *cons.* 6, fols. 31ra–32va.   [12] Pellegrini, *cons.* 22, fols. 70va–73ra.

STATUTES AND CASES

Getting the Goods

Once the recipient of an inheritance had been determined, there was still the matter of acceptance or rejection of the estate and the possible composition of an inventory. Not every city saw reason, by any means, to legislate into these areas covered in *ius commune*, but some did. Repudiation of inheritance especially raised problems against the expectations of heirship, most so when the presumed (by kin, neighbors, creditors, and officials) heirs remained on the property.

Florence attempted to regulate repudiation of inheritance with a statute that ordered any *haeres* of age eighteen or older to forsake all possessions in an estate within fifteen days if he intended to abstain. Possession after that point was taken as tacit acceptance (*aditio*), even despite any formal notarized repudiation to the contrary, even if the goods were ostensibly held under pretext of belonging to a maternal dowry or by benefit of inventory. Effectively that law propelled the decision to accept to a fast track (fifteen days), while it restricted the inventory, as a device to limit liability, to heirs under age eighteen. This contrasted somewhat with the Tuscan communities of Arezzo and Montepulciano, which similarly took possession as tacit acceptance, even in the face of a formal repudiation, but made exception for maternal dowry and permitted citizens to make use of benefit of inventory. Florence in the redaction of 1355 added the requirement that all repudiations be registered with communal authorities (at the same time ordering registration of emancipations as well). In 1415 finally, Florentines who repudiated were also allowed to retain maternal dowry property – a grudging recognition of the legal distinctness of spousal holdings.[13] Siena later established a complex procedure for repudiating before town officials and a related arbitration process to mediate between the heir who wished to retain maternal dotal property and the creditors on the estate.[14] Siena's moves were to preclude the problem of fraudulent repudiation of the sort that Bergamo's statutes of two centuries earlier had to address, declaring one who still held property to be heir and liable for debts on the estate. Bergamo, like Florence, also effectively forbade recourse to benefit of inventory, except for minors.[15]

---

[13] On the Florentine statutes, Kuehn, *Heirs, Kin, And Creditors*, 53–57.
[14] Siena, 263–65.   [15] Bergamo, 109.

Ferrara's early statutes (1287) took the curious tack of demanding, "as it is not proper that what is done by fathers or their predecessors be revoked," that sons had to abide by sales or alienations made by their fathers, even if they had repudiated the estate (as most notarized deeds of sale specified that the seller pledged his heirs to abide by the sale). Sons were allowed to keep their mothers' dowries and even, in contrast to abiding their fathers' activities, were allowed to recuperate anything that was obligated for maternal dowry.[16] Forlì apparently found no particular reason to regulate or register repudiations, but legislators there were alarmed at the errors that crept into inventories. So a format for inventories was laid out in one statute, which also set penalties on heirs who "omitted" some goods from the list. Inventories were to be completed by a notary before a judge of the podestà's court following proclamation to neighbors, or before the parish church in the case of a woman of good repute (*honesta domina*). Then another rubric was assembled "because often widows remaining in the house or needing to leave the house of their late husband, especially when they do not have children by said husband, strive to hide their trousseau [*coredum*] and even the goods of their husband, on account of which heirs and creditors of the husband are sometimes unduly defrauded." It ordered that on the day of such a husband's death two *consanguinei*, or, lacking them, two neighbors, proceed to the house with a notary and draw up an inventory of all *mobilia*. This provision, moved by what it saw as female deception (conceding nothing to supposed gendered weakness), reversed in some sense the meaning of inventory, in that here it was designed to protect the interests of creditors, including the heirs, rather than the heirs alone. The widow, of course, was not her husband's heir; she was another and privileged creditor to him.[17]

Acceptance or rejection of an estate raised the sorts of problems that led to disputes and the intervention of jurists. *Aditio*, mere acceptance of an inheritance, became a problem when it did not occur or did not seem to have happened. A Tuscan named Giambattista inherited from his father and then died. His estate passed to his mother, Lucrezia, though there was a paternal uncle. It did not matter whether or not the son had "inmixed" himself in the *haereditas* of his father (thus tacitly accepting it, according to statutes in some communities). Either the patrimony came to his mother through such *inmixtio* or it had not been legally accepted, and

---

[16] Ferrara 1287, 215–16.   [17] Forlì, 373–76.

then she was "creditor of the paternal estate" for her dowry. However, she had been given goods to satisfy her dowry claim by the uncle (her brother-in-law) acting as heir, even if in fact he was not heir. Was her acceptance of dowry then tantamount to a repudiation of the estate in favor of the uncle? The problem was further complicated by the fact that Lucrezia did not know that the estate fell to her. While ignorance was not usually presumed, in this case it could be because women were generally presumed to be ignorant of the law and because "it is not likely that this monna Lucretia would want to refuse the advantageous estate, as the gender of women is most greedy." As this was in fact her husband's property, and wives did not normally succeed husbands, her ignorance was likely. Women were probably well aware of their weaker, postponed inheritance rights, and a presumption that a close agnate male was heir would have been sensible. But as her acceptance of dowry from him as heir was done in ignorance, her act could not be construed as an equivalent to repudiation.[18] So the jurist Pierfilippo da Corgna backed her claims. The uncle was unlikely to relent, however, and probably had his own attorney craft a reply. At the least, one would think he could retrieve what he had given her as her dowry.

The brothers Marco and Pollonio di Francesco de Venda, through their mother's right, sought pieces of land their grandfather held at the time of his death. Alessandro Tartagni opined that the mother's failure to formally enter the estate did not affect direct heirs (sons), and in any case, formal acceptance might be inferred from an instrument by which the mother had settled some debts on the estate back in 1461. The lack of a formal *aditio* by the sons was not an obstacle, as they had thirty years by law to accept a maternal estate.[19] Paolo di Castro too faced a problem of no *aditio* on a case from Parma. There he determined that local statutes failed to take effect, so that a fourth-degree agnate did not exclude the deceased's sister or her sons. She had not formally acceded to the estate, as she died in a few days, and in the interval she had been occupied with *pias causas*: "namely to have her brother buried and to close the house as custodian and similarly to carry goods to her house that also as custodian she can be seen to have done." In some sense she had acted like an heir, and certainly like a good sister. Her infant sons fell heir to her right, and they had plenty of time to accept the estate that she had had no time to take.[20] They, of course, were not agnate to the other claimant. The quick

[18] Corgna, *cons.* 226, fols. 173rb–vb.   [19] Tartagni, 2 *cons.* 89, fols. 62rb–63va.
[20] Di Castro, 2 *cons.* 33, fol. 16va–b.

demise of an heir before formal acceptance was the source of such problems here and in many other instances.

Bartolomeo Cipolla declared that the question was "trite and vulgar" and the *communis opinio* was clear that a paternal estate *non adita* still transmitted to the next in line, a young male cousin in this case. Where an infant daughter had been heir but then quickly died, the issue was whether her rights went to her mother, for if the estate was the father's, then it could not go to his wife but would go to a male agnate. If the infant had accepted the estate through a tutor, being thus nominally its owner, however briefly, then at least her mother would gain a legitimate portion. If not, then the estate fell to agnates and the mother was excluded by statute of Colonia. Some of the estate lay in the jurisdiction of Ferrara and its statutes precluded inheritance by the cousin's mother, as it generally precluded all women in favor of agnate males.[21] In either case, the cousin gained.

Florence's statutes, as we saw above, looked with brutal clarity at ownership and liability. Angelo degli Ubaldi in 1399 took a look at a case in which two men were still in their *palazzo* after their father's death. The father, it was claimed, did not own the place; it belonged to his brother, who had let him live there. A second issue was, if one son married and bought a house and moved into it, did he do so with his father's money, which was liable to his creditors? Angelo declared that the statute "varied greatly from common law" (*fortiter exorbitat a iure communi*) and so deserved very strict construction. First, the two sons did not fall subject to the statute, if indeed the property was not their father's. Their presence in the house was simply tolerated by the true owner. Second, as for the purchased home, even though the son was *in potestate* when he bought it, it was not from his father's property as "he had his wife's dowry and was an assayer or banker keeping an exchange table publicly and openly, in which he daily gained his living, as bankers and assayers assiduously do." In other words, the son had access to his own funds. Third, the father was in the *palazzo* by a right of *familiaritas* only; at most he had a right of *detentio*, which was not the same as possession or ownership, both of which were transferable rights.[22] So Angelo concluded, despite the Florentine statute, that the sons' residence in a dwelling that had not, in fact, belonged to their father and the one son's purchase of a house with his wife's dowry and his own earnings did not amount to *aditio*, with its consequent liability for the father's debts.

[21] Cipolla, 2 *cons*. 7, 27a–29b.   [22] Angelo, *cons*. 386, fols. 217vb–18rb.

A complicated scenario came years later to Mariano Sozzini, although he claimed a resolution was simple and straightforward. A monna Antonia, wife of the noble Daniele Carugrano, mother to Pietro and Carlo, passed away in 1457 leaving a hefty 1,600 ducat dowry that Daniele kept, according to the terms of Florentine law (as we will see). Daniele remarried and had another son, Francesco, and at his death around 1470 he left his estate in equal portions to all three of his sons. They divided it, though continuing to live in common. Pietro died at age 76 in 1515, leaving a son, Daniele. Carlo died at age 73 in 1517, leaving Vincenzo. The youngest son, Francesco, was still alive in 1526, when his nephew, Vincenzo, claimed his grandmother's estate for the portion falling to him (nominally 800 ducats). In the intervening years, among Pietro, Carlo, Francesco, and Vincenzo, there had been business ventures, settlements of debts and credits, in common, without any mention of Antonia's dowry. Francesco, therefore, moved against Vincenzo's claim, even though he was not Antonia's son. Sozzini backed him and denied Vincenzo any recourse. So much time has passed, said the jurist, that any right of deliberation to accept the maternal inheritance, which Carlo had never formally accepted, had lapsed. No right was transmitted to Vincenzo. After all, it had been sixty years between the deaths of Antonia and Carlo, and although not all those years might count against the time limit to accept an estate (e.g., during an heir's minority), certainly at least thirty had. Even if someone could demonstrate a way that Carlo supposedly accepted the maternal estate as such, though it remained in the hands of his father, there was still a prescription of any rights after thirty years.[23] The 1,600 ducats simply disappeared into the estate of Daniele and as part of the patrimony came to three sons, with nothing separate as a maternal estate to those descended from her.

Inventories were a legal device to limit liability for debts on an estate for the heir who accepted it, but they could also be abused and used to cheat creditors. Luigi Layolio had been condemned by a judge to pay what he owed to Giovanni and Cardinale de' Poleti, though he objected that he had taken the inheritance with benefit of inventory and his exposure was limited to what was in it. Baldo had none of that. He said instead that Luigi "heedlessly and maliciously" litigated and it was "absurd" and "ridiculous" that he be able to do so under cover of inventory, for otherwise he could litigate perpetually and dissipate the

[23] Sozzini, 3 *cons.* 14, fols. 24va–25vb.

inheritance "to the great inconvenience of the creditors" (*in maximum dispendium creditorum*). Mainly, the expenses in this case were not incurred by the testator but by the heir, and so unprotected by an inventory, which had not been a thorough list of goods in any case.[24] Jurists had to leave protection for creditors.

They also had to protect licit inventories. Angelo di Nardo of Borgo, said to be old and sick, had a twenty-five-year-old natural son, Giovanni, and three legitimate younger sons. He had Giovanni draw up an inventory of all his possessions. About three months later Angelo made his will, which included some bequests, and named all four sons as equal heirs, with Giovanni as guardian of the three minors and faced with the obligation to make an inventory. The aged Angelo in fact did not die for five years, but when he did Giovanni (legitimated by being named heir in his father's will) accepted his role with regard to his half-brothers and drew up the inventory. It declared that a number of people owed his father money but also that he, Giovanni, was a creditor to the estate for sums of money that had appeared on his first inventory of five years before, including large bank deposits. When the brothers reached age of majority, they wanted an accounting to finish the *tutela*, and certainly one issue was what was not listed in the second inventory but had been in the first. Benedetto Capra conceded that *mobilia* and money were more easily lost than ownership of lands, for example, so one might argue there was no basis to assume that those sums not entered on the second inventory were still part of the estate after five years; but he argued that ownership was continuous and presumed unless acquisition by another could be demonstrated: "if possession of *mobilia* is useful and lowly (*utilis et abiecta*) and may be more quickly lost than possession of *immobilia*, still it is not presumed lost unless some accident is given or other act leading toward loss of possession." Capra went on to entertain the idea that Giovanni had deliberately tried to conceal assets, but he also conceded that he be given opportunity to show where and why they were no longer part of the estate – to mount a defense, in other words.[25] There may have been less willingness to trust an illegitimate child with guardianship of his legitimate siblings, but there also always had to be an accounting from guardians of their stewardship, and in that regard Giovanni was not being treated any differently than any guardian.

[24] Baldo, 3 *cons.* 73, fol. 19rb–va.   [25] Capra, *cons.* 161, fols. 195va–97ra.

Dowry and Women's Inheritance

The multiform legal situation challenged each community to come to grips with it. Roman, Lombard, and feudal laws were quite different and the potentials quite diverse. But in fact there emerged a surprising level of uniformity in their approaches. The main object of statutes was to modify the order of succession from the rules of *ius commune* in a direction that made more sense to the societies enacting these statutes. There was one vital common dimension to all these modifications. Almost without exception, as Franco Niccolai observed decades ago in surveying statutes from Lombardy, Tuscany, Piedmont, Veneto, Liguria, and Emilia, there was application of a lesser status (*deterior conditio*) for women.[26] In its essence, women with a dowry were excluded from seeking anything further in favor of agnate males. This *exclusio propter dotem* was so widespread that jurists, such as Alberico da Rosciate, one of the first jurists to turn systematic attention to statutes, took note that there were many "commonly in force throughout Italy that if men exist women do not succeed."[27] He and a predecessor, Alberto Gandino, identified these norms as customary in Lombard law. Bartolo da Sassoferrato simply identified as custom of his time that daughters at the time of marriage made agreements not to seek more than their dowry, which agreements had been confirmed as licit in a decretal of Boniface VIII, as long as there was a solemn oath and no force or fraud present in the act. Such widespread customary practice became statutory law. By the sixteenth century these statutes and the issues they raised were subject to regular and systematic legal treatises.[28] Jurists tended, in fact, to see such statutes not only for the *odium* they seemed to hold toward women (daughters, sisters, mothers) but for the contrasting *favor agnationis* or *favor masculinitatis* they showed to men and their (mainly male) descendants. These contrasting – positive and negative – sides as to the effect of such statutes would figure in when jurists had to interpret these rules in light of the cases brought to them.

The key statutory provision was that the woman was dowered. Were she not, statutes tended to leave her on the face of it with a pretty strong

---

[26] Niccolai, *La formazione del diritto successorio*, 2–3.　　[27] Quoted in Romano, 47.

[28] As Lorenzo da Palazzo, *Tractatus super statuto communiter per Italiam vigente quod extantibus masculis foeminae non succedant*, and Giovanni Campegio, *Tractatus de statutis excludentibus foeminas a successionibus*, in *Tractatus universi iuris*, 28 vols. (Venice, 1584), vol. 2.

right to have a dowry that was suitable to family rank and wealth. Once she had a dowry, a woman did not necessarily lose all right to inheritance, it should be noted, but her claims were generally postponed in favor of any arising from a fairly closely related set of agnates, mainly males. Nicola in Sozzini's case was able to assert her claims for lack of a close male agnate to preclude her. That set of agnates that excluded a dowered woman might vary a bit from place to place, and the language terms in which exclusions were posed varied even more widely. What local historical and social factors lay behind these differences are hard to pin down without detailed research into them. From a wider perspective, it is their overall congruence that is interesting.

The most evident outlier, but even then only partially, was Venice. On intestacy dowered daughters were excluded by sons (though they might enter a claim that their dowry was not suitable and seek supplement, as was true elsewhere). Daughters yet to be married could inherit with their brothers, but only *bona mobilia*. They were nominally kept from owning more permanent assets. However, as Anna Bellavitis points out, in a city so dependent on trade, *mobilia* could be the most important wealth and the distinction between *immobilia* and *mobilia* was not so simple or open, such that pieces of real estate could be classified as *mobilia*.[29] Descendants in female line were excluded in Venice. The main difference in Venice from what was found most everywhere else was that daughters were not excluded by uncles and nephews and cousins – those largely outside the same house. In Venice the range of exclusion was narrow. Venetian girls also inherited from their mothers equally with their brothers, whereas so many places – Genoa, Florence, Pisa, Siena – excluded women from maternal property in preference to their brothers, at times extending that to their grandmothers' property as well. Also Venice kept the basic Roman rule of no inheritance between spouses, whereas other communities would come to give husbands claim on at least part of their wives' estates.

Venice's statutes of the thirteenth century (1242) remained in force throughout our period. But already earlier Volterra had stated that a dowered woman could not take from her father's or brother's estate if he had left children (legitimate), unless she was in need of basics such as food and clothing. In a revision of a few years later, a clause was inserted broadening the exclusion in favor of a brother of the deceased or his son.

---

[29] Bellavitis, *Famille, genre, transmission à Venise*, 35–38.

A second statute declared that no woman could succeed her child (the nearest in male line did), though the child could leave a limited amount to the mother in a will, depending on how modest the estate was, keeping the sum to no more than one-fifth on more lucrative estates. The next rendition of statutes cut that to a tenth. Another statute dealing with intestacy declared the heirs were to be the closest in paternal line for those dying without legitimate children. The maternal line came into consideration if no paternal relatives were to be found in the city. The statute was essentially unchanged in the next redaction.[30]

Milan's earliest statutes (1216) treated intestacy with incredible brevity. In succession to agnates "all women" were excluded, sister and father's sister excepted. Mothers did not succeed if agnates, even sister and aunt, existed; wives did not if there were any agnates or cognates. Sister lost to brother as long as he dowered her, which was the only clause in that early law that even mentioned dowry.[31] The Roman dowry may have been late becoming a social norm in a city so influenced by Lombard customs. But by 1330 dowry was fully enthroned in Milan and justified the exclusions of various types of women. Mothers were excluded by agnates to seven degrees. In succession to ascendants, males *ex linea masculina* were preferred to females at every degree, while they were bound to provide dowries to the women they excluded. The later statute of 1498 was more thorough and prolix but essentially the same.[32] The interesting provision that came into Milan's laws was that if the male who excluded a woman later died without legitimate issue, she could collate her dowry back into the inheritance and take a full share.

The university towns of Padua and Bologna confronted the Roman rules quite directly. The old Paduan statute of 1222 had approved the "custom" that a dowered daughter did not succeed her father if she had brothers, though he could leave her something more in a will. She could not inherit from her mother in favor of brothers. If she were unmarried, the brothers had the obligation to dower her. This rule was inserted under the rubric *De mulieribus*, along with one from 1277 by which a mother could not leave her property to anyone other than her sons and daughters or their progeny.[33] In contrast to Padua's weak statutory display in the thirteenth century, Bologna treated intestacy at length in two statutes. The first, broadly, was about inheritance by descendants. Daughters who were dowered were to remain content with their dowries, if there were

---

[30] Volterra, 9, 10, 52, 125–26, 129–30.   [31] Milan 1216, 94–95.
[32] Niccolai, 77–78; Milan 1498, fols. 82r–86r.   [33] Padua, 189–90.

legitimate sons or other descendants in male line, not otherwise in the clergy or religious orders. Daughters could not take anything from their mothers in the same circumstances, even *ex testamento*. They could exercise *ius commune* rights to succeed only if none of those males accepted and immersed themselves in the estate. Undowered daughters should receive a dowry equivalent to that of married sisters, unless the *bona patrimonialia* had been diminished in the meantime. If none had been married by the time inheritance arose, six near relations on the father's side had to determine an amount for dowry. The same rule applied for all granddaughters and other women descended through men. Those descended in female line, men and women, were excluded by those in the male line. Finally, dowered and excluded women were not to be counted in determining the legitimate portion due to each male heir.[34] That was the kind of contingency that would come to the mind of a trained jurist that the less learned legislators would not think of (and did not, as such a provision does not occur in other statutes).

Succession of ascendants on intestacy in Bologna went by the same logic: from one dying without children but leaving brothers (agnate) or ascendant males, the estate passed to the total exclusion of the mother or sisters. A woman got usufruct on the paternal estate if the only surviving males came from a wider kinship circle (nephews, sisters, uncles, cousins). Those related in cognation were excluded by any surviving agnates. Brothers and their sons were preferred to sisters; but sisters split equally with paternal uncles, though not with uterine sisters. The fitting coda was that "in cases not covered in this statute, *ius commune* is to be used" (*casibus hoc statuto non comprehensis, ius commune servetur*).[35]

While not as comprehensive with regard to various contingencies, statutes of many places followed similar lines. Foligno excluded a dowered woman from her father, mother, grandfather or great grandfather, grandmother or great grandmother, in lieu of any legitimate male descendant in male line. Mothers could not inherit from a child if there were other children or grandchildren or paternal uncles. There was no inheritance from brother or sister, if there were a brother or his children.[36] At Forlì, mothers (or grandmothers or great grandmothers) lost out on inheritance to their children or grandchildren dying without children to any brothers or sisters or the brother's children (both sexes). Father or other ascendant also excluded the woman, as did a paternal

---

[34] Bologna 1335, 563–66.   [35] Bologna 1335, 566–68.   [36] Foligno, 87–88.

uncle. Women's possible succession to father, or grandfather, to mother or brother failed in the face of legitimate male children or grandsons, always remaining content with dowry. If one died intestate without children or grandchildren, the property went to the father, secondly to brother (excluding sister), then, lacking either of them, to sisters with their mother. All else lacking, then property went to paternal uncles and their sons. Insertion of sisters before paternal uncles or their sons was fairly generous in comparison to other cities. Finally *ius commune* was said to set the order after that point. Rights to dowry and *alimenta* for the unmarried were firmly upheld.[37]

That each community had its own peculiarities, however minor at times, can be seen from a close comparison of Tuscan cities. Florence directed its intestate statute at women, using the word *mulier* in the rubric. The persons excluding dowered daughters and sisters, or their children, included the deceased's legitimate children (both sexes), or grandsons or brothers, in male line. Mothers and grandmothers were excluded by sons or males descended from them, or by father, brother, sister, or nephew, grandfather, or uncle. If none of those survived, a mother could get a quarter of the estate, not to exceed 500 *lire* in value and not to consist of houses or buildings. Women could inherit from their mother if there were no sons or their descendants. These rules, dating from before their repetition in the first full redaction of 1325, persisted in 1355 and 1415, with some extensions. In part from the intervention of Bartolo da Sassoferrato in a case of 1351 at the behest of communal officials, the 1355 statutes extended the exclusion beyond mother and grandmother to cover the entire maternal line in preference to agnates for eight degrees of relationship – a very extensive set of excluding males in potential that probably seemed sensible in the aftermath of the plague of 1348.[38] The usual rights to dowry and *alimenta* were included.

In 1327, Arezzo, often at odds with its close and more powerful neighbor, worked a narrower set of exclusions on dowered women. Daughters were excluded from ascendants by sons or their male descendants in the male line, not necessarily by brothers or uncles of a deceased. Any male descendants kept a woman from succeeding her mother or grandmother. Mothers or ascendants in maternal line were precluded in favor of brother or sister or their children, or uncle or his sons, from

---

[37] Forlì, 177–78, 354–57.
[38] Florence 1325, 128–29; Kuehn, *Law, Family, and Women*, 241–43.

inheritance to their sons or daughters. Sisters lost out to brothers or
nephews, but not to nearly as wide a group as for mothers. To protect
the rights of undowered women, the heirs were required to make an
inventory within a month.[39] Montepulciano's contemporary redaction
kept a dowered woman and her heirs from paternal, maternal, or fraternal estate in favor of sons or male descendants or brothers or their male
descendants.[40] Cortona's statutes pushed aside a dowered woman from
inheriting from her father, grandfather, great grandfather, grandmother,
great grandmother, mother or her parents, brother, sister, or their male
offspring, legitimate or not, or others in the male line. They could succeed
siblings who left no children.[41] In contrast Colle Val d'Elsa in
1341 deployed three rubrics pointedly at succession by different sorts of
women. Dowered women were forbidden succession to father, mother,
brother, grandmother or grandfather, uncle or cousin or any ascendant or
male line descendant, if the deceased left a legitimate male descendant or
brothers or other collaterals who were agnate within four degrees (by
canon law). Mothers could not inherit from sons or daughters if there
were any agnates (even female) within five degrees, though they could
have usufruct on the property for life if living with their children. For
brothers and sisters with common father but different mothers, where the
deceased left no children and the sisters were not dowered, there could be
equal division.[42] So five communities within the same region, over a
period of less than twenty years, each came up with divergent extensions
of the same basic principle of exclusion of dowered women. All five
favored males and agnates (who were sometimes women), just to different
extent, in more remote relationships.

So it is not hard to understand that other communities – Belluno in an
extensive rubric in 1392, Ferrara dealing with only paternal inheritance
much earlier (1287), Verona in 1327, and Perugia – had their quirks and
variations.[43] Yet they also essentially did the same as the others we have
seen. A notable eccentricity is found in Verona in 1339 and 1345, where
there was an extensive revision of the statute that extended it to brothers
and others and was exclusive of most of the female line. It allowed that in
succession to father or mother, a brother and sister would split the estate
unequally, three parts to him to one for her, or similar ratios depending

---

[39] Arezzo, 169–70.   [40] Montepulciano, 141–42.   [41] Cortona, 334–36.
[42] Colle, 304–05, 306.
[43] Belluno, 2:31–38; Ferrara, 214–15; Verona, 351–52; Perugia, 406–08.

on how many of each sex there were. Unequal as that was, it was a rare concession to both sexes at the same time.[44]

There was also language in the Veronese rubric, not in the body of the statute, that offered a motivation for the law, about preserving the family: "paternal property is kept with male children and other descendants in male line for the conservation of houses and for sustaining the burdens of the commune of Verona" (*pro conservacione domorum et pro oneribus communis Verone substinendis*). Treviso's extensive statute, covering both intestate and testamentary matters, and leaning regularly to males in the male line over females or males in female line, began with an interesting, if brief, rationale:

We believe that it pertains to the honor and glory of the city that it have wealthy subjects and that by the groups of women the possessions of men not be diminished, especially as the acts and counsel of women are found sometimes to work against good practices and their own benefit.[45]

This text invoked the ideological touch point about female weakness, alluding as well to family and the commune's need to tap family wealth. Cortona, which offered no justification for the initial exclusionary statute of 1325, was more forthright later. A revision of 1378 stated that any agnate, even female, within four degrees eliminated any more closely related cognate, "considering that the memory and honor of the house of the deceased is kept (*memoria et domus defuncti honor retinetur*) through agnates of the deceased, but not through cognates." A few years before (1375) the statutes had simply declared it "absurd" that cognate women succeed in preference to agnates.[46] In 1378, therefore, the absurdity was spelled out.

These statutes are exceptional in citing an ideological justification for the exclusion of dowered women – in terms of gender or in terms of family. In the long run, it was the sense of family that would be increasingly invoked in statutes limiting female inheritance and, as we will see, in juristic opinions interpreting those statutes. Still, furnishing such a rationale in the statute itself remained rare. That of Viterbo in 1469 did not rely on ideological justification.[47] Even later Siena's set of workmanlike statutes laid out the usual exclusions without making an ideological statement.[48] But the 1567 statutes of Ferrara did not hesitate to explain from the outset that the rubric on intestacy was designed "so that dignity and

---

[44] Verona, 354–56, 398–99.   [45] Treviso, 369–74.   [46] Cortona, 516–18, 520–21.
[47] Viterbo, 140–41.   [48] Siena, 253–54.

greatness of the family be maintained, that it might not be impoverished by women, as most do, going to other families" (*non depauperetur propter foeminas transeuntes ut plurimum ad alienas familias*).[49]

It is worth noting that Jewish law too excluded daughters in favor or sons, which was a provision in line with many local laws but contrary to *ius commune*. In general, here as with so many other matters of law, jurists recognized Jewish laws as authoritative custom. They thus tended to back the application of what they were told were Jewish inheritance rules. There was nothing said on this score about a rationale of preserving property and agnatic lineage.

In essence, for jurists, dowry was thus left in an uncertain status, dangling between the legitimate portion allotted women in *ius commune* and the limitations devised in local statutes. Thus Laura Turchi has characterized dowry as

an anomalous property title, because it was arranged at the intersection of sexual difference, ties of kinship, and the true and proper right to possess property, actually not exercised in presence of a husband, who administered it for the duration of the marriage. The woman could not decide even the ultimate destination of her own dowry, since statutes regulated all possibilities in that regard.[50]

The statutes, however, were not nearly so airtight, as we will see. The pervasive statutes limiting female inheritance to dowry and excluding women from estates in favor of agnate males generated more lawsuits, it is safe to say, than any other type of statute (except perhaps the countless procedural issues that could be and were raised to delay or derail all suits).

According to Antonio Marongiu, jurists, wedded to the gender-equal inheritance of the Roman law as a standard of reason and justice, strove to limit the exclusion of dowered women. They pointed out that exclusion was relative (to categories of surviving related males, by and large) and not absolute. But they also recognized the bias in the statutes.[51] So the binary opposition *odiosum/favorabile* would come to be routinely applied by jurists to communal intestate inheritance statutes, and jurists would be able to fashion widely varying interpretations around that binary. A quick perusal of court records and *consilia* confirms this.

---

[49] Ferrara 1567, fol. 115v.   [50] Turchi, "L'eredità della madre," 164.
[51] Marongiu, *Beni paterni e acquisti*, 246.

CASES INTERPRETING INTESTACY STATUTES

Far and away the biggest issue in intestacy, and even in some testate cases in the period 1300–1600, was making sense of the different statutes governing the process of inheritance in all the various communities. Once jurists came to be called on with some regularity to contribute their expertise to inheritance cases, they developed an armament of forensic weapons to unravel social and legal meaning from texts that differed substantially from those they met in law school. It took a little time to get there.

Some of the earlier jurists whose *consilia* were prized, collected, and even subsequently printed, had surprisingly little to say about intestacy. Most inheritance cases they saw involved wills, which provided their own intricacies. Dino del Mugello, for example, whose surviving *consilia*, it must be admitted, number only in the few dozens, left no intestacy case of any substance. A slightly later figure, working in the early decades of the fourteenth century, and who left a few hundred *consilia* in a later printed edition, Oldrado da Ponte, had only a few intestacy cases. And the questions raised were not difficult, nor was the treatment given them elaborate. For example, from a place named Sinodrio came a suit in which a married daughter sued her brother over the patrimony. Her dowry had been 100 *lire,* but the patrimony, which went to her brother by statute, was said to be worth 1,000. She wanted to collate her dowry into the estate and split the entirety equally with him. The local statute, as so many others, disqualified her as dowered, but it also stated that unmarried children of both sexes split equally. Giving back the dowry would seemingly render her undowered and gain her five times as much (one revealing instance of what was supposedly a fitting dowry in relation to the entire patrimony). The brother argued that he did not have to do that, citing as well another statute that said dowries, marital gifts, estates, and such "do not go by equal steps" (*aequis passibus non ambulent*). Oldrado defended the intestacy statute as within the prerogatives of the community and, though it might be said to be contrary to *ius naturae,* "a certain quota is not owed to children by natural law, which appears because things vary," as in the example of Lombard law of succession. As the daughter did not succeed, she could not collate with the heir.[52] This was a brief text invoking no general principles of interpretation, though making a rare reference to Lombard law. And it dealt with the

---

[52] Oldrado, *cons.* 135, fols. 49vb–50ra.

most obvious of instances of exclusion, of a daughter by a son. Its main contribution was to preclude collation, which, if allowed, might indeed frustrate the purpose of the statutory dowry exclusion. The jurist was probably advising a judge or government body.

Bartolo too did not deal so frequently with intestacy, as opposed to wills. One case, however, made an obvious and irrefutable point. If a dowered woman, excluded otherwise by statute, was not mentioned in her brother's will, could she contest the will and gain the patrimony? A woman's brother left a will naming his wife as heir and leaving bequests to his daughters (undoubtedly as dowries). By statute of Perugia his sister was excluded, both from the paternal estate and from those of any surviving sons. But her brother had died without sons, so that was the sister's opening. Bartolo closed it. She had no right to seek overturn of the will. He pointed out that the son had taken his father's estate and thus it ceased to be the father's and became his. There was no recourse for her after that. He did not go into an analysis of the statute in any further terms.[53] Interestingly he did not reference family as an object of the statute. Bartolo himself had equated family and substance precisely in commenting on a text dealing with intestacy, which noted how automatic was the passage of property from father to son. But he did not bring it into play in statute interpretation.

AFTER THE PLAGUE

The tremendous mortality occasioned by the cataclysm of 1348 and revisited at intervals thereafter left many estates in doubt. Intestacies were frequent. The deaths of presumptive heirs left the identity of the eventual heir uncertain and the relationship between deceased and heir more distant than might otherwise have been the case. Unsurprisingly, cases came to courts and thus to jurists, who were, as a result, more regularly confronting local statutes about inheritance. Certain principles of interpretation came to be applied and entered the armament of judicial decision making. The pivotal figures in fashioning and disseminating these interpretive devices were the brothers Angelo and Baldo degli Ubaldi, who faced cases from a variety of places.

Two major modes of statute interpretation developed, largely at their hands, that would have a long career. One was that the typical intestacy

---

[53] Bartolo, *cons.* 20, fol. 8rb–va.

statute excluding dowered women was intended to preserve family, which in turn rested on the twin poles of property and agnation (as Alberico da Rosciate had noted). This rationale could be invoked to give a statute an expansive reading in favor of agnates. The other was that the statute was contrary to the learned law as a standard of equity, a basis from which one might argue against such statutes, or at least for a narrow reading that would seek to exploit gaps or omissions to restore inheritance to women or those related through them. These interpretive poles became steady but not necessary features of intestacy cases, especially when women's claims were pressed.

So, as a first example, Angelo examined Lucca's statute, which favored descendants in male line, after them ascendants, and after them brothers or sisters. Niccolò Anguilla had died leaving his brother's daughters and male cousins (sons of his paternal uncle). Angelo affirmed that by common law the girls, related in third degree, excluded the boys who were in fourth degree. The statute varied from this

because thus it pleased posterity to prefer the line of agnates and males, so that the dignity of their line might be preserved, which cannot properly be preserved unless the goods and the agnates' patrimony flow and run to males (*quae conservari commode non potest nisi bona et patrimonium agnatorum confluant et decurrant ad masculos*), but not to females in whom the line of agnates is ended. . . . Nor also can the honor and dignity of the same agnation be preserved unless by an affluence of worldly things, since wealthy individuals and affluent citizens are ascribed the ordinary dignities and honors and they support with their own [wealth] the burdens of the government of their city, not those who are vile and abject in body (*viles et abiecti in corpore*).

That was why the statute put brothers and their sons before sisters or their offspring. The cousins were capable of preserving the honor and dignity of the line; the nieces could not. Even though the statute did not mention sons of an uncle, and thus the situation might be said then to fall under common law, Angelo cited the statutory rationale to exclude the girls.[54]

The case of Martino di Giovanni of Florence provoked three different *consilia*, one by Baldo, two by his brother. They variously employed both interpretive devices. Martino's widow, Nente, had taken guardianship and accepted the patrimony for her infant daughter, who soon died. The only other possible claimant to the estate, other than Nente, was Sandra, Martino's sister. So there was no male involved, and no male line to preserve. Did the mother get it all? Or did Sandra get it, with less a

[54] Angelo, *cons.* 221, fols. 118vb–19rb.

quarter for the mother (not to exceed 500 *lire* by the statute of 1355, which was reproduced in a manuscript version of the opinion)? Baldo noted that there was no expressed rationale in this statute (nor was there in most such measures, as we saw above), but he argued that the intent (*mens legis*) could be conjectured and applied, to be restricted only lest it result in unjust enrichment or loss. The rationale Baldo hit upon was, of course, to preserve the dignity and honor of families in agnation and in its memory, for the good of the city and its offices, which were for the *virilis sexus*. One proof of that was the clause precluding a mother from realizing dwellings and such (*domus et casamenta*) in her quarter,

which exception properly concerns the favor of agnation consisting in male offspring, for which it would be most injurious to see the house of their ancestors and the sites in which the form of their agnation had arisen from old (*situs in quibus antiquata est sorte agnationis forma*) and which were accustomed to retain the name of the agnation devolve to strangers and the images of their ancestors, arms and insignia, removed.

But preservation of agnation did not seem to be at stake where only one of two women was possible heir. It was admitted that the second part of the statute was ambiguous as to what sort of persons excluded a mother. Baldo opted to read in *ius commune* at this point and to favor the mother.[55]

In the second opinion on the same case, Angelo applauded his brother's subtlety, but pointed out that the statute not only favored agnation, it also favored men. So the issue to him was the right of a cousin, Lamberto, fifth-degree agnate, to inherit from the dead infant. Such a distant agnate was not expressly mentioned in the statute as excluding a mother. On the other hand, Angelo noted that by the most ancient rules in *ius commune*, agnation was so favored that mother and child had no inheritance rights to each other. These had come in only by later legislation. In the end, Angelo opted for the mother's claim precisely because an agnate past third degree did not exclude her according to the statute. She got it all, he said.[56] In the next *consilium* he went further into why a sister, agnate to the deceased, excluded a uterine brother, who could not perpetuate agnation, as the statute desired. The sister was able by its terms to exclude the mother and, since 1351, the entire maternal line, so why not a half-brother from the mother's side? In either case, there was

---

[55] Angelo, *cons.* 281, fols. 154rb–55ra. The exact same text is attributed to a Francesco Becchi, Aretine, citizen of Florence, as *cons.* 344, fols. 192va–93vb.
[56] Angelo, *cons.* 282, fol. 155ra–b.

not going to be the preservation of agnation the statute aimed at. So he concluded expansively:

because this reason of perpetuation and preservation of the descent is the final cause of the statute, and this alone was in the legislator's mind, perhaps it can be said that where an agnate male who is yet unsuited by nature to preservation and is the end of his descent, or unsuited by chance, as because he entered a monastery, may not exclude the mother.[57]

All three opinions found for the mother, both by stressing that the goal of preservation of agnation was not possible in this situation and by noting omissions that favored her.

Baldo otherwise took on a number of cases in which he defended the statutory rationale and extended the statute to unspecified instances. In one such case from Assisi he began by quoting the local intestacy statute which, rare for the breed, gave a rationale: "For preservation of whatever house in the city and community of Assisi and lest the estate and successions come into possession of others who are not of the house by the male line." By its terms no dowered woman nor her son could inherit if the deceased had a son, grandson, great grandson, or other male heir of legitimate birth. He considered how this law "corrected" *ius commune* and whether it precluded transmission of an inheritance right or merely delayed or deferred its acceptance. The issue was inheritance by a woman's son to her father. Baldo decided that the fact that the mother did not transmit to him a right to inherit from his maternal grandfather was not an issue thanks to *beneficio statuti*, because, while he was precluded if there were male descendants, he was contrarily provided for if there were not: "and this opinion is a friend of nature and equity, although by strict law it can be greatly doubted on account of the rigor of the words and the rules of law." No male heir meeting the terms of the statute had come forth in a timely manner, so the grandson could succeed.[58] Baldo saw his decision as equitable, even if tendered at the behest of the party he backed, while recognizing that a stricter interpretation could have been applied.

In other cases Baldo operated close to a statute's wording. In Perugia, when the noble Filippo de Giacani died with no male heirs, and no other branch of the lineage had a male heir, but there were various men of other lineages related through their mothers or grandmothers, Baldo entertained the idea that Perugian law did not keep women from claiming a

---

[57] Angelo, *cons.* 283, fols. 155va–56rb.   [58] Baldo, 2 *cons.* 111, fols. 24vb–25ra.

legitimate portion. True, what they received was dowry, but it was also supposedly "congruent" and, as "rarely is support lacking for dowered women, this dowry is thus the legitimate portion" (*mulieribus dotatis raro deficiunt alimenta, hanc ergo dotem esse legitimam portionem*). Then again Florentine lawyers (he named Tommaso Corsini, Francesco Becchi of Arezzo, and Antonio Machiavelli) had determined that the law did not simply exclude women but did so because of the existence of a certain set of persons and only as long as such persons were around. Moreover, women's right to a full legitimate share was only suspended, not removed. But was it transmitted to their offspring when they never got to exercise it? Baldo said it was, because failure to exercise the right arose not from something intrinsic to the women but as a result of the statute, and the impediment was removed when the males died. So he allowed that cognatically related males could now step forward and seek a *supplementum* of the *legitima* that had been limited to their mothers' dowries.[59]

In another instance a statute of Arezzo extending masculine gender to include feminine (i.e., declaring that terms like *filius* meant child indiscriminately and not just sons), by Baldo's reading, meant that two nieces on the paternal side excluded the deceased's mother. He agreed with others that such a statute, placing the more distantly related nieces before the mother, was hateful (*odiosum*) and should not receive an expansive interpretation. But here the nieces were agnate and kept the mother, who was not, out. Here the extension of male gender to include female worked.[60] But here too, Baldo was arguing the opposite of what we saw in the case of Nente in Florence. To do so required that he mention the statute's inclination to agnation without, however, further linking that to a desire to preserve agnation, which was not going to be served by the nieces any more than it would by the mother.

Even when he had to face a contrary argument, as he did with a case from Cortona, Baldo stayed pretty much with the statutory text. A Cortonese died intestate with two sons, each by different mothers, one of whom subsequently died. Did the dead boy's share go to the brother or the mother? Two *consultores* had already taken opposite positions, so Baldo proposed that the truth lay in the middle. He divided the statute into three parts. He recognized that while, in excluding mothers, it ran contrary to *pietas*, it was in line with public utility in

[59] Baldo, 1 *cons.* 70, fols. 23va–24va, and 3 *cons.* 426, fol. 121ra–vb.
[60] Baldo, 5 *cons.* 47, fols. 13vb–14ra.

favoring agnate males and preserving families. Alluding to a bias toward the same blood (*favor sanguinis*), he struck down the others' arguments.

This statute has the root of its words and reason in the paternal line, it excludes the mother by the apt nature of the words, and so the consultor advised perversely contrary to the words, reason, and intent of the statute; he tried to gloss it, to destroy (*destruere*) the statute, when the truth is that the mother does not succeed, because the determination is general.

The blood relation of the brother, from the father, was what counted.[61] He was agnate and he met the conditions for maternal exclusion set forth in the statute.

Expansive and restrictive readings of inheritance statutes were available in every case, and there would continue to be plenty of them. But over time the rationale of preservation of family and agnation would come to dominate the legal discourse and leave fewer openings for female inheritance.

FIFTEENTH-CENTURY CASES

In the fifteenth century and beyond, following the vital formulations employed by Baldo and Angelo, a veritable torrent of intestacy cases hit jurists such as Lodovico Pontano, Paolo di Castro, Filippo Decio, Giason del Maino, and more. While the opinions they wrote often supported the interests of clients, rather than the needs of judges, they disposed of a finite array of interpretive tropes to do so. Increasingly their arguments enlarged or more creatively confronted the demands of agnatic heirs and the senses of family and kinship that bolstered the resolve of litigants to pursue their rights.

Lodovico Pontano found that a daughter dowered by her father after her mother died, but before she took possession of the maternal estate, was excluded from it by the terms of the local statute. But her son too was thereby excluded.[62] Here Pontano clearly diverged from the opinion offered by Baldo in the Florentine case above. In another case in which the two grandfathers contested the estate of the maternal grandmother, who, after all, had been married to one of them, Pontano read the statute as privileging the maternal grandfather. As the grandchild had never accepted the estate, it was the mother's, and on that her father's claim

---

[61] Baldo, 4 *cons.* 205, fols. 46vb–47rb.   [62] Pontano, *cons,* 442, fol. 236va–b.

was strongest.[63] On neither of these did he make any sweeping pronouncements of statutory intent. He just construed statutes against the facts before him. Giovanni d'Anagni did much the same. While admitting the statutory exclusion of the female line was so "that males linked in the paternal line be not deprived and that they could sustain the burdens and honors of the house," he simply presented language from two statutes. The result he came to was that the statute could take away a mother's right to inherit from a child.[64]

Paolo di Castro recast the statutory rationale in a way that was more prejudicial to women, it would seem. He hinged his argument in one case on the fact that the statute listed off various relations from whose inheritance it excluded a dowered woman. Had it simply said that a dowered woman did not inherit, he noted, then it could be argued its effect was limited to the estate of the person who provided the dowry. Instead, the statute's concern had to be seen as broader, to exclude her from a number of males, not solely to see she had a dowry, which was the concern of a different statute of the same city (possibly Florence). More broadly, not only was the dowered woman excluded; even men of the female line were excluded:

> for the statute truly did not have respect for agnation but for the male sex and for the desire of the parents, which flourishes equally in the mother as in the father (*pariter viget in matre sicut in patre*), because they choose that male children and grandsons and great grandsons descendant from them succeed to them universally, as by them is preserved their memory more than by women who are of another family, namely that of their fathers. And we see this by experience that women just as men institute [in wills] as universal heirs male children not female, whom they want to stay content with a dowry.

As the statute spoke to both male and female ascendants, its scope, he said, was not preserving agnation but preserving men, otherwise it had no reason to mention the maternal line.[65]

In another case he formulated an argument that a daughter might inherit, though there were sons, because she was not dowered, and that was the basis of her exclusion. But he then proceeded to demolish that straw man. The statute wanted her excluded, even as it demanded a dowry be provided. She was excluded not because of dowry, which would be "absurd", (his thinking behind that assertion not being at all clear), but because of the presence of male heirs. After all, another statute also

---

[63] Pontano, *cons*. 40, fol. 20ra–va.   [64] D'Anagni, *cons*. 4, fol. 3ra–b.
[65] Di Castro, 2 *cons*, 91, fol. 41rb–vb.

excluded her from the estate of one brother who had since died.[66] Similarly when he argued that male agnates succeeded an infant rather than the child's mother, he argued that the statute was not *odiosum*, though it could be for the excluded woman, but was in fact rational.[67]

The language of a statute from Castello provided some basis for fine distinctions. A statute could say that if there were a male heir, a daughter could not inherit but was owed a dowry, or it could say that a dowered daughter could not inherit if there were a male heir. In other words, either the exclusion was based on gender alone, or it was based on dowry, plus gender. Among the older jurisprudents (*antiquos*) di Castro found that someone like Riccardo Malombra had based the exclusion on gender and the lessening of *legitima* by dowry. The statute of Castello clearly excluded dowered women. The immediate issue was the dowry left a woman by bequest in her father's will, which had never been collected, as she did not live to marry. Marrying was thus an unfulfilled condition of the bequest. Now the question was: Did it revert to the estate of her father, and thus to his heirs, as an intestate estate, or was it a legitimate portion that through her went to the heirs she had designated in her testament? Di Castro, following a lengthy treatment of the issues, decided that the bequest of dowry was not conditional but pure and simple. The property was hers whether or not she married.

> But if the bequest was conditional, it could happen that she would not have it if she did not marry or because she did not want it, or because prevented by death, and so she would be without both bequest and succession [to herself], which would be greatly inequitable and inhuman and against the statute's intent, because the testator could not consider placing a condition and so take away by indirect means what the statute wanted her to have.

So the bequest went to the daughter as heir and the consequence in inheritance followed.[68] Di Castro was willing to defend a woman's right to dowry, but her exclusion otherwise was not based solely on dowry. In statutes where most jurists found a bias to agnation, he found at times a defensible bias more particularly to males.

An intestate man, Francesco, left a full sister and a half-brother (paternal). He and his brother had dowered the sister. Who inherited in the presence of a statute that privileged males only within two degrees of relationship? While it was true that the statute was *odiosum* to women

---

[66] Di Castro, 2 *cons.* 7, fols. 4va–5ra. [67] Di Castro, 2 *cons.* 276, fols. 132vb–33rb.
[68] Di Castro, 3 *cons.* 25, fols. 30ra–31rb.

and on that argument was due a restrictive interpretation, Benedetto da Capra claimed the statute overrode the sister's better right in *ius commune* and wanted the brother as heir, because the statute "arose for preservation of the line of the house" (*ad conservationem cippi domus emanavit*). The statute, indeed, was favorable (as opposed to odious), as it gave greater access to a half-brother. No less than four times Capra repeated the rationale of the statute to drive home his point.[69]

Luca di Bernardo of Nuceria left a widow and two young sons, each of whom died in the course of the next two years after Luca's intestate demise. Luca also had a brother and sisters, and his widow, Gabriela, had a brother and two sisters. It was noted that while the sons were still alive neither their mother nor their paternal uncle moved to take guardianship or accept the inheritance or draw up an inventory. So the mother's siblings and the uncle's sister advanced the case that such negligence stripped the others of inheritance and left it to them. The uncle, Jacobuccio, for his part, claimed there had been an oral will before witnesses, empowering him to take care of the boys, so he did not need to assume guardianship in any formal manner and should not lose the property, though he seemed quite content with stripping his sister-in-law of any share. Capra had to go estate by estate: who succeeded the father? Who succeeded the first son to die? Who the second? The father was easy. His sons inherited. The second was not too tough. A surviving brother inherited both by *ius commune* and statute. If one tried to make a claim that the mother got part of that, her failure to act as guardian cost her any such claim. The whole problem lay in succession to the last son. As Capra saw it, local statute would then devolve the estate on the mother and uncle, but as they had not acted to take guardianship they were equally repelled from the estate for their negligence. Capra took the father's dying declaration not as a bestowal of guardianship on Jacobuccio as an office but as a simple request to take care of them (*custodia*). But then arose the problem that the statute seemed obviously to prefer the agnate uncle to the aunts and maternal uncle. Capra concluded that there was statutory exclusion of the uncle for his neglect of *tutela*, which dropped the case into the realm of *ius commune* and put the estate in the hands of the maternal uncle and aunts, divided equally.[70] Had the paternal uncle had sons, however, one cannot help feeling that they would have won out, though certainly Capra would have used his expertise on that issue as well.

<hr />

[69] Capra, *cons.* 8, fols. 18vb–20ra.   [70] Capra, *cons.* 148, fols. 182vb–83vb.

A dowered daughter from the village of Stronconi tried to inherit from her father, as every other potential heir had died, except some nephews. The local statute could be read as excluding a woman only from the estate of the one who had dowered her, so if her rights were posed in terms of her brothers and mother, who had all died, it might be a different matter. Also in her favor was always the argument to restrict the "odious" statute. The jurist who weighed in on this matter, Pierfilippo da Corgna, however, read the statute as nonetheless excluding the dowered woman from all the relations designated in it. He cited a number of *consilia* as having taken parallel positions to add their weight to his partisan opinion. And he concluded that the statute was not odious, but was favorable by reason of preserving the house and deserved more liberal interpretation.[71] In a case from Assisi, Corgna did not have to conjecture as to the statutory rationale. The statute did it for him. On that basis it would seem that Jacopo, brother to messer Mazico, succeeded him to the exclusion of two grandsons by a daughter – an effect of the statute being contrary to *ius commune*. But Corgna's clients were the grandsons and they needed a different argument based on the "exorbitant" nature of the statute. He thus contrived to read it as not putting an uncle among the list of persons excluding a dowered woman, let alone her two sons. The weak argument he fashioned against the statutory rationale here was that the exclusion of dowered women was not general, "that in vain would legislators restrict themselves to dowered women or those to be dowered, if their general desire was that estates not go to others who are not of the house of the male line and in jest would be posed all the following words" (*ludibrio fuissent apposita omnia verba sequentia*).[72] He had to take the statute as exclusionary of all women, and his opportunity to do so was furnished by its vague reference to the male line.

In a suit from Lucca there were conflicting claims to Jacopo Schiatta's estate from his sister's son and from agnates from the wider Schiatta lineage. These were descendants from Jacopo's father, who had been emancipated back in 1417. There was an argument that an emancipated son and all descended from him were not agnate to the other kin, disagnation being one legal consequence of emancipation. But there was also an argument that the later Roman civil law had changed that, and agnation endured despite emancipation. The statute was in favor of agnates and begged for a wide reading in that regard. So the results of

---

[71] Corgna, *cons.* 127, fols. 109va–10ra.   [72] Corgna, *cons.* 88, fols. 80vb–81va.

emancipation for agnation were critical. Filippo Decio defended the
nephew, probably his client, as closer in degree, though part of the house
of Interminelli, not the Schiatta. The emancipation had terminated agnation between Jacobo's line and the Schiatta, and among all the cognate
contenders for the estate, the nephew was closest. Had Decio's intent been
the other way, one trusts the agnatic intent of the statute would have
figured more prominently in his text.[73]

Decio had a much harder time arguing against a *consilium* of Paolo di
Castro (long dead by then) in accord with which a case had been decided
in Pavia. When first approached on the issue di Castro had been, said
Decio, pressed for time, and while he had his own opinion he did not have
opportunity to draw it up. The case had involved the claims of Camilla
de' Barsii, as presented to him by messer Girolamo Zunta. Di Castro had
decided that existence of male heirs was enough to disqualify a daughter,
she need not also be dowered. We have seen di Castro make such an
argument. Decio's argument, in contrast, was that the woman had to be
dowered at the time of her father's death in order for exclusion to apply.
Otherwise it was an even harsher statute, effectively excluding a woman
without dowry.[74] Yet we have seen others who did not put so fine a point
on it and simply stressed the right to a dowry. In a Sienese case a woman
excluded from her father by statute, and by her renunciation of paternal
inheritance, tried to succeed her brother, who had accepted the paternal
estate. Her contention was the statute did not exclude her and the renunciation no longer applied. There were no men to exclude her, and the
purpose of the statute was to preserve property in agnation and family,
which was no longer possible. There was only a daughter to share with
her aunt. But Decio argued that the exclusion was not limited to the
existence of male heirs but was perpetual, because it was a simple exclusion by the terms of the statute. Here his view of the statute was not
restrictive. Even if she were not excluded by statute, she was by *ius
commune*.[75] In contrast, in a case from Cortona, when asked by the
cardinal from there to look into a matter that had already garnered
contrasting *consilia*, Decio decided that the local statute's language did
not cover the case where the surviving agnates were brothers of ascendants only linked on one side or where there were ascendants but no full
brothers. In this instance there was a paternal grandfather. And Decio's
decision was in his favor, only after he went in great detail through

[73] Decio, *cons.* 13, fols. 17vb–19rb.　　[74] Decio, *cons.* 261, fols. 281ra–82vb.
[75] Decio, *cons.* 309, fols. 338rb–39vb.

arguments for the contrary view in order to give the sense of thoroughness and justice that the cardinal had asked him to bring to the case. The statute clearly wanted to eliminate a mother in favor of the male line. Decio did not miss the opportunity to invoke the agnatic bias in the law, but he also held it out as merely the fifth argument for reading the statute as he did.[76]

The statutes of Pavia said women could not inherit with their brothers or their sons, and that male agnates in remoter degree still precluded women of closer degree within three degrees by canon law. The immediate issue was if the heirs to Giovanantonio de Berreti were three girls, daughters of the deceased's sister, and thus cognates, of the Turti lineage, related in second degree, or men of the Berreti related in three degrees. At first blush there was no problem. The men should inherit in line with the purpose of preserving agnation and family. And when there was only one rationale to a statute, it was argued, by interpretive rules it should be extended to cases not overtly included, so it should be seen to cover not just brothers in first degree but their cousins (*fratres patrueles*) too. The reference to third-degree agnates in the second statute seemed to seal the deal. But Giason del Maino contrived a way to uphold the nieces' claim. Of course common law was in their favor. The statutes had to work two changes to it: preferring agnates to cognates and remoter degree to closer. While he noted that there were all sorts of obligations on jurists to follow statutes and to read them with their intent in mind, he asserted that "the statutes really and truly, and according to what they say literally, never lead to these two corrections of common law, unless by listening beneath (*subaudiendo*) or otherwise interpreting than the words of such statutes allow." Here he leaned on a third statute, which forbade interpretation, demanding that statutes be understood as they read (*ut litera sonant*), to repeat that the exact situation in his case was not covered explicitly by the statute. The first statute did not refer to cousins and, by common opinion, he said, it could not be extended to them, despite the statute's rationale to preserve agnation.[77] This is a rare instance of a jurist conceding the agnatic bias of the statute and still trying to blow past that.

In another case Giason del Maino faced the "new" statute of Brescia that privileged men in succession to ascendants. The issue was whether that extended to the estate of a maternal grandmother. The statute clearly favored *masculinitas*, and that was not unusual. And behind that stood

[76] Decio, *cons.* 333, fols. 361va–62vb.   [77] Maino, 2 *cons.* 205, 678a–85a.

the fact that "males support greater burdens, public as well as domestic, than women, as experience teaches." But men were not agnatically related to the maternal grandmother. The statute, in fact, referred indiscriminately to ascendants, as Paolo di Castro had noted in discussing the earlier statute of Brescia. Nonetheless, Maino said it should not be interpreted in an overly literal fashion, and part of his argument was "that in statutes the intent rather than the words must be attended to more, although ignorant and gross men, often do the opposite, adhering to the words, like Jews" (*sicut Iudaei*).

Raffaele Fulgosio had also decades earlier argued that the statute of Brescia did not include the grandmother. Maino went over all the verbal changes between the old version of the Brescian statute and the new, which were designed to eliminate the doubts Fulgosio had exploited. But he agreed with Fulgosio that the men were related to their grandmother in maternal line, which was excluded by the statute. The usual argument for a restrictive reading of a statute contrary to common law was invoked, but mainly Maino stuck to the words that excluded descendants of females. In another curious move, at the end of the printed version of the *consilium*, Maino noted that this was how he interpreted this one statute of Brescia and that in another *consilium* in volume four (in fact, volume one) he interpreted another statute of that city in a different sense.[78] There he followed on a *consilium* of Francesco Corti (d. 1495) to the effect that Antonia and Lucia Astulfi, related on their father's side to Jacopo Torti in second degree, were preferred to Antonio Torti in fourth degree. Common law put the inheritance in the girls' hands, so the issue was the statute, which Antonio and those acting for him wanted to interpret as saying that agnates even of remoter degree excluded cognates. They wanted the words "ex parte patris" to mean agnates only, which Maino declared an absurd idea. The statute looked to the problem of controversy between those on the paternal side against those on the maternal, thus subsuming agnate and cognate. He also invoked another tactic of statute interpretation to the effect that a general assertion made in the rubric was not restricted by later language in the body of the text (*in nigro*). In this case the word *consanguinei* in the rubric was not to be restricted to agnates: "however *consanguinei* are understood as agnates and cognates from the father's side, to which [understanding] even the

---

[78] Maino, 3 *cons.* 55, 200a–05b.

common mode of speaking agrees, also that of the learned, as plainly demonstrated the same lord judge [Corti]."[79]

SIXTEENTH-CENTURY CASES

The next generation grappled with similar questions, but now with a whole other generation's citations to add to their arguments and the display of their legal erudition. Mariano Sozzini and his student, Bernardino Buoninsegne, agreed that Cassandra, niece of Bartolomeo Venturi, succeeded to him along with her uncle Girolamo, brother of the deceased. That was the result in *ius commune* and by Siena's statute, which said that brother's sons inherited with their uncle. The first point had to be that the rule was that the masculine noun *filii* also included daughters – in other words, that here it was not gender specific, but meant children. The statute was then in line with common law. A second statute, however, spoke of brothers and, by the logic that a masculine noun subsumed feminine, seemed expressly to cover Cassandra. Sozzini claimed instead that hers was a *casus omissus* and thus fell under *ius commune* and not the statute. She was not dowered or married at the moment Bartolomeo died, so the reason for exclusion was not in place. He cited in support, among other commentaries and *consilia*, one of his uncle Bartolomeo Sozzini dealing directly with Sienese statutes. What he did not state, of course, was the agnatic rationale behind the statute.[80]

In a case from 1550 involving Cortesia di Marco Grossi of Ravenna against their uncle Pietro, the college of jurists of Padua had found for him, but on appeal the jurists of Perugia had found for her. So Sozzini faced the professional problem of determining where the truth lay. He considered the arguments in her favor. *Ius commune* clearly favored her as daughter over an uncle. A renunciation she had made when dowered by her uncle did not hold, because by statute in Ravenna the legal act of a woman under twenty-five had to be enacted in particular forms that had not been observed. But the arguments against her were also solid. She could not claim property Pietro held, which admittedly had been Marco's, because it was held by particular grant on an emphyteotic lease (a long-term lease specifying the lessee keep up or improve the property) from the bishop of Cerveteri. By that token she also had no right in the emphyteotic lands held by her uncle Gregorio that were not also in Pietro's hands.

---

[79] Maino, 1 *cons.* 52, 161b–63b.   [80] Sozzini, 2 *cons.* 5, fols. 10rb–11rb.

More broadly, Sozzini sided with the Paduans who had determined that Cortesia had no rights of succession to her uncle, Gregorio:

for it is much explored among jurisconsults construing the statute, as in other similar [statutes] excluding women in favor of men, to have the intent that goods be preserved in agnation, and so such statute is said to be enacted in favor of agnation in wealth and preserving dignity, by a certain public utility considered in it and in this stands the true reason of such a statute of this sort.

The same sense of statutory intent continued to propel judgments in the sixteenth century. Though it was not good to women, the statute was an enactment favorable to agnate men, and that was the general and common opinion. So the daughter of a brother was excluded by a brother. Sozzini went on at some length here, mainly, it seems, to show the Perugian jurists why he did not agree with them. At one point he challenged directly three of their conclusions, one of which was that a brother's daughter was agnate and so not so clearly excluded as, say, a mother. While it could be said that any woman failed to perpetuate agnation, as she was *finis suae familiae*, it could also be said that "even an agnate woman, as long as she lives, is said to preserve the family name." But as the statute clearly excluded sisters, for reasons of agnation, so much the more so nieces.[81] He had a much easier time in 1552, in contrast, agreeing with a colleague (Girolamo Tornielli) that grandsons and granddaughters succeeded to equal shares of their maternal grandfather's estate, both by *ius commune* and by the intestacy statute of Ragusa. While the statute seemed conventionally to leave a granddaughter only a dowry, it spoke only to paternal grandfathers.[82]

It was the generation that followed Sozzini that finally saw a reduction in contentious intestacy cases, probably because more estates were transmitted through wills, and there were fewer heirs (something to explore in the next chapter). Pietro Cavallo had a couple cases of some substance. In one he ordered a judge of San Terenzio to have the defendant, Marchino di Giovanni d'Antonio, as heir, provide a "congruent and competent dowry" to his sister, Felicita. It was simple to point out that it was a *paternum officium* to dower that passed to son and heir, that became the son's duty when a statute made him heir and excluded her.[83] The reluctance of an heir to dower a sister seems to fit an age in which proportionally fewer women, among property-holding elites at least, married, and the

---

[81] Sozzini, 4 *cons.* 10, fols. 24va–27va.   [82] Sozzini, 4 *cons.* 53, fol. 96rb–vb.
[83] Cavallo, *cons.* 43, fol. 37rb–vb.

values of dowries were correspondingly higher. A suit from Fivizzano saw a son and daughter seek the estate of their mother's sister from her husband. It came to Cavallo on appeal and he upheld the court of first instance. The local statute did not exclude the niece and nephew, as it did not consider inheritance to a sister, so that fell under common law. Unless there were a local statute saying that masculine terms included their feminine counterpart, there was no license to read brother as including sister. The statute in question in fact ended with the assertion that all other instances it did not cover were to proceed by "la ragion commune de' Romani." So Cavallo was content to make that the case.[84]

Inheritance by Illegitimates

Women were not the only category disadvantaged in inheritance. Those related through them, including men, were also excluded or postponed in favor of agnates. Even uterine siblings felt the prejudices embodied in intestacy statutes. So did bastards. They were already hit by various provisions in *ius commune*, especially falling on those in the category of *spurii*. Most communities did not feel the need to take special account of bastards. It was sufficient to state, as almost all did, that heirs by intestacy were those born legitimate and natural. Such language would on face of it preclude not only bastards but adopted and legitimated children as well, as they were not born legitimate. Some cities, however, addressed potential succession by bastards or to them, in some instances allowing them limited rights to succession.

Perugia, for example, allowed fathers of illegitimates of all types and both sexes to leave them something by testament, gift, or codicil; such largesse, however, could not exceed one-sixth of the estate.[85] Nothing was said about the presence or absence of legitimate offspring or other agnates, and no right to succession in intestacy was conceded. Colle Val d'Elsa allowed succession of *spurii* by testament, not setting any limit on paternal generosity and specifically citing the text of Roman law thus effectively being set aside.[86] Montepulciano and Arezzo both allowed fathers to leave goods to bastards in the absence of legitimate male descendants. If there were both legitimate and illegitimate children, the share left to the latter could not exceed a sixth. Florence in the mid-fourteenth century, soon after the great plague, legislated a right to inherit

---

[84] Cavallo, *cons.* 54, fols. 49ra–50ra.   [85] Perugia, 409–10.   [86] Colle, 305.

on intestacy for *naturales* in the absence of other heirs. Those related to bastards were affirmed to have succession rights to whatever the illegitimates possessed.[87]

Legitimation of bastards gave rise to inheritance rights in *ius commune*. The emperor or his counts palatine were authorized to legitimate children. Statutes had some interest in regulating such possibilities. Arezzo, for example, authorized its podestà, on petition from a father, to legitimate his bastard as if it were an act of the pope or emperor.[88] The 1498 statutes of Milan required that any legitimation had to occur with the undoubted consent of the father or other ascendant male in order for it to enable the illegitimate to inherit anything. That capacity to inherit applied to the estate of the consent giver and no other – meaning no right could be gained through an illegitimate's father to brothers, half siblings, uncles, and so forth. Milan also sought to have legitimations published and registered and to control their format before counts palatine or civic officials.[89] These precautions were needed because the subsequent inheritance rights of legitimated bastards were to be honored. Ferrara in 1567, perhaps conceding to an atmosphere of Counter Reformation morality, followed Milan's lead in allowing legitimated sons to succeed their fathers or "other agnates" on intestacy only with expressed paternal consent at the legitimation if there were legitimate heirs.[90]

Inheritance by illegitimates, though rare, both because of social prejudices and of disabilities in the law, still raised perplexing legal issues. Baldo degli Ubaldi seems to have caught an inordinate number of cases in this area, arising in the midst of plagues and other catastrophes of the later fourteenth century. In one instance a man had two legitimate daughters and a *spurius* son, whom he legitimated so as to succeed him and his widow, without the half-sisters or grandmothers present. The girls died and the grandmothers had their property. The legitimated son sought the estate, arguing to exclude the grandmothers and their heirs, which were charitable institutions. A bastard son was thus in litigation with two ecclesiastical bodies. The counter to his suit was a challenge to the validity of his legitimation on a number of formal grounds. Baldo defended it, even against the argument that the prospective heirs had not been summoned to appear, as usually required, because succession to women was not so immediate and automatic that clear rights of others were in

---

[87] Kuehn, *Illegitimacy*, 74.   [88] Montepulciano, 142; Arezzo, 170.
[89] Milan 1498, fols. 136v–37v.   [90] Ferrara 1567, fol. 117r.

view and needed to be honored.[91] In other words, Baldo was willing to see the estate go to a legitimated (and thus agnate in some way) son in preference to grandmothers or charitable concerns.

In another case messer Pietro Salimbeni of Siena had a son by an unmarried woman whom, however, he had not kept in his home. Their relationship thus did not rise to the status of concubinage in Roman law, and thus the child could not be termed *naturalis*. Pietro later married a suitably noble woman. He did legitimate the boy, who succeeded on his father's death, but he gave a castle to one of the Salimbeni. Baldo defended the legitimation. He also tackled the status of the son before legitimation. A *naturalis* was born of a concubine kept in one's house without the honor of a wife: "and this is introduced for the sake of having certainty of offspring [*certitudinem prolis*]; otherwise women could easily feign that they have sons by some magnate and true noble and our successions would pass to strangers and others." A more vulgar mode of meaning was that a *naturalis* was born of two unmarried parents, and it was an appropriate fiction if the father recognized such a child as his own and treated him with affection, even if the result of a furtive, less socially certain relationship. Thus he argued to give the illegitimate child something of the status of a *naturalis*, rather than the more ignominious quality of *spurius*. The son could inherit the patrimony but not fiefs or noble dignities, according to Baldo. The father's gift of the castle thus stood; it could not be voided on the argument that it was an act of a known prodigal who consumed his substance wastefully.[92] In Solomonic fashion, he thus split the baby (patrimony) in two.

For later jurists, illegitimacy still raised issues, if not as frequent and urgent as a century earlier. Pierfilippo da Corgna had to consider whether the legitimate son of a *spurius* could be named as heir in his grandmother's will. His response was affirmative. The "stain" of illegitimate birth from the father did not pass to the son legitimately born.[93] For Mariano Sozzini, working in Padua in 1532, the problem was that the father of two *spuria* had legitimated them, one during his life and one by his will, but the next in line (*venientes*) by intestacy (who were his sister's daughters) had taken formal possession of the estate. It could be argued that the legitimations showed that the father preferred his daughters to his nieces as his heirs, and as these *venientes* were not his descendants but transverse cognates, they could licitly be deprived by the legitimation,

[91] Baldo, 5 *cons.* 99, fols. 29vb–30ra.   [92] Baldo, 2 *cons.* 129, fols. 29va–30ra.
[93] Corgna, *cons.* 25, fols. 24vb–25va.

enabling his girls to succeed. But Sozzini agreed with other jurists called to consult on the case that the nieces were the heirs. A *spuria*, he claimed, citing a number of *consilia* by others, could not truly be legitimated but only received a dispensation, which was effective against claims by the fisc, by the deceased's wife, or by relations further than four degrees, but not against nieces. The fact that the father had not used his will to institute his girls as heirs was taken to mean he preferred the nieces (as opposed to trusting the language of the instruments of legitimation). And whatever he preferred, it was not enough to overcome the disabilities on *spuria*:

in our matter the will of ser Bernardino, given that it was established properly, is not of itself sufficient that after his death the daughters were able to be legitimated in prejudice of these nieces, because we are dealing not with simple legitimation but with dispensative legitimation; and so that it may be done, and by it the right be removed from these nieces of seeking actual possession, it is required that there be present and expressed a rationale regarding public utility.

Sozzini simply did not see public utility served by inheritance by *spuriae*. He did not find a *voluntas* to make them heirs because there was no will.[94] In the instance of intestacy, Sozzini saw legitimacy of birth as stronger than the legally nonagnatic blood of *spuria*. Such prejudices against illegitimacy ran deep at that time, so Sozzini's opinion could meet with the approval of more than his clients. But his argument that legitimation of *spuria* was merely a dispensation to permit them to exercise certain abilities, even if he could cite *consilia* of others, was weakly contrived and effectively gutted a legal institution, legitimation.

Spouses

The other area of succession that had to concern municipalities, and did so more than inheritance by illegitimates, was inheritance rights of spouses. In *ius commune* spousal inheritance was low in the pecking order (spouses inheriting from each other only in the virtual absence of all other possible claimants). Given the agnatic bias we have seen in inheritance statutes, it is not surprising that communes did little to establish any right of a wife to inherit from her husband. Many of them, however, did move to establish a right of a husband to claim inheritance of his predeceased wife's dowry (*lucrare dotem*). Meanwhile, almost

[94] Sozzini, 2 *cons.* 120, fols. 167vb–70va.

without exception they all took care to spell out the wife's rights for return of her dowry on dissolution of marriage and interim claims to support. These two elements – a wife's right to retrieve her dowry on her husband's death and a husband's right to at least part of his wife's dowry on her death – drove most of the disputes that arose regarding spousal inheritance.

One of the problems in every community was how to render the dowry into a form – cash, movables, or even immovables – that did not hurt the household and the husband's heirs. The best choice for the household could well be that the widow remain there and simply use and enjoy her dowry, embedded into the patrimony, which would pass to her children, mainly sons in many places, but to both sexes in Venice and some other communities. In essence, the best choice for households, as Isabelle Chabot has demonstrated in great detail for Florence, was that the widow remain in her husband's household and not execute a return of dowry, though its legal return might be advisable to substantiate what it was and that she managed it. The difference in age between spouses, especially among the wealthier, meant that a city like Venice or Florence would contain a good number of widows having years to go to live off their dowries but being ripe, the youngest of them at least, for remarriage.[95] Delays in restoring the dowry could become common, even strategic. Laws and the courts of Venice confronted such delays and enforced women's rights for return of dowry.[96] Venice, however, could also come down hard on women. A widow had a year and a day to vacate the husband's house, unless he had left her a right to stay so she would care for minor children or unless she had some unpaid dowry, which, once paid, left her with two months to vacate.[97] Venice did not give the husband any claim on the dowry of a predeceased wife, it seems.

Often cited as the opposite extreme from Venice, with some exaggeration, is Florence. Statutes there limited the *donatio propter nuptias* to 50 *lire* or a quarter of the husband's property if less than that. On the husband's death the wife could seek the *donatio*, but if there were any children, she could not. So a widow had little claim on what was her husband's. But she had a highly enforceable claim to seek her dowry and anything her husband might have left her. The court was supposed to move in summary fashion and give her goods of her husband's and

---

[95] Bellavitis, *Famille, genre, transmission*, 57–72, who uses the word "imperfect" for Venice; Chabot, *La dette des familles*, 273–309.
[96] Venice 1242, fols. 25r–30r, 50r.   [97] Venice 1242, fol. 76r.

constrain his heirs and the guarantors of the dowry debt if they had not acted in two months.[98] Florence's intestacy statute also gave widows the right to return to live with their brothers or fathers. On the other side of the ledger, in Florence a husband had right to his predeceased wife's dowry if there were no children, and he then also got one-third of nondotal goods, the rest going to the nearest relatives in her father's family. However, if there were children, then sons and daughters inherited from their mother, even to the exclusion of her children by a prior marriage, with the husband holding usufruct.[99] Girls succeeded their mothers, however, as Isabelle Chabot has correctly pointed out, only if they had no brothers. Later in 1415 their exclusion from the entire female line in favor of brothers would be made apparent.[100]

Other Tuscan communities had variant rules. Arezzo gave a husband's heirs six months to affect restitution of dowry; if there were children, the widow was due support during the six months. The restitution of dowry in cash had to be accepted if that was how it was offered, even if originally the dowry had consisted of things or real estate. If the wife died first, the husband enjoyed half her dowry, from which he had to meet expenses for her funeral.[101] Montepulciano did not entirely follow Arezzo's lead. If the dowry had consisted of or been turned into *immobilia*, it was to be returned immediately. If it were in the form of cash or *mobilia*, the heirs had one year to return it with *alimenta* in the interval, along with any nondotal property (even the price of anything her husband had alienated with her consent). In imitation of Arezzo, Montepulciano's legislators ordered that a dowry restored in cash instead of *immobilia* had to be accepted in that form. On a wife's predecease her husband gained two-thirds of her dowry if there were no children. If she had children by a previous marriage, the husband got half and the wife could dispose of the other half. If she died intestate, children of the last marriage got two-thirds and of the first got the other third.[102]

In Cortona the husband without children realized one-third of the dowry of a predeceased wife and the *donatio propter nuptias*.[103] Siena in her 1545 statutes raised some peculiar notes, possibly arising from practices and resulting cases. No widow was to receive her restored

---

[98] Florence 1325, 91–93.

[99] Florence 1325, 130; Chabot, *La dette*, 13–20; Kirshner, "*Maritus Lucretur Dotem Uxoris Sue Premortue*," 120–22.

[100] Chabot, *Le dette des familles*, 19.   [101] Arezzo, 173–74.

[102] Montepulciano, 137–39.   [103] Cortona, 336.

dowry without first refusing her intestate legitimate share of one-fourth from her sons or grandsons and also swearing that the restitution of dowry was not an act of fraud – for which concession she did not need the authorizing consent of anyone else (no limitation of female agency in this regard). When a woman died without children, her husband gained half her dowry and the *donatio* he had given her. If there were children of both marriages, they succeeded equally per capita, the husband gaining nothing.[104]

Milan decreed the dowry be returned when there were no children or male descendants. When there were children, the widow still received all her furnishings and clothing, except the ceremonial outfittings for marriage (including dress, ring, jewelry, and so forth, which were typically furnished by the husband) and the marital bed, but including mourning clothes. She regained only two-thirds of her dowry if her husband had children by a previous marriage, which was equated to what her husband would have gained on her predecease with children of her previous marriage. He gained it all if there were no children. Other property she brought to the marital home stayed with him, children or no, though it was shared per capita with any of her children by a previous marriage. Husbands inherited on intestacy from wives even if they had a brother or sister or uncle or nephew.[105]

Saona postulated that if a wife died without children, her husband realized a quarter of her dowry and extra dotal goods, but if the husband predeceased and there were no children, she got a fourth of his property. She got nothing if there were children.[106] Bologna gave a surviving husband half his wife's dowry if there were no children. If there were children of her first marriage, the second husband retained a *virilem portionem* and the rest of it went to them. A surviving wife with children received her dowry back and they in turn got it following her death.[107] Treviso also gave a surviving husband with no children half his wife's dowry and anything she left him by will was in addition to that half; but when he predeceased she could get nothing but her dowry.[108] Forlì saw reason to explain that a widow who remained in her husband's house was understood to direct all *fructus* from her dowry there, as she had even by statute during marriage. The surviving husband without children obtained a third of his wife's dowry, beyond any bequests in her will, in compensation for marriage expenses. Children got the dowry otherwise,

---

[104] Siena, 244–45.   [105] Milan 1498, fols. 86r–88r.   [106] Saone, 182–83.
[107] Bologna, 571–75.   [108] Treviso, 381–82.

and those from multiple marriages split equally.[109] At Belluno the husband in absence of children received half his wife's dowry, while the other half returned to her father or grandfather. Were her father dead, the wife could dispose of that half of her dowry as she saw fit. To the contrary, on restitution of dowry to a widow, aware as Belluno's legislators were that "in restitution of dowry women meet with not a little aggravation and lest they suffer doubly," they decreed that the one facing restitution had to lodge a monetary security. And husbands received the fruits of the dowry and used them as they saw fit and could not be taken to court over their management.[110]

Viterbo prefaced its statute giving husbands of a childless marriage a quarter of a predeceased wife's dowry with an explanation:

Because husbands at the instigation of wives are forced to make and do make from their property for their wives, during marriage, unrestricted and just about insupportable expenses, we consider it worthy and fitting that in compensation of such goods husbands gain some return.

If the marriage produced children, he got only an eighth. If the husband passed away first, his heirs had a year to return the dowry to his widow, with *alimenta* in the interim, of course, at a specified ratio of two *denarii* for each *lira* per month (amounting to 10 percent over a year).[111] One would think, were such expenses really so intolerable, that Viterbo might have given its husbands a bigger share. It is revealing, nonetheless, that there was offered a rationale to the modification deliberately made to *ius commune* inheritance rights of husbands.

Quite different from Viterbo was the faraway southern city of Bari. There the wife's position as owner of her dowry was affirmed. If there were no children from the marriage, or if they were minors, her dowry then went to the one who had furnished it. Either way it did not go to the husband. Such a rule paid no attention to the disruption to the husband's household from restoring the dowry. Pugliesi sometimes modified these customary rules through the insertion of clauses in dotal contracts, and at times women themselves overrode these rules in their testaments. But at least in the fourteenth century in southern communities, husbands did not have as much control over dowry as in northern cities like Viterbo.[112]

In addition to the exclusion of dowered women, which rendered dowry as a distinct type of inheritable interest, there were distinctions drawn

[109] Forlì, 146, 317, 352–54.   [110] Belluno, 232, 236–37.   [111] Viterbo, 142–44.
[112] Mainoni, "Il potere di decidere," 219–22.

with regard to other types of property. These included *peculia*, property transmitted through male and female lines, and property acquired during one's life, as opposed to what had been inherited. Some southern communities, such as Naples, Sorrento, Syracuse, and Catania, made clear that an owner had broader discretion of use and disposition of what he had acquired by his own "industria" than over what he held as inherited patrimony. At least relatives had no right to repurchase acquired property later alienated. Sons, as heirs, could move to reacquire patrimonial holdings, but also were not free to alienate from their *peculia*. Southern locales, like Naples, were more lenient with regard to filial disposition of property, including what they gained from their mothers (which fell usually under the heading of *peculium adventitium*).

Frankish law had introduced the differentiation of paternal and maternal property and the rule "paterna paternis, materna maternis" (essentially, father's property to sons, mother's to girls). This rule was left to apply in southern communities, especially where statutes otherwise did not address intestate succession by collateral relatives. By this sort of rule women would at least retain a solid claim to inherit from their mothers. But this distinct characterization of property as paternal or maternal generally did not last beyond a generation, except perhaps with regard to outsiders.

Dowry restitution usually occurred when the husband died, but also at later points, when the wife or her heirs acted to extract her dowry from the patrimony. The understandable reluctance of his heirs to hand over a piece of household wealth, even to their own mother, if nothing else, could generate disputes. These were even more likely after time passed. To take a fairly early case, Angelo da Pietro Lunardoli of Castropoggio died intestate, leaving two sons, Petruccio and Giovanni, and a pregnant wife, Andreuzzia, who soon gave birth to a girl, Angeluzzia. Andreuzzia remained with her sons and daughter for five years before taking her modest 65 *lire* dowry and her young daughter to her remarriage. When Petruccio died at an age between twenty and twenty-five, Giovanni and his mother came to a division of the patrimony, now fifteen years since Angelo's death. Was Andreuzzia due her dowry and *alimenta* for the fifteen years, and did she gain any portion of Petruccio's share? Baldo degli Ubaldi stated that she deserved *alimenta* for the period she stayed as a widow in the house, "because in marriage is devised a goal [*causa*] that it preserves the honor and reputation of the husband in widowhood." So she was owed *alimenta* for the five years spent together with the children; but if she wanted *alimenta* for the daughter thereafter, she had no claim, as her second husband could afford it. It is interesting that Baldo saw the stepfather obligated for the support of a girl he admitted to his home. As for her dowry, there was no doubt that "dowry is the patrimony of the woman and is given as this."[113] She was entitled to get it back.

Two centuries later, parallel problems still arose. The noblewoman Camilla de' Grassi of Bologna married her first husband with a dowry of 1000 Bolognese *lire*. After his death she remarried to Teseo Bombelli with no mention of a dowry, though by the statutes of Bologna it was presumed that she had one and it was to be the same as in her first marriage. Teseo moved to retrieve her dowry and obtained possession of a farm, which he held for eight years until his death. His brothers then took his estate, while his widow took herself to a third husband. The brothers wanted to keep the farm. Camilla wanted to take the farm to her third husband, but Mariano Sozzini (in 1548) said she had to take cash or other objects as statutory law held. The title to the farm was Teseo's and it passed to his heirs.[114]

Second marriages further complicated dowry restitution, and in view of demographic realities, were at least a frequent possibility. If a wife left children behind as she moved to a second marriage, rights and claims between her and them had to be determined. Baldo found that Asti had a statute by which a widow could take her dowry and all else left to her and take it to her second home, while her children got nothing. Mother and all related through her were, in consequence, excluded from any inheritance to children of prior marriages, including from guardianship, with an express exception if the mother were named heir in a testament. So an Asti merchant, Antonio de Nivei, named his wife, Simoneta, as one of two guardians for the four daughters who were his heirs; and Simoneta, as guardian, accepted the estate for the girls and had an inventory made. But after her year of widowhood she remarried and took her dowry and some bequests left her by Antonio. When later one of the daughters died, Simoneta moved to claim half of her share on the basis of a substitution in Antonio's will. Baldo was not prepared to let her be heir when the statute precluded the children from being heirs to her. Though she had been named as a substitute, that was not the same as being instituted heir, which was what the exception in the statute meant.[115] In effect Baldo was arguing to keep the property in the hands of the girls, where it could serve as their dowries.

---

[113] Baldo, 2 *cons.* 86, fol. 19vb.   [114] Sozzini, 3 *cons.* 118, fols. 188rb–89vb.
[115] Baldo, 2 *cons.* 216, fols. 62va–63ra.

We have the instance of Venanzio da Fabriano, who married Gentilesca, and they had Bernardino, Caterina, and Marchigiana. Gentilesca subsequently died, and after her Bernardino and Caterina. Venanzio remarried and subsequently sold part of what came to him as the shares of his son and daughter in his wife's estate. Marchigiana (someone for her) contested her father's claim to title or even usufruct on her mother's property on account of his remarriage. The children succeeded their mother, so each had a third. Father and daughter in intestacy split the estates of the children. So Marchigiana had two-thirds, and Venanzio one-third. On her direct share, Marchigiana had full ownership, beyond doubt, but on the third that came to her by way of her siblings there was doubt. Benedetto Capra said she had full ownership, and on the share Venanzio inherited from the children, as a result of his remarriage, he had only usufruct, with title passing to his daughter. His alienation of those properties, then, was invalid, not only as to title but even usufruct, at least without his daughter's consent (a reverse of generational expectations). The parties were told to accept the arbitration of a local judge as to an appropriate amount for Venanzia's dowry.[116]

There were untold stratagems employed by a husband's heirs and kin to keep dowry or at least delay or string out its repayment. Yet not all delays were deliberate or deceptive. Paolo di Castro was asked to weigh in on the case of a man who had accepted a dowry, along with his insane (*mentecaptus*) father. Who was responsible for restitution of the dowry after the father's death? According to the widely accepted teaching of Bartolo, a father obligated himself and his property for restitution of a dowry for his son. His mental condition did not stand in the way: "because this happens by reason of necessity on account of the defect in his consent, lest the public utility of marriage and marriage itself be impeded, the law requires it be treated as if he had consented." When in doubt, one had to opt for dowry and marriage, and one should keep in mind that even during the father's life the son was, as Bartolo had put it, *quasi dominus* of the patrimony.[117]

Alessandro Tartagni had to determine if a statute governing restitution of dowry applied not just to a wife dying without ascendants but to a widow, such that a third of her property had to be left to her brothers. There were arguments that the statute applied only to a married woman – for

---

[116] Capra, *cons.* 46, fols. 68vb–70ra.   [117] Di Castro, 3 *cons.* 14, fol. 18ra–b.

example, the statute spoke of dowry and one had dowry only if one had a marriage. Paolo di Castro had argued that a statute that allowed a woman to bequeath only one-quarter of her dowry, leaving the other three parts to her children, applied to married women. But for all that, Tartagni waxed eloquent in his opinion that the statute did cover widows: "as is said the statute speaks absolutely of women and otherwise would follow the absurd result that a widow who is more independent [*sui iuris*] than a married woman, is more subject to her husband ... and it is absurd to say that a wife more subject [to the husband] is less impeded so as to be able to testate than she who is less subject." The statutory clause requiring that a woman who had remarried and had two sets of children provide for each set equally, which would seem to apply to widows, only held for married women. They were the ones in position, under the influence or from fear of the second husband, "because a wife has reverence or fear of her husband," to disadvantage the children of her first husband in favor of those of the second. That was what the law sought to prevent. But it also had to prevent some sort of ungoverned use of testaments by a widow. In either case Tartagni was relying on the restitution of dowry to make the statute operate in fact.[118] In this and other cases, the requirement to return dowry was seemingly absolute. The legal problems revolved around who was responsible and for what dowries. Other matters – timing, content – were things that could be and were best handled in direct negotiation or arbitration.

Pietro Brolas had three children, a son and two daughters, by his first wife, who died intestate. He remarried and later married off one daughter, Anna, before the other two children died. Succession to these two was the issue. By *ius commune* Pietro and Anna would split it, but for Anna it was argued that Pietro's remarriage disqualified him to be heir and that that part of the property that was the mother's dowry should go entirely to her. Pietro's response was that the civil law disqualification on remarriage applied to mothers, not fathers, and that Anna had formally renounced any share in her mother's property. Into this situation waded Filippo Decio, flourishing a raft of citations, especially to others' *consilia*, to the effect that the *communis opinio* was that the law also applied to remarrying fathers. The issue then became Anna's renunciation. Decio dismissed it largely on the grounds that she had renounced inheritance from her mother but not to her brother and sister, while she received a dowry that was undoubtedly assembled from a portion of her mother's.[119]

---

[118] Tartagni, 3 *cons.* 101, fols. 81ra–82rb.   [119] Decio, *cons.* 230, fols. 248va–49va.

In contrast to di Castro's case, here everything tended in the direction of the (then married) woman. In such a case, pitting father against married daughter, her husband, and possibly his family played a role in pursuing the matter, looking effectively to enlarge what she brought to the marriage. On the other side, the father had no other children, so his wife's dowry would go to his agnates.

The opposite situation was a case that later came before Marcantonio Pellegrini, for there the question was the right of succession of a remarried mother to her son when there was also a daughter. The statutes of Padua did not favor agnate females (i.e., the sister), "because the statutes sprang from favor to agnation and to maleness, by reason of preserving families, and thus they do not favor women, because by them agnation is not preserved." What of remarriage? The *iura novissima* held that a mother could not succeed to what was *de paterna substantia*. But Pellegrini gave these a strict rendering. "A dying son had [the estate] immediately from his father," but succession was not immediate for what came indirectly from a brother or grandfather. Such an indirect succession was the case here, so Pellegrini determined that the mother got half in usufruct on paternal goods and ownership on other goods.[120] The daughter's share from her brother was considerably reduced in favor of a remarried mother, so the property came within control, one assumes, of the second husband.

Even simply what the dowry was could be disputable. For example, what if a widow nominally had no dowry (that is, none was specified at the time of marriage or no notarized record existed)? Statutes in a number of cities declared that in such cases whatever a woman brought to the marriage was to be considered dotal property, even if it had not been specified as such. One woman married without dowry and had three daughters before her husband died, leaving by will one-third to those girls and the other two-thirds to two of her husband's agnates. Those two gave some things to the widow, who was "destitute," and the daughters also contributed to her through guardians and a judge. It was determined by arbitrators that this widow was still owed 600 ducats from a total of 1,200 as settlement for what she had brought to the home, so the agnates assigned her some properties as equivalent, as did the girls. As someone then in full possession of 1,200 ducats, this widow was a prize catch for some man in the community. So after a

---

[120] Pellegrini, *cons.* 78, fols. 211va–14va.

widowhood of twelve years, at age thirty, she remarried to a man from another city. No dotal instrument appeared this time either, though the property she had been given was sold off with her second husband's consent. When she later died, this widow (only the letter K is used for her in the *consilium*) left a will that gave a small amount to the daughters of the first marriage, much less than a legitimate portion. The two daughters by the second husband were named her universal heirs, with lifetime usufruct to their father. After his death there was to be a division of half to the woman's brother and half to the girls from her first marriage. Effectively, by the will, the girls from the first marriage inherited only if those from the second died without remarrying and only after the second husband died.

The legal problem for Paolo di Castro was whether what had been handed to her from her first husband's property was to revert to their daughters, and in what proportion. He declared that it all went to the first set of daughters, as it came from their father. The widow by law could take it so as to facilitate a second marriage, but municipal law should not overtake *ius commune*. He also offered the idea that the widow was consciously defrauding those girls, with the connivance and to the benefit of the second husband:

> More so as this testatrix strove to cheat the daughters of the prior marriage and totally exclude them, by alienation made with their consent and perhaps better by the urging and begging of the second husband, an outsider, against the municipal laws, because she left them just about nothing, leaving the daughters of the second marriage as universal heirs, substituting the husband. The daughters of the prior marriage should succeed, as through deliberate fraud she strove to transfer her property to the second husband against the disposition of law.

The clauses in the acts of transfer that stated that the widow had full and free rights of control over the property did not mean she could perpetrate such a fraud. She only had possession and usufruct until she died, because the goods in question were subject to restitution.[121] In some ways this was a weak legal argument, which could stand as long as di Castro did not bring into play the fact that she clearly brought something to the marriage, for which she was compensated and had firm dotal rights. The real factor here may have been the fact that the second husband was a foreigner to the jurisdiction of the first husband and the daughters, who seem to have been di Castro's clients.

---

[121] Di Castro, 2 *cons.* 149, fols. 63rb–vb.

When a wife died, her surviving husband had to see to the household, especially if there were children. It was not at all uncommon for such widowers to remarry, but as the children were those of the prior wife, statutes often directed that her dowry remain with him and the children. Jewish law too directed the wife's property to the husband, not the children.[122] Jurists upheld this rule. Either the husband was designated her heir on intestacy, or he had usufruct and the children were nominally heirs. Some communes went so far as to name even a childless husband heir to his wife's dowry, in total or in part (*lucrum dotale*). Still, this statutory right of a husband to his wife's dowry was not always clear-cut. Baldo, working with an Aretine, Rosello de' Roselli, had no problem deciding that in the situation where the wife died before being taken to the husband's home, even though a dowry had been legally arranged, he received nothing because he had not for an instant sustained the burdens of marriage.[123] That household burdens persisted and that dowry was intended to meet them would seem to have been the rationale behind the husband's statutory claim. The same rationale held in Baldo's examination of a case from Castro Sarzana, when there too the wife had never made it to the husband's home. The statute there, he said, held for a real marriage and not one in name only (*nudo nomine*).[124] Supporting the costs of marriage was what Bartolo had cited as the overriding reason a husband could hope to retain at least a portion of a deceased wife's dowry.[125] By the same token, Baldo demanded that the dowry be real. At Spoleto, where by statute a surviving husband retained a quarter of the dowry, there was a case in which the dowry had never been paid, though promised and "confessed" as a matter of four yearly installments. Baldo simply denied that the statute applied. A dowry "confessata" was not a dowry "data."[126]

Around a century later Giason del Maino faced an unconsummated union in similar fashion. Here it was unconsummated because the husband, Giorgio, never had the opportunity to do so on account of crimes he had committed that seemingly landed him in exile, rather than the marital bed. Although authoritative jurists, including Baldo, had said that actual intercourse was not required to gain the dowry by the Pavian statute, that *copula carnalis* need only be "in potentia," Maino, along

---

[122] Colorni, *Legge ebraica*, 208–09.   [123] Baldo, 1 *cons.* 290, fol. 88ra–va.
[124] Baldo, 4 *cons.* 447, fol. 107rb–va.
[125] Bartolo, Quaestio 7, *Consilia, Quaestiones, et Tractatus* (Venice, 1581), fols. 81va–82va.
[126] Baldo, 4 *cons.* 333, fol. 75rb.

with other jurists and in accord with ducal decision, determined that there
was not any such *habitus* or *potentia* in this case. The wife had been led to
Giorgio's house, and thus there might be an argument that some marital
expenses were incurred; but those were covered by the dotal *fructus* and
did not justify keeping the entire dowry. The husband was not there and
thus the marriage, for purposes of the statute (so that it "correct" *ius
commune* the least), was not essential and complete, as there was never
the possibility of having children. The dowry thus should pass back to the
bride's family, which was in accord with *ius commune*.[127]

Dowry had to have some certain configuration also. A man who had
held his wife's home and a farm for many years "tanquam dotalia," on
her death, childless, claimed a statutory third. His claim was countered
with the argument that nothing had been promised or handed over as
dowry. Baldo noted that Aristotle had said that anything a wife brought
to her husband was dowry, but the gloss noted that wealthy wives would
hold much back as their own. So, in the absence of a statute establishing
that anything brought to the husband's house was dowry, there was
legitimate doubt as to its value. An amount that was thus uncertain, along
with mere "patientia" in a husband's management during marriage, was
not tantamount to ceding him title to what had come with her. Still, Baldo
forged a path to dowry by leaving the amount to judicial discretion while
declaring that there was indeed some dowry, "for a general custom is that
marriage is not contracted without a dowry, so establishment of a dowry
is presumed, which is to be referred to the discretion of a good man." The
wife's "patience" counted for something for "the husband is the image of
the wife (*vir imago uxoris*) and represents her in dowry."[128]

Bartolomeo Cipolla looked at a situation in which, at first glance, he
would have to agree with Baldo and the language of Parma's statute that
the dead wife had to have been *transducta* in order for the husband to
keep her dowry. Instead, he agreed with Alessandro Tartagni, who had
spoken first on the case, that one had to look carefully at the statute
because "the intent of the legislators does not consist in the words of the
statute alone but in the sense, not in the surface but in the marrow, not in
the air of speech but in the root of reason." He aimed to make a sweeping
interpretation. The *onera* of marriage arose at three points: in the
exchange of vows, in *ductio* to the groom's house, and afterward. He
took the statute to mean all three, for in any of them the husband had

---

[127] Del Maino, 1 *cons.* 58, 186a–88a.   [128] Baldo, 4 *cons.* 102, fols. 25va–26ra.

expenses, and the statute did not look at how much or how long he bore them. In the case at hand there had been an exchange of vows, consummation, cohabitation for five months, but in the wife's house, and then travel to the territory of Parma, where on account of the plague they turned back to her home in Luna in the Trentino, where two years later she died. So technically she had never set foot in his house, but he certainly had had expenses, and those justified his keeping the dowry.[129]

If by this calculus the *transductio* might be somewhat virtual, the wife's dying without children could not be. One man, in a community in which by statute he could gain half the dowry (indeed half of all her property brought to him), if his wife died childless, argued that his wife had died childless, though there was in fact a grandson whose father, their child, had died. The grandson argued that he was equivalent to a child for the purpose of the statute. Cipolla was disinclined to swallow the husband's disingenuousness. The statute ran contrary to *ius commune* but to the husband's benefit; yet it also liked children by making them exclusionary. He took *nepos* (grandson) as equivalent to *filius* in the terms of the statute for a variety of reasons, not least because doing so resulted in less departure from the terms of *ius commune*, and because, if a daughter excluded the husband, why not the grandson?[130] Paolo di Castro received a case involving a statute that gave a husband his wife's dowry if she had no descendants, ascendants, or collateral relatives, nor even mother or sister. He carefully examined the statute's wording and concluded that the husband was his wife's heir and through her also heir to her mother and sister.[131] Here there indeed was no son or grandson.

For Giorgio, by his mother's first marriage, the question was if the statutes of Asti gave him remedy against her second husband to claim half her dowry. The stepfather, Odone Lupo, whose marriage had produced two children, contested him on the basis of the statute, though by then the two children had died and he had long since remarried and fathered other children. Paolo di Castro, consulting along with another lawyer, found that the mother's dowry at her death split into three parts, one for each child alive at that moment, for their existence excluded the second husband. The shares of Odone's children from Giorgio's mother, furthermore, devolved on Giorgio and not on the agnate half-siblings from their father's second marriage.[132] Giorgio, not those siblings, was blood-related

---

[129] Cipolla, 2 *cons.* 18, 83a–84b.   [130] Cipolla, 1 *cons.* 7, 24b–28b.
[131] Di Castro, 2 *cons.* 14, fol. 7ra–va.   [132] Di Castro, 2 *cons.* 358, fols. 168vb–69rb.

to the mother whose property was under consideration, and that was the strongest point in di Castro's opinion in his favor.

By Florentine statute a surviving husband kept all the dowry. So though Baldassare Rossi had no *confessio dotis* for the dowry from Contessa, it could be assumed he had the same 1,000 florins she gave her first husband (as the terms of *ius commune* stipulated). He, of course, wanted to keep it. Pierfilippo da Corgna, after rehearsing many reasons why the husband's consent at the promise of dowry did not violate Florence's requirement for a *mundualdus* to protect the wife's interests (in which he was also an interested party), argued that such an "exorbitant" statute had to be restricted. One way to achieve that was to demand that the dowry be real and not merely tacit. Moreover, Contessa could not obligate herself for a dowry without a *mundualdus*, especially that as a woman her ignorance of the law, including the statute giving her dowry to her husband, could be presumed.[133] The effect of his argument, if accepted by a court, would be return of the dowry to the first husband or children by him.

A woman named Filippa married Federico de' Boschi and had a son, Mariano, before becoming a widow and remarrying maestro Felice, with a dowry and 100 florins for clothing and other paraphernalia. And Felice did provide her with several outfits during their marriage. On her death Mariano sought all her property as her heir; and Felice opposed that, citing the statute ordering the dowry of a wife who died after five years of marriage without children fell to her husband. Dowry was one matter; the 100 florins and other property were another. Benedetto Capra first distinguished festive and expensive clothing, which the husband paid for and kept, from daily wear that belonged with and to the wife, which was the case here. As the statute only considered dowry, these garments in their substantial value passed by *ius commune* and thus fell to the son. The dowry stayed with the second husband.

Such issues generated by second marriages and dowries continued to crop up decades later. Pietro Cavallo in 1578 found that a father who gained a portion of his wife's dowry, the rest going to their children, did not lose it by remarrying. He retained usufruct, though the reigning opinion was he did lose title, which went to the children.[134] The problem of *ductio* too did not go away. Marcantonio Pellegrini faced it on a handsome 4,600 ducat dowry between Francesco Bucciacareno and

---

[133] Corgna, *cons.* 254, fols. 191vb–93ra.   [134] Cavallo, *cons.* 8, fol. 6rb–vb.

Cornelia Dondi al Orologio, as they had exchanged vows and celebrated their marriage, but she died before he could get her home in Padua and consummate their union. Strictly speaking they were married, so the statute could be said to apply, even though it was not in line with *ius commune*. But Pellegrini fell on the side of Baldo and others who insisted that the husband had not sustained the *onera matrimonii*. The statute, he claimed, took marriage as *carnalis copula*, which had not happened here. The husband could gain the dotal *fructus* in compensation for such expenses as he incurred. Moreover,

> many doctors said in this sort of statute about gaining dowry not only is respect to be had to the burdens of marriage but the contract of marriage and the person of the husband are to be contemplated, by which hope of gain men more easily are enticed to contracting marriage, in which lies the public good.[135]

There was thus more than sustaining burdens as a *causa* to this law. And this rationale did not need to be expressed. The social good of marriage was evident.

CONCLUSIONS

In this chapter we have examined some recurrent features of inheritance (such as filiation and legitimacy, acceptance or repudiation of estates) and particularly the playing out of intestate inheritance, lodged in *ius commune* and statutory rules concerned with the place of dowry and claims of dowered women in the estate. Across the early modern era legal practitioners commonly saw at work in such statutes an ideology of family and agnatic preservation, the heart of which lay in keeping substantial holdings in the hands of agnate males across the generations. With the passage of property thus secure, the rest – name, memory, honor, and reputation – would be taken care of. In the hoped-for normal course of events, when a man died with a son or sons, waiting in the wings to carry on the patrimony and memory, intestate inheritance raised little problem, at least as to who was heir and for how much. Some issues, such as the return of maternal dowry or the provision for dowries for sisters, might raise legal difficulties, which sometimes came to court (but also were directed to arbitrators). When there was no son, however, things got interesting. Almost every case we have seen, of the hundreds in the sampling of juristic *consilia*, arose in the absence of an obvious direct male heir.

---

[135] Pellegrini, *cons.* 85, fols. 232ra–33vb.

Such instances were far from rare, given the realities of births and life expectancies in Italy in the era, for which factors also lay behind the continuing impact of intestacies.

In such trouble cases, women and more distant male relatives were both the self-interested immediate claimants of property and, to a greater or lesser extent, depending on circumstances, the hoped-for perpetuation of the agnatic line and its honor and memory. Any one inheritance, moreover, was subject to the consequences of previous moments of inheritance or intervening legal acts, not the least of which were dowries. Some patrimonies moved between intestate and testate transmission. They moved as well from male to female hands and back again. The narratives behind families combined to produce situations far beyond what legislators could anticipate or judges find comfort in confronting. Jurists had to step in again and again.

One other consequence of these complex and largely unanticipated situations was that claims of women were advanced with some regularity, by themselves or others (men) in their name. No one, at least in the cases we have looked at, expressed any dismay that women would try to lay claim to property and had the legal rights to do so. We have encountered frequent recourse to the clichéed justification that women were the most avaricious sort of people in the course of arriving at judicial arguments. That bit of gender discourse is found much more than any reference to physical or mental weakness in these cases.

Intestacy cases allow one seemingly to say little about the dead. They left no instructions, leave alone explanations, as to the disposition of assets after their deaths. Intestacy points one at those seeking the property. The perspective shifts when we consider testaments.

6

Inheritance

Testaments

Testaments produced their own problems, supplementing, as they did, the rules of law concerning inheritance. Yet many people of all walks of life were eager to make their last wills in order to leave a variety of bequests, including those for the good of their souls, for their burials and memorials, and to give directions to their heirs, as well as designate who the heirs were.

When they were linked with other testaments, as a patrimony passed through several generations, the fate of an estate could become incredibly complicated. As our introduction to this area of law and practice, we will consider a case that came before Baldo degli Ubaldi from the Apennines town of Borgo San Sepolcro. Even this fairly early example from the fourteenth century shows how complicated things could get. The legal matters began with the testament of Matteo di Vani di Neri, who named as heirs his son Barnaba and his grandson by another son, Cristofano. Matteo added substitutions to either of them if dying without a legitimate heir. Following Matteo's death, both men accepted the patrimony, although Cristofano never fulfilled the condition placed on him to ratify Matteo's acts (probably those as guardian of Cristofano), so that Cristofano's acceptance could be said to be of no import for not meeting that condition. His failure activated a clause of substitution in favor of Barnaba. Cristofano then died, leaving a natural son, but naming his maternal uncle Benedetto his heir in his testament, with specific bequests to the illegitimate son. Barnaba then died, leaving a son by his concubine, monna Billia, whom he married on his death bed. He named his mother, Beatrice, his heir and left bequests to the son. He made it clear in his will that he wanted the substitution left in his father's (Matteo's) will to remain firm and valid. Thus the estates at issue were themselves the product of a congeries of deaths and passages of property, passing through men who both left illegitimate progeny (one legitimated by deathbed marriage) and named heirs from the maternal line. Here, and with every estate we will see, there was a history that actively impinged on the present.

This set of events generated eight distinct legal questions for Baldo. It is hard to tell from his text if he was acting as counsel to the court or to Barnaba's mother. First was whether the death bed marriage effectively legitimated the son, as Barnaba was ill at the time, though *mente sanus*, and had acted through an agent. Baldo quickly determined that legitimation in such circumstances was efficacious. Second was whether Cristofano, who had "inmixed" himself in Matteo's estate and sold off many items, was heir or not. A negative answer would put his share in Barnaba's hands. Baldo upheld the condition that Cristofano had to confirm his grandfather's legal dealings and thus declared Cristofano not an heir. It all went to Barnaba. The remaining legal problems concerned the substitution in Matteo's will that would come into effect, or not, following Barnaba's death. The substitution had expired, said Baldo, because there was a legitimate heir, as marriage made the offspring honorable (*matrimonium honestat prolem*). Property was supposed to go to descendants, which in this case meant it passed through Barnaba's legitimated son, although he too had died. Finally, Vanni di Neri, Barnaba's grandfather, in his will had prohibited alienation of the houses in Borgo San Sepolcro, "because he wanted the houses . . . to go in perpetuity to his children (*posteros suos liberos*) or to those descended from them in the male line," and he wanted any property sold off to be repurchased. As all Vanni's descendants had now died, except for the natural son of Cristofano, did this son have a claim against the alienation worked as a result of Barnaba's will (in favor of his mother)? Baldo rehearsed the argument that the bastard was covered by the term *liber* (child). His conclusion is an eloquent treatment of the differences between bastards and legitimate children:

the intent of a testator which is common [to favor] a natural and legitimate son is changed to the natural son . . . or at least one is to recur to the distinction of § *si quis rogatus* whether a testator may make mention of children by this unburdening children, as 'if my son should die without sons, I substitute so and so,' in which case natural children are sufficient to free the estate from the burden of a trust, as in these laws, or whether in reverse a natural son makes worse the condition of legitimates, as when we are heavily burdened by their existence, which we would not be without them, as is here. For if natural children are included, the legitimates are more burdened because they cannot alienate the houses left to them, and then the prohibition of alienation made in favor of children would turn back against legitimates in favor of natural children, which is not equivalent; because such a sense is not to be presumed about natural children, that the testator would want to tie the hands of the legitimates on account of bastards, through whom neither the honor of the house nor the dignity of families is preserved, for which the testator had respect, and especially because he was a nobleman.

The testator was also concerned about agnation, whereas the bastard followed the mother, not the father, and so was not agnate. The houses, said Baldo, could not go to the bastard; they went to Barnaba's mother, Beatrice, who was hardly agnate herself.[1]

In this situation, then, the agnatic line failed. Legitimacy and honor were upheld paradoxically by a woman, in preference to a bastard. The use of testaments across three generations, all forbidding alienation of the family's houses and employing other devices, like bequests to specific individuals and substitutions, had failed to overcome biological misfortune. Property ended up contested between a mother and a bastard grandson. It was all made possible by the devices of Roman and canon law, to which we must now turn.

LAW OF TESTAMENTS

A Roman testament had as its first role the naming of an heir. It was not valid if it failed to appoint an heir. Typical testaments then also provided legacies to particular recipients, and in this way became a vehicle for charitable and *pro anima* bequests. So a testator could designate both heirs and legatees. Validity of a will also rested on the capability of the one making it (e.g., one had to be of "sound mind") and the fulfillment of proper form. Capability meant the testator was a citizen, adult, and *sui iuris*. Those qualifications were required in order to respect the testator's wishes. In Roman law women initially lacked capacity by those terms. Law allowed them eventually to draw up a testament with a guardian's consent, but as that consent could be compelled, many women obtained an unrestricted right of testation.

Women were prohibited by the *lex Voconia* of 169 BC from being heirs to the wealthiest Roman citizens, seemingly guaranteeing a sizeable portion of that wealth went to males. More than one heir could be named, generally to share equally, but the testator could differentiate if he or she chose. The rule that a person could not die both testate and intestate

---

[1] Baldo, 4 *cons.* 319, fol. 71ra–vb.

meant the whole estate was available to the heirs, minus specific legacies. Heirs could be named subject to a condition to be fulfilled first, which could not in the nature of things be impossible, immoral, or illegal. One of the more productive areas for testamentary innovations (and complications, as in the case we have seen) was the provision for substitutions. Lest the appointed heir die first or otherwise fail to take the *haereditas*, and thus throw it into intestacy, it was possible to appoint a substitute (*substitutio vulgaris*). The substitute was thus conditional, and it was possible to be both *haeres* and substitute (to another *haeres*) at the same time. Substitute to a minor heir who succeeded but died before puberty (and thus be able to make his own will) was termed pupillary (*pupillaris*).

Rights of heirs and legatees commenced at the testator's death, but a legacy was not enforceable until the heir accepted, as the legacies were generally charged on him to fulfill or deliver. The balance between bequests (*legata*) and the estate of the heir (*haereditas*), to ensure some minimum gain for the heir, was set by the *lex Falcidia* (40 BC) as one-quarter minimum to *haeredes*. The senatus consultum Trebellianum (56 AD, revised under Justinian) extended the provision of a quarter to the heir named in a substitution (*fideicommissum*). In its way this Falcidian and Trebellianic quarter was one limitation on what was otherwise a considerable freedom of testation. But there were others. Testators had the ability to disinherit (*exhaeredatio*) children. But disinheritance had to be done expressly; simply failing to mention a child or passing over him (*preteritio*) only rendered the testament invalid. This was a complicated area of law, and in the late Middle Ages disinheritance was a practice not much in favor in legal doctrine. Only a limited set of reasons was allowed for disinheritance, such as apostasy, or violent acts against one's father, and it became much simpler for jurists such as Baldo degli Ubaldi to advise testators wanting to disinherit a child in effect to leave him or her a small amount rather than try absolute disinheritance.

There might be little then to keep the disadvantaged heir from turning to a legal remedy, the *querela inofficiosi testamenti*. This was the way in which a *sui haeres* or others who would have been heirs on intestacy could challenge a will that passed him over without mention or left him too little, both seeming breaches of the duties of a good father. It allowed dispute over inadequate provision in a will, though one had received something. Justinian reshaped the remedy to be a right to a *legitima portio*, the lack or deficiency of which could be contested, but success of which claim did not invalidate the rest of the will. If there were four or fewer children, they were entitled to a minimum of one-third to be shared among them; five or more were guaranteed half to be shared. *Legitima* and the Falcidian quarter, combined, led to some legal confusion and furnished an opening for heirs to contest the results of a testament.

It is important to note the social/familial ethic that underlies this set of affairs around testaments. In theory, at least, the will of the testator was circumscribed by the existence of persons, children mainly, whom the law considered possessed of a right to at least part of the deceased's wealth. Testators could not give it all to whomever they wanted. No medieval or early modern Italian could leave everything to a charity, for example, if there were direct and immediate heirs who possessed an inheritance right by law. Means like the *querela* allowed disinherited persons a way to press their claims. The testament, then, was about the testator and those around him or her, not about the testator alone.

The law's dislike of disinheritance points to a certain reluctance to embrace the full potential individualism of the testament. Testaments were not a feature of Lombard law; they were not a deeply ingrained practice in the earlier Middle Ages. The testament, well into the first decades of the fourteenth century, was a device whose use was limited.[2] Some communities eased the way to use of testaments by legislatively accepting wills witnessed by only two or three people, versus Roman law's insistence on seven witnesses. The Church too was a force in this direction, as testaments were the way to affect pious bequests, which would be one important area in which a testament could modify intestacy rules.

While canon law and some statutory rules made the making of wills easier, it was the reception of those instruments in courts and their conceptualization by jurists that truly helped insert them into the fabric of Italian life, and death. Jurists perforce lectured and commented on all the many sections of the *Codex* and *Digest* that dealt with elements of testamentary succession. Their contribution to law in practice was inestimable. In the same way that their interpretations of statutes excluding women gave them operational and theoretical validity as acts benefitting the perpetuation of family dignity and honor, through property, their interpretations of testaments fused the desires of discrete testators with the laws, particularly those regarding *fideicommissa*, and created an effective law of family trusts. This development, coming a bit later, coincides with what Romano, for one, posits as a shift in the conception and concerns of family in Italy:

[2] Romano, *Famiglia, successioni e patrimonio familiare*, 50.

With the end of the Middle Ages even the idea of the 'medieval family' united in its personal element weakened. For the conception of a patrimony to be held firm in the name of family solidarity for common defense and advantage of each was substituted the idea of the indivisibility of the patrimony, intended functionally for the continuity of the house, which was identified with male descent, especially in the person of the firstborn. The focal interest thus shifted sensibly from the personal to the patrimonial (for all that was always present).

Beyond every sentiment and in the light of a new ethical key, succession was seen as the transmission of the family patrimony across the generations, a sort of restitution of the property to the sons or to the kin disposed in a way that 'lest the base of the family or of the name of the family die out' ...[3]

The fideicommissary substitution was just the device to affect this result, if the jurists could facilitate its acceptance and use. They did so, though not without some difficulties.

Beyond the *substitutio vulgaris*, replacing an heir who did not want to become heir, and the *pupillaris*, replacing an heir who died too young to take over (in which case the substitute was in fact heir to the heir, not to the testator), the third form of substitution in Roman law was the *fideicommissum*, which imposed an obligation on heirs or other beneficiaries to hold property (usually to transfer it) for benefit of other(s) designated by the testator. These became quite popular in Rome once Augustus recognized them, as they were a way to circumvent other restrictions on the movement of property. They were useful in making family settlements, as to posthumous children, for one thing. Early glossators distinguished *fideicommissum* as an indirect substitution, to which some also applied the term *obliqua*. Bartolo's contemporary, Raniero Arsendi (d. 1358), in an extensive treatise, divided substitutions into six types. All but the last, *fideicommissaria*, he termed direct. This was the legal basis for the sort of entailing of property that we will see becomes common in Italy around and after 1500. *Fedecommessi*, to use the vernacular, became regular and expected, especially among the nobility, but even among aspiring families not so well off or socially entrenched.

Two key elements made the *fideicommissum* into a common feature in early modern Italian testaments. One was the linking of substitutions in order in male line, specifying which collateral branches stepped in when an entire line of males failed, importantly allowing those substitutions to persist over untold generations and not just a more easily foreseeable progression of three or four generations, as laid out by Justinian.

---

[3] Romano, 59.

The other was the addition of a general prohibition against inherited real properties being alienated "extra familiam." This included the provision that heirs not separate out their legitimate portions and thus diminish the patrimony. The rules for construing such trusts became so transparent that it was possible to generate them from contracts other than wills, notably in gifts. It was also possible, through the work of jurists like Bartolomeo Sozzini (1436–1506) of Siena and Giason del Maino of Milan, for law to swallow the very un-Roman notion of primogeniture and accept it into substitutions in *fideicommissa*.

The possibility of primogeniture was just one consequence of *ius commune's* de facto acceptance that the heir by *fideicommissum* had full ownership of the *haereditas* that fell to him, but he did not have full rights to use and enjoy it, including not having his right of free testation on it in turn, not even on his legitimate portion, if he in turn faced a substitution in favor of another (even his own son). It was on that score that some jurists termed the *fideicommissum* "odious," while those who saw it in a favorable light fixed their sights on the preservation of family *dignitas* as the sole sufficient justification for thus tying the hands of subsequent heirs. Seeing it as favorable, jurists throughout Italy sketched out a functional ideology of agnatic family identity and the tools with which to realize it. They took advantage of those tools in their own strategies, notably so in their testaments, where they too burdened vital family properties with prohibitions against their alienation to others outside the family. The property made the transition across generations not by a sort of natural process, but by the will of a founding *de cuius*, which bound the wills of all inheriting from him. Patrimony was rendered indivisible, inalienable, and only temporarily under the management of each successive heir or set of heirs.

As Renata Ago has said of *fedecommessi*, "such acts were not attempts simply to preserve goods but to render them inalienable, thereby elevating them to a level superior in value to those ordinary things that could be exchanged with impunity."[4] Family continuity became tangible by the transmission of treasured lands and objects that were also vital material support. While somewhat successful in amassing property in the hands of more well-off families, these trusts also limited the liquidity of patrimonial assets, blocked their market availability, and generated countless lawsuits. Along with the statutes excluding women, *fideicommissa* became

---

[4] Ago, *Gusto for Things*, 59.

a powerful shaping force in early modern Italian societies, even despite the undoubted problems they also created.

Such substitutions and restrictions also, if in less distinct ways, had to affect the emotional and companionate life, or its potential, for families, more so in areas where primogeniture took hold. The nominal titleholders in each generation really did not have ownership, only possession. They were stewards of a family trust. They might rent or pawn objects, including open-ended annuities on real estate (*censi*) that became popular in cities such as Florence in the sixteenth century, precisely because they did not alienate ownership and gave the owner great flexibility in handling his debt. By the end of the sixteenth century some of the first hesitant attempts to place a limit at least on the duration of *fideicommissa* made an appearance. We now have some excellent studies of these trusts and the laws and courts that supported them in Florence, Rome, Milan, and Naples. Almost without exception, however, these studies do not examine the problems and disputes generated by this device.

The spread of practices such as these also raised concerns about women's roles in inheritance. Substitutions could be and were devised to pass family property to males. Only when all lines of legitimate males died out (as happened in Baldo's case) were women generally eligible to be heirs. And then their claims might be limited by the statutory regulations of a given municipality or principality. Beyond women as heirs there were also bound to be concerns about them as testators. Roman law gave women extensive abilities to devise testaments (again, further encouraged by the Church and canon law) that were not always contemplated with equanimity by Italian legislators. Statutes placed some limitations on these capacities, adding to those already in place that restricted women's possibilities of owning property (beyond dowry) and on their capabilities to use and dispose of it.

STATUTES AND CASES

Formal Elements for a Valid Testament

Most of the law relating to testaments, in contrast to intestacy, came from *ius commune*. Communal legislation tinkered around the edges, with notable attention to women's wills and issues related to the agnatic bias of intestacy statutes. Statutes certainly did not overlook testamentary issues because the testaments were rare. Historical research in different communities shows widespread use of testaments, across all social classes, in the cities and the countryside, notably from the time of the fourteenth-century plagues on. The contemporary advice literature to prepare for death even generated what some have seen as a dread of dying intestate. Certainly there were Roman texts expressing such a sense and they remained enshrined in the *Corpus iuris civilis*. Still, there were communities such as Florence that paid little statutory attention to testaments. In 1325 Florence did publish two brief rubrics demanding that *legata* be paid out without delay with the oversight of the podestà's court.[5] Arezzo and Montepulciano did not even have rubrics on that score. Otherwise there was no overt legislating in these Tuscan cities on the form wills took, number of witnesses, or other details past the solemnities required of notarial acts.

Some statutes addressed formal requirements for a will. One area of some concern was to establish the number of witnesses needed for a valid testament. Communities such as Milan, Novara, Pisa, Lucca, and Siena reduced the seven required by *ius commune* to two or three, even including women among those eligible to be witnesses.[6] Other communities opted for more (e.g., five) or kept the Roman law requirement, especially for nuncupative testaments (initially oral declaration as to who was *haeres* but by statute, for example at Novara in 1277–89, having to be written and subscribed by two notaries or by one notary with seven witnesses).[7] Cortona legislated that wills needed only five witnesses, and empowered judges to complete payment of legacies in one month.[8] Treviso in 1385 required seven witnesses, five in rural areas.[9] Perhaps that was also the rationale behind Treviso's and Padua's similar blessing of the last will over any prior ones.[10]

Bologna dedicated an extensive rubric to the making and validating of testaments. A male testator had to affirm personally that he was *sanus*; women or invalids had to do so too or through an agent, specifically established to do so; and for their wills a priest from the neighborhood had to be present, beyond the required number of witnesses. Notaries were required to keep both a cursory set of notes (in a *liber denunciationum*) and an extensive and complete copy (in a *liber memorialium*). The notary also had to send a herald to proclaim the fact of the will before at least two neighbors. If a male of twenty or over wanted to have a will that would remain private and secret, he could follow the *formam iuris* before

---

[5] Florence 1325, 2:113.   [6] Niccolai, *La formazione del diritto successorio,* 266–69.
[7] Niccolai, 272.   [8] Cortona, 339–42.   [9] Treviso, 368.
[10] Treviso, 368–69; Padua, 188.

seven witnesses and a priest or two religious and by hand of a notary; the will then had to be deposited at one of eight religious institutions of Bologna named in the statute. Following the testator's death, two of the monks or friars would take it to the podestà to be read publicly and have copies made by a notary for whomever wanted one. Witnesses to the will had to appear and attest to their signatures for the publication of "secret" wills.[11] In a city in which notaries took an active political role and tensions arose between them and the academic jurists and the courts, this rubric seems almost a paranoid attempt to keep some control on notaries and their clients.

Siena two centuries later also exercised oversight on the making of wills. Because "often the will of a testator is perverted, which yet must be observed insofar as it is possible," and to remove doubts that arose about testaments, they had to have three male witnesses and all the solemnities required of any valid notarial act. If the will did not take the form of a notarial act, then four male witnesses were needed. The most recent will carried the day, even if the last will posed any derogation or nullification of previous wills only in general terms. No will was valid without token bequests to the *Opera* of the cathedral and the hospital of Santa Maria della Scala. Three witnesses sufficed for codicils, notarized or not. But if the codicil contained substitutions (*fideicommissa universalia totius haereditatis*), it was valid only if it fulfilled all requirements for a testament. *Legata*, for pious or other purposes, were due immediately without necessity of an acceptance by heirs. A testator could leave sons and daughters or their descendants equally or unequally, by *legatum* or institution as heir. As long as the *legitima portio* was obtained, the will could not be contested. Falcidian and Trebellianic shares could be set aside by a testator.[12] In effect, while striving to reduce uncertainties in form, Siena's legislation looked to guarantee the wishes of the city's male and female testators, including the provisions they made for their spouses.

In Italian societies, where property was seen culturally as a family possession but legally as belonging to individuals, where wills allowed an individual some freedom to temper the rigidity of intestacy rules but not to forget one's kin, testaments were a frequent source of conflicts. They raised many legal problems. Too much was at stake in terms of tangible and symbolic values, and by their nature they were working changes on intestacy rules and expectations. The only way to disinherit

---

[11] Bologna 1335, 554–60.   [12] Siena, 249–52.

anyone was by will. The only way a prospective heir was passed over (*praeteritus*) was in a will. The only way bequests could come to other than heirs was by a *legatum* in a will or a *donatio causa mortis*. And against all that were various rules of law placing the will of a deceased in a quasi-sacrosanct position to be respected and enacted, unless it proved "unduteous" or illegal.

Studies of wills have uncovered an endless variety of strategies and tendencies on the part of testators. A strictly agnatic strategy, for example, would propel a father without legitimate sons to direct his property to brothers, nephews, or paternal cousins. They would be the ones in the community with the same surname and coat of arms, an overlapping set of relatives and friends, and possibly possession of contiguous properties. Instead some men in such a situation chose to benefit other relatives, even those connected by marriage who were not agnate, or wives, or illegitimate sons, or even daughters. They might fraction a substantial patrimony into numerous bequests to religious and charitable bodies, possibly also leaving handsome dowries or supplements to existing dowries to daughters and other female relatives. As Anna Bellavitis has reminded us, while wills are extraordinarily expressive, they are also deceptive. They can be read for testators' intentions and perhaps the circumstances of their lives, but "not as the proof of the reality of transmission of property from one generation to the other."[13]

In countless suits the simple formal validity of testaments was challenged (e.g., number of witnesses), though these sorts of challenges generally went to notarial guild courts of other local judicial panels without much in the way of learned intervention. Litigants' desires to change the outcome of wills led them to attack them on a variety of levels, and picky formal details were fair game.

The earlier jurists, faced in general with less complex testaments, had more fundamental matters of validity to struggle with. Testators sometimes left multiple testaments, each crafted at a different life moment. Children were born or, unfortunately, died; fortunes flourished and waned; one traveled or one remained more constantly at home. So many factors could persuade one to make a new will. Though more recent wills usually carried clauses abrogating earlier ones, and the rule was to take the most recent as the one to follow, there was always the possibility of challenge. In a case that came to Dino del Mugello, a testator made his

[13] Bellavitis, *Famille, genre, transmission*, 97.

first will in favor of an *extraneus* (in this context simply one who was not
suus et necessarius – namely, not a child, but possibly otherwise related)
but disinherited his son, citing one of the causes of disinheritance allowed
in the law. In his second will he named a different heir but in general
language affirmed the first will, and thus seemingly the disinheritance
contained therein. Dino argued that the second testament voided the first,
but as in the second there was no mention of the son, he was effectively
praeteritus and not *exhaeredatus* and could act against that will.[14] We see
here also some of the law's bias against disinheritance, if not against
testaments too greatly altering the default landscape of intestacy. Neglecting one's son in a testament ran too much against the grain. When another
man left *legata* to an emancipated son but passed over in silence the
grandsons who were still in his *potestas* by law, leaving his other two sons
as heirs in specific objects that he designated, Oldrado da Ponte overturned
the will for passing over the grandsons. They should have been necessary
and direct heirs for being *in potestate*. All the property then fell by intestacy. The *legata* were a dead letter, leaving their father, the emancipated
son to press his claim. The same son, who after his father's death had
effectively seized the family dwelling, was not subjected to the penalty set
out in the will if he did not remain content with its terms.[15] He had simply
secured his inheritance. Here again the basic validity of the will was
contested and here did not stand up to the challenge.

When the lord of Monte Lauro, Ponzio, emancipated his son Guido
by his first wife, he gave him lands and castles. Ponzio had two sons by
his second wife and he dedicated them to religious life. Yet when he
made his will, he named the younger of these two, Guglielmo, his heir,
and left some bequests to Giovanni, with direction to honor his wishes
and enter religious life. Giovanni ignored that directive, married, and
had a daughter named Delfina, who subsequently moved to gain at least
one of those castles and possibly quash the grandpaternal will. Paolo di
Castro declared that the parents could not dedicate children to religious
life by their vows, that Ponzio's will was invalid for not also instituting
Giovanni as heir, and the emancipation gift to Giovanni, though it
bound his hands with regard to making a will concerning those properties, stood, as both the testator's desire and as in accord with public
utility and the dignity of family to keep castles in male hands.[16] Delfina

[14] Dino, *cons.* 51, fols. 63vb–65va.   [15] Oldrado, *cons.* 138, fol. 51rb–vb.
[16] Di Castro, 1 *cons.* 375, fols. 196va–97rb.

got nothing from her grandfather, whom, after all, her father had disobeyed, even if di Castro saw that as his right.

The omnipresence and rapidity of death from plague raised spiritual concerns for at least one Florentine, who confided his last wishes to the abbot of Santa Croce, who was a kinsman (*consanguineus*). In his haste to see to his own salvation, his daughter, however, went unmentioned, and Baldo had no trouble quashing the entire will on that ground.[17] However admirable the father's desire to take steps for the good of his soul, it did not justify neglecting the very existence of his daughter (seemingly his only child), no matter the assurances he may have been given by his kinsman, the abbot.

Apart from a possible increase in the use of wills, triggered in part by the enormous increase in deaths, which both impelled bequests for one's soul and the need for substitutions (even more lengthy and thorough), the demographic effects put many estates in doubt and difficulty. No jurists in that period were more influential than the brothers Ubaldi. One of Angelo's *consilia* illustrates these demographic effects nicely. A will of 1385 saw a man divide his estate into five equal parts for his four sons and his wife. Later, "at a time of great plague" (*tempore magne pestis*), the parents died intestate, and a bit later so did one son, also intestate, leaving two children, ages sixteen and fourteen, though the elder son soon died. With the plague at large, the three surviving brothers made a common will, naming their sons (each had one) and their nephew by their dead brother, with all going to a sole survivor, if that was the case. Indeed, death did not stop there: first one of the brothers, then one of their sons, leaving his sister, and then another infant son, and then his father (one of the original four brothers), then the young girl. In all that time the survivors held in common, the last of the original brothers dying childless. The remaining nephew had a will drawn up containing various *legata* and naming as heir his nephew on his mother's side. Angelo needed to figure out how much came to the last brother, given their common will, and how much to his will-writing nephew, and thus to his named heir. After a narration that Angelo could only label "multum prolixa," he waded in, figuring who got what in order of death. Along the way he voided the will of the three brothers, as each only named his own son as heir and thus overlooked the others. The whole idea of a collective or joint testament just did not fit well into the individualistic framework of *ius commune*.

---

[17] Baldo, 4 *cons.* 114, fol. 29ra–b.

The nephew in fact ended up with over half as heir to all the others, while the surviving grandson retained the other quarter, even though he was deemed *mentecaptus*.[18]

When a Lucchese wrote his will, he had a pregnant wife. If she bore a son, he was heir; if a daughter, she got 500 florins. The estate otherwise went to the church of San Michele in Foro of Lucca. The wife later bore a girl who died during the testator's life. The wife again became pregnant, but the husband passed away before the birth, and indeed the wife died in the eighth month of her pregnancy. Her womb was cut open and the baby extracted, and the boy lived long enough to cry. San Michele and the intestate heirs contested the estates of father and mother. The will could be declared null for failure to make the daughter heir, but Baldo upheld it for instituting the son who lived to emit a sound. Of course, if the will stood, the church inherited because it was substituted to him. Then there was the argument that the will only referred to the first pregnancy, the one in course at the time the will was crafted. But Baldo invoked the idea that when in doubt a will should be interpreted so as to preserve it, and thus it had to be maintained here that the testator was thinking of all pregnancies.[19] The result then was that the church, not the kin, inherited.

As these few cases show, inheritance was a process, playing out over time, including in lawsuits and arbitrations, involving the dead but mainly the living. What heirs and legatees did was part of it. Their immediate problem was appraising a *haereditas* or a *legatum* for its worth (not all of that monetary only) and deciding to accept or reject it. But even before all that, there was the little matter of being aware of the death and of an inheritance or bequest. The hypothetical clock running down the interval in which an heir had to act or lose the claim to the next in line did not begin to run until the heir was aware of it. One man contested the claim of ignorance of the paternal testament on the part of a daughter. If her delay in accepting her portion of the estate was not licit, then he stood to gain by pressing the claim of his wife, her aunt. Baldo rehearsed a number of arguments that in law children were presumed to know a father's will. Even mere *consanguinei* were said to know the dealings of their relatives, more so as "father and son are considered the same person" (*patris et filii eadem persona censetur*). Conversation was presumed. Cohabitation meant they should know what happened in the house, where the will was made. *Conversatio*, *cohabitatio*, and *convicinitas* all told against her

---

[18] Angelo, *cons.* 54, fols. 27va–28ra.   [19] Baldo, 5 *cons.* 113, fol. 28rb–va.

ignorance. In fact, knowledge of a testament did not matter for a child as direct heir (*suus haeres*), only for a more distantly related heir (*extraneus*), though knowledge of its exact content (as of *legata*, *fideicommissa*, *tutela* and other matters) could not be presumed. In the end Baldo sided with the daughter, in part because she was not in fact a *suus haeres*, because by statute she could only get a dowry and *legata*. Even being in the house did not mean awareness of all that went on there, especially about a will that could be done in secrecy in a closed room. Above all, there was a general presumption of ignorance on the part of a woman. A mother might know of some things, but not a daughter.[20] In this case, Baldo upheld her inheritance against any right of the aunt.

When Cecco di Niccolò of Narni wrote his will, he made his two sons his heirs, substituted to each other, with a bequest of 500 *lire* and widowhood rights of habitation to his daughter, Masia (who in fact became a nun). At his death there were two sons and four daughters. That was thirty-three years before the case came to court. In the interim the sons died (at age fourteen, twenty-four years before; the other only ten years before, leaving a daughter with a bequest of 100 *lire* and a wife he had named his heir, also since deceased). Masia, who had also gained a bequest in the will of the brother who survived, stood to receive her father's bequest to her; but by statue at Narni she had six months to accept or repudiate it, and she had done neither because she was ignorant of the bequest. Only now did she come forth and try to claim what her father and brother had left her. There was also the problem of succession to her mother's dowry (dead forty-six years). Baldo took this case and dismissed the phalanx of questions it raised with amazing brevity. If she was indeed ignorant, then the statute could not harm her interests. She and her sister were heirs to the brother who died while yet a minor. She also had her rights to the bequest from the other brother and to the mother's dowry (in part because Narni was in an ecclesiastical state and canon law, rather than Roman law, rules of succession applied). However, as she had not married, she could not claim the dowry left her in her father's will.[21]

Testaments in the fifteenth century were still challenged on their fundamental validity from time to time. The Lucchese woman Mattea, formerly married to Giovanni di Simone da Viano and later to the physician Baldassare di Cristoforo di Borgo Muzano, sued Antonio di Piero of the

---

[20] Baldo, 3 *cons.* 245, fol. 83va–b. [21] Baldo, 4 *cons.* 145, fol. 36rb–va.

local convent of spirituals over the inheritance of her son Francesco. She argued that there were no surviving relatives who could exclude her from the intestate inheritance by the statute of Lucca; he replied that there was a testament naming him heir, and he produced it. The jurist Giovanni da Imola proceeded to defend it as valid, noting, among other things, that it was not void for passing over the mother, as there was no requirement she be mentioned, and in any case she had been provided for her widowhood. But he also went on to defend Mattea's right to a legitimate portion, as she indeed was not statutorily excluded in the circumstances.[22] So she did not gain it all but she still came out ahead as a result of her suit. In another case Paolo di Castro said that a daughter could not break her father's will because she had been dowered, even if not from his property but from maternal goods. Statutory law commanded that she remain content with that dowry. This woman had, in fact, received an additional 300 *lire* from her father, and he had male heirs who precluded her, and her sons, not just from the paternal estate but those of her mother, uncle, and grandfather.[23]

A later case demonstrates other sorts of problems that could arise, and here teased the talents of Giason del Maino. Paolo Costabili of Ferrara, a noble and doctor, directed his property to his wife as heir, as long as she remained a chaste widow. Following her, came his son Alberto by substitution, showing that her claim was in fact envisioned as a lifetime use. If Alberto failed to have heirs, the substitute was the testator's brother, count Raynaldo. Subsequently Alberto died following Paolo's death, while the mother was still alive. It was asserted that Alberto had drawn up a will in his mother's favor, supposedly by the hand of a notary and seven witnesses, but "as is believed, dictated previously by the mother." It was also reported that the son had later changed his mind and made another will with a different notary, but it was not produced in evidence. Meanwhile, the mother made a will in favor of her daughters, ostensibly leaving Raynaldo the patrimony with an obligation to fund 500 for each girl, plus some other bequests that he would lose if he "molested" the girls about their title. At her deathbed the mother was asked before those present to clarify that she wanted her husband's estate to go to his brother, and she provided that. As Ferrara had a statute excluding women in favor of agnates within four degrees, the problem was whether Alberto had died intestate and thus opened the door to the statute. In other words,

---

[22] Imola, *cons.* 114, fols. 65va–67vb.   [23] Di Castro, 1 *cons.* 196, fols. 99rb–100ra.

was his rather shadowy will valid? Did the mother get the property, then to give it to Raynaldo with conditions attached, or was it his free and clear of those by substitution to Alberto? Maino threw himself into a maze of technicalities by which he could determine that Alberto's will was "imperfect" and did not hold.[24]

The burden of *legata* could leave too little for heirs, and that provoked a category of cases. For example, Gregorio of the noble family of Cesenate de Fabris had as heirs his wife Francesca and an agnate named Onofrio. Each received a house worth 1,000 scudi, among other *legata*, which, all told, consumed the estate, such that the Falcidian quarter had to be carved out. At the time of Gregorio's death in 1529 Francesca was thought pregnant, and any son would have superseded her and Onofrio as heirs. They settled various of the *legata*, setting aside a Falcidian portion; and then when it emerged that she was not pregnant, Francesca took possession with benefit of inventory, completed March 3, 1530. On her death in 1542 her brother Sebastiano became her heir but was faced with a situation where half was due Onofrio and half to Cristoforo de Fabris. Could he at least get a Falcidian quarter for himself? Because she had not reserved herself a Falcidian quarter before paying out so many *legata*, and because she had made the inventory well after the thirty days allowed, it looked as if Francesca's heir had little recourse. But Mariano Sozzini found him some legal arguments. An heir burdened with *legata*, for whom not even a quarter remained, had a right to deduct from the bequests and get that quarter. That right was not diminished or lost by the passage of time. Francesca had paid *legata* without knowing the extent of the estate, and so in error paid them off in their entirety. She could have sought some of that back. The timing of the inventory was also defended, noting that it had to be done before a judge (notary) and the thirty days counted the time allowed as his "useful" days and not a continuous run of time. By that count, she initiated the inventory at the time she formally took possession, the first point she truly knew it was hers, because she was not pregnant.[25]

Another factor that could be invoked against a will was if it directed property to an otherwise disadvantaged class of persons, such as illegitimates. Wills could often override statutory disabilities placed on intestacy, but the prejudice behind them remained to affect judgments about wills. To take a fairly late example here, Aloisio de' Tacoli of Reggio

[24] Del Maino, 2 *cons.* 148, 645a–52a. [25] Sozzini, 3 *cons.* 19, fols. 28va–29va.

made his son Francesco heir with prohibition on selling the family home, which he wanted to stay with "confratres de Tacolis." If Francesco produced no heirs, then the estate went to two daughters for life and thereafter to other Tacoli, though the house should go to Piero de' Tacoli alone. Francesco fathered an illegitimate son, Vincenzo, on a certain Magdalena. As both parents were unmarried, the boy was termed *naturalis*, and his father had him legitimated by a count palatine. But in his will, having about exhausted his wealth in a number of *legata*, Francesco instituted Vincenzo as heir to a third, "so effectively to almost nothing" (*et sic effectualiter quasi in nihilo*). Vincenzo then tried to realize the entire estate on the basis of the substitution in Aloisio's will on the grounds that he was one of the Tacoli. Against him it could be contended that he was not in fact *naturalis*, as his mother had not been a concubine kept in the home, and so the pretense to the legitimation was false and the act null in consequence. Giason del Maino took his side, arguing he was *naturalis* and thus called to inherit by Aloisio's will. He noted there were two forms or meanings of *naturalis*. One indeed hinged on the housed and loved concubine, which held "on account of having certainty of offspring (*propter habendam certitudinem prolis*), otherwise women could easily fake having sons by any magnate and noble and so our inheritances would pass to strangers." The other was a more vulgar sense that the parents simply were unmarried, though they could have been, and the parents recognized the child as theirs and raised him. At least by canon law and common speech Vincenzo was *naturalis*. By terms of Aloisio's will it did not matter that Vincenzo's legitimacy was somehow "minus."[26]

In all these instances jurists came to take part when the legal issue was something more substantial than the number of witnesses or similar formal details. Possible disinheritance certainly called for juristic intervention.

Women and Wills

The one area regarding testaments in which Florence took a lead was in restricting women's ability to receive by or have a testament. Generally there was more attention, in Florence and elsewhere, to what women might do with a testament than with what they might obtain by one. That women might have a will was conceded only obliquely in the first

---

[26] Del Maino, 3 *cons.* 51, 183a–87a.

redaction of Florentine (1325) statutes at the same point it leveled a restriction, when a husband of a predeceased wife was said to receive a third of nondotal goods if there were no children, despite his wife's will.[27] Of course this statute followed on that concerning intestacy, which also specified that where succession was, in fact, testate and something had been left to a woman who had a *ius commune* possibility of inheriting, "she is and must be content and may in no way seek more." That provision carried through to the later redactions.[28] That of 1415 noted that a woman with inheritance rights left nothing in a will could seek the portion she would have received on intestacy, but without otherwise voiding the other provisions of a valid will, which is what would result if a man were to contest such a will. That same redaction also inserted a rule that wives could not make a testament or a *donatio causa mortis* to the harm of their husbands, children, of other descendants.[29] The contrast to Venice was clear, as there a law of 1474 stepped in to keep husbands from being present when their wives made their wills, which were the only means by which husbands could inherit from their wives, so they were present as self-interested parties. But it was also the case in Venice that husbands did not get their wives' dowries, and procedures were readily available for widows to reclaim their dowries. So Venetian husbands seemed to want to gain by testament what Florentine husbands had by statute.

Genoese women too enjoyed wider freedom of testation, although fathers or husbands were often present. In both maritime cities testaments of women, married or widowed, tended to single out other women as beneficiaries of bequests. Women there also frequently found themselves the managers of family property as a result of a husbands' absence on business or on their deaths. Their activities and their wills demonstrate what capable managers they could be.

Women in southern Italian regions also generally "enjoyed juridical-patrimonial conditions more favorable with respect to that of the women of central and northern Italy."[30] While these areas saw a conversion to a more patrilineal family model, closer to that of the north, in the course of the fourteenth and fifteenth centuries, following the plague, influence on and control of property by a woman's family of origin continued to be felt. In contrast to north and central Italy, married women had testaments more often; they did not have to wait for widowhood (as Chabot finds

---

[27] Florence 1325, 130.   [28] Florence 1325, 129.
[29] Chabot, *Le dette des familles*, 52–53.   [30] Mainoni, "Il potere di decidere," 214.

was generally the case for Florence) to be free to write a will. Women around Bari had property rights that became the frequent focus of disputes, if only because those rights often resulted in title to houses and other real properties. Women's wills directed property to husbands and to daughters, as well as sons.

Other communities controlled women's testamentary activities in like manner to Florence. Belluno decreed that a woman with children had to leave her property to them, and in such a way that sons or their male descendants received at least half, less a "just" amount for pious bequests.[31] On the other hand, Foligno promoted the testamentary rights of women without children, even against interference, nonconsent, or fear of one's father, brother, mother, or other kin.[32] But if a woman had children, she could not make a will without spousal consent, and *consanguinei* could stand in for the husband if he was away. A mother in Foligno could not keep property given to her by a son after his death, but she had to restore it to his heirs.[33] Similarly an unmarried woman left a dowry in a *legatum* had to remain content with that.[34] Lucca too limited the portion of her dowry that a woman could dispose of by testament, reserving the lion's share to husband and children.[35]

Saona saw a regulation to void all testaments made by women, in writing or not, executed in any church since February 1294. In fact, women were forbidden to do any contract in a church.[36] So in this community there was some wariness of what clergy, especially friars minor, might get women to do. Otherwise, as we saw in chapter three, this community was rather accommodating to women's contracts and legal actions. While Saona looked to what came from women, Colle Val d'Elsa looked at what came to them and quite simply affirmed that women could inherit *ex testamento* from any of those from whom they were excluded on intestacy by Colle's statute.[37] Along those lines Montepulciano enacted that any woman left something in a will, and later given something by the testator, such as for her dowry, had to count that gift toward the testamentary bequest and not seek more.[38]

Bologna stated that daughters or other females left something in father's, mother's, or other ascendant's will, even if not sufficient as *legitima*, could not move a suit against the will. Women named as heirs, as opposed to mere legatees, could seek more to the point of a whole share

[31] Belluno, 235, 238.   [32] Foligno, 2:93–94.   [33] Foligno, 2:148–49.
[34] Foligno, 1:88.   [35] Paterni, "Le leggi," 65–66.   [36] Saone, 186–87.
[37] Colle, 304.   [38] Montepulciano, 142.

of *legitima*. Women here too were to remain content with any dowry left them.[39] Treviso legislated that a married woman could make a will with two of her kin present (or one man and one woman or two women, if there were not even one man available) within six degrees of relationship. If these kin refused or simply did not exist, the podestà could officiate a woman's will with a notary recording, and no one present could interrupt or change her mind. A married woman of Treviso who was outside the city could proceed to establish a will without anyone and, provided she reaffirmed it fifteen days later, it would stand.[40] Trevisan women were permitted by statute to leave their husbands whatever they wanted, and it did not count in the half that husbands were already entitled to by statute from predeceasing wives.[41] Forlì also allowed women free testation as long as children of a first marriage were not thereby defrauded. But a widow could not seek anything from her husband unless there was a *legatum* in his will to her.[42] Women given dowries in a will had to be content with what was left them.[43]

Viterbo prohibited a woman with children, especially from multiple unions, from testating to others than her children, allowing 10 percent for pious bequests. Such a woman was permitted, on the testimony of two close kin, to alienate from her property for necessities. And her sons were to have equal shares, no matter what she might have put in a will or codicil. Similar constraints fell on a childless woman who had a brother or nephews, as she could make a will but only with their consent. There was a parallel restriction on men with a second wife and children, from leaving the second wife more than a quarter, beyond her dowry and "habitationem condecentem" and *alimenta* for life, which came to the same percentage a wife with children could leave her husband. Fathers with children by two marriages were constrained to leave an equal amount to both, "because stepmothers often are accustomed to plot against step-daughters" (*quia noverce sepe solent insidiari privignis*).[44]

Milan's statutes of 1498 said wives could testate property other than dowry, which was to profit the husband by terms of other rubrics, without spousal consent. A childless woman could not testate until she had been married ten years.[45] A husband by will could leave his wife one-quarter which was a provision consistent back to 1216.[46] Vicenza in 1425 directed that a woman with children could leave her husband

---

[39] Bologna, 561–62.   [40] Treviso, 374–76.   [41] Treviso, 381.   [42] Forlì, 353.
[43] Forlì, 354.   [44] Viterbo, 145–47.   [45] Milan 1498, fol. 88r.
[46] Milan 1498, fol. 87r.

something, but she had to leave the same amount to her children, who could in turn realize the father's share after his death.[47]

Many communities thus sought to limit the testamentary capacity of women or limit what spouses could leave each other, or even leave as pious and charitable interests.[48] The general success of these rules, at least with regard to married women, emerges from the low percentages of them among a community's testators. Married women who had wills were mainly women without children. Venice was an exception, as were southern communities. Widows had more opportunity to make wills, but they still faced whatever restrictions their community might have erected. Jurists would have plenty of business adjudicating women's wills or bequests to them.

Surviving testaments disclose that women were less frequently in the position of testator than men, although it is also remarkable how frequently they did write wills. They show up in *consilia* rather less than one would suppose, possibly because their wills disposed of less value (and thus less dispute) or because they were simpler in their terms on the whole. Statutory concerns emerged at points.

Assisi had a statute to the effect that no woman could make a will unless in the presence of her son(s), or grandsons, or brothers or their sons. Angeluzia had three daughters, all dowered, and one son who was in exile (*exbannitus*), as well as three granddaughters by one of the daughters, and two adult nephews from her brother. She made a will without son or nephews present, making bequests to the daughter with children and the exiled son, but naming someone else, Becco Accoli, as her heir. The testatrix soon died and later her exiled son did as well, leaving a dowered daughter. As a man in exile could not be present at the making of the will, his absence was not at issue. It was that the nephews were not present. On that basis Baldo declared the will null and concluded that her property went to intestate heirs. That was the exiled son who could not come forward to claim it, so it went to his heir, who was his daughter, to the exclusion of the same fisc that had exiled him.[49] Angelo, for his part, upheld a similar statute and also voided a woman's will, rendering her estate intestate and, in this case, giving a dowered daughter access to it, as no longer excluded by statute because the mother was not the dowering party.[50] So too, when another woman ignored the

[47] Niccolai, *La formazione del diritto successorio*, 290.
[48] Niccolai, 285–93; Chabot, *Le dette des familles*, 53.
[49] Baldo, 3 *cons.* 399, fol. 113ra.   [50] Angelo, *cons.* 226, fol. 67ra–b.

statute, confecting a testament without the presence of her grandson, to whom she left 100 florins among various *legata* to other persons and to pious causes, Angelo struck down the will. The solemnities attached to the making of a will were elements of positive and civil law and thus open to change by statute, and there was no *odium* attached to that, indeed it served the public good, "lest an account of the weakness of the sex and the coaxing of others by threats or terror sons may be defrauded of the maternal estate on account of their absence."

The statute was not made to the woman's favor, it was to the son's and the *res publica's*.[51] There was an evident unwillingness to see the combination of testaments and statutes deprive a prospective (on intestacy) heir. It was better to quash the testament.

In another case from Castello, where the issues were whether dowries left in a mother's will were in fact from her property (so a *legitima* might yet be claimed from the father), and whether the wife's will was valid, when done not in the presence of her husband, due to the plague, it was the local language of the statute and not ideological principle that decided. In defending the wife's will at the time of plague, Pierfilippo da Corgna conceded that the social effects of plague had to be accommodated by the law, as "men are not accustomed to want to invite the presence of someone sick with this disease, so that it happens commonly that neighbors and others are not able to be had but commonly are avoided."[52]

Closely related to the validity of wills was the issue of testamentary capacity, which mainly applied to women's wills – or at least that was where statutes would collide with learned law and raise interesting issues. Siena's statute prohibiting women from alienating goods to the prejudice of their children came under scrutiny by Pierfilippo da Corgna. It seemed that a woman had given away more than the quarter allowed by Sienese law to the harm of her daughter's son, although the testament by which she had acquired the property gave her total freedom of disposition. That was the basis on which Corgna backed the gift, for the testator had set a condition contrary to municipal law. Yet a testator could "forbid that his goods be transferred or alienated to another." The testator's will (in a valid testament) was law.[53]

When a mother left her married daughter a sum of money and named her son as heir, the son resisted his sister's claim on the grounds of statutes forbidding a mother to make a will to other than *filii* or bequeath more

---

[51] Angelo, *cons.* 88, fol. 45ra–va.   [52] Corgna, *cons.* 316, fols. 250rb–51vb.
[53] Corgna, *cons.* 132, fol. 112ra–va.

than 10 percent *pro anima*. The sister appealed to the common law freedom of testation and to the gender-inclusiveness of the word *filii*. Paolo di Castro defended the terms of the will, noting that this mother had not provided for anyone other than her children and that the statutes also mentioned daughters, so *filii* was inclusive.[54] He defended a woman's claim against her brother, albeit on the mother's estate, not the father's. In another case looking at the same law, di Castro said that the statute created a situation "as if this mother had two patrimonies, one free, in which she can establish anyone as heir, in a fourth of her goods. The other by disposition of the statute reserved for children, which reservation is of no less vigor than the institution of the mother, and this lest this mother be defrauded by disposition of law, and so that the intent of the statute is to be served and absurdity avoided." In this case, the sons actually ended up as heirs neither *ex testamento* (for they were not covered by their mother's will) nor *ab intestato* (as she left a will) but by a third mode *tanquam successores utiles*. For the rest, di Castro argued that the statute excluding a dowered daughter still held, especially as the statute here voided the maternal will.[55]

Bartolomeo Cipolla faced a different and somewhat unique set of circumstances in another woman's will. This *rusticana* was a widow with a 200 ducat dowry, who remarried to a poor peasant. During the several years of their married life the return on her property went to household expenses; but she controlled and administered her wealth herself. She wrote a will leaving her husband as heir, with condition that if he died without children (tacitly accepting, it seems, the potential for his remarriage) her money would be distributed to the poor. The husband survived her for twenty-seven years, using the property she had left him. His heirs (not children) tried to claim half of it by virtue of Verona's statute giving a husband half the dowry of his predeceased wife and forbidding her testament to alter that proportion. But was this dowry? Cipolla said no. There was no presumption here that this was dowry, even though she had brought this into the marriage. A woman was not obligated to dower herself, and in this case the wife had not even tolerated her husband administering her money. He conceded, however, that a wife did owe her husband for marital expenses, such that a testamentary settlement to a husband could be said to derive from a desire to repay (*animo compensandi*). In the event, at a standardized rate of 5 percent per annum, the

---

[54] Di Castro, 1 *cons.* 427, fol. 220rb–vb.   [55] Di Castro, 1 *cons.* 441, fols. 227rb–28rb.

husband had been fully compensated after twenty years, so he gained an extra seven years' worth and his heirs gained nothing. All the property was to be made available to the poor.[56]

Remarriage complicated women's wills too. Monna Vanna had one married daughter and in her will she named Jacoba and her father Giovanni as heirs. If Giovanni died first, she substituted Jacoba and she also enjoined Giovanni from alienating any of her property. After she died, he remarried and had several children. He also sold off a farm that was Vanna's without Jacoba's knowledge. When Vanna died, Jacoba repudiated her share and the half-siblings took their father's estate. But she sought the farm back, which she and her husband in fact worked, though the purchaser claimed she had repudiated it. Capra easily dismissed the sale by Giovanni as invalid, noting also that by the substitution in Vanna's will, Jacoba was heir to the entire farm, not to mention that remarriage cost him title, so he only had usufruct from that point. That lack of title was also why his children by his second wife had no possibility of claiming a trebellianic portion from the estate of Vanna through him. Bartolomeo Capra also absolved Jacoba and her husband of charges of theft leveled by the purchaser of the farm.[57]

In Treviso, master Pietro, a surgeon, had married off his daughter to her first husband with a 400 ducat dowry and an agreement that the survivor between the two spouses would realize a gain of half that value. So when the daughter outlived her husband, she received her 400 and another 200 besides. She then remarried with no dowry promised to the second husband, although she had also made a will following the specifications of Treviso's statute about married women's wills, leaving all she had to her husband if she died childless, which she did. The second husband claimed all 600 ducats or, failing that, half by another statute about dowries and paraphernalia. But did he get anything, especially as she had been *in potestate* and made that will without permission from her father? It seems, having been married already and living apart from her father, this woman had simply taken some control, and her father seems not to have felt a need to intervene in a second marriage. Her testament, by statute, had been executed in the presence of two *propinqui*, because her father and brother had not wanted to participate. As dowry was *patrimonium filiae*, she could dispose of it. But in law a *filiafamilias*

---

[56] Cipolla, 2 *cons.* 5, 23a–25a.   [57] Capra, *cons.* 93, fols. 133va–35rb.

could not make a will, not even on the dowry, because she was not *sui iuris*. The statute did not validate it, even though she had met its terms, because it had to be understood *secundum ius commune*, which regulated testaments of women able to make one, which a daughter *in potestate* was not. The statute was merely intended to restrict *ius commune* by adding a consent requirement. With the will a dead letter, the next concern was if the same agreement about half the dowry value going to the survivor carried over to the second marriage, and on this there was a statute to take account of. Bartolomeo Cipolla labored long and hard on this aspect of the case, concluding that the statute was for the benefit of the father or whomever established the dowry, not the husband. So the second husband netted nothing. If it could be shown that the wife had explicitly promised a gain of half her dowry to her second husband, that would be invalid by *ius commune*, because she did not have her father's permission. Informed, however, that Treviso had a statute that a woman *constante matrimonio* could not alienate, except with consent of two or three agnates, Cipolla briefly put it, "If that is the case, the promise may not be valid unless the solemnities are observed. . . . And because I did not see the statute I do not insist about anything else in regard to this."[58] Here *ius commune* and not statute invalidated a woman's will, but it was also a will in favor of husband in the absence of children and not father (or his heirs).

Near the end of the sixteenth century Geronima Papafava left a will in favor of her four sons, with substitution *in infinitum*, then to daughters if all male lines failed. Her will thus betrayed an agnatic bias that her husband would have understood. When one son died leaving a daughter, the three brothers got a decree on 27 September that his share was theirs; but the daughter got a similar ruling in her favor on 8 November. Marcantonio Pellegrini argued that the testator's intent was clear; she was thinking of all male descendants and thus was setting up a reciprocal *fideicommissum* among the brothers.[59] The daughter was not heir. That case almost seemed too easy, but the daughter (or someone for her) had a moment of success around a different reading of the testament, as Pellegrini was arguing on appeal against the finding in a local rural court of first instance. This case is a good example how far people might go to dispute a will, with much to gain and seemingly little to lose, as the daughter does not seem to have had much of a case.

[58] Cipolla, 2 *cons.* 39, 162a–67a.   [59] Pellegrini, *cons.* 54, fols. 149va–51vb.

Women as Heirs

This case also reminds us that property coming to women was also a frequent and difficult issue across the centuries of concern to us. Generally property came to women in the form of a bequest, but on occasion women were also designated as heir to the testator. We will begin with those cases.

Typically, when women were named as heirs, there was no son or other close male available to take the estate. That was the situation a man named Matteo found himself in. He had two girls by his first wife. One, Benvenuta, ceded her rights in her mother's dowry to a messer Angelo for 165 florins and the next day was married with a 200 florin dowry. Then Matteo remarried and had three more girls, the last born posthumously. Matteo left dowries of 250 florins for each of the three girls alive when he died, along with the bequest of restitution of dowry and another 100 florins to his second wife. The as yet unborn child was given a 200 florin dowry, if a girl, or the status of universal heir, if a boy. Lacking a male heir Matteo named all these five daughters as heirs, requiring the married Benvenuta to collate her dowry. The first problem for Baldo degli Ubaldi was whether her cession of rights at marriage kept Benvenuta out. But her father had included her in the substitutions among the daughters, indicating that he saw her as an heir, and her cession had been to the maternal dowry and not the father's estate. She also won when Baldo said she did not have to return into the estate the 165 florins, simply the 200 florin dowry. One presumed that the father's concern for his daughter had seen him use the 165 to make the dowry. The other girls all had to confer their dowries into the estate, which would leave them all even and not lead to envy (*invidia*). The one sister who had died young was to be succeeded equally by her two full sisters. The mother was left out, but there was an equal division otherwise.[60]

Failure to mention a daughter, especially when there were no sons, was liable to invalidate a will. When a grandfather left his granddaughter nothing from his estate but a bequest from her dead mother's estate, and the granddaughter sued to break the will, Baldo decided that her argument had merit. Local statute, it was true, seemed to disinherit women, but only on condition they were dowered. In a strict reading, as the statute did not mention granddaughters, they were not covered by it,

[60] Baldo, 2 *cons.* 37, fols. 8rb–9ra.

even when fortuitously dowered from property in the maternal line.[61] In the absence of a male heir and with the statute not applying, the grand-daughter had full status as *haeres*.

In October 1377 Angelo degli Ubaldi addressed a case in which Piero left his daughter Spineta a dowry of 1,000 florins and 50 more annually "as long as Spineta does not seek her legitim." He otherwise named his hoped-for future sons his heirs with a substitution to two hospitals. There was no provision in the will for a subsequent daughter, Maria. At some point after the will was written, an arbitrator settled affairs between Piero and Spineta by giving her her mother's dowry of 400 florins, because Piero was required to dower his daughter "in accord with the capacity of his patrimony" (*secundum facultatem sui patrimonii*). The arbitrator further directed that Piero pay her another 645 florins for her dowry, with stipulation that she and her husband not seek anything more. Spineta's dowry in actual payments of 400 and 475 came to 875. After that arrangement, Piero married off Maria with a 400 florin dowry. Maria died leaving a son, Giovanni. On his behalf the will was contested to keep Piero's property from going to the hospitals he had substituted as heirs.

This testator seems to have been fairly ignorant of the law or at least negligent, because he never incorporated Maria into his will. Nor did he make provision for his grandson by her. That was where the will, according to Angelo, failed. Recognizing that the institution of an heir was the essential function of a testament, the failure to mention Maria and her son, who at his grandfather's death was first in order of intestate succession, broke the will. The "ruptured" testament meant the estate passed in intestacy, but the expression of the deceased's desires could not be entirely ignored. The testator knew he had a daughter and her son and yet had done nothing to change his will or otherwise accommodate them, so it might seem that his resolve was firm regarding the substitution to the hospitals. But it was hardly realistic (*verisimile*) to believe the testator would have wanted to prefer such outsiders to his own descendants. Angelo found that Piero was both prudent in stipulating that any sons born to him in the future gained the estate and yet also imprudent for not taking account of a grandson he knew. This interpretation, Angelo claimed, coincided with four rules of nature and presumptions, among which he included "the common wish to have estates go to descendants" and "the rationale of presumed duty and paternal advice, for duty of a

[61] Baldo, 1 *cons.* 2, fol. 2rb–va.

father or grandfather is always to use healthy advice ('salubre consilium') for children." He went on then to declare that Spineta and Giovanni, as Maria's heir, should share the estate equally, while she kept her mother's dowry, but her own dowry (the part actually paid) and Maria's dowry were to be factored back into the estate.[62]

In the fifteenth century Bartolomeo Cipolla upheld a will in which a daughter was named heir under a condition, with a nephew in her place if the condition was not fulfilled. If the condition were against the law, the will might be voided, but one had to presume the notary had been accurate and the testator wanted what was written, which was not against the law but "most honest and tends to concord and marital honor" (*honestissimam et tendat ad concordiam et honestatem maritalem*). The condition? That within one month her husband expel from his house his concubine. While her status as heir might well be an incentive for her husband to put an end to de facto bigamy, to see her realize the estate, it would seem that fulfilling the condition was out of her hands; and Cipolla noted that it was not just to deprive her for the acts or failings of a third party. Cipolla, however, upheld the condition on analogy to a bequest on condition that the slave it was directed to had been freed. Indeed, the key to this provision, after Cipolla ran it through various possible objections, was that "in view of the fact that the son-in-law and his father were alive, to whom usufruct must be attributed, the testator wanted to punish them and not the daughter or her descendants." The daughter in fact got a legitimate portion in any case, so she was only hurt for whatever the difference was. The testator could have left her heir with simply the condition that usufruct not go to the husband as long as the concubine stuck around, but Cipolla said that move would incite marital discord, because husbands commonly wanted and had usufruct of their wives' paraphernalia.[63] One wonders what happened in this household, even as a nephew seemingly walked off with the bulk of the estate.

Another testator made his daughter Dolceta and her children his heirs, and when he died she and her two daughters succeeded, including to a separate bequest of 50 florins. It was not clear if they all succeeded at once or the girls succeeded to their mother. In any case, after the mother's death, one daughter was married off by her father with the promise of a 400 ducat dowry from her mother's estate, for which, though she was less than twenty, she was made to renounce on oath any right to seek any

---

[62] Angelo, *cons.* 364, fols. 204ra–5ra. [63] Cipolla, 2 *cons.* 61, 220a–25a.

more, when in fact there was both more in her mother's estate and the
400 was never paid. The husband was due usufruct on her parapherna,
but as he was *in potestate*, it would go to his father. She too was *in
potestate*, so could she compel her father to give her her share? Did she
need to accept the maternal estate? Paolo di Castro went through these
issues one by one. It was a successive estate. The mother was sole heir. If
she did not want to be heir, the girls took over by a vulgar substitution; if
she became heir and died they succeeded by *fideicommissum*. The husband who had not received the promised dowry had every right to act, but
so did the daughter/wife, as the father was supposed to dower from his
goods and he had not, and so he still faced that "natural" obligation. The
girl's renunciation was void, as it had not followed the prescriptions in a
statute for contracts of minors and because it "enormously" harmed the
girl, as she gave up much more than the dowry. The husband's father
could not gain usufruct because it was a personal right. The daughter
would stand in full possession of her mother's property and could invoke
the protection of inventory.[64] Here di Castro clearly had no sympathy for
a father who had exercised all his power to his benefit, even against the
wishes of the testator – in this case the plaintiff's grandfather.

One wife was instituted heir by her husband, with a portion equal to
her daughters' to carry her through widowhood; but she also received a
specified part of the estate if she remarried. Her portion should devolve to
the daughter or others of the testator's lineage after her death. Substitutions to the daughters also declared that their death without children put
the estate to the paternal lineage (*ad cippum domus*). The portion of a
daughter who died should go usually to the uncle rather than by substitution to another daughter, but the existence of such a substitution showed
that the testator loved his daughter more than his brother and wanted his
property to remain "to his descendants not to outsiders or transverse
kin." A daughter was undeniably *de domo patris*. According to Bartolo,
in Tuscany *domus* was "taken for all descendants from one stem (*ab uno
stipite*) and so also for a daughter who immediately descends from the
paternal branch." Despite that, Pierfilippo da Corgna finally sided with
the brother's claim. *Domus*, he argued, had many meanings: agnation,
potestas, sharing insignia and arms:

for often we see that they are said to be of the same house and same clan or lineage
(*de eadem domo et de eadem consortoria seu casata*) those who share no blood

---

[64] Di Castro, 2 *cons.* 455, fols. 211rb–12rb.

among themselves, as the common form of speech has it. Yet commonly many of the same house are agnate to each other, therefore it is no wonder if house is taken for agnation, and especially in a last will when agnates truly are more loved of the testator than others of the house not agnate.

So those who were both *de domo* and agnate were the most loved and preferred, as opposed to the *familiares* and *servi* who lived there. Women did not preserve agnation and, if dowered, were often excluded by statute everywhere in Italy. The *mens testatoris* was here presumed to be consonant with the *mens iurislatoris*:

In similar appellation of the house of the line taken for family agnation or clan (*cippi domus sumpte pro familia agnatione vel consortoria*) do not come all those of the house or the agnation or the clan, but those persons through whom family or clan powerfully receive stability, foundation, and greater perpetuity (*stabilitatem fundamentum et maiorem perpetuitatem*), understanding line properly proceeding from like to like.

Women were like the leaves and fronds of the family tree, which easily fell away. The women in this instance were married and in the homes of others. That was the custom: "at Perugia are termed of the same house all residents who bear the same arms and are dubbed with the same name and they are accustomed here in Perugia that married women commonly are named by the husband's house and not the father's and to use the husband's arms in these matters in which women use arms, as happens in signing letters and offering rings." Pierfilippo da Corgna claimed to have been consistent in this regard in cases from Assisi and Foligno. The dead sister's share went to her uncle.[65]

Gemma's father left everything to his only daughter. If she died before age twenty-five childless, he directed the proceeds from sale of a house be spent for his soul and his parents'. In that case too his dead wife's dowry should be returned to her father's family. Gemma lived to marry and have her own daughter, Elizabetta. Then at age twenty-four, being ill, Gemma made a will giving her husband her 200 ducat dowry and usufruct of the house, naming Elizabetta her heir, though the girl in fact soon died, even before her mother. When her husband too died, his father was his closest relation. So he took over the estate of Gemma's father. The charities that were to step in by the father's will contested the father-in-law's possession. Benedetto Capra waded into this, first determining that Gemma was her father's heir, but then deciding that the substitution came into play,

---

[65] Corgna, *cons.* 55, fols. 50rb–51va.

even though she seemed to have passed *pubertas* and had a child, though Elizabetta had preceded her mother in death. His argument was that the testamentary clause was to be "construed and should be construed in a way that may result perfect prose and good Latinity" (*oratio prefecta et bona latinitas*), such that any judge would figure the testator wanted substitution at any age if Gemma had no children. There was also a tacit burden in the will on Gemma to preserve the estate for the substitute heirs. The *legatum* returning the maternal dowry to her family was invalid, as Gemma had inherited that and her father could not give it away. Gemma's own will did not hold because her heir, little Elizabetta, died before her, but the "institution" of her husband in the bequest of her dowry elevated him to heir by *iure codicillorum*, and his father was clearly his heir.[66] So Gemma's father's will was cast in a particular direction while her own was rendered moot, except to benefit her father-in-law with her dowry, while her father's property went to the unnamed charities.

At the end of the sixteenth century Marcantonio Pellegrini was still looking at women as heirs. A case came to him from Basinensi, where Marietta, heir by testament to her husband, sought title to property by virtue of her efforts (*industria*) and not as part of her husband's business, which was directed to the local priest as heir. Marietta, Pellegrini found, had only a modest holding, her eighty ducat dowry, so it could easily be maintained that whatever she had was her husband's. But he backed her claims, not just because she had been named heir and the intent of the testator deserved enforcement, but because she realized the fruits of some fields her husband owned and she exercised the cloth trade with him.[67] Of course, there were no sons or agnates waiting in the wings, so it was easy to support the wife's claims.

Bequests to Women

So different were the designs of testators, in the face of seemingly rigid rules of succession, that it becomes truly difficult to identify tendencies and characterize their moves. The interpretive grid of the law, laying atop the formulas imposed by notaries on testators' expressions, imposed some degree of coherence to these. By far the commonest theme in juristic interpretations was that of giving expression and consequence to the *mens*

---

[66] Capra, *cons.* 66, fols. 93ra–95rb.   [67] Pellegrini, *cons.* 54, fols. 149va–51vb.

testatoris. While historians are indeed well advised not to take wills as the blue prints of actual property settlements, they can take the interpretations of jurists as at least powerful suggestions as to what they thought an inheritance settlement should look like.

A will allowed for the confluence of legatees of all sorts alongside heirs, and the potential for conflict among them was ever present. Bequests were a perennial problem for jurists and at least a confusing factor for historians. Many of these were directed to charitable or religious bodies or uses. Many were directed to friends, relatives, or even to some of the heirs. But an enormous proportion was destined for women, quite often as provision for a dowry, or as widowhood support for a wife. Where property went to women, it seems, there were bound to be other interests in conflict.

Bartolo faced a case concerning the estate of Massio di Martino of Assisi, who left a bequest of a piece of land to his daughter with the stipulation she seek no more. He named his son Marcuzio as his heir and if he were to die without heirs, pieces of land were to be distributed to a fraternity, to the Church of San Francesco, and to the testator's sister. In the event Marcuzio died young. The problem was the sister's legitimate portion. Bartolo determined that it was half of the third she would have shared with her brother on intestacy, and she could seek more, counting the two pieces of land she had gained, if they did not amount to that fair share.[68]

A fairly famous example of a man who died without a male heir was that of Francesco di Marco Datini, whose patrimony, among other things, provided for the founding of the Innocenti hospital in Florence. The case in question, which came before Giovanni da Imola, involved not his bequest to the Innocenti in Florence but to the Casa del Ceppo in Prato and the provisions for Datini's illegitimate daughter, Ginevra. Actual parties to the suit were Antonio Bertini of Prato on behalf of his sister-in-law, Brigida, Datini's daughter's child, wife of Giovanni Bertini, and the administrators of the charity. Datini's will carried a bequest of a 500 florin dowry for the first granddaughter, but for any more girls the amount was whatever the administrators of the Ceppo deemed appropriate. The first granddaughter, Peracina, was seven when Datini died and lived for several more years, dying unmarried. Brigida was born ten years after Datini's death. At the time of the suit she had been married for two

[68] Bartolo, *cons.* 34, fol. 11ra–b.

years and was trying to get the 500 florin dowry. Imola noted the ambiguity of the "first" – first born or first to marry? The term should be construed "according to what is credible the testator had been thinking" (*secundum quod credibile est testatorem cogitasse*). Datini may have meant birth order, "from the strong affection that the testator is said to have had toward Peracina," whereas he never knew Brigida. There was also the fact that Brigida had proceeded to marry without the 500 florin dowry, so the purpose of a dowry to facilitate marriage was moot. But Imola rounded on this line of argument and found for Brigida, because the word first was used in connection with dowry and marriage and not birth. The fact that Brigida went to her husband with a dowry from her mother's property did not mean she could not get the *legatum*.[69] So here the charitable institution lost, even though the testator could possibly have been said to have affection for it too.

When a father left provision in his will for unmarried daughters to have 500 florin dowries, one daughter, who had married before he died, asked for a supplement to bring her dowry up to 500. Pierfilippo da Corgna, however, declared that in this will daughters were not heirs entitled to equal shares and that fathers were concerned with their daughters' marriages, not the marriages of their heirs. The daughter did not get as much as her sister did, while her uncle and cousins received the rest of the patrimony.[70]

Another father left 1,000 *lire* to his daughter on condition that she marry. A further amount was left for her widowhood on the idea "that a widow marrying needs a greater dowry than a virgin" (*quod vidua nubens eget ampliori dote, quam virgo*). If she died without children, it went to male kin; if her brother died without heirs, the bequest was hers to do with as she liked. As "paternal charity and love for the daughter gain expression were there no sons," and "lacking males the father's affection is consolidated in the daughter," the *legatum* was said to be hers.[71] A niece left less than her aunt as dowry, because she was already married and was told to remain content, did not have a right to seek a supplement. By statute of Mantua she was excluded, even by a restrictive reading, leave alone the usual expansive agnatic rationale; but mainly because the legitimate portion was not a matter of natural law, but civil law, and so was subject to change. She was not eligible to succeed (*successibilis*) by the terms of the statute.[72]

---

[69] Imola, *cons.* 113, fols. 64ra–65va.   [70] Corgna, *cons.* 288, fols. 224va–25rb.
[71] Baldo, 4 *cons.* 139, fol. 34ra–b.   [72] Baldo, 3 *cons.* 465, fol. 135ra–va.

Legata to widows were their own headache. Antonio da Butrio (1338–1408) laid out a case in which a testator gave his two daughters use of the family home as their dwelling in widowhood along with their mother. After her death one of the sisters alienated the house without the consent of the other, who in fact had married for the third time and no longer lived there. Following her third husband's death, however, she sought to regain habitation in the family home. The purchaser argued that the *legatum* in the father's will was satisfied in the first widowhood. Butrio, however, maintained that the term widowhood in the will was used indistinctly and meant any widowhood – first, second, or third. There was no reason to conclude the testator was thinking only of the immediate widowhood, just as a bequest of a dowry was not confined to one marriage. Then there was the quality of the persons, father and daughter:

because the daughter is the cause of the bequest, because the distinction, honor, and paternal dedication are maintained when a daughter lives in the paternal house rather than with strangers, with many problems and dangers, which reasons uniformly apply to all widowhoods, this bequest is not restricted to the first widowhood but [applies to] the last.

Necessity was the mark of widowhood from its inception and was the father-testator's concern:

first because, given that they have the houses of husbands, many things arise in the homes of husbands in which there is trouble, then because as they have their origin, having concerned persons and friends, neighbors, near kin, by whom they are protected and defended from bothers and aided in their tribulations, testators contemplating such necessities of widowhood in practice suppose widowhood is a situation of need (*viduitatem habere causam annexam necessitatis*).

There was need for the widow to find herself in the arms of friends and those who cared for her (*inter brachia amicorum et attinentium*). Effectively in this bleak image of widowhood Butrio created a rationale for them roughly equivalent to that of agnation for the privilege of men in inheritance, of which such widowhood was one result.[73]

Angelo degli Ubaldi and Filippo Corsini of Florence faced the *legatum* by Arculano to his two daughters and his granddaughter of usufruct in widowhood on all his possessions at Cerello and Sant'Arculano outside Perugia. The granddaughter, Alleuntia, married, but after only six months she was left a widow. She remarried after another six months and during

---

[73] Da Butrio, *cons.* 30, 48a–49b.

that marriage her aunts died. As Alleuntia was not a widow at that
moment, there was doubt about her rights. To these jurists, after rehearsing arguments about the temporary nature of this *legatum* and of widowhood, the answer was that the terms of the will simply meant that
widowhood triggered the right to use of the properties. It did not ask
for persistence of that state, notably because there was also reference to
the widow's possibly entering a convent. This case was also different from
what a son or husband might have in mind in such a *legatum* to a mother
or wife.

Finally I say what truly conformed or had to conform to the testator's wish be
considered, for if widowhood conformed to his wish, as that a son bequeathed to
his mother if she remain a widow, and then it is not adequate she remained a
widow, if later she marries, as by subsequent marriages injury is done to children
and their memory (*filiis et filiorum memoriae fiat iniuria*). . . . Also in a bequest
made by the husband if his wife remain a widow, for it conformed to his wish that
she not marry, as by her marriage his soul is saddened (*sua anima contristetur*). . .
it is not similar therefore that the testator by existence alone of widowhood would
want such women to have a bequest, unless they persevere in widowhood, by
which by lack of perseverance injury be done to their soul and memory.

They stayed a bit close to the text and did not rise to the same general
rationale Butrio did, but they also clearly had their stereotypes of
widows.[74] To realize bequests of this sort they had to remain widows,
as they were part of the deceased husband's house thereby (as Isabelle
Chabot has shown for Florence).

The noble Jacopo da Faitano of Rimini had two sons by his first wife
(one a minor), whom he named his heirs, and daughters by his third wife,
to whom he left bequests for dowry. To his wife he left her dowry,
100 ducats he got from her mother's dowry, and *alimenta*, as long as
she remained a widow and lived with his heirs. On his death she saw to an
inventory and the sons, with the minor acting through his *tutor*, took the
estate under benefit of inventory and later divided it. The stepmother then
sought her legacies from the adult son, including *alimenta*. Baldo used the
case as an opportunity to categorize bequests. Some *legata* had a specific
quantity, and the heir without inventory was open to demands to fulfill
those claims, as there was even a presumption that failure to make an
inventory arose from a desire to hide things from the legatees. Other
legata were uncertain but could be given some quantification from the
testator's assets, such as bequests of *alimenta*. The inventory done by the

---

[74] Angelo, *cons.* 34, fols. 17va–18rb.

wife did not protect the son, because though she acted in good faith, there was still the possibility he could disguise assets. Considering the persons and assets, the *alimenta* were to be moderate. It was not credible that the testator would want to leave the stepmother in a better position than the children. Neither of them should go hungry to the benefit of the other, so there should be a division, "even if there is only one pint of grain" (*etiam si esset unum solum sextarium frumenti*).[75]

Several communities, as we have seen, enacted statutes regulating how much, to whom, and under what conditions women could receive by testament. Unsurprisingly these raised additional problems in contrast to *ius commune*. A Pisan testator left land and houses to one fellow while leaving his wife usufruct on all the same properties, as long as she remained a widow, with the condition to his heir that "they might not molest nor disturb her but they are to suffer her having and holding and enjoying, using, and possessing in peace." Suit arose as to who had usufruct – mother, another legatee, or heir – in view of Pisa's law limiting bequests to wives to fifteen *lire*. The bequest was perfectly licit by *ius commune*; it was the statute that provided an opening for a challenge. Baldo recognized the statutory limit, which argued that the legatee had *proprietas* and half the usufruct, whereas the other half went to the heir beyond what the wife was allowed by statute. But the heir was held to a *naturalis equitas* toward her. By the terms of the will itself, it was evident that the testator did not want the legatee to have any usufruct as long as the widow survived, so that was the conclusion Baldo reached.[76] The intent of the testator here overruled the intent of the legislator, it seems.

Francesco Zaberella upheld a will in favor of an heir, seemingly unrelated to the testator, against the claims of a daughter. His was a quite different take on such matters than we saw the Ubaldi brothers take earlier. Quagliotto de' Bonomi of Trigesto named his minor son Paolo as heir, along with the yet to be born son of his pregnant wife, substituting them to each other if they died without heirs. If the posthumous child was a girl, she got 150 marks when she married. If both sons died childless, he substituted ser Francesco de' Bonomi and his heirs. In the event, the child was a girl and Paolo took the inheritance through his guardian but died, still a minor. The question was who had better claim to be Paolo's heir, as Trigesto had statutes that legatees had to be content with what was left them and that all statutes were to be taken literally, "without any

---

[75] Baldo, 4 *cons.* 221, fol. 50rb–vb.   [76] Baldi, 1 *cons.* 204, fols. 60vb–61rb.

interpellation, glossing, interpretation." The girl had not been instituted heir, but she was not *preterita* either, because she was left something, and by statute (whose validity and applicability Zaberella also upheld) she could be left with a differential sum and had to remain content with that. He also declared that ser Francesco, the substitute heir, had a stronger claim than the daughter/sister. The desire of the testator was apparent, and it was to keep his property in the hands of an agnate "to preserve his line and the testator's memory," just as so many statutes also wanted. The girl simply got her 150 marks.[77]

On February 1, 1410, messer Niccolò di Jacopo di Pagello of Vicenza wrote his will. It featured a bequest to his granddaughter, Dorotea, of 300 ducats as her dowry, with which she was to be content, and support "to be treated honorably according to her status in the hereditary home." If she died before marriage, the funds went to his heirs. The heirs were his son, Guido, for a fourth, a grandson, Bonzilio, of the late son Piero, Dorotea's brother, for a fourth, his grandsons by his son Antonio for a quarter, his son Cardo for a quarter (different mother). The grandsons were substituted to each other and generally any descendants to any who had none, with no deduction of a trebellianic portion. On April 11, 1415, the dowry was paid to Dorotea in the form of an assignment of certain lands. On May 21, 1429, as a result of Guido's death, the other heirs delivered a third of the *haereditas* to Leonardo di Cardo Pagello, in which were included the properties previously deeded over to Dorotea, who had died after Cardo and wrote a will in favor of her nephew Bonzilio. Could she make a will? Did Leonardo not already hold the properties assigned to Dorotea, so he was due some more? Was her property to be split? Could Leonardo claim some of Guido's estate by virtue of the substitution in Niccolò's will? This was a marvelously complex situation into which Paolo di Castro was thrust. He stayed close to the details and technicalities, but one fact stood out. Dorotea never married, so the assignment of lands as her dowry was empty and it went back into the common estate, from which Leonardo took his share.[78] There was no thought of her gaining something simply as a daughter.

In a different sort of case, Paolo di Castro faced the fact that monna Antonia had for a long time managed the properties and revenues of her ailing husband, Bartolomeo, being the one who in fact paid moneys to merchants. So her household role was well known in the town.

---

[77] Zaberella, *cons.* 60, fols. 52va–54rb.   [78] Di Castro, 2 *cons.* 225, fols. 104rb–5va.

Bartolomeo's will absolved her of all obligation in that regard, not to be held to account by his heirs, adding that all animals managed by Giovanni Pivello on his farm at Vallunga in fact belonged to Antonia, bought with her money obtained as heir to her mother. Antonia had been dead four years when Bartolomeo finally died. They had a daughter, Anzolina, who was heir to her mother, but Bartolomeo named as his heir his nephew, Francesco, who would have been his heir on intestacy by local statute. Francesco claimed sums Antonia had paid out to various merchants. Di Castro had to concede that the *legatum* in Bartolomeo's will was a dead letter because Antonia had predeceased. Francesco had no obligation not to molest her heir for sums paid out. Bartolomeo had not drawn up a new *legatum* taking care of the daughter (had he even thought of that? And how much of his will may have been his wife's fashioning?). Di Castro even hinted that there was possibly good reason to investigate Antonia's handling of the property: "And she is detected to have been in fraud, making instruments and writings posed in her own person with no mention made of her husband, and so she wanted to appropriate to herself what was not hers and by this device remain in her possession or her heir's."[79] Actually, how this was to make a difference in household accounts was not explained. But Antonia's reputation in the markets created doubts. The agnate heir was being conceded latitude to undo her dealings from years before. In this instance, however, and in keeping with how we have seen Paolo di Castro treat women, the uncertainty or revocation of legal acts, including the bequest to her, was not based on allegations of womanly weakness but on the quite opposite assertion of financial trickery and marketing astuteness.

Lodovico Pontano tackled a statutory prohibition on women seeking a supplement, as *legitima*, to the dowry that might be left them in a paternal will. He upheld the "exorbitant" statute and ruled against a supplement for the women. The statute had the goal of seeing that a testator's wishes were enacted, and thus was favorable to him. It also had the rationale we have seen so many others ascribe to it, "certain agnation is preserved by the wealth of families as by it might be preserved the honor of the same, which is lost by penury."[80] He and others were not open to adding to bequests, but they upheld them.

Maestro Giovanni da Esculo's will carried generous provision for his widow Marina: domicile and effective control of all his property while

---

[79] Di Castro, 2 *cons.* 402, fol. 186ra–va.   [80] Pontano, *cons.* 16, fol. 7rb–vb.

living with their children. If she chose to live separately, then she got specified amounts of grain, wine, oil, wood, and ten ducats annually. Giovanni's sons were his heirs, substituted to each other. On his death the five boys entered into the patrimony and lived with their stepmother. Two of them later died, the second leaving a will with a bequest to Marina of a house that came from his father's holdings. He left half a shop to one brother and the other half of a farm under the same conditions, with the privileged brother, Giovanpiero, bound to return 300 ducats to the estate, which was capital from the father for their business. Otherwise, his heirs were the three surviving brothers, who continued to live with Marina, though soon there came a division and she lived only with Gianpiero. She then sued for the *alimenta* left her in the will and for the house the one son had bequeathed to his brothers. They cited a statute that kept mothers from inheriting from their sons. The whole situation was complicated by three deaths and two wills. Benedetto Capra had an unenviable task before him. Marina, he concluded, was entitled to *alimenta*, as the housing arrangement was not her idea but the result of division among the brothers, in light of local custom (*attenta consuetudine vulgari*). Succession to the first brother, intestate, meant in *ius commune* shares for each brother and the mother. By statute, however, she could seek only *legitima*, which was a third of her share, and the boys were also substitute heirs. But the house bequeathed by the second son to die was not in her rights, as it was not part of the patrimony but an acquisition he was free to assign. It came from the sons' business in wool, which was also the capital he called on Gianpiero to restore.[81]

Remarriages further complicated the disposition of estates and their bequests. Benedetto Capra seems to have caught a number of cases involving remarriage. In one he dealt with a man who married three times. His will left 800 *lire* to three daughters as dowry, which was the same sum he had already realized as dowry of his second wife. The usual clauses enjoining these girls to remain content accompanied the bequest. He died leaving his third wife and a boy and girl by her, the son by the first wife, the two girls from the second. The two older girls married brothers, with no dowry specified. One gave birth to a daughter and then died. The second died without children, leaving her half siblings and a niece. What those women could have claimed and who had claims to them was the crux of the matter for Capra. He judged the 800 *lire* to be

---

[81] Capra, *cons.* 4, fols. 12ra–14va.

compensation for the maternal dowry, because the girls were ordered to seek no more. The one daughter did obtain the right to a portion of the 800 from her dead mother. Her father obtained no rights in his wife's unspecified dowry by local statute, because there was a child who inherited. The other brother, however, gained half his wife's dowry, as there were no children. His wife's heir by *ius commune* would be the niece, who was related through a full sister, as opposed to the half-brother, and that was the case here as the "exorbitant" statute did not cover succession to a sister, and the rationale of conserving agnation was not in question in female succession.[82]

Finally, for Capra one widow's suit became an occasion to confront civil versus canon law. Catino left his wife, Lucentina, in control of his property as widow and 200 ducats, with another 50 in someone else's possession, plus a silver necklace and clothing, naming their daughter Baldina as heir. Within a year Lucentina remarried but sought what had been left her. In opposition it was alleged remarriage made her *infamis*, inflicting civil penalties on her as a result, and cost her those rights. The response was that the penalties in civil law had been removed by canon law; but to that the retort was that it was all a civil matter under local statute. Lucentina had ended her widowhood and thus her rights to the *legata*, and she had administered the property for her daughter like a *tutrix* without formally ever becoming one, and then ran off without giving an accounting of her stewardship (as required of all guardians). Still, Capra backed her claims to the money, jewelry, and clothing. Those were extended in other clauses of the testament not explicitly directed at widowhood. Canon law did indeed remove the stain of infamy and other penalties in civil law for remarrying, in order to encourage or at least ease remarriage. He argued for canon law also to be served in a secular forum, but that is an issue well beyond our concerns.[83] Consistently remarriage, it could be argued, attenuated rights of the remarrying parent, depending on local law. Results of suits seem, on the basis of what we have seen so far, to have been uneven.

One man left the son by his first wife as much as he had given her, but he later changed his will, leaving the son less, and instituting as heirs that son's sons. Pierfilippo da Corgna conjectured "that he did that in order to defraud the heirs of the recipient [the wife] who had predeceased, as truly the donor did not love the heirs of his wife as he did his wife"

---

[82] Capra, *cons.* 62, fols. 85rb–86rb.   [83] Capra, *cons.* 70, fols. 99rb–100vb.

(*ita diligebat heredes uxoris prout ipsam uxorem*). The family had also been wracked by violence, which lay behind the second will, as the son had killed his father's second wife. As Corgna concluded, "there remain two truth-like conjectures why he changed the testament, because he could doubt lest on account of the murder of the stepmother the goods of the homicide son become public [confiscated]. Likewise he changed the testament from the indignation the testator had against the son who killed his wife."[84] Beneath this domestic tragedy there was the reduction of the bequest to the beloved wife and the inheritance by the murderer's sons.

Even Venetians had problems with bequests. Vincenzo Valier, in his holographic will, left his wife clothing and his villa at Ganbarare for life; thereafter it went in halves to her brothers Andrea and Zacharia Foscolo. Vincenzo's heir otherwise was his cousin Andrea Valier. In the end, the widow Helena and Zacharia's son Marco were the survivors. The Valier were intent on limiting Helena's share and claimed Marco had only his father's half. Mariano Sozzini read the will more expansively. Helena had the villa, gardens, animals, courtyard, and so forth. He also defended Marco's claim to the entire property as heir to his uncle and cousin.[85]

SUBSTITUTIONS

In comparison, the statutes paid less attention by far to the entire area of substitutions and *fideicommissa*. Franco Niccolai found only a few statutes dealing with substitutions, generally to allow explicitly substitution to a son or other male heir who died young and left no children of his own. As we have seen again and again, many wills contained substitutions. They were one of the most useful and attractive features of wills, allowing for affirmation of alternatives to intestacy rules that would operate if a designated heir were dead or refused the inheritance and there were no designated substitute (and thus at times favoring women more so than local statutes, especially in the absence of sons). The testator could lay out contingent lines of succession that met with his or her desires. By the fifteenth century notarial protocols for wills had become consistent and elaborate, taking account of technicalities of law with fulsome language. A substitution was said to be vulgar, pupillary, or fideicommissary, whichever applied to the circumstances of application, death of the heir, or whatever. In similar fashion heirs and legatees were all said to be

---

[84] Corgna, *cons.* 118, fol. 104rb–vb.
[85] Sozzini, 1 *cons.* 139, fols. 258ra–59vb (Padua 1536).

"instituted" so as to employ that vital word for a will's validity; and a further clause stated that if the will could not stand *iure institutionis* then it was said to be by *iure codicillaris*, in order to save its provisions from any technical deficiency. In the course of the fifteenth century, substitutions became more common and elaborate, and jurists had their hands full.

Although substitutions were not the object of much legislation, they were an endless source of litigation. Given the vagaries of mortality, the identity of the substituted heir in the face of imprecise testamentary language was a constant problem. Substitutions were another means by which women might become heirs, among other things. Those cases are always revealing of social prejudices and domestic realities. Even as substitutions became more complex and there was more general awareness of the appropriate terms to use, legal cases involving them became no less frequent. Among them were a surprising number where inheritance devolved to or through women. Despite all the agnatic bias of local laws, of social practices, even of jurisprudence, jurists were faced with and able to champion the causes of women.

Substitutions always seemed to tail off into a vague area where the identity and/or prerogatives of the heir were in doubt. Problems of this sort arose early on and were constant. Dino del Mugello faced a case in which a man named his two daughters as heirs in equal portions, and if either did not have a legitimate heir, he allowed her to testate half of her share while the other half went to the survivor. If there were heirs they were free to bequeath their entire share. If neither had an heir, he named someone else. In all, a not unusual situation in which coheirs were substituted to each other, and then there was a further substitution if neither survived or accepted the estate. In the event, here one daughter died before marrying. Dino declared that the condition for final substitution failed, as one girl had lived to marry. The substitution went into effect only if both had died, whereas the substitution to the surviving daughter did go into effect.[86] Her later death did not change that; the property passed through her to her heir.

One early fourteenth-century substitution was set up like this. The testator named his nephew, substituting, if he died without legitimate heirs, his father (the testator's brother), and after him substituting the nephew's wife. His nephew and brother both died during the testator's

[86] Dino, *cons.* 40, fols. 48va–49va.

life, so on his death there were the nephew's wife and her sons. Oldrado da Ponte quickly determined that the substitutions to father and then to nephew's wife had never happened. Nephew and father had predeceased the testator. Failure of the substitutions, however, threw the estate into intestacy, and the mother inherited as closer in degree than her children (who still might get it from her).[87] It is not clear from the *consilium* who was pressing the suit, but if it was a more distant relative, Oldrado was not intent on keeping the property in the hands of the agnate but more distantly related nephew's sons.

When a father left his minor son as heir, with a substitution to the testator's brother, the issue, on the death of the young heir, was if the substitution to the brother was direct, which would exclude the boy's mother, or fideicommissary, which would get her something, less a half for *legitima*, as her son would indeed have been heir while he lived. Oldrado decided it was a direct substitution, as the testator was concerned that his heirs have heirs: "it happens that the father wanted to arrange the effect of substitution even during the time in which sons might have sons, and while they should die without them, as the testator's words show, whose intent is powerfully to be attended to in the judgment and discretion of those substituting in."[88] There was nothing for the mother in such a direct substitution. The testator had displayed no concern for her.

The canonist Giovanni Calderini (d. 1365) looked at a will in which the testator substituted charitable distribution to the poor if his son died childless. In that event, did the mother get to claim anything as a "portion owed by nature"? The executors who were to see to the distribution were not substitute heirs, so Calderini claimed some sort of *legitima* was owed to the dead son, to which his mother succeeded. It would have been different if the poor recipients of the largesse had been named substitute heirs.[89] Then the testator might be said to have cared for them and not his widow.

Less bound to the technicalities of labeling the substitution was Bartolo's handling of a complex case from Tuderto. Tebalduccio's testament left handsome dowries of 1500 *lire* each to two daughters. To their married sister went 100 in addition to her dowry, with the order to seek no more. His son was designated heir, and a niece got ten *lire* in addition to 300 she had already received. Tebalduccio's wife got usufruct of a piece of land, suitable *alimenta*, and the right to remain in his castle, all "as long

---

[87] Oldrado, *cons.* 141, fol. 53ra–va.   [88] Oldrado, *cons.* 99, fol. 36rb–va.
[89] Calderini, *cons.* 27, fols. 67vb–68ra.

as she lived chastely and honorably" and she did not try to recover her dowry to remarry. If the son died a minor, the three daughters became substituted heirs in equal portions, with the obligation to deliver 1,000 to religious uses for Tebalduccio's soul within two years of his death. As it happened the two unmarried girls and the son died, though he had managed to accept the estate through a guardian. The mother then sought the one eighth share available to her according to local statute. Bartolo declared the substitution to the daughters to be a pupillary, and thus direct, substitution. The mother was cut out, as she was also by statute law in Tuderto. The niece also posed an argument to seek more than the small sum left her, alleging that the statute was about intestate succession, but the testament and substitution meant that both Tebalduccio and his son in fact died testate. But even if that argument worked, Bartolo said she could only claim up to a third of what would have been the legitimate portion to her on intestacy, and in fact she would have had nothing on intestacy.[90] It is not possible to tell what sum the niece may have realized. In this case and the others we have seen to this preliminary point, the lack of a son as direct heir, or his death at a young age, threw the estate into doubt. That would remain a major factor in inheritance disputes. Plagues and other mortality factors only increased the likelihood that substitutions might come into effect, but also that the substituted heirs themselves might have died.

When Simone di Neri of Siena made his will, he named his son Biagio his heir and left his two daughters 100 florins with admonition to remain content with that. If his son died without issue, he substituted the next in agnatic line, being no more specific than that. Father died and so did son, having reached age thirty but childless. That left the daughters and the sons of Simone's brother Giovanni, and these were the parties to the suit. The cousins alleged they were the ones to fulfill the substitution, which had used the masculine *agnatus*. The girls countered that they were agnate in closer degree and the male term encompassed the female. Baldo essentially took two steps that precluded these daughters. The first was to deny that they were "ex paterna linea," "because agnation did not arise between them and the testator, who was called the stem and root and first principle of agnation (*stirpes et radix et primum principium agnationis*) as far as his daughters were concerned. The second was that the substitution was deemed merely pupillary, going into effect if the heir died young,

[90] Bartolo, *cons.* 8, fol. 5ra–b.

but the brother had inherited and lived to adulthood so the pupillary substitution was extinct.[91] The cousins, it seems, would inherit on intestacy then, if not by the substitution. Had the substitution been labeled "vulgar," the result might have been different.

When "a great noble" with "many castles" made his will, he gave his three daughters bequests and named his brother heir. Should he die without male heirs, substitution went to the daughters or their sons. The brother in fact had a son by his daughter. Was this transverse male the heir? While this grandson was indeed a male heir, Baldo did not put him ahead of the testator's daughters. His first reason was

in testaments and substitutions when in doubt we must look at the order of affection, as he is preferred in whom affection is more strongly found (*inspicere ordinatam charitatem, ut illi preferatur in quo vehementior charitas*), all else being equal . . . But by ordered affection the testator is affected more to his daughters and their granddaughters than to transverse kin, thus in doubt daughters are to be preferred.

Of course the testator could also be taken to be concerned with the *honor* and *dignitas* of his family, by putting his brother first. Then the fact arose "but these his grandsons descend through a female, rather their descendants are said to be of their paternal line rather than maternal, and so is it by habit of speaking, because denomination is by male sex as the more worthy." One had to attend to the idea that the heir was a *prudens homo* and see what such a man would want. Was this testator prudent? Baldo assumed he was prudent and diligent and preferred his agnatic relations; but the terms of the substitution were deeply ambiguous. He came back to the imperative of affection and opted for the daughters of the testator versus the son of the daughter of the heir, if only because "in doubt is always to be made an interpretation for the children" (*pro libes*). Althogh he had to concede that the first *lex* of C. De conditionibus insertis seemed to make a strong case for the potential male heir, Baldo went with what he took to be the testator's intent.[92]

Second marriages further complicated substitutions and dowry restitution, but in view of demographic realities, these were at least a frequent possibility. If a wife left children behind as she moved to a second marriage, rights and claims between her and them had to be determined. Baldo found that Asti had a statute by which a widow could take her dowry and all else to her second home, while her children got nothing.

[91] Baldo, 4 *cons.* 115, fol. 29rb–va.   [92] Baldo, 3 *cons.* 40, fol. 17ra–va.

Mother and all related through her were, in consequence, excluded from any inheritance to children of prior marriages, and excluded from guardianship, with an express exception if the mother were named heir, not just a legatee, in her first husband's testament. An Asti merchant, Antonio de Nivei, named his wife, Simoneta, as one of two guardians for the four daughters who were his heirs and had substitutions to them that included Simoneta. She, as guardian, accepted the estate for the girls and had an inventory made. But after her year of widowhood she remarried and took her dowry and some bequests left her by Antonio. When later one of the daughters died, Simoneta moved to claim half of her share on the basis of a substitution in Antonio's will. Baldo was not prepared to let her be heir when the statute precluded the children from being heirs to her. Though she had been named as a substitute that was not the same as being instituted heir, which was what the exception in the statute meant.[93] In effect Baldo was arguing to keep the property in the hands of the girls, where it could serve as their dowries and to keep the families of first and second husbands distinct.

Again and again, these issues of phrasing became the crux of jurists' determinations of succession to testators. In one case Giovanni d'Anagni coped with the will of a testator who left his wife her dowry and left her and his mother rights of use and support on his estate, as long as they lived as chaste and honest widows. Beyond these bequests, his sons Guido and Francesco were his heirs, substituted to each other, and if both died without heirs, a further substitution named the mother and wife equally. Guido in fact died within three hours of his father at age fifteen, intestate, to be sure. The two women lived together for three months along with the mother's brother. Then the testator's widow remarried. For seven years she took care of the young Francesco, though she did not move for a formal *tutela* and was not challenged on that by her mother-in-law or anyone else. The mother-in-law/grandmother passed away in 1449, Francesco six months later. Who was heir? Was the wife due compensation for the expenses she incurred for the two dead sons? Telling against the wife/mother was her failure to seek formal guardianship and her remarriage within a year (not completing the legal mourning period), but Giovanni d'Anagni brushed that aside with the argument that the testator's substitution showed he wanted her to inherit. This substitution was fideicommissary to the testator, not direct (and thus to the son).

[93] Baldo, 2 *cons.* 216, fols. 62va–63ra.

The wife then could claim as mother, despite the guardianship issue. And all the learned doctors agreed there was no longer a penalty on widows remarrying within a year. But because this was a fideicommissary substitution, the trebellianic quarter was due to the uncles.[94]

A Bolognese noble left dowries to daughters and three sons as heirs, substituting them to those dying without sons. If all died without sons he substituted his brother's son; if that line failed he substituted his brother. In the event, one son died leaving two daughters. The problem for Alessandro Tartagni was whether they or their uncles inherited. The girls seemed excluded, as the *mens testatoris* was about agnation and family, while girls and their dowries left the family. And the presumption was that the testator would have greater affection for his own daughters, whom he excluded, than for granddaughters, so their claim in this case seemed weak. Then there was the usual issue whether the masculine noun *filius* covered female also. Tartagni brought forward an interpretive rule from an earlier jurist, Pietro d'Ancarano, that "wherever there is a different succession of a son and daughters then by the term son of a son daughter is not included." The agnate concerns of the testator had to be honored even if he had not added the helpful adjective *masculos* "and it is the same and greater equity and in all regards its equivalent is required so that the substitution is limited if without male children, which in our case is eternal memory of family dignity (*sempiterna est dignum memoria*), it therefore follows that so much the more it is limited to male children." The uncles won out. The notary's mode of operation, using more words than the testator, even using often "clauses in testaments which they do not understand" was also noted.[95] Notarial practice should not annul the obvious desires of the testator.

One man instituted his three sons as his heirs, along with any sons yet to be born, "and sons of his sons, and great grandsons, and into infinity according to prerogative of degree," with substitutions if they died young or had no sons. If the entire male line failed, then his daughters and their descendants stepped in. In the event, all the boys died without male issue, though there were some daughters. One sister survived her brothers, and there were children of the other two girls, grandchildren of the testator. The dispute was between the remaining daughter, Antonia, and her nephews and nieces over the inheritance to the last of the three sons to die, who had been substituted heir to his brothers. The sisters' children

---

[94] Anagni, *cons.* 102, fols. 55vb–56ra.   [95] Tartagni, 4 *cons.* 52, fols. 36va–39ra.

argued for two shares equal to that of the aunt on the basis that the substitution was in line with intestate rules, whereas for Antonia the argument was that the substitution wanted the *gradus prerogativa* that gave her the right alone to the last brother. Paolo di Castro quickly determined that there were three shares to be allotted: one to Antonia, one to the girls who were descendants of the brothers, the third to descendants of the other sisters. Although, quaintly, the testament did not mention female descendants of the sons when it came to substitution for lack of male heirs, it certainly seemed absurd that the testator would privilege female descendants through females to the disadvantage of females through males.[96]

Ser Asquino de Subragavacca named his sons ser Marcore and ser Bertoldo as heirs, and if they died or did not have sons, he substituted "nearer of the kin and his house, namely de Subrovacca." Some years later ser Asquino remarried and had Rizzardo and Bartolomeo, who were about four years old when he died. The two older boys entered the inheritance and lived with their half-brothers and their mother, "as brothers in the paternal home they ruled, governed, and provided" (*rexerunt, gubernaverunt et alimentaverunt*). The younger boys both died not long after growing out of their minority. Their mother survived, but Marcore and Bertoldo held and managed the property for ten years without contest from anyone. The rupture in this domestic situation occurred when the second wife ceded her rights to be heir to her two sons to a monna Bartolomea, who turned around and sued the older sons to get what was thought to come to their half-brothers. Marcore and Bertoldo responded that they were not intestate heirs but were heirs by virtue of the *fideicommissum*, which obligated their half-brothers to restore the estate to them by substitution. Now those two sons had not been alive at the time the will was written, so Bartolomea was relying on the *preteritio* of them to quash the will and remove the substitution. But as the forgotten sons themselves had never challenged the will, was it still valid? Paolo di Castro had to cope with some opinions of jurists already tendered in the case, which was on a highly disputed and dubious area of law. If a mother had a right to inherit from her sons on intestacy, could she challenge a will that seemed to take that right away from her sons, and thus from her? He found one *consilium* advising that the mother did receive half. More importantly, even if the will were invalid, the

---

[96] Di Castro, 2 *cons.* 454, fols, 210va–11ra.

substitution remained in force by virtue of its open-ended language and was meant to cover other sons.[97] So the second wife inherited nothing from her dead sons. We cannot say how Bartolomea reacted to finding out she had gained nothing.

When one testator's descendants all died without sons, his substitution to his daughters took effect. One survivor, however, was a granddaughter, Gabriela, who claimed the estate by virtue of the substitution of surviving sons to those who died. Of course it could be argued that by the same logic by which he excluded his own daughters, the testator wanted to exclude any other women. Though he found varying opinions among Perugian jurists, and it was a Perugian case, Filippo Decio found, as he said others did, that substitution of daughters showed the testator thought of more or other than agnation and, as a result, the granddaughter should exclude her aunts.[98] The estate had passed to her father, to whom she was more closely related than her aunts, even though the estate was governed by the testament of the aunts' father, to whom they were closer than their niece. Although the domestic and marital statuses of these women are not disclosed (as legally irrelevant), it may have been that the granddaughter had greater need of the assets for her own dowry, in comparison to older aunts who were at least socially situated.

In the very first opinion in the 1570 edition of Filippo Decio's *consilia*, hailing from early in his career (1497), he grappled with a murky matter of substitution, while also fending off professional jealousy. His initial opinion had elicited a rebuttal from a colleague, which Decio took umbrage at:

> as the Comic says, as many heads as there are, there are that many opinions. But yet it was customary among professors of law of typical modesty (*solitae modestiae*), before correcting my *consilium* to indicate something to me. Which, as it was not done, I am forced by the natural law of defense and not by any injury to write the reasons by which it will easily appear below that I have responded for truth and justice, and the lord consultor who wanted to correct me walked in darkness.

This benighted colleague had declared that the substitution in the testament of Francesco Manueli directed his estate first to his son, Berto, then to his (Berto's) daughter, Vagia, and finally to a granddaughter, Lisa, who had been born to Berto's deceased son. Decio argued that only Vagia inherited, because the substituted heir was put in place of the testator.

---

[97] Di Castro, 2 *cons.* 392, fol. 180 rb–vb.   [98] Decio, *cons.* 370, fols. 395rb–96ra.

Because her father had predeceased his father, there was no right realized through him that came to Lisa. Decio's reasoning was thorough, as he had a professional rival to silence. The other jurist conceived of the case in terms of intestate inheritance to Berto, while Decio maintained it was a matter of fideicommissary substitution to Francesco.[99]

Giason del Maino, who was Decio's professional rival throughout his career and perhaps the object of his pique, had a very active practice in inheritance cases. Messer Niccolino de' Vayroli named his grandsons, Piero, Giorgio, and Filippo di Giovanni, his heirs with substitution to each other. Piero died first with no issue; Filippo left sons; Giorgio died last, leaving two daughters as his intestate heirs. Filippo's sons contested the girls' inheritance on the basis of the substitution in their grandfather's will. Maino began touching all the right chords about agnation and family wealth lying behind the testator's provisions. But he held for the granddaughters, mainly because Giorgio had outlived Filippo, and so Filippo was not substituted to him. Filippo's sons had no claim on Giorgio's property. A substitution was to move from one person to another when the same presumed intent of the testator was at work. But there was no further substitution extending to the girls' father. This "ardua et difficilis" matter rested on the *mens testatoris*, of course, which was said to prefer the near relative (*coniunctus*) to the *substitutus*. Filippo's sons' case certainly seemed to be strong. There was the expressed intent to keep property in the hands of agnatic males and the "exclusion" of the dowered daughter of the testator's son. Splitting various legal hairs, Maino arrived at no less than twelve arguments in the women's favor. In the end, Lucia, Giorgio's daughter, stood as heir to her father, so there was no substitution to him. The argument that *filius* also covered female was an old and standard one for him to rely on. More interesting was the assertion that Piacenza did not have a statute privileging males and agnates; men and women inherited equally, as the rules of *ius commune* held sway there, and the *mens testatoris* was to be interpreted as in accord with the rules that prevailed locally. The testator had not used the term *masculus* in his first two sets of substitutions as he had in the third, though obviously he could easily have done so. It seemed a telling omission. Inheritance by Lucia did not constitute alienation outside the family, neither by birth nor by her marriage to someone of the Fontana family. Maino acknowledged and rehearsed at some length powerful arguments

---

[99] Decio, 1 *cons.* 1, fols. 2ra–3rb.

in a *consilium* of Paolo di Castro in favor of a substituted transverse male against a daughter, but again pointed out that in Piacenza there was no such statute as that of Florence, which ruled in di Castro's case.[100]

Paola de' Piscari had a dispute with her uncle Galeazzo and his sons as a result of the will of her great grandfather, Cristoforo, who had named his three sons, Andrea, Astolfo, and Battista, his heirs with substitution to each other. Andrea's sons and heirs were Galeazzo, Rugerio, and Guerrerio. Rugerio was Paolo's father. Guerrerio entered religious life, meaning he had no claim on the estate and no children. Paolo's suit was over Galeazzo's claim to that part of Rugerio's estate that had come to him through their father, Andrea, which was a third of Cristoforo's estate, in whose will there was the substitution. Here Maino, despite good arguments for Galeazzo in such a "beautiful and subtle" matter, argued for Paola. There was no clause prohibiting alienation or privileging agnation. The jurist saw only a simple vulgar substitution that was satisfied in the first generation's descent and that did not continue past the acceptance of his inheritance by Andrea.[101]

From 1550 in Bologna came the case of the will of Bartolomeo di Giannozzo Antonelli de Sancti, a Florentine, naming as heir his son and any future sons, with 200 florins for any girl. Substitute to the son were his uncles, Raphaele d'Antonello and Amphrione d'Antonello, for halves, with instructions to provide 200 for females. Charities came in if all else failed. His son survived, as did a daughter who was dowered. The son left a daughter, who predictably saw the uncles' heirs dispute the inheritance. Did the substitution include women or only men? Mariano Sozzini said it included women. Even if there were an agnatic bias to the testator's wishes, he had not used the term *masculus* in the substitution. Further, "a predeceased is not said to be bound by a *fideicommissum* to his brothers, through whom rather any of them must be said to be bound than the sons of the uncles with respect to preserving agnation, as they are more remote in agnation."[102] So the daughter was substitute heir because a closer relation, who happened to be agnate herself. In another case Sozzini simply faced the mutual substitutions among three sons, with dowries for girls. If the sons all died without sons, the estate passed to three monasteries. He simply found no recourse for the sons' daughters. The key was that "if the testator were asked whether he wanted a reciprocal *fideicommissum* to exist among those male descendants, on account of

---

[100] Maino, 2 *cons.* 142, 432b–42a.   [101] Del Maino, 1 *cons.* 134, 398a–400b.
[102] Sozzini, 4 *cons.* 26, fols. 50va–52va.

which succession by women would be impeded and the estate transfer to strangers, without doubt he would respond that he wanted that, for notice that he always called males, and if there were none, holy institutions, and never women.[103] Here use of the term *masculus* in the testament and not the gender-vague term *filius* put things in male hands only, at least licensing Sozzini's misogynistic reading of the testator's mind.

Women's wills may not have been misogynistic, but they could be every bit as agnatic in their bias as men's. When monna Gilia de' Prothi wrote her will, she named her grandsons, Bartolomeo and Daolo de' Dotti of Padua, by her deceased daughter, with mutual substitution to them and their heirs. These two had a sizeable progeny (necessitating a family tree in the printed text of the *consilium*). Over the ensuing generations, Daolo's share had passed to Antonio, whose son and heir was Francesco, whose son and heir was Antonio junior, with substitution to the son of his sister Lucrezia. To Bartolomeo the heirs were Antonio and Jacopo and then the latter's sons. Two of these contested what went to Lucrezia's children in the other line of descent on the basis of Gilia's will, which lay four generations back. How long did a *fideicommissum* last? It could be argued that the agnatic line descended from Daolo was ended with Antonio's death, as Lucrezia was not even legitimately born, and all descended from her were in any case not agnate. Sozzini, however, said the property belonged to her sons in accord with the intervening will of Francesco. Gilia's substitutions had been obviated by the heirs having sons. The substitutions stopped there. Even if one argued that there continued to be an agnatic trust passively in the presence of sons and heirs in each generation, by the time it got to Antonio junior one was looking at a descendant in fifth degree from Gilia:

For a *fideicommissum* is not usually stretched beyond the fourth degree from the testator who made it, just as we say of the prohibition of alienation, so that goods transfer within the family. For that [prohibition] and the *fideicommissum* contained in it does not last beyond the fourth degree, unless in the prohibition was added the word perpetually, as I want that they come perpetually in all descendants (*quod perpetuo veniant in omnes descendentes*).

It was a very precise and limited reading but also understandable.[104] Sozzini was not going to extend the sense of family any further than the

[103] Sozzini, 3 *cons.* 110, fols. 177va–80va.
[104] Sozzini, 3 *cons.* 81, fols. 132va–34ra (Bologna 1546).

testator, here a woman, had seen it. And this was a woman who clearly had a limited concern with agnation, but in legal terms the telling lack of concern with agnation lay in not appending the term perpetual to the substitution.

Carlo de' Uberti of Mantua named his nephew heir, substituting the nephew's sons in turn. If they all died childless, then their sisters came in, and after them a hospital. He also allowed his nephew to leave one of his sons, Lodovico, more than the other two. The nephew indeed took the estate and soon died with his own will, containing various *legata* and a prohibition on alienation, with the explanation to keep it *in posteros* in male line. Substitution to his sons for half went to the Uberti living in Venice. If they failed, their half went to the testator's daughters or their sons. The hospital got this half if all else failed. Two of the nephew's sons died without issue, so the favored son Lodovico fell heir to all and passed it to his son, Antonio, and then to his son, Giovanfrancesco junior, which is where the male line ultimately failed. There were two daughters. These hoped to claim inheritance by terms of Carlo's will, not his nephew's, as it allowed for sisters. Or did the Venetian branch profit? It could be argued that the nephew was no longer burdened with a *fideicommissum* once he became heir. The substitution lapsed at that point, and so his will would govern. Sozzini took the other side, seeing the nephew bound by the fideicommissary substitution in favor of his sons in turn. The testator clearly wanted those sons to get his property, and he looked past them to the hospital in what was a deep substitution. That in turn meant that the nephew could not craft a will on this estate. With that will out of the picture, the estate went to Giovanfrancesco's daughters. Sozzini defended their claims against the Venetian Uberti. A second *consilium* argued that by terms of the nephew's will the grandson of his daughter Margareta, who was Carlo Malatesta, could inherit by the terms that allowed male descendants of daughters in the absence of sons, which also showed that this particular will did not consider the preservation of agnation.[105]

The jurist Leonardo da Thiene of Vicenza left his daughter her handsome 5,000 ducat dowry and a dowry to his granddaughter, while his four sons got the patrimony. Substitution *in infinitum* was set up among them. Should his line fail Leonardo substituted his brother's line and thereafter "other near relatives of the family of Thiene." When one of the sons later died without sons, but with two daughters with 3,000 ducat

---

[105] Sozzini, 3 *cons.* 1 and 2, fols. 2ra–7rb.

dowries, the question arose if his share went back to his brothers. Did the language about heirs include women in those masculine nouns? Did it include granddaughters, who were agnates? Was the testator only concerned with agnation in that last substitution of anyone from the Thiene? The huge dowry of 5,000 showed the testator was no less fond of his female offspring, it might be argued. For all the mental agility it took to offer a series of arguments for the women, Sozzini was much more at home defending the male claims. What mattered were not abstract arguments whether *filius* was a more generic term also including women, but the intent of the testator. The treatment accorded his own daughters showed the testator's concerns, which would be no less with granddaughters. His concern for preserving family dignity and honor was palpable. That concern excluded the daughters in this trust to the brothers and their sons.[106]

A late and final example of substitutions involving women, comes from the *consilia* of Pietro Cavallo. Monna Benedetta Cini of Barga went to court against Giovanna de' Pucci about the testament of Antonio Cini in favor of his sons Michele and Giovanni, to whom, lacking heirs, Benedetta was substituted as the testator's sister. Giovanna was her sister-in-law, mother of the boys, and in possession of the estate that Benedetta now tried to claim. A judge in first instance had ruled against Benedetta, because the condition for her substitution was lacking, as she seemingly was substituted for any nieces, not her nephews. But there were no nieces. Pietro Cavallo in 1585, however, upheld the substitution with the proviso that usufruct went to Giovanna for life and the legitimate portion should be deducted (presumably to go to Giovanna outright).[107]

Fideicommissa

The essence of what became the pivotal feature of so many Italian inheritances, the *fideicommissum*, consisted of the wedding of two elements – perpetual substitution in the male line and the prohibition on alienation of property, or certain properties, outside that line. It took time for *ius commune* and its practitioners to bring themselves to accept this combination of elements, which on face of it bound the legal hands of the heir in any one generation. With regard to *fideicommissum*, a bare handful of statutes dealt with the first heir's right to a Falcidian or Trebellianic

---

[106] Sozzini, 2 *cons.* 168, fols. 238ra–44ra.   [107] Cavallo, *cons.* 164, fols. 213rb–15ra.

quarter, as he was burdened with the charge to return the property to
the next heir. Only a late statute like that of Siena in 1545 dedicated a
specific rubric to *fideicommissa*. There the concern was that property
could not be claimed before the condition in the *fideicommissum* had
been fulfilled, and the one with the burden of restoration of the property
to the substituted heir could be asked to make an inventory in the
interim and provide sureties for ultimate delivery of the estate. That
security was not required where the heirs were children or other direct
descendants of the testator.[108] That clause seemed to indicate that the
tricky moment was when the *fideicommissum* was going to land property in the hands of collateral and more distant heirs (possibly even
women), who would not have firsthand knowledge of all the different
holdings and assets and, perhaps more important, of the different debts
and charges on the estate and the identity of the creditors. Siena's statute
was concerned, then, with procedural issues, while otherwise (as in so
many other jurisdictions) placing no limits on making *fideicommissa* or
how long they could last.

Fifteenth Century

Prohibitions on alienation were matters jurists accommodated even back
in the fourteenth century, but within limits. Baldo took a case that can
be seen as an early expression of the desire to preserve family property
that animated the law and practice of *fideicommissa*. In his will a father
forbade sale or alienation of his homes, as he wanted them to remain
permanently in the hands of his heirs and their children. If someone
wanted to sell, it could be worked out with other kin at a set price. But
could it be sold to anyone else? Baldo noted at first that the answer
seemed to be no, but he decided otherwise. The testator had allowed
sales, after all, even if of a certain type. Once a thing was bought, it was
in the nature of the contract of sale for the purchaser to be able to
alienate in turn. In contrast, what was received in inheritance was
supposed to go to one's sons or next of kin by the usual routes.[109] So
allowance of sale of any sort seemed to obviate the prohibition on
alienation, at least past the heirs and their children, who were mentioned
in the will. Baldo was not yet ready to go too far in tying the hands of
heirs as property owners.

---

[108] Siena, 252.   [109] Baldo, 5 *cons.* 85, fol. 23vb.

Some decades later another testator named his sons Francesco and Antonio heirs, with provision "that any of them cannot sell, give away or alienate anything (*vendere, donare, aut aliquid alienare*), any possession, as long as they were not yet twenty-five years of age. With this condition, that if one should die without legitimate and natural male sons, then the estate of the deceased should pass to the other or his male heirs." They could not give any female a dowry of more than 1000 ducats. After the testator died, Francesco lived to an old age, leaving two sons, Paolo and Antonfrancesco, neither of whom seemed to have entered into their father's property. Antonio too left a son, Jacobo, who lived well into adulthood and left one son, Francesco, who also seemed not to have entered into Jacobo's estate. "But the aforesaid Francesco and Jacobo at or near a very senile age alienated many goods and lands." The first legal problem was if the grandsons and great grandson were substitute heirs to the original testator. If they were, then could they claim restitution of the sold properties as liable for the substitution? The allegations advanced by the attorney for the descendants, probably in fact by one of them, Paolo, who is described as "doctus," argued for the continued validity, and thus governing role, of this fideicommissary substitution. Paolo di Castro declared that a tacit fideicommissary substitution was indeed in play, and the testator simply wanted to burden the sons with return to the substituted heirs. If this had been a simple vulgar substitution, meaning there was not *aditio* to the testator, then grandsons could not come to the inheritance by substitution to the grandfather but only by intestacy to their father. But in this case there were other words referring to further descendants, and the testator prohibited alienation, substituted the heirs to each other, and set a cap on dowries. That all added up to a tacit *fideicommissum*:

So we conclude in this first issue that the grandsons and great grandson of the testator were tacitly substituted to said Francesco, son of the testator instituted heir, . . . And this under the opposite condition, namely if his sons should die with children, for the express condition, by which they were substituted to each other, was if any one of them should die without children, and under this it cannot be said that children of the deceased seem to be substituted, because it would be to imply a contradiction.

On this basis it was then possible to argue that these descendants did not have the right to retrieve sold properties, as they did not gain them under substitution. After all, by the will alienation of property was allowable once the heir reached twenty-five, so it was not totally prohibited. The bigger question was if there was, nonetheless, a legal prohibition, because the property was under obligation of restitution to substitute heirs. As the testator had placed a substitution in the will, he had to want the property to be available to substitute heirs or his intentions would have been frustrated. The jurist also blew away the argument that Francesco may have been ignorant of the prohibition on alienation. In the end "rather said Francesco had understood the contrary because he took care and tried to have his sons ratify the alienation, and so he supposed that they could come against his power, and so it seems and is presumed that he was aware and so the contrary cannot hold . . . that the alienation may be retractable on account of ignorance."[110] In essence Paolo di Castro was not going to let presumed senility or a substitution undermine legal acts of sale. The claims of male descendants were not, in his eyes anyway, enough to overturn the loss of ancestral properties. The testator had, perhaps strangely, allowed alienation after reaching age twenty-five, so the jurist could as well.

The will of ser Viviano di Neri Viviani of Florence raised a host of issues about substitution and the reservation of property subject to it. Giovanni da Imola and Benedetto Accolti (1415–64) had already weighed in on the case before it came to Lodovico Pontano. The first two seem to have argued that the substitution among the sons of ser Viviano's first marriage was fideicommissary, but Pontano said it was *vulgaris* and direct. The substitution of the four sons by first marriage to each other was in simple terms, while that among the three sons of Viviano's second marriage was phrased as being "vulgariter et pupillariter per fideicommissum," thus covering all bases. The insertion of these adverbs and the precise placement of them mattered. The testator, himself a notary, highly involved in drafting Florentine legislation and other government business prior to his death in 1414, could easily have added such a clause to the first substitution, but clearly chose not to. Direct substitution did not require "restitution" of the estate to substituted heirs. In this case, then the testament of one of Viviano's sons, who was a papal protonotary, which had named only one brother as heir, establishing that he only had usufruct, made clear there had not been alienation of anything from his other brothers.[111] The substitution, which might have been applied to a cleric dying without legitimate children, was direct and so he was not obligated to restore things to substituted heirs.

The will of messer Giovanni de' Salgardi of Feltro favored cousins: the brothers Sandro and Bono, sons of ser Francesco di ser Sandro de'

---

[110] Di Castro, 2 *cons.* 263, fols. 119va–20rb.
[111] Pontano, *cons.* 403, fols. 267rb–68rb.

Salgardi (substituted to each other) for one half, and the brothers Vittore and Zandaniele, sons of ser Antonio de' Salgardi, also substituted to each other, for the other half. A broader substitution worked across those halves. Alienation by one brother was subject to redemption by the other, or if not, by the other set of brothers, "so that said goods may remain in the house of the testator." So this testament employed both substitutions and prohibition of alienation. The first pair died without issue, so their half went to the others. Vittore then sold two possessions to an outsider, Sandro da Petracho, while Zandaniele was alive. Zandaniele had two sons by different mothers. When Vittore died without sons of his own, could Zandaniele's sons, seemingly heirs to all messer Giovanni's patrimony, act to retrieve the sold properties? Paolo di Castro faced the fact that Zandaniele had not acted against the sale and that the testator had allowed each set of brothers to step in against an alienation of ownership but had said nothing about their sons. So it could be argued that there was no right to retrieve (*vendicare*) that had been transmitted to the grandsons. But di Castro was in fact sympathetic to the rights of the sons to retrieve family property, and he left his biggest weapon for his last argument:

But to the contrary works the reason that the testator used, namely, that said goods may remain in the house of the testator. And so he made the prohibition in contemplation of everyone of the house, thus the sons of Zandaniele seem called after death, though they were not specifically named.

This *mens testatoris* was to be honored, leaving aside legal issues of transmission of rights.[112] The testator was capable of contemplating a seemingly infinite line of descent, or at least the logic of di Castro's argument left the door open to such an infinite line. Here then we see a jurist willing to construe the law to the benefit of agnatic lineage and its property.

Pierfilippo da Corgna in a similar situation took the prohibition of alienation as perpetual, from a desire to see property go to descendants rather than others. Against the position that such a perpetual prohibition restricted the freedom of testation of the heir, he argued that the prohibition clause did not restrict freedom of testation, because one could always name any heir, even an *extraneus*, just not to those goods inherited under the substitution. The presumption was that the testator loved those who were closest as set by intestate order of succession, whether that

[112] Di Castro, 2 *cons*, 238, fol. 111va–b.

order was set by local statute or by *ius commune*. In the case at hand where, in fact and ironically, all the remaining descendants were female, sisters were in the advantage as closest, because the estate had become *haereditas fratris* and no longer the father's.[113]

Later Fifteenth and Sixteenth Centuries

By the end of the fifteenth century and increasingly throughout the sixteenth, *fideicommissa*, specifying substitutions and prohibition of alienation of at least key family properties, became commonplace in wills, except in Venice. Legal cases involving these testamentary substitutions also became common and occupied, almost monopolized, jurists' attentions. These devices did so in part because they also carried with them a profound contradiction. As Renata Ago notes, "by introducing encumbrances these instruments impeded the exercise of property rights by the title holders at any time, denying them that same power that the duty of head of family attributed to them. The contradiction is so strident that jurists could not confront it to seek to resolve it at least on a theoretical level."[114] In cases, however, some accommodation had to become actual, if not theoretical. The *consulens* and the judge had to accede to the prerogatives of individual head or to the larger family imperative.

There were thus broadly two modes of interpretation of *fideicommissa*. One was in line with the interests of the heir against the burdens and prohibitions placed on him. The other was in accord with family interests, asserting *favor agnationis* against the individual. The power of the latter was such that juristic doctrine was content to construe existence of a *fideicommissum* in a will even without direct expression, as long as the testator spoke to concern for preservation of family. And that concern and the *fideicommissum* it gave rise to were taken to be perpetual.[115]

Mariano Sozzini (elder) gave exemplary (for us) handling of a will that prohibited alienation. There was a complicated set of multi-generational relations to be considered. What it seems to have boiled down to is that Francesco di Niccolaccio di Petrone Accorridoni of Siena, in keeping with his father's will, which had left half to his brother Giovanni and the other half to his nephews Francesco, Andrea, and Jacopo di Guglielmacci, also gave half of his shops and loggias and a palazzo in Siena to these nephews as heirs. He imposed the condition that no one was to dispute his uncle

---

[113] Corgna, *cons.* 97, fols. 90ra–92va.   [114] Ago, "Ruoli familiari," 127.
[115] Zorzoli, "Della famiglia e del suo patrimonio," 160–63.

Caterino's rights to live there, and that his uncles and their sons *in perpetuum* could not alienate those properties. Anyone who did would be deprived of their inheritance share. At Francesco's death three-quarters went to Ricciardo di Andrea di Guglielmacci, one nephew's son, and the other fourth to Lodovico Salimbeni and Petrone di Francesco di Salimbene di Francesco di Guglielmacci. Ricciardo's death, in turn, left his son Antonio, and four years later his widow Nessina sued for return of her dowry. To realize her claim she took the palazzo, although there were other properties on which she could have capitalized her dowry. Meanwhile Lodovico and Petrone sold their quarter part. Caterino, still alive and in possession of the palazzo, disputed with Petrone that the quarter of the building Petrone had sold should be his by the clause of the will forbidding alienation.

Sozzini first defended the prohibition in the will as the testator's valid desire that it "remain in the house and family." But Sozzini ended up permitting the alienation as the way to meet the demand for Nessina's dowry (a reminder of how powerful the right to dowry and its restitution could be). For sons burdened with the obligation to restore a patrimony to their heirs, an alienation for dowry was permitted, especially on a parental obligation, but for *haeredes extranei* it was not (*extranei* in this case were still part of the wider family, such as cousins). True, the dowry could be settled from other belongings not subject to the prohibition. But the prohibition was *mens testatoris* and so it was the rule to follow, and it applied not only to the heirs but to the heirs' heirs. The prerogative to revoke the alienation fell to the next in line to the testator among the Accorridori, on analogy to laws that wanted women's contracts approved by the nearest *consanguinei*. In this case that was indeed Petrone who had done the alienation.[116] Sozzini thus found it possible to uphold a prohibition of alienation, which he insistently labeled "pure and simple," even in the face of alienation for necessary debt, such as restitution of dowry. Petrone had the right to refund the purchase price on the fourth and to retrieve the rest of the palazzo, even against great-uncle Caterino's claims to ownership (as opposed to a right to use and reside there, which seems to have been all he had).

In another case Filippo Decio wondered how the noble Carlo di Forbino could sell a house subject to a conditional *fideicommissum* in his father's will. Carlo's brother Michele was coheir and substituted to

---

[116] Sozzini, 5 *cons.* 50, fols. 63rb–65rb.

him (to each other), so the first need was to have Michele's formal, notarized renunciation allowing the sale to go forward. There was also a secondary substitution in favor of three nephews if both brothers died without children. So the next requirement was to get each of the nephews to renounce it with the same formality, if they were of age, or by promise of another that they would do so on coming of age. There were also heirs to those nephews, but there were limits. The substitution lapsed with them (fourth generation).

> Whence for those males yet to be born within the fourth degree or within the tenth it [the sale] cannot prejudice their rights, but it is necessary that some suitable person promise to preserve the purchaser of the house unharmed in case it happen that he is molested under that form as was said above about grandsons, and this difficulty would cease if Michele or Carlo should die leaving children, because the condition of the *fideicommissum* would fail.[117]

Decio was not reading the prohibition as absolute or as perpetual. All interested parties could agree and the sale would go forward.

Prohibition of alienation in wills, coupled with substitutions to descendants or, failing them, collateral agnatic kin, turned into something more, rendering a *fideicommissum* an enduring trust. Filippo Decio, for example, had the problem of determining if Giovanpietro de Cathena's prohibition of alienation of the *domus paterna* rose to the level of a fideicommissary substitution to Jacopo de Cathena, his closest agnate kin. He took note of a very common juristic opinion that prohibition of alienation did not of itself give rise to a fideicommissary substitution, unless there had been an actual alienation to an *extraneus* (still possibly related, though not in direct line). A testator could not prevent the fact that an heir's intestate heir might be an *extraneus*, or that the heir could institute that *extraneus* as his heir. So inheritance by an *extraneus* was not covered by the prohibition. In the case before Decio, were the *communis opinio* to hold, the son of the testator, having no children, could name his mother as his heir and she could inherit, notwithstanding the prohibition in his father's will against alienation outside the family. Decio, however, decided "that *fideicommissum* arose to favor family at least in this respect, as those inheriting on intestacy who are not of the family of the testator are excluded from such property." A *fideicommissum* could be conjectured, tacit, from the words and *mens*:

---

[117] Decio, *cons.* 323, fols. 351va–52ra.

For from these words it seems a *fideicommissum* is induced because as he wanted these goods to remain always in the house and kindred of the nobles of Cathena, thus expressly disposing, and it does not seem that this can take place except by way of a *fideicommissum*, as otherwise they may pass outside the family.

The goods could not remain in the family without the obligation to pass them along through the generations. The very verbs "volo" (I want) and "iubeo" (I order) conjured up a *fideicommissum*. And if the terms of the prohibition were general and universal, such as "perpetually to remain among his descendants" (*perpetuo remanere apud suos descendentes*), then the *fideicommissum* was *in infinitum*. To achieve this end,

> that this will of the testator, which is established, may take place, it is necessary that the *fideicommissum* arise absolutely, otherwise the prohibition of alienation is considered simply if anyone of the family should die leaving a stranger heir on intestacy.

So in this case the nearest agnate could claim the property and keep it from going to the testator's son's mother (the original testator's wife), who was not of the testator's *familia*. The prohibition of alienation prevented *extranei* and *venientes ab intestato* who were not of the family. Whatever the *communis opinio* may have been, it was superseded by the indubitable will of the testator and an opinion that was said to be greatly in accord with reason (*magis consona rationi*). The common opinion held where there was a simple prohibition of alienation, but not when there was an additional dispositive passage about keeping property in the hands of kin as a rationale. Decio's opinion was given June 20, 1502, on a case from Asti.[118] Nowhere does he question the value or ethics of keeping property in the family. He easily extended that desire into an infinite progression. Here then was the needed juristic forensic support for a major shift in inheritance practices through much of Italy.

In another case, following on the determination of his colleague, Bartolomeo Sozzini, that a prohibition of alienation induced a *fideicommissum*, not only if the prohibition were specifically broken by an act such as a sale but absolutely, Decio pointed out that as the prohibition allowed alienation with the consent of all the agnates, it did not contain the absolute desire to favor family against outsiders and thus impose the burden to restore goods to family. "Whence this testator does not seem to consider the dignity and honor of the family but rather an affection for the persons (*potius affectionem personarum*) of whom he speaks by

---

[118] Decio, *cons.* 23, fols. 29ra–30ra.

name." Decio, however, agreed with his colleague, and in doing so revealed an abiding presumption about family inheritance. The testament in question contained a *fideicommissum*, as the testator was clearly concerned that the property remain among his sons and theirs in turn, and that led to a wider presumption of his motives. So too

having considered the quality of the palace and the goods in question, whose preservation is a matter of the honor of the family and the testator, it is fitting that the testator seems to have made a prohibition of alienation by way of a *fideicommissum*.

A social and economic presumption thus seemed to anchor the legal one. The allowing of alienation with consent of others was attributed to the fact that those who had the power to consent would instead buy the property and thus keep it in the family. There really was no desire to have alienation. The alienation that had taken place at the hands of receivers settling debts had not had the consent of those named kin and so was invalid in terms of the will. The receivers' power, even to satisfy legitimate debts and serve the interests of creditors and the civic markets in which they operated, did not override the will. Their power, as set by statute, was said to apply to the goods of a bankrupt (*bona cessantium*). But the testator, Carlo, was not "truly" *cessans*, as he had not been properly tried and found *cessans*. He had merely been condemned in contumacy for not appearing before the court, so his sons were not (yet) liable for the 600 florins he owed. The statute of Florence in question was, said Decio, extremely harsh on the sons (*valde odiosum*) and merited the strictest reading.[119] Having rigorously tied prohibition on alienation to agnation, Decio (no more than Sozzini) could not let stand the institution of a mother as his heir by one son, as that was an alienation outside the family.

Giovanni de' Nicelli's testament and those of his ascendants provoked the question whether they contained a tacit *fideicommissum*, such that Bartolino could pursue his grandfather's property. Bartolino was substitute heir to a substitute, so his inheritance claim was hardly direct. If there was a *fideicommissum*, including prohibition of alienation, Bartolino's hands were tied as to disposition of the estate. Giason del Maino said that the will of the testator was clear, not at all subtle, and "law follows the will of the testator just as a hunter follows a hare" (*sicut venator leporem*). The will set up an order of substitutions of males of the Nicelli family, to keep the line going always and to exclude women always. So it

---

[119] Decio, *cons.* 38, fols. 47va–49va.

was proper to construe that heirs faced a burden of keeping property intact and passing it along. It was a reciprocal *fideicommissum* to each succeeding generation. When the prohibition of alienation was given an agnatic explanation, as in this case, "that such goods never leave from our name or our family" (*quod talia bona nunquam de nomine nostro vel nostra familia exeant*), it implied a reciprocal arrangement. There was provision of 800 for each female to marry in each successive generation, which proved again the male agnatic bias of the first testator and set a limit for women to be content with. The Trebellianic portions were not even to be removed, as the will prohibited that as well.[120] Here in a manner similar to Decio, *fideicommissum* was construed largely on the presentation of a rationale about family in a prohibition of alienation. The seeming perpetuity or open-endedness of it all was conceded.

In another instance, where a male line had failed and possession of the family dwelling was contested between aunts and a granddaughter, where one might presume the testator would prefer those closer in degree to those more remote, Giason del Maino went with the remoter female because, he said, she more closely fit what the testator had in mind. Violante was the daughter of Niccolò, who was the last of the male line. The house lay under a perpetual prohibition of alienation. Although such a prohibition did not extend normally past the fourth degree, "yet when the prohibition is made for all children and descendants and in perpetuity, then all descendants and males in infinity are deemed prohibited [from alienating]." By that logic the house descended until it ended up in the hands of the last male, and from him to his daughter.[121] The aunts were closer to the testator, but not to his line of descent.

The central position of the prohibition of alienation is clearer when one looks at cases in which it was not present. Enemundo Fabri made his brother "et suos" his heirs by testament. The brother died leaving two sons and two daughters. In what way were they heirs to Enemundo in view of the cryptic "et suos"? Filippo Decio saw three possibilities: a vulgar substitution, a *fideicommissum*, or simultaneous installation of brother and his offspring. He came to reject the first two. There was no need to name "et suos" for a substitution, as the brother's sons would succeed him in any case. And a *fideicommissum* would leave the brother burdened with restoring the estate to his heirs, but in fact he had accepted it and managed it freely. So only the simultaneous heirship made sense,

---

[120] Del Maino, 4 *cons.* 108, 393a–98a.   [121] Del Maino, 1 *cons.* 4, 25a–28a.

but that also had to be taken as successive, sons following father. So Decio concluded that once the elder took possession, any vulgar substitution was ended.[122] He could manage the property as he saw fit and had no obligation to pass it intact to "suos." The same sort of issue arose in 1513 with the will of Giovanni di Genasio that named as heir Francesco, minor son of Lodovico de Genasio, the testator's brother, "et suos liberos masculos." Again Decio argued that such a direct institution of the sons was not a *fideicommissum*, but a vulgar substitution that was ended when the youngster grew up and entered into the estate. So his heirs were not bound by a *fideicommissum* and were free to dispose of the property.[123] In these two instances, then, Decio was ruling for free disposition of property in the hands of an heir when there were no clauses prohibiting alienation outside the family.

The physician Giovanni da Tolentino had four sons. He left maestro Niccolò his books; Pandolfo got 70 ducats per year for eight years; and all four were named heirs, with substitution "vulgariter, pupillariter et per fideicommissum." They were forbidden to divide the patrimony for fourteen years, and the younger ones, Antonio and Jacopo, had prerogative before all to 800 ducats each as equitable compensation for what went to the other two for their studies. After many years, with Giovanni since dead, Antonio died childless and left a will in favor of Jacopo's sons, also claiming that Niccolò owed him part of the paternal estate. The 800 ducats due to Antonio were at issue, subject to *fideicommissum* and to be restored (giving half to Pandolfo, in effect), or under Antonio's control to be left to the nephews? Giason del Maino took the 800 ducats as a bequest to Antonio that was outside the scope of the testamentary *fideicommissum*. Maino did not fail to point out that the 800 ducats was also compensatory in view of the moneys expended on the other two brothers.[124]

Later Sixteenth Century

Mariano Sozzini the younger, working in the first half of the sixteenth century, was of the generation of jurists who solidified the *fideicommissum* as a standard feature of so many Italian inheritances. He handled many such cases, and we can only look at a few interesting ones. The first example arose from a set of events over several decades. Silvestro Trenta of Lucca set up a will in favor of his two sons, substituting, should both

---

[122] Decio, *cons.* 253, fols. 273va–74rb.   [123] Decio, *cons.* 125, fols. 223va–24va.
[124] Maino, 4 *cons.* 175, 614b–16b.

die without heirs, his nephew Cristoforo for two-thirds, with the rest to
the poor. If Cristoforo died without heirs the testator's daughter stepped
in. Silvestro's two boys took the estate, one later dying without children,
so it all fell to his brother, Giovanbattista. Meanwhile, the nephew
Cristoforo left three sons. In 1486 Giovanbattista died childless, leaving
his widow life rights. After her death, his estate was to go to the poor and
for dowering poor girls. Cristoforo's sons died in 1509, 1511, and 1517,
leaving in total four sons. All those boys moved to get Cristoforo's two-
thirds, basing their claims on a substitution then two generations old and
on which their fathers had not acted. Despite a lapse of over thirty years
in which a woman, not agnate, had held the property, Sozzini had little
difficulty asserting that Silvestro's governing will was that Cristoforo's
sons take his place, and their sons in turn. Beyond the usual close reading
of the will's terms, he claimed there was undoubted desire to preserve
property and agnation: "The evident basis of the preservation of this
agnation [is] his property and wealth, without which the honor and
dignity of families is besmirched and declines, as experience teaches"
(*sordescit et decrescit honor et dignitas familiarum, ut experientia docet*).
Sozzini was characteristically long-winded and tediously detailed.[125] But
in a way he had to be, because there was no single clause explicitly
mentioning the desire to preserve family and agnation; there was instead
the powerful general presumption that such was what testators wanted
and what lay behind substitutions to agnates.

The Ragusan ser Francesco di Stefano de Benessa left his two nephews
as heirs. If they died without heirs, Francesco wanted his "casa grande" to
go to Antonio d'Andrea Benessa. He also ordered one nephew not to
alienate anything so it all descended perpetually in the male line. The heirs
took over and the death of one put it all in the hands of the other, who
also died childless. So the sons of Antonio de Benessa advanced their
claim to the entire estate, not just the house. They seemed to have a good
case resting on the agnatic preference of the testator as expressed in the
prohibition of alienation falling on one of the nephews. But Sozzini in
1542 cast them aside, as there were daughters who were descended from
the testator and could be called *haeredes* (*ab intestato*). And despite local
statute, the daughters were next in line, as there was no statutory exclusion by such distantly related agnates. The testator also had given the
brother only the house, not the rest of what was under a prohibition to

---

[125] Sozzini, 2 *cons.* 141, fols. 194va–96vb.

alienate. Other than the house, whose destination in Antonio's hands was precise, the substitution was ended with the end of the male line. The distant male agnates gave way to the true meaning of heirs as *haeredes sanguinis*.[126] Sozzini licensed his reading of the *fideicommissum* in Ragusa as being in accord with its rather generous statutory allowance for female intestate succession.

In a case from 1539 Pietro de' Pompeati of Tridento named four sons as his heirs with the usual substitution to each other. If all lines failed then the estate went to the "the nearest relations of his house" (*proximiores de domo sua*). The four sons inherited and all four had sons of their own, though one's line finally failed with his grandson, who left his share to a notary. The agnates sued to retrieve that as subject to restitution under the *fideicommissum*. Sozzini conceded that the matter was not simple, but in the end he denied that there was a reciprocal substitution to the agnates. There had been heirs to the original heirs and the substitution was ended. There had been no prohibition of alienation or perpetual possession, so there was no testamentary recourse against the notary.[127]

By the later end of the sixteenth century, approaches to the issues raised by *fideicommissa* were well worked out, as the cascade of citations in *consilia* of the era testifies. Marco Antonio Pellegrini provides us with the example of messer Stefano Centurioni, one of many Genoese with interests in Spain, who made his will there in 1530. The case came to Pellegrini from the officials of San Giorgio for his decisory opinion as to whether Stefano junior, son of Domenico di Simone Centurioni, uncle of the testator, was free of the *fideicommissum* and its substitutions to the sons of the testator's three sisters, to their daughters, if need be, and then to the Misericordia. Could Stefano freely dispose of houses in and out of Genoa and of a deposit with San Giorgio? Pellegrini's plodding approach called forth eight reasons the substitution was extinguished and one-by-one refutation of all eight. For example, the will mentioned only sons and grandsons, so it did not extend past them; and it mentioned the eldest son, so it did not cover younger ones. To the contrary stood the fact that

We believe the trust is not ended in the first and second generation of Simon, but the most remote among his major male descendants is preferred by the nature of the trusts [*maioratium*] which the Spanish frequently use, as many Spanish authors have left in writing.

---

[126] Sozzini, 2 *cons.* 187, fols. 280rb–81va.   [127] Sozzini, 2 *cons.* 176, fols. 254vb–56ra.

Beyond the custom of that region, which applied to the elements of the patrimony situated there, Pellegrini appealed to the deposit with San Giorgio as evidence of the testator's desire to make that perpetually available to his heirs, and thus he thought of perpetual substitution, especially in view of the prohibition of alienation attached thereto.[128]

A testator from the Giusti family of Verona set up substitutions, if he had no sons, to his brother, count Vincenzo and his heirs, failing them to Annibale, Carlo, Leilio, and Zenovello, the sons of Leilio, as transverse agnates. He had a son, so the substitutions were ended, but the boy died young without heirs. The second main clause of the will was a prohibition of alienation of the palace at Broili, near Santa Maria in Stelle outside Verona, so that it always remained among the Giusti. It was not easy to say if that prohibition gave rise to a perpetual *fideicommissum*, especially in regard to those Giusti who ended up not as heirs (the young son was), and so not bound to something that seemed to be a personal matter for heirs. In other words, it did not seem to tie the hands of Annibale and his brothers, though by order of succession they ended up with the property. Pellegrini argued that they were bound, that the intent of the testator, which was in favor of anyone from the Giusti, was clear. He also argued that the prohibition was general and applied to all property, not just one palace, though "as this palace with its adjacent holdings and lands is most noble and of great splendor in the illustrious family of Giusti, [it is] no wonder that the testator cared especially for it."[129] Though his substitution had been obviated, the testator's sense of familial prerogative on such noble property was not to be set aside in Pellegrini's eyes.

Pietro Cavallo also had little trouble handling *fideicommissa*. In the name of Pietro and Bernardo Carnesecchi, Benedetto Rucellai sued the brothers Durante and Cristoforo Carnesecchi as substituted heirs according to the will of a senior Bernardo Carnesecchi. They were seeking to have deducted from the estate their *legitima*, trebellianic portion, and maternal dowry, as well as the costs of improvements. Cavallo argued for these and more on multiple grounds. *Legitima* was due Pietro as a son, by right of nature (*iure naturae*), not by paternal beneficence; Pietro as son and heir had the right to deduct trebellianica from the patrimony he was burdened with restoring; maternal dowry was owed by the father who had contracted to restore it to his wife or her heir. Funeral expenses for the testator and the costs of meeting any bequests were also to be

---

[128] Pellegrini, *cons.* 38, fols. 104ra–06vb.   [129] Pellegrini, *cons.* 45, fols. 124vb–28ra.

deducted. Creditors were to get their share (*aes alienum*). And improvements were to be paid for.[130] Not all property was family property, in this case. There was a host of obligations that fell on the heirs to meet. Cavallo gives us an indication that there were those who were not so open to perpetual patrimonies and the harm they potentially did to various classes of claimants or creditors.

CONCLUSIONS

Because we have proceeded by means of legal cases, we have necessarily focused on moments of dispute and the (statistically) non-normative situations. We have seen that jurists, comfortable as they were doctrinally with privileging the agnatic line of descent, were also able to argue against certain substitutions and to put property in women's hands. True, those were moments when the obvious agnatic connection was ruled out, but it was still possible to argue for agnates in some instances. Invoking the intent of the testator as the lynchpin of interpretation, they in fact had to hand a malleable tool.

Testators who forbade alienation of particular holdings were elevating something to a significance beyond its market value. A possession thus became durable, was lifted from the realm of circulation (though it could return to it), objectifying a lineage and its people. In the course of the sixteenth century noble families in particular would generate inventories of belongings, not just as a legal protection against debts when an estate changed hands, but as an affirmation of ownership in all the many different items. Women's relations to objects, in contrast to men's, remained more utilitarian, Renata Ago has noted, except when women had a contribution to make to perpetuation of the (usually marital) lineage in inalienable objects.[131] Women identified with the languages of lineage and engaged in transmission of objects that made family continuity visible, even as theirs were the hands by which property might pass from one lineage to another.

Jurists provided an important means to foster such inalienability by construing prohibitions of alienation and substitutions as perpetual, at least when the right language was employed. Yet they also remained profoundly aware of the contradictions and conflicts between individual prerogatives of ownership, including freedom of testation, and the

---

[130] Cavallo, *cons.* 83, fols. 80va–82rb.   [131] Ago, *Gusto for Things*, 220.

prerogatives and demands of family and inalienability, and those of creditors. Those conflicts were most apparent when the obvious cases of continuity, especially biological survival and legal heirship of sons, were lacking. It was in such moments that they could and did argue for the prerogatives of individuals, including women, and against the perpetuity of substitutions, or not.

In the cases we have tracked in the *consilia* of more than a dozen jurists across three centuries, we can see that the testament itself was an object of concern, in its formal elements, but mainly as an individual's modification of intestacy. As time passed, jurists seemed to become more comfortable with the uses of testaments in the service of agnate relationships and a durable sense of identity. These included reassuring women of their dowry rights, even if the testament left them nothing or too little or too much. With appropriate limitations, they came to accommodate the intentions of testators as the privileged grid of property transmission across the generations. These, in turn, were honored as fitting with the dignity of heads of household and public utility.

Paternalism

Family and State

In the mid-sixteenth century Mariano Sozzini was confronted with a not-uncommon issue. The noble Simon de Fregua, citizen of Faenza, had died intestate, leaving a nephew, Cesare Gandolfo, by his sister, also Faventine, and Lancelotto and Stefano, paternal cousins, who were from Brisighella, and thus as foreigners to Faenza did not pay taxes there.[1] These three disputed the inheritance. Faventine statute favored male agnates within four degrees, specifically placing paternal cousins ahead of sisters or their issue. But another statute declared that outsiders come to live in Faenza could not enjoy the immunities and privileges of Faventine citizens, unless a civic council expressly granted such. Sozzini noted that the statute on intestate inheritance was common to others in Italy that "were favorable to preservation of agnation, which is preserved by wealth as otherwise dignity of the family would be besmirched and decline because of poverty" (*decrescat familiae dignitas ob paupertatem*). That they were not Faventine could be finessed by the argument that an inheritance law which did not dispense a privilege, but shepherded a line of succession, did extend to foreigners. But Sozzini did not agree with that line of thought and determined that Cesare inherited to the exclusion of his cousins. That was consonant with *ius commune*, as Cesare was closer in degree to the deceased. And the inheritance statute did not apply in this case, as the cousins were *forenses*, in the sense of being subject to a different forum. They should not gain from a statute contrary to *ius commune*, that was a *ius proprium* to Faventini but not to Brisighellini.

---

[1] Sozzini, *cons.* 80, vol. 4, fols. 135va-36rb.

He backed this position with citations to numerous *consilia*. The rationale behind the statute, conservation of agnation, was not in play either: "this reason is considered with respect to agnation for someone existing in his city by a sort of public favor, namely so that burdens of his city may more easily be sustained." That did not apply to foreigners. The statute of one city could not make the persons of foreigners legitimate to succeed against the rules of *ius commune*. The cascade of references he drew up was designed to demonstrate that this was the (by far) common opinion among the doctors of laws.

In the end Sozzini was subordinating agnation to the state. The rationale of family preservation (at least in intestacy) gave way to the shouldering of civic burdens and the kinship of one's fellow citizens. The city's interest in fostering agnation (as we saw in the examination of intestacy statutes) was in providing itself with well-endowed officeholders and taxpayers. Cesare's cousins, for all that they had his uncle's name, did not fit that description. They were not part of the greater household that was the city.

CIVIC INTERESTS

The sources available for investigation of family life and economic circumstances are generally fiscal in nature. Certainly that is the case for the most well-known of such sources, the catasto of Florence. These sources have to be approached with care so as not to confuse fiscal with legal responsibility, or fiscal association with actual living arrangements.[2] We have seen such problems arise in considering the dissolution of *fraterna*, for one thing. In a larger sense, these fiscal sources demonstrate governmental interest in family and its possessions, in a continuity of officeholding and taxpaying.

The growing paternalism of governments in Italy was one of the features of the period from 1300 to 1600 (and after). Governments weighed in on social and moral issues. They provided food to the poor, care for abandoned children and widows, for abused and abandoned women, and simply (perhaps more crucially) for fatherless children in need of legal guardianship. They took oversight of religious charitable institutions. They legislated to prevent practices contrary to family and civic well-being (such as sodomy and other moral matters, including prostitution). They passed sumptuary laws to curtail expenditures and

[2] Leverotti, *Famiglie e istituzioni*, 146.

ceremonial spectacles at weddings and funerals. They provided laws to limit officeholding to legitimate offspring (thus promoting marriage) and even, as in the case of Florence, to furnish dowries in response to sufficient investment by a family.

These paternalistic steps were in keeping with the self-conception of governments throughout Europe, leave alone Italy. To all these, families were the essence of the *res publica*. Their wealth was the basis of state wealth. Defense of families was therefore an important governmental function. Every bit as much as it was the function of fathers. For their part, jurists and theologians tended to reject any mindless equation of king or emperor with *pater*, but the fact that they seriously entertained the possibility, as Luca da Penne (ca. 1325–1390) did in regard to the southern Italian monarchy, shows how common and easy such an equation could be. It worked in reverse too, as by the maxim that a man was king in his home (*quisque in domo sua dicitur rex.*)[3] The modeling of rule on the role of the father – whether by the collective "fathers" of an oligarchic council or by the benevolent prince of a ruling dynasty – was a common idiom. This is what Isabelle Chabot has characterized as the "government of fathers," in which even only the responsibly married were to be eligible for important offices. Preservation of family wealth was also a political imperative, which generated inheritance rules and the disciplining even of sexuality. So there was a particular image of family at work in political discourse, one in which paternal power was supposedly beneficent, but uncontested.

The patriarchal dimension of the state became patrimonial in the cases of princely dynasties, where the household and government overlapped and the fiscal and private treasuries were often promiscuously intermingled. This is not to deny that tensions could and did erupt between the prince and the corporate elite entities of any state. Representations of relation between fathers and sons as dominant and subordinate male gender roles elided the real tensions that could arise between prince and heir or between prince and subject.

The linkage of household and government went back at least as far as Plato and Aristotle, and thus was common across Europe. James I in England notably adopted a rather absolute model of his paternal authority over his childlike subjects, although there were other, less absolute versions of paternalism. Still, the obedient acceptance of the citizens/

---

[3] Cavina, *Il padre spodestato*, 49–51, 53.

subjects (children) was expected. The concern for the good of the whole on the part of the ruler (father) was presumed. The failures of the children could be punished. As a disobedient son might be cast from the family home, the rebel was sent into exile. But, as there was no sanction a son might hold over a failing father (except to hope somehow to dodge the consequences of his failings), there was no sanction (or very few and weak) against the tyrant or incompetent ruler.

In these depictions of family, women were largely absent, or at least subordinate, just as they were absent from oligarchic governance and only occasionally prominent in principalities, in the absence of men. But treatises on household governance, as they placed paternal actions under careful scrutiny, also began to concede more to the maternal role. There was no corresponding broadening in theory of women's political role. In fact the notion that political power was an attribute inalterably gendered as male meant that rule by women could only seem "monstrous' – famously so to the Scottish Calvinist, John Knox, but hardly to him alone.

Just as wealthier families might expect more ready obedience from their sons, as the cost of disobedience was greater, governments might also expect such obeisance, because for such families access to political offices or favors was an important prop to family preservation and enhancement of family prestige. In this regard the narrow vertical dynastic dimension of that preservation yielded, however tacitly at times, to a larger sense of family in collateral and even cognatic relations, as a network of fundamental support for political needs and ambitions, as well as the welfare of the family.

We might consider one case of exile as an example of the ways in which citizenship and kinship crossed. In 1482 Bernardo (a doctor of law) and Niccolò dei Borghesi, sons of messer Galgano, were exiled from Siena as rebels and their goods were confiscated. Their mother, monna Cia, obtained her sons' property from Sienese officials in order to restore dowries to their wives and cover all debts and obligations. As part of this Cia gave her son-in-law, the physician Francesco Nivo, for dowry and support of his wife, Lucrezia, the sum of 600 ducats, which took the form of a house and two shops. A renewal of the ban of exile in 1484 demanded return of exiles' property to their owners, even if given over as a dowry. Niccolò, the surviving son and exile, along with his nephews, moved in 1499, despite their silence on the matter to that point, to retrieve the house and shops, offering Francesco Nivo the stated sum of 600 ducats. Francesco refused and went to court alleging title to the property from the lapse of time (a process known as prescription in law).

Giason del Maino was handed this complicated case. He had to consider that by *ius commune* the mother's alienation of property without the knowledge or consent of her sons was not licit. He also faced the 1484 act that demanded exiles' property be returned to their owners. Also in Niccolò's favor was the argument that prescription did not apply, as there were not a full ten years from the rebanning of 1484 to the death of the exiled brother, Bernardino – intervening years not counting, because his sons, as heirs, were too young to act to retrieve their title. But the arguments against Niccolò and his nephews militated more strongly for Francesco. As heirs to Cia they could not abrogate her acts (the cession of the house as dowry), if only because "the heir is reputed one and the same person with the deceased" (*haeres reputatur una et eadem persona cum defuncto*).[4] And her act was to settle a true and just obligation of a dowry. Finally, there had been more than ten years between Bernardino's death in 1487 and 1499, when the redemption could have been offered (had they had the cash). So prescription did apply. In this case Maino upheld the Sienese legislation against the interests of a family that had experienced exile. But the main legal point seems to have been that no move was made to regain the house until more than enough time had passed to allege prescription. Without saying as much, Maino was penalizing the Borghesi, not as exiles but as poor managers of their economic assets and legal rights. Had the brothers acted sooner, Francesco would have had cash, not the real estate they wanted. Yet it is also the case, here as elsewhere, that the prerogatives of exiles were not entirely lost, even in the face of confiscation for rebellion. Rights of wives and children, at least, retained validity and some force.

Political exile struck at families, depriving them of persons and property. The political struggles that preceded sentences of exile were most apparent when cities such as Florence designated families as magnates and hit them with penalties and extensive liabilities. In the case of Florence as well, rehabilitation of branches of some magnate families to full rights of citizenship required familial acts of secession from the broader disenfranchised kinship, notably by changing the family name and coat of arms. Exiled families returned from time to time, as the ever-shifting politics of their city turned in their favor, and the legal recovery and disposition of their assets became a distinct political and legal problem.

---

[4] Maino, *cons.* 238, vol. 1, 798–801.

The central feature for many of these families was that "in struggling to ensure that their sons, their patrimony, and their name endured and prospered, elite family heads also created family mythologies honoring their own lineages and their right, as fathers, to govern."[5] As political authority could vary from place to place, so did the family and the image it might present. In many cases, in central and northern Italy, the differences on all these scores could be relatively minor. The large similarities are seen, for example, in the prevalence of rules of intestate succession, advantaging male agnates and limiting women to dowry. The broadest distinctions probably arose between those areas and the kingdoms in Sicily and southern Italy, which in turn rested to a good degree on the distinct paternalism of feudal political power and property succession. The feudal pattern, however, could also be found in the princely states to the north, such as Milan or Tuscany under the Medici dukes. It was the case, then, that "the agnate status of the family does not have the same value and is not disciplined in the same manner everywhere."[6]

CITIZENSHIP AND JURISDICTION

Whatever the powers of the father as defined in law, his effective control lay generally within the walls of his house and required that his children be near at hand to experience that power and his will. The city or prince faced an analogous situation. Jurisdiction had its physical as well as legal limits. Baldo degli Ubaldi had posed, in a case involving municipal concessions by Perugia, that the term territory had three senses: circumscriptive or terminal (set by its boundaries), subjective or material (set by jurisdiction of its courts), concessive or rational (set by privileges).[7] This distinction was employed in a case in which a son was born in the city to a man who was a rural resident, and thus liable for taxes, duties, and burdens imposed on *comitatenses*. The Perugian government maintained that the son could not be considered a citizen, except by express act of the priors. Status of the parent, not place of birth, *origo*, set one's status. Clearly it was better to be a citizen than a countryman: "the distinction about rural dwellers is not made merely with respect to fiscal burdens, because countrymen are presumed to be denser and dirty (*gravioribus et sordidis praesumuntur*) and are burdened with duties unlike the citizens who are better and worthier than they." Perugia had a statute affirming

---

[5] Adams, *The Familial State*, 34.   [6] Mineo, "Stati e lignaggi," 60.
[7] Baldo, *cons.* 293, vol. 4, fol. 63va–b.

fiscal privileges for *comitatenses* living in the city for ten years, but it did not mention their sons. That omission meant the sons lay under *ius commune* and the son in this case gained some protection from having his *origo* in the city:

> by reason of his own origin he has some similarity with the citizen, and so it is easier for him to change as thus in sons there is a certain quality of difference from fathers which is in question, a quality natural as much as civic provided against fathers is not extended to sons ... and although this seems to be the truth yet I do not want that officials put him in the list of citizens without the advice of other doctors, because it is more deleterious if one errs in this ... the catasto is a care of the Perugians and must be guarded as a most sacred thing and shrine and life of the city.[8]

Baldo conceded something to *origo* as somehow softening the harsh edges of the rural yokel, but he was not eager to insert rural folks into urban citizenship on his own.

Perhaps the most frequent manner in which citizenship became confused and confusing was in consequence of the marriages of women to men from other towns. Take the case of a Perugian woman who married a man from Assisi, whose city had a statute forbidding wives to have a testament without their husbands' consent. During her long married sojourn in Assisi, she made a will with her husband's consent, but she later returned to Perugia without him and made another will there, where there was no comparable requirement of spousal consent. Which of these two wills was valid? And therefore, which city's statutes came into play, as those of Assisi gave the husband claims on the dowry of a predeceased wife? Baldo argued that the woman's *origo* was immutable, even though marriage drew her to that of her husband. Marriage, it is true, made her a citizen of Assisi, but only in a fictive manner; and a restrictive statute such as that of Assisi circumscribing her ability to testate and dispose of property should be restricted and not apply to fictive citizens. Nevertheless, Baldo seems to have been retained by the husband to advance his case, so he determined that her citizenship in Assisi by its statutes was real, not fictive. He added that she was in the *potestas* of her husband, as she would be by Lombard law, and so could not dispose of her dowry because of the statute, even though by *ius commune* she could.[9] The realities of her marital situation carried the day, instead of her *origo* or separate domicile.

---

[8] Baldo, *cons.* 294, fols. 63vb–64ra.   [9] Baldo, *cons.* 139, vol. 5, fols. 35vb–36ra.

Cornelia, a Genoese by birth, married a Mantuan, resident in Ferrara. She died childless. Her sister, Lucrezia, married to a man from Armino, had a son, Giordano, in third degree of cognation to Cornelia, who contested Florio, son of Cornelia's father's brother, fourth degree in agnation, for Cornelia's estate in Ferrara. Thus neither litigant was Ferrarese. Florio alleged the Ferrarese statute favoring agnates in intestate succession; Giordano alleged *ius commune*. Florio's claim had merit. But Giordano himself was a foreigner to Ferrara and its laws could not apply to him. Alessandro Tartagni, who took this case, enlisted the example of England, where primogeniture was the rule. If such a rule held *circa rem*, then one who died with property in both England and Italy would see the property in England pass in accord with the customs of England, where the property was situated. But if the custom applied *circa personam*, that is, to the primogenitus, then if the heir was not English the rule did not apply to him. If the heir were English, then primogeniture would apply to property there and *ius commune* elsewhere. The problem was to figure out if Ferrara's statute applied to things or persons.

The intestacy statute, he decided, applied to the person of the woman being deprived of inheritance. If its goal was to keep her from property, then it applied to her, as the property was in Ferrara. But if the statute intended to keep her from *haereditas*, "for some reason and by some right," that is, to keep her from a universal right acquired in *aditio* to represent the person of the deceased, then it applied to things and was not confined to a territory, but extended wherever the things were that had belonged to the *de cuius*. That reading, however, would seem to make a mockery of the statute, unless the local idiom (*consuetudo loquendi*) in fact equated *haereditas* with all its *bona*. If property lay outside Ferrara and the intent was to deprive the woman of *haereditas*, then she could not act to get the property. But as she was not Ferrarese, the statute did not apply to her. So it did not apply to her nephew Giordano, even though the goods were in Ferrara. Here Tartagni relied on Pietro d'Ancarano's judgment that a statute enabling or disabling someone in law did not apply to a foreigner, even for property within the territory, because the *bona* were accessory to persons. As long as the statute applied to persons and not to things, that was the case. An example of a rule applying to things was the power of a judge to appoint guardians to a minor not otherwise under his jurisdiction, because then it was a matter of managing and protecting the property. If Cornelia had written a will in Ferrara, it would have to be treated in accord with *ius commune* and not local law, even if it followed the prescribed steps for a valid will in Ferrara.

The parallel was emancipation. A town could set the formalities to be followed in one, but it did not emancipate. The father did by law.[10]

Angela from Bitone, outside Bologna, married a man from Foligno and lived there with him. Finding herself childless as death approached, she made a will and named her husband her heir. She had a female cousin on her father's side, two nephews on her mother's side, and two female cousins also on her mother's side – all of whom came forth to prevent the husband from realizing Angela's estate. Their case rested on the fact that property lay in Bitone, which had a statute demanding that a woman's will be made in the presence of her husband and two *consanguinei*. Angela had not had the two relatives, though she could have found some in Foligno. But that was also the husband's defense. The will was done in Foligno and need not follow Bitone's formalities for a valid will. Benedetto Capra, seemingly employed by the nephews, argued that Angela's will was not valid. The statute of Bitone, "was enacted to the benefit of the woman," so that she not be deceived or defrauded unknowingly, and it was to be observed, especially as she had kin to hand in Foligno, and the statute had a clause explicitly applying to a woman "nupta extra territorium." Quashing her will left her property intestate, and intestacy favored the relatives over the husband. Bitone also had a law forbidding alienation of land to foreigners, such that one wanting to leave something to a foreigner had to sell the land and hand over the cash. The law did not like seeing local land in the hands of outsiders. Capra sidestepped the argument about not extending a statute outside the territory with the notion that a jurisdiction could legislate for its subjects outside the territory when it did so "in their favor." In broadest terms,

although this woman married elsewhere is made a citizen of her husband's city, as she follows his forum and ceases to be a citizen or a native of her place of origin, as far as those [things] by which this woman may be drawn away and separate from the service of the husband, yet as far as others she does not cease to be native of her place of origin, where she drew origin, as it cannot be changed ... as in this case it is not a matter of statutes, which separate her from the service of the husband, but of the statutes disposing in her favor on the manner of the capacity to make a testament. Such statutes seem to take effect and bind everywhere she may be and peculiarly as far as goods situated in the said territory of Bitone.[11]

She could not alienate property to her Fulginean husband. It went instead, said Capra, by *capita* to each of the relatives in Bitone. All began with a right to succeed by *ius commune*.

---

[10] Tartagni, *cons.* 44, vol. 5, fols. 39vb–41ra.   [11] Capra, *cons.* 21, fols. 36vb–38rb.

Camino di Pasino claimed two-thirds of his cousin's estate by virtue of Verona's statute privileging agnates. The deceased's mother and sister opposed him on the grounds of *ius commune*, saying the statute did not apply, as Camino was a foreigner and they were certainly closer to him in degree of relationship. The statute worked for Camino, provided a valid argument could be had for its extension to a foreigner. A colleague of Bartolomeo Cipolla, Bernardo Brenzono, rehearsed several such arguments, including that legislators could extend a benefit to those not otherwise subject to their jurisdiction. But he found them unconvincing, first of all because the women's claims were stronger in *ius commune*, and second because the statute did not extend to foreigners. The statute's rationale, that the city had an interest in preserving agnation, was not served by foreigners. Other statutes showed that Verona's legislators wanted to keep outsiders from owning land, so they would not have wanted them to inherit it. Cipolla too raised the example of English primogeniture and concluded that the statute concerned the person of the heir (as agnate by its overt terms) and not the objects to be inherited. In this case, in fact, the mother and sister had entered their formal claim to the estate, and only after that did Camino come to Verona and set up household and then enter his claim. If he was allowed to make a claim on the basis of domicile, it would render the law ineffective, as "it is easy to set up their domicile in the place and thus seek the goods of the deceased" (*facile esset eis constituere domicilium in loco et ita petere bona defuncti*).

Cipolla himself also gave a lengthy treatment to the issues raised by the case. He noted that the statute spoke indistinctly of agnates and did not distinguish citizen from foreigner. But he quickly turned that argument against Camino. A *casus omissus* in a statute modifying *ius commune* remained under *ius commune*, which was the basis for the women's claim. He agreed that the *familia* to be preserved by agnation according to statute had to be a citizen's. Had the legislators been quizzed as to their thinking, whether they would want to disadvantage a Veronese mother for a fifth-degree agnate foreigner, certainly they "would have said no." The Veronese republic as a whole would be harmed by the passage of wealth to an outsider. That was the sort of interpretation that made broad sense, that "resonated in vulgar ears" (*sonat in auribus vulgi*). Had the laws been intended to cover foreigners, they would have and should have done so explicitly. General language about agnates was not enough.[12]

[12] Cipolla, *cons.* 19 and 20, 85a–92b.

Here the exemption of the foreigners in the statute worked against Camino, and the sense of belonging to the large "family" of the citizen body carried weight.

Brunoro and his son Niccolò Spinola contested the sisters Franchetta, Nariola, and Peregrina over the estate of Girolamo Spinola, more specifically over those assets in Mongiardini which, the women claimed, were not subject to Genoa's statute advantaging agnates. Giason del Maino gave no space to any argument extending the statute outside Genoa. Instead he poured considerable energies into labeling the statute *irrationabile* and *odiosum* and drawing the parallel to restricting the reach of England's custom of primogeniture. He flatly rejected the claim of Brunoro and sons, supposedly backed by witness testimony, that it was customary to extend the reach of the statute outside Genoa.[13] Genoa could advantage agnation within its walls, but no farther.

Fiscal matters could be a different issue. Baldo, along with Signorello degli Omodei (1308–71), a Milanese, considered a case in which the question was whether a son took the "accidental" (as opposed to original) domicile of his father as far as fiscal obligations (*munera*). There were seemingly simple arguments that a son who lived apart from his father had his own domicile. The two jurists, however, said a son was constrained by the paternal domicile, accidental or original. One part of their argument was that a father did not establish domicile in a city by his act and intent alone but also by the consent of the city or its rulers. A son by his will alone could not change that but was "immutably" bound to the paternal city. By analogy one could not become a guildsman of a particular craft by his own choice, but such also required acceptance by the guild. One could not be a doctor of law by one's own choice but had to undergo procedures to receive a degree. They could give many other examples along these lines to the same effect, "mainly by the infinite qualities that flow from the person of the father to the son" (*maxime per infinitas qualitates que ex persona patris transeunt ad filium*).[14]

MEZZOGIORNO

Where monarchy provided an element of continuity, though its ability to control its aristocracy varied enormously over time, having an active relationship with the monarch was paramount. Other elements of family

---

[13] Maino, *cons.* 163, vol. 1, 535a–37b.   [14] Baldo, *cons.* 415, vol. 5, fol. 110rb–vb.

cohesion, such as found in northern cities – celebration of family memory or rights to preferment in other arenas – were disarticulated from the dynamic of princely patronage in Sicily. There urban inheritance patterns were more bilateral, but the aristocracy was feudal. There was also a Byzantine legal heritage, overlaid with Norman elements and, in the fifteenth century, Spanish influence with the arrival of the Aragonese dynasty. There was also a body of royal legislation, mainly the work of Frederick II, which, with regard to inheritance, admitted both daughters and sons, but advantaged males.

One result of this diverse legal heritage was the existence in the late Middle Ages of two different regimes of marital property: *alla latina* and *alla greca*. The "Greek" form followed the rules of *ius commune*, in which the wife had a dowry that remained a separate fund from the husband's property; the "Latin" form allowed for a communion of property in the family with a consequent partition into three shares (father's, mother's, children's) at the birth of children. A child could not in fact manage his third separately or demand it, unless he were emancipated. However, once a son reached eighteen and married, he might be emancipated and receive his quota into his direct control. Likewise the father could exercise considerable control over his third, even to the point of bequeathing it for religious purposes, for the good of his soul, or even to leave it to a daughter in preference to a son. The mother could bequeath the moveable goods in her third, but *immobilia* had to pass to her children. Effectively, even her dowry ceased to be distinct. It melted into the common pot on the birth of children. They, in turn, ended up with possession of two types of property; their third that came to them by a natural right (*iure naturae*), and all or part of the parental thirds, that came to them *iure sanguinis*. The family communion of property thus ended with the household, as it could at any point by a voluntary but formal and public act of separation. "On the whole and limited to Sicily up to the fifteenth century, one draws the impression of a society not formed by 'extensive families', rather (at least in urban areas) by small communities that with marriage achieve their patrimonial autonomy."[15]

For such families, a father's will was in fact the directive disposing only of his third; and with equal division among the heirs, a paternal will was mainly concerned with burial and pious bequests. In Naples and other mainland communities, more latitude was accorded sons to manage and

---

[15] Romano, *Famiglia, successioni e patrimonio familiare*, 114.

dispose of their *peculia*, especially whatever they might have received from their mother or her kin, than was the case in Roman law.[16] On face of it, the wife in this situation stood on a level of parity with her husband, as she too had a third share of the common holdings. As Andrea Romano cautions, however, any such parity was more formal and hypothetical than real in most cases, as the weight of custom and the authority of the husband could serve to rein her in and to limit any real autonomy of the children as well.[17]

In Sicily the laws of Palermo and Messina, in their insistence that property of husband and wife "are mixed on the birth of children and made into one body" reveal, according to Igor Mineo,

that an effective agnatic discipline was weakly practiced and that the propensity to involve collateral relatives of the same name on succession was very rare. That confirms that the exclusion of women was generated as a rule by a moderate need to protect the patrimony: to contain the dispersion produced by the regime of common holdings, to be sure, but not to the point of privileging one line of succession (male) alone or to consent to the participation of collateral males to the detriment of the direct female heirs.[18]

In other communities, such as Syracuse, such communion of goods was limited to property acquired during the marriage, whereas *patrimonialia* remained distinct, to pass by the rule of *paterna paternis, materna maternis*. It is not surprising then that through the fourteenth-century recourse to testaments seems to have been fairly rare in Sicily.[19]

The agnatic direct line was served by various devices, but there was not as much sense of a larger lineage linked by a name and symbolic patrimony. When the direct male line failed, women in the Regno and Sicily were more likely to become heirs, and jurists trained in *ius commune* were ready to back their rights. The fragmentation of holdings on inheritance that such shared patrimonies predicted could be countered by the legal right of blood relatives, recognized by many locales, to regain property. The so-called *ius prothimiseos* (which supposedly had its origins in a decree of the Byzantine emperor Romanus Lecapenus) was extended in the course of the fifteenth century beyond blood relatives to neighbors. Drawing limits to that range of potential holders of rights, so as not to interrupt titles constantly, was one dimension of further legislative revisions.

---

[16] Marongiu, *Beni paternali e acquisti*, 150.   [17] Romano, 169.
[18] Mineo, *Nobiltà di stato*, 234.   [19] Romano, *Famiglia*, 145.

An example of the need for such limits arises from the pages of *consilia* of even a later jurist, Francesco d'Antonio Costa (d. 1656). In 1604 Caterinella de Baldo, by judicial decree, obtained a house from another Caterinella, la Magistra. The house was then sold to a Giovanbattista Musulino, with a right to buy it back (*cum pacto de retrovendendo*), and he in turn sold it to Antonino la Magistra, Caterinella's son, who was exercising that right to retrieval of the property. He was also Costa's client. Antonino's brother Joseph then purchased from the other Caterinella (de Baldo) the right to retrieve the house (*ius luendi*) and declared his intent to buy it back, undertaking the public steps he was required to do by statute in Messina to force the holder to sell to him. Joseph claimed the right to do so on the basis of both blood and vicinity, in accord with the statute and with a decree of King Alfonso that allowed a neighbor with more contiguous property to be preferred to one with less, even if the other was a closer relation.

Costa noted that the Messinese statute indiscriminately accorded repurchase rights to blood relations and neighbors, but he argued that the closest in degree should receive preference. Repurchase in his mind had the same purpose as a *fideicommissum*: "and in all it compares to *fideicommissa* established for perpetual preservation of goods in the family, in which the nearer relation is admitted to recover the goods, even in the meantime acquired by a remoter relative ... where it concludes the legislators gave the relatives the right of retaking, so that goods are in the family and are reunited, and so there is one rationale to all, *fideicommissum* and retaking.*" Antonino had the compelling card in his hand against someone no more closely related than he was. He had possession (nine tenths of the law in some places). So a couple months later, May 5, 1618, the court of Straticotiale gave judgment to Antonino.[20] This is a rare sample of a dispute between brothers that got to court (rather than the common recourse to arbitration to affect division of property). In this instance, there was clearly no family solidarity to hold this house in common. Each brother was looking for an advantage to himself.

The sense one gets from Costa's case is that the rule of proximity would operate most of the time, but that as long as one went through with the formal steps, including a monetary deposit as a sort of earnest money for the sale, it was at least possible to hold up a sale or throw it into doubt. Messina's marital practices had a similar effect, as by law there the birth of children melded all the property into one, with one-third

[20] Costa, *cons.* 46, 292–96.

shares. The marriage between Giovanfrancesco Soprani and Giovanna Marra in 1571 ended with her death four years later, leaving a son, Joseph. Giovanfrancesco remarried in 1578 to Portia Barrili, this time according to Roman law and not the *usus Messanus*. The second marriage produced two children before Soprani died. Joseph then sought a third of the estate. Costa added two legal facts to the narrative: the inheritance was intestate and the *societas* of father and minor son could be said to have continued into the second marriage, including in the household's possessions what had been Joseph's mother's share.

As the statute declaring that property became common on the birth of children was "exorbitans a iure," Costa argued to restrict it. It could be maintained that the first wife's share became an acquisition of the father. The *societas* that was the first household did not continue past the mother's death, for all that the son and father lived in the same house as before. This particular son was too young to have agreed to the situation, and the share that fell to him (with usufruct to his father) fed him but did not implicate his labor and potential profit or loss. Perhaps the best argument that there was no continuity of *societas*, said Costa, was the fact that Giovanfrancesco had remarried in the different legal model of *ius commune*, thus the underlying basis to domestic life had changed. Also, had there been a *societas* in existence, why in 1599 did father and son draw up a contract mingling labor and capital for four years? They obviously did not see themselves in a *societas* prior to that point.

So the remaining issue was whether Joseph had been satisfied in his claim to his mother's property. Here the depositions of witnesses left interesting information:

through them shines the truth in a wonderful way, for they testify that no goods at that time remained by reason of the scarcity and calamity of the time, by which the greater part of the Regno was oppressed by plague, then also by the fact that in effect he had nothing and the marriage lasted for four years, in which brief space he could gain nothing [as] it is said from nothing is nothing made.

The 100 uncia it was said the father set aside for Joseph was somehow to cover his *legitima* (the third in his share) and his mother's share. Costa piled up reasons to see that Joseph had all that and had come away with more of the profit of the second *societas* with his father from 1599. So Costa's clients (seemingly the children by the second marriage) were cleared of any obligations to Joseph.[21]

21 Costa, *cons.* 57, 343–49.

Into the fifteenth century, elite families in Sicily could attempt to pursue power and protection by adopting instruments that kept people and property together in an extended, mainly fraternal form, "a patrilinear divisible model of inheritance transmission." These instruments included agreements not to inherit (*pacta de non succedendo*), usually tendered by daughters marrying out (thus achieving by contract what elsewhere was done by statute, though these too came increasingly to be adopted in Sicilian cities), but sometimes also from sons, as well as testaments and substitutions. Fragmentation of holdings among sons on inheritance was, however, always a possibility. Only from the later fifteenth century did such an extended family structure give way to a more vertical aristocratic family that was "patrilinear indivisible," in favor usually of one son (and the influence of Spanish inheritance practices through the Aragonese monarchy aided the process).[22]

But for many of the Sicilian elites, social and political authority was assured, and family identity, individual and collective, was beyond discussion. When men in direct line were lacking, it was more likely a female would inherit than that a patrimony would go to collateral males (though husbands of heiresses might be expected and commanded to adopt the names and coats of arms of their families). Keeping a patrimony intact and in transmission through a line of male descent became more common, though it was more dynastic than agnatic (in that collateral agnates were accorded weak rights, if any).

Even without picturing a rigid causality, there is no doubt that the weakness of lineages and the discontinuity in their processes of reproduction, the diffusion of logic of bilateral transmission and the scant significance of family memory and genealogical discourse as instruments of self-awareness and legitimation are all interconnected phenomena at least in part determined by the fragility of the signorial tradition.[23]

The bilateral nature of customary inheritance patterns in Sicily set a base line from which later norms and practices worked a certain amount of modification, mainly on the part of the feudal aristocracy and the urban elites. Testaments provided one means, for example, by which some things might be held *pro indiviso* or one line of descent might be privileged. But self-consciousness of families, a sense of identity – "traces of private elaborations, internal to the families, of identity and the sense of self are practically absent."[24] Families still had many agnatic elements,

---

[22] Romano, *Famiglia*, 178–79.   [23] Mineo, *Nobiltà*, 296.   [24] Mineo, *Nobiltà*, 196.

but they did not project a sense of social superiority more prominently until 1400. From that point, more marriages were constructed *more greco*, in which the wife received a dowry that substituted for the legitimate portion due her from her father's belongings. The material basis to marriage and household, at least for landed and urban elites, became increasingly similar to that found in communities in central and northern Italy.

Sicilian testaments began to use the *fideicommissum*, directed in narrow line, in the course of the fifteenth century, as agnatic consciousness increased. The term *domus* was conceded to encompass *familia*; the family name became an evident badge of belonging. "One identified with the *domus* and the *substantia*, having as immediate consequence the search for instruments more suited to tie the patrimony to the family and to guarantee perpetuity (even fictive)."[25]

So, from a situation in which there had been one dominant form of families marked by a shared patrimony, there arose two prevalent family models – one marked by the more customary communitarian forms, the other feudal, aristocratic, and patrician, dominated by the *paterfamilias*. The shared property of the household by *mos latinus* became the mark of the closed, relatively impoverished rural world where all components of the family shared its economic life. For the rest, there was the model of the urban family and that of the feudal aristocracy. Ideological and symbolic elements identified the lineage and in a more Europe-wide fashion identified family with patrimony and relied on those legal instruments that placed its unity "in a person destined to perpetuate the dignity and honor of the house."[26] Progressively the testament changed from an instrument to dispose of belongings *pro anima* into a political statement that also left little room for testators' initiatives in the face of *fideicommissa* and rules of succession.

Jurists in Sicily became quite comfortable with the *fideicommissum*. One of them, Niccolò Intriglioli (1562–1604), penned a treatise on substitutions in which he gave expression to the widest validation of perpetual *fideicommissa* one was likely to find from any jurist: "When the testator after substitution adds the prohibition of alienation, with added reason that he wants the goods be preserved in the agnation and family, then it is presumed the testator wanted the goods subject to a *fideicommissum*." He was likewise clear in his finding that women did not

---

[25] Romano, *Famiglia*, 162.   [26] Romano, 176.

fall under the term *familia* because they could not preserve it.[27] For elites, at least, the prevalent family model, north and south of Italy, tended to take the same form. The main difference was that in some regions, more so to the north, primogeniture still remained rare and out of favor.

An important ingredient in the Sicilian aristocratic family, in addition to its embrace of the marital model of *ius commune*, was the feudal basis of much of its property. To be sure, as Mineo says, feudal possession was not in itself enough to foster an ideological and political cohesion of the Sicilian elite. But feudal property did pass by distinct rules. Royal decrees from the late thirteenth century opened fiefs to succession by women in the absence of men and gave rights of alienation of fiefs, including by testament. Still, fiefs were indivisible and preferably to be transmitted to one heir in primogeniture. This was the position repeated in treatises and *consilia* by Sicily's most prominent jurists. Women could inherit them, but they were inferior to men in the misogynistic eyes of the law. Those eyes also came to see the founding act of investiture as controlling in the succession to any one fief. If the lord, who conceded the fief, did not specify that women could inherit, the tendency in law was to deny them succession. This was true of Sicilian jurists and of cosmopolitan north-erners such as Baldo degli Ubaldi. They also endorsed the use of fidei-commissary substitutions, which inserted agnate collaterals ahead of women in direct line of succession to feudal properties and to what the Sicilian jurist Mario Cutelli (d. 1654) called *res egregia*. The so-called "new" fiefs of recent royal investiture were inheritable only in direct line, while so-called "old" or "paternal" fiefs that had been inherited already could pass to collateral male descendants. New fiefs became paternal after the initial recipient or initial heir.

In Naples too feudal law influenced the development of an aristocracy and its inheritance practices. It was not always so, as feudal holdings, at least in Naples itself, were fairly modest in the Angevin period. Rather, it was entry to the *familiaritas* of the monarch that distinguished a man, and could elevate one whose loyalty could be useful to the court. But such men aspired to possession of a fief, with rights of justice and hereditary transmission. Matrimonial strategies allowed court officials access to fiefs. Some also succeeded in occupying the same offices across gener-ations. Frederick II's laws had limited transmission of fiefs to the direct line, enhancing the crown's prerogatives to retrieve a fief when the line

---

[27] As quoted in Romano, *Famiglia*, 163, 161.

failed. Division of fiefs and inheritance in collateral branches of a lineage were what feudal lords sought in the fifteenth and sixteenth centuries, and generally gained the latter, though limited to "old" fiefs (held by one's grandfather). Urban families had more freedom of testation and could devise to collateral branches and develop an autonomous lineage, but they also faced the progressive parcelling of their patrimony over generations. The infusion of the great feudatories of the realm in the Neapolitan elite worked a profound transformation. Families projected their presence in the urban space, in their *domus* and in patronage of local ecclesiastical institutions. They were part of the social and civic order, if also at times disruptive forces from antagonisms with other families.[28]

By the end of the sixteenth century Neapolitan aristocrats used testaments to keep the feudal patrimony intact and in the hands of the eldest son, while also detailing substitutions to collateral lines, seeing to younger sons and dowries for daughters. "It is the beginning of a process of closure, of withdrawal, of formalization of privileges and of rules that will culminate in the second half of the seventeenth century, that will be accompanied by an effort of theoretical rationalization and of ideological justification."[29] The honor and services attached to the fief justified its indivisibility and family continuity. The pattern spread from the great feudatories to smaller holders. The families became more linear, having or recognizing fewer branches. Innovative solutions were tried, as *fedecommessi* were generally used at first on only a portion of a patrimony, but over time were extended to the rest. *Fedecommessi* were not only intended to keep an estate intact. The *fedecommesso* was "an instrument to stem a growing indebtedness and to try to avoid the ruin of a patrimony."[30] By the end of the seventeenth century the rigidity of such devices had clearly become a problem. Steps were taken to free up property for sale and allow aristocratic families some means to adapt to markets and economic needs and opportunities.

We can gain some sense of the legal problems associated with fiefs in a case that came to the Venetian Marc Antonio Pellegrini (1530–1616), in May 1598 from Naples. Pellegrini was also author of a popular legal treatise on *fideicommissa*.[31] The royal council in Naples and a number of jurists had already examined the claims of Gabriele dei Castelli to the castle at Pedisluce, originally granted by Pope Nicholas V to

---

[28] Vitale, *Élite burocratica e famiglia*, 152.   [29] Visceglia, *Il bisogno di eternità*, 15.
[30] Visceglia, 53.
[31] Marc Antonio Pellegrini, *De fideicommissis tractatus frequentissimus* (Venice 1665).

Matteo Poiano and his descendants, even those born out of wedlock but legitimated, and men descended through women. Pellegrini began then with the observation that this grant had not concerned itself with agnation, but only with gender, keeping the estate in male hands. He also observed that properly speaking this was not a *feudum*. It carried merely an annual payment of a silver bowl, for one thing, and it had been conceded in consideration of the 8,000 ducats the Holy See owed Poiano at the time. So feudal law did not preclude women and even male outsiders from inheriting this property. Gabriele Castelli was the son of a daughter of the last Poiano heir, Giulio. Both because the castle was not properly a fief and because the grant had not been concerned with agnation, he seemed to be heir. But Giulio had an illegitimate son, Giuseppe, who had been legitmated by decree of the prince of Massa and by Gregory XIII, not by subsequent marriage of the parents (as he was *spurius*). Pellegrini let the arguments of others on this point stand without comment from him, striking down Giuseppe's claim, and proceeded instead to the rights of women to inherit fiefs. Normally they could not render the services attached to the fief. Their oaths of fidelity may have fictively asserted fulfillment of *servitia* in their persons, but in fact they had to use a substitute. A woman who had a fief, though also presumably incapable of exercising jurisdiction, to the contrary in fact had jurisdiction and performed it by herself or through another. But even the minimal annual tribute on Pedisluce had not been paid for several years, so the question arose whether the fief reverted to its lord. Pellegrini went with the view he labeled as commonly received, which was that there was no rule in feudal law that said the fief reverted for such nonpayment.[32] In his opinion the castle passed through the daughters of the last heir to her son, Gabriele.

In another instance concerning the same fief, Pellegrini considered whether a father could divide a *feudum antiquum* between two sons, favoring one with two-thirds. There was the argument that this father did not own the fief and could not devise by contract or testament, so that it passed neither in intestacy nor by testament, but by feudal law.[33] But Pellegrini relied on Baldo to assert that fiefs had hereditary quality when they were inheritable by terms of their investiture. It was licit for the feudatory to exclude one son in favor of the other, which also made sense for a fief that had jurisdiction, that it be exercised by one person and not

---

[32] Pellegrini, *cons.* 6, fols. 31ra–32va.   [33] Pellegrini, *cons.* 10, fols. 45ra–46ra.

several. Because this was not properly a fief, it could be left to those otherwise ruled out by feudal law.

In all, the agnatic bias to inheritance and marital practices in the northern and central areas of Italy was attenuated to the south. Feudal law was more prevalent, for one thing. But mainly the drive to privilege agnation arose later, ran into more entrenched prior practices, and was not as open to collateral branches. The southern kindreds seem to have been narrower. The image of the domineering *paterfamilias* seems only to have prevailed among the wealthier and more noble. Women's claims met with support from the professional legal community.

JEWS AND THE LAWS

Jews, it should be noted, were subject to their own law, at least on domestic matters, though Christian jurists and courts might become involved. Generally Jews were subject to civil and penal laws and to the Christian courts that adjudicated them. Giovanni Calderini rehearsed all the texts and agreements of church and emperor to that effect to support the simple finding that by Mosaic law sons did not succeed equally with daughters, but excluded them. He nowhere noted that this rule in fact ran closely parallel to so many municipal statutes.[34]

Jews were covered by Christian laws of domestic life too, if only because of local courts. Specific customs might differ from the patterns of civil law, as was the case in seventeenth-century Livorno's fairly sizeable Jewish population, where procreation became a determining moment in emancipating a married son from paternal power.[35] Jewish sons were otherwise emancipated on occasion to take advantage of the cessation of liability between fathers and sons, as did Christians. Fathers' prestige was enhanced by such measures. Familial control of marriage was as consistent for Jews as for Christians, and the significance and amount of dowry ran parallel, including the exclusion of daughters from further family wealth. Talmudic and Roman texts could equally justify such matters. Engagements and dowries were the occasion for disputes, made more complicated for Jews living in the small communities they established in different cities by the fact that a bride frequently came from another community at some distance. The role of matchmakers was thus, if anything, more vital in Jewish communities than in Christian ones. But the same concerns tended to mark marriage negotiations in both

---

[34] Calderini, *cons.* 30, fol. 68rb.   [35] Cavina, *Il padre spodestato*, 61.

communities, ancestry, appearance, family reputations, and dowry. Jewish wills were also similar to Christian as long as a rule or practice did not compromise religious identity.

Legal issues for Jews invoked halakhic traditions and were presented to rabbinic courts. The *responsa* of experts before these courts occupied for Jews a position parallel to the *consilia* of jurists in Christian courts. Jews, for example, also had questions as to the validity of particular marriages and standards of proof. Just as a Christian marriage had a strong, if not total, presumption of validity if there was a dowry, the Jewish marriage stood if there was a *tenaim* writ, which made the event public and demonstrated that it had not taken place outside the aegis of the family.[36] In the dense spaces of the ghetto area to which Jews were confined in a number of Italian cities, the framework of family and adults' control of the young were weakened to some extent. But among Jews, as with Christians, the more material interest transacted in the marriage, the more the choice of partners and much else remained in parental hands. In much else, besides, the living conditions and legal conditions for Jews were little different from those of their non-Jewish neighbors.

Jewish women, like Christian women, faced restrictions on their ownership and disposition of property. Widows had more such rights, though they ordinarily could not inherit from their husbands. Historical investigations, however, indicate that Jewish women were able to act quite independently, on a par with their fathers and husbands, and even were able to receive property in inheritance from husbands, despite strictures in law and rabbinic opinions. Jewish women had the same sorts of interests in managing dowries. More interesting were the occasions on which men devised property on inheritance to women. Sales, leases, and other elements of property management by Jewish women can be found in legal records, albeit infrequently. Women's acts were useful to them and their families, much as they were for Christian women.

One of the ways by which a family dispute among Jews would get to Christian courts and jurists was when a discrepancy between the two laws emerged. Otherwise much of adjudication among Jews happened in their own courts and outside the purview of Christian jurists. One rare example that came before a secular court arises in the *consilia* of Felino Sandei. The case came from Reggio, where a man had given assets to his son, who was not emancipated. The gift, however, had been validated by

---

[36] Weinstein, *Marriage Rituals Italian Style*, 123.

an oath the son swore to the father in accord, supposedly, with Mosaic law. Later, for no apparent reason, the father sought to revoke his gift. Sandei began with the lament that he could find no *iuris interpres* who had handled such a case, which had been sent to him from the court of the capitano of Reggio, "so this difficulty was treated by past legal commentators as both rare and in places not customary."[37] Sandei rehearsed both sides of the issue. First, that the gift could not be revoked but stood as valid. There were no reasons given for taking the property back – nothing about ingratitude or fear. It seemed the father simply wanted it nullified on the grounds that there could be no valid gift between a father and a son *in potestate*. However, it was argued that a Jew did not have his son *in potestate*, that, as a Jew was a *servus* (slave) of the prince, he was under the power of another and could not have power over someone: "Therefore he does not have sons in his power, as being in the power of another he cannot have another in his power." The other argument was simply that the Mosaic oath was valid and could be enforced in Christian courts. Still, Sandei then launched the reverse arguments, which were easy to see. Jews lived by Roman law and had the same rights and powers, including *patria potestas*, which also arose from the fact that their marriages were valid. Nor were Jews the *servi* of the prince; what they acquired remained theirs and did not belong to an overlord. No gift between father and unemancipated son could hold, even by an oath, even between Jews. Jews could not be compelled to keep such an oath because the matter in hand was "reprobata" by the civil law. So Sandei's judgment turned on denying the difference between Jews and Christians and making them both subject to the same (civil) law. He backed the father's revocation of the gift.

A Jew named Lazarus left a pregnant wife, two daughters, and two wills, the first naming any legitimate children, male and female, present and future, as his heirs. The pregnancy yielded a son, who came to an equal division of the estate with his sisters when he reached fourteen. Lazarus' second will had followed Hebraic law and was composed in Hebrew. It commanded that the girls be married locally (Padua) and not in Germany. It also specified that the girls inherit equal shares, but that if a posthumous son was born (as was the case), each girl's share was to be half the male's ("mezzo maschio"). This unequal division in the Hebrew will had been translated into a properly notarized will *more Christiano*. The confusing conjunction of the two legal traditions opened up the

---

[37] Sandei, *cons.* 30, fols. 40ra–41rb.

possibility for the daughters to try to claim shares that were equal to their brother's, and not half as much (i.e., to end up with thirds rather than quarters), by contesting the validity of the Hebrew will in Christian courts. The Christian jurist, Paolo di Castro, defended the validity of the second will, for though Jews nominally had to follow civil law, which demanded seven witnesses for a valid will and not the mere two required by Jewish law, the will had been drawn up by a Christian notary and had the required *solemnitas* to be accepted as a valid legal document in Christian courts. But di Castro rejected the inequality between the heirs, saying that, though the second will contained language supposedly annulling any previous will, and it seemed that a final will should be followed in preference to any preceding will, the second will in Hebrew had not specifically overturned and rejected the equality of heirs of either gender in the first. In fact, it flew in the face of Jewish law's tendency to leave more to women than to men, who would later realize greater wealth in their mercantile activities.[38] Di Castro could thus seem to be defending the general law against one father's preferential adjustment of it. Also, the *fructus* on that portion the daughters had not yet claimed (beyond their quarter) was due to them.[39] The son did not fare well at his hands.

One type of law Jews were subject to was sumptuary legislation. Regulations about Jews' clothing marked them off in some cities, as did rules as to what aristocrats or those of lower status could wear. Typically laws demanding special clothing for Jews were the only sumptuary laws that mentioned them expressly. Otherwise Jews were not specifically singled out in sumptuary laws until the sixteenth century, as sumptuary laws swung to concerns with social hierarchy more than matters of public morals. They were expected to conform to regulations constraining Christians as well. An exception is legislation from Bologna in 1474 that explicitly mentioned Jewish women and distinguished those who belonged to banking families from others. The former were allowed more elaborate dress and jewelry, setting them off as from a superior and socially useful social order.

In point of fact, Jews were as likely to indulge in luxury dress as Christians were. Jews therefore also promulgated their own sumptuary rules in some communities, such as that from Forlì in 1418 issued by representatives of a number of Jewish communities. These seem generally also to have been driven by a desire not to call down attention on themselves by displaying

---

[38] Cavallo, "Family Relationships," 24–25.   [39] Di Castro, 2 *cons.* 377, fol. 175ra–va.

luxuries that might only incite adverse reactions from their Christian neighbors. There was also an element here that seemed to assert that Jews were at least as capable, if not more so, of moral rigor as were Christians.

Jews' civic status reveals in a different way the conceptual tensions between belonging to a group by virtue of blood or belonging by virtue of proximity. Jews could be genuine citizens of places like Pisa and Florence, which meant also contributing to civic taxes and other obligations and having the use of the courts, though without officeholding privileges (but then there were plenty of Christian citizens in roughly the same circumstances, also incapable of holding office). Still, Jews were much more likely, even when citizens, to be identified not as such but as residents (*habitatores*) who had established domicile in the city (as one's central and permanent abode and where one had the bulk of one's "fortune"). Yet their rights were virtually identical to those who were citizens by birth, and their religion had no bearing on that. Bartolomeo Cipolla defended the right of a Jewish father to come to the defense of his son, accused of a capital offense against a Christian, on the grounds that Jews lived by Roman law and a Jewish father had the same paternal rights as any Christian father wherever civil law did not derogate from Mosaic law.

The existence of commerce between Jews and Christians, most evidently in forms of banking and pawn loans, led to legal disputes that unsurprisingly generated *consilia*. In an era that saw anti-Semitic preachers and later the founding of pawn banks, *monte di pietà*, intended to undercut the business that went to Jews, there was some remarkable display of tolerance and equanimity in these texts. The polemics concerning usury found their way into many of these, as Jews sought to defend their practices and profits. The pawnbrokers operated generally under contracts with civic councils, and renewal of such contracts always allowed for discussion of the pros and cons of usury as well as the venting of anti-Semitic views. In any case, Jews were resident in many cities, where they provided services and obeyed local laws, but they remained at best an ambiguous part of the larger "family" that was the city or principality. Their clothing, their place of residence, and their activities, beyond even their religious practices, marked them as different.

SUMPTUARY LAWS

Perhaps no measures taken by governments and rulers in our period seem more paternalistic than sumptuary laws. With these governments were intent on meddling in what people ate, wore, or otherwise consumed, especially on ritual occasions. Above all, such laws were "concerned with various manifestations of excess," especially of luxury goods.[40] Women's clothing was the most targeted object, but the expenses of funerals and weddings were also frequently targeted in legislation. Dissipation of capital and the resulting decline of families, including a decline in the number of marriages and births, were often cited in preambles to such laws as the reason for their existence. Take, for example, a Perugian law of 1318, addressing women's dress:

> on account of the superfluities of pearls, gold, silver, and other ornaments of clothing of wool and silk that are lavished and made by spouses and husbands for their spouses and wives, from which dowries are consumed and wasted, the status of husbands is thrown into disorder, dishonorableness arises and many people are easily reduced to poverty, and among women envies arise and scandals are generated.[41]

Legislation in Foligno in 1426 was content to reference "insupportable expenses" incurred by citizens in weddings and funerals.[42] Todi in 1346 labeled such expenses onerous and indecent.[43] Cortona's statutes forbade certain ornaments and clothing to women and ordered husbands to pay any resulting fines from their wives' dowries, notwithstanding legal assurances for return of dowry.[44] Orvietan laws of 1350 lamented the indignity and shame to the city arising from the fact that women of ill repute mingled among the "good" women and dressed like them, and so ordered that such evil women should not dare to wear the outfits of honest wives (*mantellum muliebrem*).[45]

Fears about the loss of economic and demographic capital in different cities and principalities were real. These were, then, in some way the reverse side of the coin from the intestate inheritance laws found in so many jurisdictions. Both sought to preserve the wealth of the most prominent agnate lineages. In that regard too sumptuary laws were, as Mario Ascheri has remarked, both negative (forbidding luxuries to certain groups) and positive (allowing them as signs of privilege and social utility to others).

Primary object of sumptuary laws was women's clothing and jewelry. Explanations of such measures, not surprisingly, have been rendered

---

[40] Killerby, *Sumptuary Law in Italy*, 2.
[41] *La legislazione suntuaria secoli xiii-xvi: Umbria*, ed. M. Grazia Nico Ottaviani (Rome: Ministero per i beni e le attività culturali, 2005), 48.
[42] Ibid., 394.   [43] Ibid., 768.   [44] Cortona, 163–67.
[45] *La legislazione suntuaria*, 1012.

almost entirely in terms of gender by some historians. The young women of leading families have been depicted as little dolls, garbed so as to display their families' wealth and their own suitability as females under male control and marriageable. Once married, their clothing changed and their appearances on the streets became less frequent, as their place became the marital home and their bodies no longer the projection of family wealth and status but the means of populating the home. Expenses from women's clothing were cut following the wedding to recover family finances. Whatever the occasion, women's clothing gave them a "public," if limited, voice at such events, but always they were "speaking on behalf of men, not on [their] own account."[46]

In fact, the concerns about expenses, in their amounts and in their types, were very real at times. As dowry values rose, the financial burdens of marriage fell more heavily on women's families, but the husbands too faced pressure to clothe their brides in fancy dresses and jewelry. Sumptuary laws tried to draw limits on the size of wedding parties and even on who could attend. The union of two prominent families would be an event of civic significance in any jurisdiction, but also a moment of potential social disorder. Funerals perhaps more so. Laws sought to limit the numbers in attendance, the size and amount of gifts, even the weeping or rejoicing that might be expected, depending on the event. People always seemed to find ways around the laws. Sometimes they merely needed to pay their fine and go on with their celebrations. In such cases sumptuary laws served also as revenue raising devices. But attempts at enforcement of sumptuary laws were real and frequent.[47]

Cities did not try to ban all luxury. Quite the opposite, if the city's economy rested on the provision of luxury items, as was the case for Florence and Venice to a good extent. In that case luxury items could embody civic honor. Luxury carried significance, but precisely because it was meaningful it could not escape government oversight. As Catherine Kovesi Killerby has said, "Renaissance women could be viewed as the ceremonial consumers of the goods that their fathers or husbands produced. If this were indeed the case, then by legislating against women's clothing, city rulers were partly attempting also to reduce rivalries between men and keep their ambition in check."[48] Perhaps to the same end laws frequently contained tolerances which

---

[46] Killerby, 116.   [47] For examples, *La legislazione suntuaria*, 52–71.
[48] Killerby, 117.

might be pushed further by the courts, or sumptuary laws might be suspended at moments of civic or religious celebration.

Such laws carried provisions for enforcement, and there were prosecutions under their terms. Places like Florence created magistracies specifically charged with enforcing sumptuary law (the Officiales super ornamentis mulierum). Enforcement efforts behind such laws, which intruded on family spaces, were also unpopular and heavily evaded. Enforcement was time-consuming and means of evasion were never ending. Families were frequently enough willing to pay the fines for violation of the laws, even in advance of the event, and cash-strapped governments were just as frequently content to take the money. One consequence, from our perspective, is that sumptuary laws did not lead to legal problems that required the intervention of jurists. *Consilia* on such laws are practically nonexistent.

The one fairly well-known example of a *consilium* concerning sumptuary legislation comes from the pen of the Florentine Antonio Roselli (1381–1466), who wrote it in 1447 when he was teaching in Padua.[49] The legislation Roselli discussed was not civic but episcopal, and he approached the topic mainly because of his teaching expertise in canon law. He was a jurist making a foray into an area mainly the province of theologians and moralists. His *consilium* considered two issues. The first was whether the episcopal ordinance regulating women's dress (elaborate and long trains, jewels and fancy embroidery) was valid. He determined that it was, as the rules were intended to promote honor and virtue and preclude sin, which was the proper domain of a bishop and his court. The second issue was the scope of the rules. Here Roselli disingenuously restricted them by a narrow reading. Only if (unmarried) women's dress was somehow intended to provoke extramarital lust, as opposed to attracting the attention of a potential husband, was it properly restrained by law. Married women's dress was presumed to be aimed at pleasing their husbands. Only the intent to use dress to spur an act of mortal sin fell clearly under the enforcement of the law.

Here a legist, acting within the realm of canon law, had no cause to consider the civic motivations behind similar legislation. In dealing with a

[49] Analyzed and edited by Hermann Kantorowic, with N. Denholm-Young, "De Ornatu Mulierum: A Consilium of Antonio de Rosellis with an Introduction on Fifteenth Century Sumptuary Legislation," *Bibliophilia* 35 (1933): 315–35, 440–56; reprinted in *Rechtshistorische Schriften*, ed. Helmut Coing and Gerhard Immel (Karlsruhe: C.F. Müller, 1970) 341–76.

bishop's attempt to regulate dress there was no question of raising the economic well being of the craftsmen who supplied the dresses nor of arguing about civic or even familial pride and honor. Roselli ended on a conciliatory note, invoking the idea of Aristotelian moderation in such "exterior things." Still, he also made clear that they were not in themselves sinful.

CONCLUSION

The thoroughly drawn and closely cherished parallels between the political community and the household, both gravitating around the father figure, generated numerous provisions and practices in the late medieval and early modern Italian societies. Everything from laws enforcing the powers of the fathers (limiting the prerogatives of wives and children mainly), or even those limiting those powers, to inheritance rules, and to sumptuary laws were intended to perpetuate families and their wealth as the basis of social order. The members of those families would be the rulers or at least the administrators of the public good, as they were supposedly of the familial good.

The laws and practices in the monarchies of the south and Sicily varied greatly from the patterns prevailing to the north, which were themselves various. Family forms were different as well. The customary patterns in Sicily, for example, made for a more dynamic situation in terms of the forming and reforming of households and patrimonies at each generation. Marriages in the customary "Latin" form dispersed property between parents and children. The flip side of this was the right of former household members to retrieve pieces of property lost in generational transmission. Intestacy rules did not so decidedly disadvantage women on the excuse of their dowry, as was prevalent in communal statutes to the north. Even the somewhat misnamed alternative household property regime of the "Greek" marriage form, which kept dowry as a separate fund and did not result in a communal patrimony, did not of itself demand the exclusionary equation of dowry with legitimate portion. Still, the process of patrilinearization of family that we have seen for northern and central Italy also had an impact in the south. The invention then of exclusions for dowry, by statutes or contract, and the interweaving of substitutions and prohibitions on alienation of property beyond agnatic kin came to mark the elite families throughout Italy. Governments and courts enforced and adjudicated these arrangements as their duty toward the social unit that was the family.

Family solidarity always had its limits. That solidarity, such as it was, was always weaker at moments when the family seemed threatened by lack of direct succession and by the potential claims of females, among other things. Disputes within families were driven by the same forces that had people looking so intently to preserve family and property. Disputes occurred within political units too, and the rights and duties of citizenship, that sprang first from one's family, were also contentious. The consequences of marriages outside the community and of the actions of unruly members of the body politic were difficult issues to resolve. Who inherited property in another community? Who paid the taxes?

Jews were both a community unto themselves, with their own legal heritage and courts, and a community on the margins politically of the larger Italian society. Jews had to operate in two legal realms and depended on their abilities and rights in the secular courts of cities and principalities. They had the same problems as their Christian neighbors – determining validity of marriages and legitimacy of children, managing debts and obligations, amassing dowries, transmitting inheritances. Some of these carried peculiar difficulties for Jews, as their communities were relatively small and scattered over the peninsula, yet also in many places enclosed and narrow. Finding suitable marriage partners took more effort, and negotiations often had a geographic as well as economic dimension. Possession of lands was much more difficult,–,in some communities forbidden – so some of the trappings of family identity were not as available to Jews as to Christians. But legal devices such as emancipation and testaments were available and used.

Whatever community we examine, women were vital to households. There they were visible. Outside the house, in the streets, they were on display as parts of family, as statements of wealth and breeding. Sumptuary laws sought to keep that display within bounds so as not to excite the ruinous envy of others or to bankrupt the family that put too much of its wealth on display rather than to in productive uses. They also aimed at keeping the women of good families distinct from all those women who were not good. But women were not visible in government, especially not in republics. They had places, a few, in principalities as consorts, ladies in waiting, and occasionally as heirs and thus rulers. As women could not, according to the maxims of law, perpetuate family (in all senses other than biological), they seemingly did not have a place in the public arena in which heads of household managed family finances and futures. Of course, women were in markets and made important decisions in many families. They did so quietly, it was hoped. Women also were in court, or men went to court for them to transact their rights. Many of the cases we have examined sprang from such circumstances. Women's property, by those same legal maxims, would eventually fade into the belongings of a marital family defined by its men, either by way of marriage or inheritance, or even by a gift. Those related to women, their agnates and cognates, hoped to gain in those situations and brought their suits to court.

8

Crisis of Family and Succession?

Italian families, in all their different permutations across the peninsula and islands over more than three centuries, nonetheless rested on certain fairly common legal bases: *patria potestas*, agnation defined by it, gender distinctions (especially prominent in local laws and customs), definitions of marriage and relationships, and, above all, dowry and its resonances in intestate inheritance rules, as well as testaments, and related devices, most notably the fully developed *fideicommissum* that became widespread in the course of the sixteenth century. These legal devices developed over time and were cleverly adapted to perceived familial needs. They were not without their difficulties and drawbacks in shifting situations, as we have seen repeatedly in numerous cases across the centuries. Yet they seem largely to have worked, allowing for the play of that "patrimonial rationality" that served, it was thought, to preserve patrilines and their honor and property across the generations, most evidently for the nobilities and patriciates of the varying corners of Italy.

Even as far back as Bartolo, it was possible to assume that any adult male, without a great deal of training or guidance, had the capacity to manage and transmit a patrimony. There was an ethical imperative, accepted into and elaborated in law, to prevent loss and fragmentation of family patrimony. Transgression of that imperative "weighed like a stone on the conscience of that foolish father of family who proved himself so wanting or guiltily extravagant as to neglect his duties, in that way putting in danger the necessary material premise for the preservation of the house and its prosperity."[1]

---

[1] Rossi, "I fedecommessi," 177–78.

This was the patrimonial rationality that Elizabeth Mellyn has recently described as "the belief held by families and governments that the prudent preservation, management, and devolution of patrimony were of supreme importance. It suggests that economic decisions could not be made outside the context of the family or independent of social concerns."[2] Those who failed to subordinate their interests or desires to those of family – prodigals and spendthrifts – came, by the sixteenth century, but starting well before then, to be seen as mentally deficient, subjected to guardianship or even incarceration in extreme cases. Courts and jurists enforced this sense of rationality. That is how deeply embedded it was in culture and law.

Whether we want to call it patrimonial or something else, what counts for rationality is socially relative and constructed. Arguably the insane were simply rejecting a sense of ownership of objects and patrimonies that made them somehow enduring entities that they could not simply use and dispose of. Theirs was perhaps an alternative rationality, one that tried to take account of relationships other than agnatic, of meanings of property as something other than family *substantia*. Patrimonial rationality had its problems and its costs.

Francesco Guicciardini (1483–1540), an astute observer of Florentine society and political behavior in general, began his active career as a doctor of law, gathered clients, and wrote *consilia*, before turning to a more noteworthy career as a statesman. Toward the end of his life, in course of several years, he composed and organized a set of maxims, usually referred to as *Ricordi*. Among them was the statement that a "dishonestly" gained estate tended to be lost by the third generation. The founder of the fortune was more attached to it, as he had labored for it, than his heirs, who did not have to learn how to acquire it.[3] But as Guicciardini elsewhere counselled that deception was always useful in one's affairs, it might be argued that any fortune, on those terms, was dishonestly acquired. Even the "natural" inclination to have children ran into the fact that "even good and wise children are undoubtedly more trouble than comfort" (including Francesco and his brothers toward their father, by his testimony); and Guicciardini felt compelled to advise that one should strive to stay on good terms with brothers and relatives, even at the cost of occasional inconvenience.[4] Whatever the law's assumptions about the rationality of property

---

[2] Mellyn, *Mad Tuscans and Their Families*, 103–04.

[3] Francesco Guicciardini, *Maxims and Reflections of a Renaissance Statesman*, trans. Mario Domandi (New York: Harper, 1965), 50 and 112.

[4] Ibid., 112, 114.

holders and heads of household, much of life conspired to undermine the preservation and transmission of property across the generations. It was not just that the external world held so many dangers with its wars, plagues, political upheavals, and economic recessions. Even one's own children could prove to be a family's undoing. Strict paternal control over them, on a daily basis and in the legal devices that fathers turned to, was an important strategy as a result. But it too had its costs.

It can be argued that, while wasting the demographic potential of their children by arranging clerical careers rather than marriage, patriarchs preserved status and wealth, stifling social mobility and drawing wealth upwards. In that sense their strategies were successful. But there was clearly also a downside. Limiting marriages, especially by the men whose agnation was defining for a lineage and its patrimony, endangered the very demographic continuity of the line. Though many lineages survived, they did so numerically weaker than they had been a few generations earlier. Entire branches might be lacking on the family tree. In other cases all lines ended. We have seen numerous cases where settlement of an estate was in doubt due to the failure of the direct line of descent. But reduction of marriages was also a strategy to reduce the number of competing claims (or simply mouths to feed and raise against increasing costs of adequate socialization). Conflicts and lawsuits could be avoided. The solidarity of the family perhaps became more real with fewer egos in the arena. Again there was a risk-reward dynamic at work.

Limitation of marriages was also part and parcel of a relentless infla-tion in dowry values. Fewer girls were married because families could not afford to assemble such large dowries. And all that wealth, following the laws, as we have seen them, would fall into the hands of marital kin, to their heirs. Greater sums nominally in the ownership of women had effects on household management, if only because husbands faced legal restrictions in what they could do with dowry.

Alongside reduction in the numbers of family members marrying, there was the reduction of much of family property into the category of the inalienable. Much as holding to the principles of the usury prohibition notoriously generated elaborate and not always effective and efficient devices to get around it, the elaboration of the inalienable possessions of Italian patrimonies similarly gave rise to inefficiencies, gimmicks, or just plain anguish. The inalienable goods that families held onto – a residence, a rural estate, art objects or other decorations in the home or in churches, or even more humble implements – anything on which a family name or coat of arms might be affixed – carried a significance that transcended the

merely economic. To be sure, plenty of things were sold, even by direction
of a testator, to settle debts. But these items were portable and seen in
some sense only as temporary possessions, containers of wealth for a
while. In contrast, the inalienable possession could not be transitory; only
a durable item could objectify a family. The *fideicommissum* was a device
to designate what was to be inalienable, "thereby elevating them to a level
superior in value to those ordinary things that could be exchanged with
impunity."[5] Such inalienable things were truly only possessed, not owned.
Renting them out (for fairly short terms) or pawning them allowed for
economic use without nominally losing the all-important title (ownership)
to them. Inventories, made at the moment of someone's death or even at
other times, were a means of tracking ownership and possession of
alienable and inalienable things, even as items might move in or out of
a household. Otherwise the surest proof of ownership would be constant
and exclusive use of something, which was not there when an object was
rented out. The right to reclaim what had been loaned out was a sign of
ownership that also precluded such a claim by the one in de facto
possession of something. Clashes of interest were always possible over
supposedly inalienable objects. We have seen more than a few examples.

In essence, by immobilizing so many lands and goods and isolating
them from the market, people were lowering risks,–,immediate risks, but
also unforeseeable risks over a longer term. Creditors were not going to
disrupt family lines, or at least not without the cooperation of that family
in pawning some items or allowing the supposedly inalienable to return to
the market. But withholding or delaying repayment of debts by shielding
behind a family trust could also threaten reputations and access to further
credit, or at least significantly raise the costs of borrowing. Again, there
was a downside to this practice.

By the eighteenth century, and increasingly over the years, important,
eloquent, and even strident voices were raised in criticism of law and
practices relating to family, notably those practices that thwarted individual choice in marriage and profession and the disposition of property,
those practices that elevated objects above the purely economic. These
critiques offered a different rationality, resting on more individualized
behaviors in relation to markets and social organizations that
transcended families. One of the first and most thorough critics was
Lodovico Antonio Muratori (1672–1750), an archivist and librarian,

[5] Ago, *Gusto for Things*, 59.

but also a prolific publisher of documents and treatises. In his *Dei difetti della giurisprudenza* (1741), which otherwise dealt mainly with issues of historical interpretation and the ethical problems of prolonged lawsuits, Muratori dedicated the seventeenth chapter to *fideicommissa*, primogeniture, and other inheritance practices.[6] He denounced as ridiculous the arrogance of trying to control the transmission of property from beyond the grave *in infinito*. Admitting that there was benefit to a polity in preserving its nobility, he nonetheless complained that the *fideicommissa* and substitutions rendered contracts, rents, and sureties uncertain, and thus paralyzed the markets. "We quite often marvel that there spring forth rotten documents and testaments that snatch estates from the hands of ridiculed purchasers. . . . and here is a horrid storm upon so many creditors, saving the debtors or at least their sons their property by bringing forth the enchanted shield of *fideicommissa*." Foresight and planning were impossible in such a situation. Families themselves were disturbed by conflicts over the unequal distribution of assets and control over them. While in some places the ruler might offer dispensation from the structures of a *fideicommissum*, in other locales there was no such luck.

Removing all the ties and restrictions on inherited property, Muratori opined, would undoubtedly reduce the number and duration of inheritance lawsuits, in which legal professionals otherwise happily displayed their subtle talents and drew large fees. He cited the great seventeenth-century jurist, Cardinal Giuseppe De Luca (1614–83), as having already noted the deleterious effects of inheritance lawsuits. And Muratori lauded the efforts of popes Clement VIII (1592–1605) and Urban VIII (1623–44) to limit their duration or at least register *fideicommissa* in Rome, so that heirs and others would know of them before probate. Muratori denounced as well the "modern" form of the Trebellianic quarter, the claim to which opened the door to countless lawsuits (examples of which we have seen) by heirs trying to get at least that share free and clear of the testamentary restriction on alienation and control.

Only the lawyers seemed to profit from this situation in law. Baldo, it was said, according to Muratori, realized 1,500 scudi in his life from estate lawsuits. At least law should limit substitutions to a few degrees of relationship and only a few generations. Or people should have to register publicly what property they had subject to substitutions or dotal hypothecs, ignorance of which harmed creditors.

---

[6] Lodovico Antonio Muratori, *Dei difetti della giurisprudenza* (Venice 1742), 145–54.

In his concluding list of suggestions to fix all the problems of law in his day (his chapter 19),[7] Muratori offered that the *fideicommissum* cease when the heir had no direct descendants, although one could continue to imply a *fideicommissum* where the testator prohibited alienation outside the *familia* or expressed concern to perpetuate agnation. In contrast, "it has to be licit for any heir to forbid the deduction of the Trebellianic quarter to the instituted heirs, saving those regions where by custom or statute one cannot forbid to sons of first degree, when one does not adopt the precaution of Sozzini."[8] The heir should be able to alienate to meet debts on his discretion, and among the *mobili* subject to bequests were not to be included jewels, gold or silver vessels, money, wares for sale, animals, grain, wine, meats, oil, or other edibles. These would remain fungible assets. In all, Muratori listed 100 recommendations, some radical, most minor, but all aimed at clarification of ownership and control and most of those dealing with *fideicommissa*.

Subsequent *illuministi* of the eighteenth century echoed and expanded Muratori's criticisms. They proved quite willing, in fact, to go beyond him and advocate not mere prudent reforms of the *fideicommissum* but its utter abolition. Foremost was Gaetano Filangieri (1752–88), a Neapolitan jurist, whose *Scienza della legislazione* appeared in 1780 (first two volumes) and advocated nothing less than the abolition of *fideicommissa*, among other elements of law that he found repugnant to free trade and social well-being. The disadvantaging of younger sons was a particular object of his rancor.[9] Equal division among all sons seemed to Filangieri a spur to labor and economic development and thus the growth of political economy, as each heir would strive to rebuild his holdings to the level that his father had had.

Broader criticism struck the legal institution seen as foundational to family, to the subordination of children and the commanding will of the testator,–,namely *patria potestas*. Francesco Dalmazzo Vasco (1732–94) and Alfonso Longo (1738–1804) inveighed against the "unnatural" and

---

[7] Muratori, *Dei difetti della giurisprudenza*, 161–80.

[8] This was first theorized by Mariano Sozzini the younger (1482–1556). The *cautela* allowed a testator to specify that an heir who did not accept the various burdens and limitations in the testament would lose everything beyond his legitimate portion. Denounced by some jurists as a fraudulent device, it caught on from the argument that the heir was under no coercion to accept the testamentary burdens.

[9] Gaetano Filangieri, *La scienza della legislazione*, 8 vols, vol. 2 (Naples 1780; reprint ed. Nabu Press, 2010), 64–74.

"irrational" powers law vested in fathers. In Longo's case, his criticism of paternal power served as the launching pad for his own assault on the *fideicommissum*.[10] Perhaps the most renowned of the *illuministi*, Cesare Beccaria (1738–94), in his famous treatise on criminal law, penalties, and torture, attacked *patria potestas* and the family based on it as an "empty idol" that was often not in the interests of anyone who was part of it.[11] He spoke of the polity based not on 20,000 families but on 100,000 persons.

The chorus of complaints in the eighteenth century, and even as far back as De Luca in the seventeenth, would indicate that perceptions were changing. The fact that regimes such as that of the Habsburg-Lorraine dukes of Tuscany introduced restrictions on *fideicommissa* (in 1747) shows that the chorus of complaints was heard and heeded. The consensus among historians is that there were inherent problems in Italian legal models of family that made themselves felt over time. Marco Cavina has noted that, while there was certainly strengthening of the *patria potestas* within autocratic regimes that saw themselves as based on a familistic social model, there was also willingness to listen to the complaints of children about mistreatment, especially regarding marital choices. French law introduced an emancipatory age of majority that released an adult son from the need for paternal consent to wed, although he was still required to inform his father of his marital choice beforehand. And treatises about paternal roles were known to urge fathers to be loving and attentive to their children's desires and abilities.

Renata Ago has pointed to subtle legal adjustments in, for instance, lessening the privileging of dowry among a family's "debts" as a way of providing greater protection to creditors. Only tacit dotal credits (for dowries actually handed over to a husband) were protected, thus undercutting express credits established in *fideicommissa*, which also shows that the norms of *fideicommissa*, while not directly challenged, faced some restriction. The protection of dowry itself ran in the face of any sense of unity of a patrimony by asserting rights of a wife or daughter distinct from the prerogatives of a patriarch. It ran parallel to the obvious

---

[10] Alfonso Longo, "Osservazioni su i fedecommessi," in *Illuministi italiani*, vol. 3: *Riformatori lombardi, piemontesi e toscani*, ed. Franco Venturi (Milan: Ricciardi, 1958), 227; Vasco, "Note all' *Esprit des loix*," in ibid., 848–49.

[11] Cesare Beccaria, *Dei delitti e delle pene*, ed. Gian Domenico Pisapia (Milan: Giuffrè, 1964), 121–22.

contradiction between the control over property set by a *fideicommissum*
and the wide latitude otherwise accorded to a *paterfamilias*. As Ago
concludes,

in favor of the individual remained only the fact that law did not succeed in getting
on top of all the contradictions that it itself had contributed, either in the practices
of families or in notarial records or in jurisprudence, the necessity to respect
contractual freedom and the desire of the contracting parties continued to create
difficulties in the corporate family concept.[12]

Studies of Bolognese marital and inheritance practices in the sixteenth
and seventeenth centuries confirm Ago's insights. Maintaining family
and its honor for the elite tended to narrow the range of both possible
heirs and potential marriage partners. Steps taken to preserve family
were a "mixed blessing: the main wealth preserving practices – *fidei-*
commissum (entail) and severe marriage restrictions,–,ignited a process
of aristocratic implosion that would undermine the very foundation of
the edifice they were intended to protect." At the least, practices
intended to preserve families tended to immobilize society and its
economic capital.

   Philip Gavitt, in a carefully drawn study of charitable institutions and
practices in sixteenth-century Florence, has used the term "crisis" to
describe the situation. A patriciate wedded to an increasingly rigidified
inheritance system, restricting marriage opportunities for children, had to
rely on increasing abandonment of children, especially so girls. It was not
an ideology of gender that led to the victimization of women, as Gavitt
sees it, but the ideology of lineage: "the roots of the crisis, the symptoms
of which are so dramatically evident in the sixteenth century, consisted of
tightened enforcement of patrilineal inheritance rules in practice in colli-
sion with the actual situations and needs of families."[13] Families were
torn apart, however unintended that consequence, by subordinating
younger children, especially where primogeniture was in force, to family
prerogatives. In this regard, Gavitt is echoing the earlier determinations
of Burr Litchfield that "the weakening of independent households and
secondary family lines continued during the seventeenth century as
branches of families became impoverished, sold property, or died out, a
development related to the demographic phenomenon of the limitation of
marriages. ... as income came to depend more heavily on immobile

---

[12] Ago, "Ruoli familiari e statuto giuridico," 119–22, 129–30.
[13] Gavitt, *Gender, Honor, and Charity in Late Renaissance Florence*, 69.

property, it became less possible for second and third sons to marry."[14] Isabelle Chabot too has taken note of a 1620 revision of Florence's statute regulating intestate succession that she attributes to a "crisis" in succession of aristocratic lineages there. The grand duke sought to simplify the exclusion of women in favor of agnate males, while also giving room to succession by mother or those directly descended from her, in the absence of agnates within eight degrees.[15] Gianna Pomata too employs the term crisis for the state of patrilineal inheritance by 1700 and the resistance arising to it from younger sons and daughters.[16]

A growing culture of consumption only added to the anxiety to preserve patrimonies, as one can see in the demands of sixteenth-century *trattatisti* that fathers see to preservation of their patrimony. In that connection Ago's recent book on the culture of consumption in Rome underlines that the transmission of goods, even by women who "fully interiorized the logic of the language men employed to the extent that they willingly identified with their husband's lineage," as an integral part of lineage continuity.[17] While not employing terms such as crisis, Ago nonetheless confirms Gavitt's intuitions about lineage versus gender and the importance of things of all sorts (not just key buildings and lands) to family preservation. Making some possessions alienable could, in reverse, allow property owners and heads of family to settle debts and restore economic credit in the face of possessions bound under perpetual trust. Devices were arrived at. In Florence, beginning in the 1580s, the *censo* as a form of security against future revenues allowed patriarchs to find credit, extending to creditors some reassurance and a tradeable asset, while not legally alienating the debtor's property (and thus violating any reigning *fideicommissa*). The debtor also retained control over the redemption of the *censo* (so it was of indeterminate duration) and thus an important degree of flexibility.

The result of inheritance restrictions and the limitation of marriages was paradoxically the extinction of many lineages. Even a man like the famed musician and singer, Jacopo Peri (1561–1633) in Florence, who left several sons, could not count on the true perpetuation of his lineage even to another generation, thanks to vagaries of disease and markets. Peri's fairly substantial estate fell to others only a few decades after his death.[18]

---

[14] Litchfield, *Emergence of a Bureaucracy*, 220.
[15] Chabot, *La dette des familles*, 27–29.   [16] Pomata, "Family and Gender," 81–83.
[17] Ago, *Gusto for Things*, 226.
[18] Carter and Goldthwaite, *Orpheus in the Marketplace*.

Women often rose to the fore at the point where the male line failed, even in the temporary interstices of widowhood coming between two male generations. Caroline Castiglione has unearthed several outstanding instances among the Roman aristocracy. One story she follows is that of the conflict between Olimpia Giustiniani Barberini and her fairly prodigal and certainly headstrong son, Urbano. Olimpia's marriage had itself righted family fortunes in 1653, but by 1697 she was faced with the prospect of using her substantial dowry to hold onto the Barberini fief of Monte Rotondo against her son's desire to sell it to cover his large debts. Urbano, it seems, operated with an absolute sense of his ownership rather than a sense of being steward of the property for the next (unborn) generation. Olimpia also was intent on seeing to the future of her daughter, Camilla, against her imperious brother. Cardinal Francesco Barberini also struggled against his brother's proclivities and claimed to have three times saved his line from financial ruin, while equally excoriating his mother's management and recordkeeping. Barberini fortunes, in any case, were clearly waning.

Another Barberini widow, Teresa Boncompagni (1692–1744), widow of Urbano, was put in the position of defying the emperor and her brother-in-law, the cardinal, about the residence and upbringing of her only child, a daughter named Cornelia. Cardinal Francesco had visions of marrying her to a cousin, a Borromeo heir from Lombardy, and recovering the fief of Monte Rotondo. Teresa, however, was intent on keeping her daughter with her and not turning her over to a convent education. The means employed in this case were legal, but also decidedly extralegal, ranging from a mother's entreaties to an eventual kidnapping of the young Cornelia. We are reminded of the emotional registers of family life, of a mother's love for her daughter, but also of direct male control (husband) as heir (son). Finally, in an even more arresting example, when the line of the Orsini of Bracciano died out with the death of Flavio (1620–98), his widow, Marie-Anne de la Trémoille (1642?–1722), who had already faced legal difficulties from her husband's creditors, entered into extended litigation to settle the estate's debts. In the end she was reviled for letting Orsini property pass out of the family hands, despite a longstanding *fideicommissum* and a more recent one, and despite the existence of a transverse lineage, the Orsini of Gravina, who considered the properties of Bracciano theirs. The Roman Rota, as the court that ultimately determined the case, backed the creditors against the failed line of Bracciano. For Marie-Anne, French by birth but also the last of the Orsini of Bracciano, it was a thankless task.

WHY THE PATRILINEAGE AND *FIDEICOMMISSUM*?

The prominent role of women and their property at fragile points in the progressions of nominally agnatic (male) lineages points not only to contradictions in gender ideology and the truly illusory quality of agnatic continuity, but also to the fragility of these lineages, which only increased over time. This crisis, to use Gavitt's term, raises the question why families turned to and stuck with these marital and inheritance practices. They were certainly aware that lines were dying out, although the lucky survivors were in position to gather up some of what the luckless left behind. They knew the anguish of children who disagreed with parental life choices for them. They knew the problems of creditors and debtors. Further, we might ask why law and jurists permitted and perpetuated such a legal situation (leaving aside the understandable motive Muratori pointed to – proliferation of lawsuits to the profit of the litigating attorneys).

The key to answering both questions would seem to lie in what they thought family was, such that laymen and jurists alike, at least in most cases, created and used a system that was detrimental to most all families, at least in the long run. Even in the short term, the frustrations of trying to raise credit or satisfy obligations had to be palpable. Still, we also need to keep in mind that the opposite practice, division of inheritance among multiple heirs in each generation, did indeed result in the impoverishment of subsequent generations. Some family lines found a way to flourish, often to the consternation and jealousy of those lines of an agnatic group that did not. A lessened sense of belonging to the group, marked perhaps by litigation with others over inheritance, was often the result. Of course, litigation only further drove the different lines apart.

The *fideicommissum* in its full form (perpetual substitutions and prohibition of alienation) emerged as a "crude solution" to the problem of dwindling shares and fractious relations over time.[19] Especially when primogeniture was applied in a trust that remained individual, as opposed to dividual, there could be the hope (frequently realized) that property would hold together over generations, without so much litigiousness (a less frequently realized result). Having such a device available to bridge across the next death of a *capo famiglia* was what mattered. What might ensue four or five generations later, that it might lead to deleterious

---

[19] Bizzochi, "La dissoluzione di un clan familiare," 41.

results, was probably not in the mind of one who established such a trust. It can be argued, as Stefano Calonaci has it, that the *fideicommissum* was an adaptation to the nature of the economy in an era of market instability that tied productive lands and meaningful structures to a family, while giving reality to that *casato* in the repetition of substitutions into transverse lines.[20] And the perpetual *fideicommissum* always functioned as a symbolic device, giving expression to family solidarity and honor across the generations, no matter the level of wealth.

One possible answer might be found in a concept offered over half a century ago by the American sociologist, Edward Banfield. His study of a poor southern Italian peasant community led him to coin the term "amoral familism" to describe the ethos he claimed to find there. The needs and prerogatives of the nuclear family were what mattered. People were suspicious of others, and so those peasants did not form cooperative associations, political or economic alliances, and thus lost untold opportunities to improve their conditions of existence and expand the future for their children. Further, with regard more directly to our interests and approach, Banfield posits that amoral familists disregard law, having no fear of enforcement, or hope in it, as the case may be. For peasants especially, law will seem only to protect the interests of the powerful, who will be able to cheat and get away with it. In sum, as Banfield saw life in the village, there was pervasive mistrust of those outside the nuclear family, scepticism about cooperation, no sense of common enterprise or shared results, no group representing and articulating a common good, fear of law and government, and apprehensiveness about the future and change in general.

Is what we have seen among the elites of early modern Italy similar? Did the entailing of property (thus precluding reciprocal debtor-creditor relationships and capital accumulation) and the restricting of marriage (thus reducing the number of possible relations of cognatic and affinal kinship) amount to an equivalent familism? Were the frequently expressed suspicions of others, legislative and contractual safeguards against fraud and theft, the disallowance in many communities of members of the same lineage from holding political offices simultaneously or even sequentially, and endless litigation expressions of a narrowing of social horizons to the equally narrowing boundaries of the agnatic lineage? Was proverbial distrust of law (as by the old saw, when the law is

---

[20] Part of the argument of Calonaci, *Dietro lo scudo incantato*, 216–19.

made the deception is found: "fatta la legge trovato l'inganno") a parallel expression for what Banfield found?

Banfield's ideas, it is important to note, have been criticized fairly widely, and were so almost immediately, although not all critics have rejected his notion of amoral familism. They find instead that an ethos of that sort is not itself a causal factor, not an explanation, in other words, but something to be explained. Banfield, they say, has imposed a logic on Italian peasants that was not theirs, and he has downplayed the unstable political situation of such a peasant community, that can make peasant actions seem precisely responsive to their situation. Others have gone further, intent on denying amoral familism altogether, or at least confining any such thing to the ranks of the subaltern classes. Families were not isolated but interdependent on neighbors, parties, patrons, even farming cooperatives. Their prestige was highly dependent on the honor accorded them by others. One had to have status in the community, and that began with being head of family, possessed thereby of certain needs and responsibilities, predictable and reliable in some manner. Debts contracted with others are an unavoidable feature of life, for poor and rich. Any family ethos, amoral or otherwise, would seem to spring from social conditions, including class. Even though it is clear at points, as in the many local laws attempting to preclude fraud, that there was distrust of others and their capacity to manipulate markets or legal mechanisms, that does not mean that there was systematic application of such distrust to all persons in all situations.

Banfield's ideas continue to resonate with those intent on explaining the relative poverty and lack of governmental integration to be found in the south of Italy, like Robert Putnam. Even an incisive critic of current Italian life and culture like John Hooper can find it useful to employ Banfield's notion, though he does so in a nuanced and careful fashion. Gregory Hanlon employs the somewhat broader term agonistic sociability to describe patterns of interaction in early modern Italy.[21] For our purposes, coming off a study of so many intrafamilial conflicts and their attendant lawsuits, it is sometimes hard even to see nuclear family as a unit of solidarity. Most all the suits we have seen pitted relatives (admittedly, not always close) against each other. But again and again the lawsuits arose when expected patterns of inheritance and even just of behavior failed to materialize. Family solidarity still rested on individual

---

[21] Hanlon, *Early Modern Italy, 1550–1800*, 26–30.

bearers of rights. At times that individuality allowed one person to save
the economic and social substance of the family. At others it allowed one
person to assert self against or, more likely, over the group.

The true limitation of Banfield's perspective is that it takes no awareness of time. He looked to families in the moment and not to past experiences and relationships. The early modern Italian families whose legal
doings and mis-doings we have examined lived on two planes. There was
the horizontal plane of the present, when family was intermediary
between the individual and society; and by extension, family furnished
strong or weak ties to collateral relatives or marital kin. There was also
the vertical plane of past and future. As Casanova notes,

the greater the network of relations was on which each person could count, the
wider was his "family", so much greater were the possibilities of receiving help in
difficult moments. What did not vary was the tie to the vertical family, which
encompassed parents and grandparents, children and grandchildren of both sexes;
into this family, of living events, of the sentiments that each felt in his life, was
injected the value of a tradition to be transmitted, of an abstract family by which
was justified the belonging of an individual to an ideology of the material and
immaterial patrimony, which represented its continuity as a good of which all felt
a part.[22]

It was that consistent vertical agnatic lineage that won out in early
modern Italy, at least in inheritance practices. While it could prove
dysfunctional in the present and often in the future (for all those lineages
that died out or fell deeply into debt), it was the lineage that set one's
sense of self in a succession of generations, in a name and coat of arms
and ancestral properties. It was a collaboration with the dead and the yet
to be born. It conditioned relations with women and with wider kin, and
with others in general. It set the ambiguous duality of the role of family
head, possessed of what Giovanni Rossi has called his "overflowing
subjectivity" and the effective and flexible means to express it, including
the testament and the *fideicommissum*, but also made him beholden to a
duty to family that restrained (or sought to) his will in favor of the family
as a whole.[23] That, in turn, enlisted the services of law, lawyers, and
courts to make sense of the world in its terms.

Family, conceived increasingly in terms of agnatic lineage, was simply
an unquestionable good. It was beyond doubt. A social critic such as
Guicciardini (above), might draw attention to the problems children
raised for their fathers, and to the tendency of later generations to

---

[22] Casanova, *La famiglia italiana*, 236.   [23] Rossi, "I fedecommessi," 181–82.

dissipate a patrimony, but that seems precisely because family and wealth were necessary to social order and one's position in society. He also composed a family chronicle to keep alive the memory of Guicciardini ancestors, with their good decisions and some of the bad, for the utility of those to come after.[24] He perhaps had some doubt as to the survival of the family (which, in fact, remains to this day), which he was trying to aid by his writing, but he was not questioning its moral and economic purpose. Family was its own justification in a society that saw larger political and social units constructed on the basis of families. With only limited recourse, if any, to government or church, family was where individuals could look for sustenance and support. Family could only be moral, it seems. The rest of the world was something else.

The law and those who taught and practiced it were part of the process and part of the problem for families, their estates, and litigation over them. Treatises, collections of *consilia*, practical manuals – all distilled the essential elements of paternal power, husbandly command, dowry, and testamentary practices that served to retain family property. The jurists too were part of society and harbored the same aspirations for their own families as did their clients.

It is interesting that, in parallel with a sense of crisis in family and inheritance one finds among historians, those who study the law's history also see a crisis in the later sixteenth and seventeenth centuries, marked by scarce doctrinal development of law, a decadence embodied in works "sealed in a mass like neglected and pedantic products of a process of progressive accentuated pragmatism and involution of jurisprudence, which shows itself incapable in Italy of regenerating itself and elaborating doctrines that are not completely flattened into the reading at the service of practice."[25] This negative assessment, which tends in contrast to exalt the progressive ideas of the *illuministi* with which this chapter began, admits the conviction among *doctores iuris* that they could render more valuable service by giving the state of the question in law on the controversial matters in practice, than by making doctrinal positions that were not binding on judges and courts. The elaboration of the learned opinion of the best jurists, the *opiniones communes*, served to fill the lacunae left by lack of consistent legislation from princes or magistracies. These gave some certainty to outcomes and reduced recourse to *arbitrium judicis* to

---

[24] Francesco Guicciardini, *Ricordi diari memorie*, ed. Mario Spinella (Rome: Riuniti, 1981), 31–75.

[25] Rossi, "I fedecommessi," 186–87.

within acceptable limits, against so many variables in actual cases. They were incapable, it is true, of elaborating theoretical alternatives, needed to face new demands arising every day in preference to bowing before an authoritative past. Their prolix opinions, as we have seen, were replete with reverent citations and would finally perpetuate a divorce between the world of law and the needs and aspirations of the lively developments of civil society. Instead of doctrinal order there were the thousands of contingent problems and the search for rules adequate to those shifting circumstances. Jurists remained deeply mired in the realm of the probable and had to address all its contingencies. Arriving at the *voluntas* behind any given testament was just one sort of quotidian problem jurists addressed.

A monument to this state of jurisprudential affairs is the *Practicarum conclusionum iuris in omni foro frequentiorum* of Domenico Toschi (1535–1626), published in Rome between 1605 and 1608. Toschi was a bishop and cardinal, a functionary in courts in Florence and Bologna. A man of forensic experience and not the classroom, Toschi offered a simpler way through the vast outpouring of judicial problems and rules to give assurance to judges who could follow his guidance and the authority of the juristic sources he cited. For the important area of law that was the *fideicommissum*, Toschi was able to offer no less than sixty-five conclusions, covering its types, what it could do, options against alienation, and prerogatives of the *fideicommissarius*. Perhaps this all assured more than the judge. Were heads of household encouraged to formulate *fideicommissa* or to take cases to court by the seeming solidity of Toschi's rules and the timeless authorities on which they rested? Were the rules easier to cope with in such form? It is time, perhaps, for one last *consilium*, from the pen of Marco Antonio Pellegrini, to hint at possible answers.

The problem in the case, he said, was simply one. Could a father, with his son's consent, alienate from maternal properties, of which the father was nominally only usufructuarius? Or could the son revoke his father's deal? Here was a case, in short, in which prerogatives of individual and family were at odds, not just the prerogatives of two individuals. Pellegrini rehearsed three arguments in favor of the son recovering the property, resting on the son's legal ownership and the father's role as manager of his son's property. A usufructuary ordinarily could not alienate title, though he could cede something termed *commoditas* to another. In support of this line of argument were cited eighteen references to Roman law texts or to learned commentaries, to four *consilia*, and to three other sources (treatises and a judicial decision). Then, in typical juristic fashion, Pellegrini reversed field and found the opposite to be true. The current holder, Don Vincenzo, had been invested by the father of Don Matteo in good faith in the life right the father had. That was a perfectly valid transaction; "indeed there is no reason and no doctor [of law] says that Don Matteo can claim these fields in law, namely with respect to ownership and usufruct." Here suddenly there was no authority to be found to back the son's case. Indeed, to the contrary the *magis communis conclusio* was that a son could not retrieve maternal property alienated by his father (and the pile of citations proved that). The "law has more confidence in the father's management than it would otherwise in anyone else" (*lex plurimum confidit de patris administratione quamvis secus sit in aliis*). He did not need judicial leave to alienate anything, as a guardian would. So, though the son had ownership, he could not contest the alienation of the life usufruct. In fact, the father had made a good business decision: "Don Antonio the father did not prodigally dissipate and ruin maternal goods, but rather he leased them for a fitting income, just as good heads of family are wont to do, and especially because the fields are few and in a very distant location." But the son ended up with what may have been a useless title, because he could not himself enjoy the property that Don Vincenzo now held.

Even alienation of property subject to *fideicommissum* could not be revoked, despite some legal arguments: "The assertion of Paolo di Castro ... which several have followed, is false, for Bartolo opposed it in the first case most vigorously, [and] commonly the doctors held that the fideicommissary heir of a burdened estate cannot for [realizing] his right revoke an alienation made by the heir himself, burdened with a thing subject to a *fideicommissum*, so that alienation was prohibited by the testator." The *fideicommissum* could only be invoked at the point of inheritance. The father's business deal stood.[26] The son would have to wait until the father's life right lapsed (at his death, obviously) to get full control of the property.

In this case the father was being a good steward of the estate, which included the maternal property, now firmly part of the patrimony. Whatever it was the son wanted to do with the property, the fruits of which were under a long-term lease, it ran counter to the father's vision. The past won out in that sense. But it was also the case that the father had hit on a legal device that allowed him to capitalize an asset (of admittedly

---

[26] Pellegrino, *cons.* 96, fols. 259-rb–60va.

limited value and at some distance). Without saying as much, it also seemed to be the case that the lessee, Don Vincenzo, had struck a deal that was good for him and his family.

Jurists like Pellegrini were always located at the point where the social met the familial. Pellegrini upheld the value and utility of a business contract against a narrow sense of family and ownership that the son invoked to void the deal, yet he could also do so by invoking to contrary effect the fact of the law's faith in fathers' management. Individuals and family – neither could do without the other or was reducible to the other. The *favor publicus* was considered as well. And all the while the law kept a deep sense of the authority of the past and its texts.

That family mattered, to the point that people could condone unethical behavior for the sake of advancing family interests, was a true fact of life in early modern Italy. To them it would be *ragion di famiglia*, as spelled out in texts like the popular dialogue of the Florentine humanist, Leon Battista Alberti, and more pointedly in Francesco Guicciardini's *Ricordi*. It was a sense of family that resonated with those of some social standing, who had some wealth and honor and interests to pursue and protect in conjunction with kin. It was, in other words, an ethos that varied by social class and community. It was an ethos that flourished in a situation of legal pluralism, that both opened up strategies and potential uses of legal devices, but that also left open a broad domain of uncertain legal meanings.

What we may be seeing in all these legal texts, as practicing jurists grappled with all those uncertainties, was an increasing development of what we may instead dub amoral legalism. This is not to say that there were no moral concerns in jurists' minds. Family was an ethical imperative. So was social order based on it. So certainly was the weight of the professional legal past and its texts. Jurists did not question all that. What we see across the fifteenth and sixteenth centuries is the deployment of interpretive rules, long lists of authorities, a gathering of them around ever more elaborate pro and con structures, a resolution of issues that revolve around matters such as choice of words, verb tense, and other grammatical and semantic matters. All of these were deployed to reach conclusions that accorded with professional law, that made sense to lawyers. Rarely have we seen a jurist question rules of interpretation, certainly not in terms of social or economic utility on a larger scale than the case at hand. No one asked, for example, if construing the will of the singular testator, let alone the precise content of that will, was generally a good way to proceed. No one asked if the regime of separate marital property, with all the complications it raised regarding control and use of household assets and the destination of ownership on dissolution of a marriage, was a socially sensible way to proceed. It is not as if they were unaware of the problems. But they only sought solution to them as they arose, not to keep them from arising in the future.

This is not all the jurists' doing. They were, as Rossi and others have pointed out, filling the lacunae resulting from anemic or nonexistent legislation. What legislative bodies as there were (singular princes or councils) tended to operate instead on the same level as legal professionals – case by case, family by family, variously dishing out favors, pardons, or rulings. The law was an imposing body of texts, principles, and rules that had to be accepted in life, then to be used or circumvented as need arose. Law was a conservative organizing force in society. It prevented chaos in the minds of those who turned to it. It was not a progressive force (or, to be fair, not outside narrow areas where new interpretation or reweighing of overlapping rules might affect change).

One consistent feature of the law and social action, and the resulting lawsuits, has been the conjunction of family and individual. They stood in tension to each other. On the one hand was the sweeping power of the *paterfamilias*, consonant with the power of his *voluntas* when he came to write his will. And yet he was not free to disinherit, although disinheritance would seem to have been the ultimate sanction to exact obedience. He was not free to leave less than a legitimate portion to his children, despite his freedom in devising a will. He could arrange his daughter's marriage and assemble her dowry, after appropriate negotiations, but he could not consent to the marriage, in the sense that his consent was formative. He could inherit and exercise the prerogatives of ownership (*dominium*), but not so much if there were a *fideicommissum* that applied. He was a person in law, but that was not an autonomous individual.

The prominence of the individual in modern Western accounts of personhood arises precisely from emphasis on judicial contexts, as well as philosophical and religious sources. As Janet Carsten, an anthropologist, has noted, the western autonomous individual found in such sources contrasts with a more fragmented non-western person, linked to others and formed by them, and not nearly so bounded and impenetrable. However, when one looks at western persons in a kinship context, they too emerge as interrelated to others and not separate and bounded. Father and son, or daughter (for gender too is implicated in kinship) are always such on a genealogical chart, or in terms of law that defines the relationships on the chart; but their relations were, in fact, more fluid. In

Pellegrini's case the son's relation to his father had to have changed when he came forward (with his father still alive, so far as we can glean from the *consilium*) to try to revoke the paternal legal act. Pellegrini had recourse instead to an unchanging legal image of the father who knows best and always does right by his children and their substance. And certainly in all the cases we have looked at, it is substance that has been the carrier of change and the matter which flows between persons in the kinship domain. Whether the substance was something like blood (in reference to procreation) or food, or in law the patrimony, it was what linked persons, in the present, but also inexorably to a past they could no longer change (barring a successful challenge to a lease or a testament or marital vows). The equation of *familia* with *substantia*, beginning with Bartolo, still powered the law three centuries and more later.

Glossary

Aditio Formal act of acceptance of an inheritance by an heir (**haeres**). Its opposite was **repudiation**.

Adoptio/adrogatio Adoption into one's **potestas** of a person subject to the **potestas** of another. **Adrogatio** was the equivalent for someone not subject to another's control but who was **sui iuris**.

Aes alienum Literally, someone else's coin. In other words, a debt. The term generally referred to what was owed from an estate of a deceased debtor.

Agnatio Relationships traced through males under **patria potestas**. A woman thus was agnate to males of her family but could not transmit agnation to her children (hence said to be **caput et finis** [start and finish] of her family).

Alimenta Generally consumable resources for one's support (i.e., food, clothing).

Beneficium inventarii Limitation of the heir's liability to the assets of the estate, provided he made an inventory of those assets. There were requirements as to time and witnesses.

Cessans One neglecting or failing to fulfill an obligation. The term came to be applied to those who went bankrupt.

Cippus Originally a boundary stone, it came to be extended metaphorically to a line of descent associated with the delimited property.

Cognatio Blood relations traced on either side (paternal or maternal) and through women.

Communis opinio The common wisdom of doctors of law on some matter. This was where jurisprudence effectively filled in the many holes left in statutory legislation, in the absence of legislative activity. Also a rhetorical device in legal argument, as departure from received wisdom was said to be hazardous.

Confessio dotis Formal reception of a dowry by a husband and/or others on his behalf, usually specifying a value of the dowry (**dos aestimata**), and obligating the recipient(s) to return the dowry on the end of the marriage to the bride or her heirs.

Consignatio dotis The return of a dowry during the marriage (**constante matrimonio**) to a wife's control on the grounds of the husband's mismanagement and imminent financial ruin (**vergens ad inopiam**).

Consilium Reasoned juristic argument suggesting a solution to one or more legal problems, sometimes hypothetical, but usually in the context of a case. **Consilium sapientis** was given in response to a request from a judge or from both litigants, in which case the finding of the jurist usually was adopted as the finding of the court. **Consilium pro parte** was offered to one litigating party, giving it supporting legal arguments while also poking holes in those of the other side. These were usually more thorough, especially in terms of citations of relevant doctrinal texts and jurisprudence, because they were polemical. Most of the **consilia** utilized in this book were probably **pro parte**. But judges could be swayed by them and could hold to them safely as fully legal findings.

Corpus iuris civilis A later title given to the texts of Roman law generated at the behest of the sixth-century emperor Justinian (527–65), those being the **Codex**, the **Digest**, the **Institutes**, and the **Novellae** or **Authenticae**. The equivalent collection of texts of canon law, completed piecemeal in the fourteenth century, **Corpus iuris canonici**, consisted of the **Decretum** of Gratian, the so-called **Liber extra** of papal decretals compiled by Gregory XI, the **Liber sextus** of Boniface VIII, and some final decretals of Clement VI and John XXII.

De cuius The deceased, "of whose" estate was in question.

Domicilium The place where one permanently resides, associated with the **domus** (house).

Dominium Legal ownership of something capable of being privately owned, to be distinguished from possession or other forms of holding. Ownership was describable as the right of "use and abuse." The owner of something was its dominus. **Proprietas** was equivalent term.

Donatio mortis causa Gift of something that becomes confirmed and effective on the death of the donor. A mode of transmission distinct from intestacy or a formal testament.

Donatio propter nuptias Material provision by a husband to his bride, constituting a lien on his property in her favor. In late medieval and early modern Italy the amount allowed or typically given was limited and did not rise to the level of equivalence to the dowry.

Dos (dowry) Goods or cash given by the bride or someone else, most likely her father, to the groom, which were intended to meet the expenses of married life (**onera matrimonii**). In civil law this stood as the ultimate proof of a marriage. The husband had title to the property but faced restrictions on his use of it (as he could not alienate landed property) and had to pledge that it would be returned on the dissolution of the marriage.

Ductio A more or less ceremonial escorting of the bride to her husband's home to begin living there. Constituted one important element of proof of a marriage.

Exhaeredatio Disinheritance, which had to follow prescribed forms and name the potential heir thus removed.

Extraneus Technically an heir who was not subject to the **potestas** of the deceased at the time of his death, so neither an **haeres suus et necessarius** (e.g., a child **in potestate**) nor an **haeres necessarius** (slave manumitted by the will and required to accept it). Given a period to deliberate and had to make a formal act of acceptance of the estate.

Falcidia By a law of 40 BC at least one-quarter of an estate had to come to the heir(s) after funeral expenses and debts were deducted. The remaining three-quarters was then available to resolve the legacies in the testament. This was also an assurance to the testator that the heir (**extraneus**) would accept the estate and an intestacy would not result, which would void all the legacies.

Fama Common repute about a person or his actions. This constituted a partial proof in court, though it could be little more than hearsay at times. One had to have a level of **fama** in order to exercise certain rights, or one was **disfamis**.

Familia In its narrowest sense, the word refers to all servants in a household. More widely it refers in law to the things subject to the **dominium** of the head and all persons subject to his **potestas**.

Familiaritas The state of being part of a family, mainly in the sense of a right of residence.

Fideicommissum Obligation imposed on an heir under a will to hold property for benefit of and usually transfer it to another (the fideicommissary heir). These were restricted, including by measure of the second-century emperor Hadrian that they could not go to uncertain persons. Addition of a clause falling on family members not to dispose of property outside the family was a way around that restriction. Justinian limited the validity of such trusts to four generations at most. That limitation was circumvented in early modern jurisprudence.

Fructus Fruits or products, generally natural produce of fields and orchards, etc. Also could include rents and interest payments.

Haereditas The whole of the goods and rights left by a deceased, and what the heir(s) succeed to, that is the **universum ius** of the deceased.

Immobilia (res immobiles) Generally land and buildings.

Inmixtio (inmiscere) The fact of an heir's possession and enjoyment of the goods of an estate with or without a formal acceptance of it (and its debts).

Insinuatio The insertion of one's activity into the recording acts of an official, such as a notary, making the act, such as a gift, public.

Ius commune Convenient shorthand term for jurists to refer to those authoritative texts and teachings of Roman civil law, canon law, feudal law, and some other elements that were "common" to the many jurisdictions of Italy or elsewhere. This provided the basic elements of most of daily legal life (e.g., testaments, paternal power, marriage).

Ius proprium Essentially the statutes and legislation of the different jurisdictions that dealt with local issues not coverable by the "common" law or that set out to modify, restrict, or preclude the operation of elements of it. Those laws that derogated from **ius commune** and were seen by jurists as contrary to its provisions were termed **exorbitans** or to be **odiosum**.

Legatum A legacy or bequest as a deduction from the estate. Could consist of most anything and be directed to anyone, so it was a prime vehicle for specifying post mortem charitable and pious donations. Could only be done by testament, and in part the importance of naming an heir lay in the fact that it fell to him to fulfill the terms of bequests, less a provision of one-quarter to him/them.

Legitima (portio) Share of the inheritance falling to each legitimate heir.

Lucrum dotis Term generally found in statutes. While it refers to the profit one could obtain from a dowry, it more particularly referred to the recipient of a dowry following the woman's death.

Mens testatoris Intention, purpose, or design of the testator, which served as the interpretive device for construing wills in litigation.

Mundualdus A term from Lombard law for a guardian. In Florence this was the male guardian given a woman before she could perform a legal act.

Naturalis (filius) Illegitimate child born out of wedlock but in a relationship of concubinage (steady state of cohabitation of two marriageable people, such that the relationship could not be termed adulterous). Such a child could become legitimate by subsequent marriage of the parents, and had some limited inheritance rights.

Obsequium Initially the respectful behavior expected of a freedman toward his patron. **Reverentia** was a parallel term. Both became linked with the idea of owed services (**servitia**) as the behavior that a wife owed her husband during marriage.

Origo Birthplace where one acquired local citizenship and faced the burdens thereof. Distinct from residence (**domicilium**).

Paraphernalia Property of a wife, beyond her dowry, brought into her husband's house. Statutes might extend to the husband rights of management of this and thus equate it to dowry.

Patria potestas Power of head of household (**paterfamilias**) that took on a peculiar form in Roman law, as power over persons did not lapse with their coming of age, and it carried important rights over children and property. It was acquired by birth of children to a lawful wife, or by adoption or legitimation. It ended at the **pater's** death, unless he chose to emancipate a child.

Peculium As children could not own anything when under **potestas**, what was conceded to be theirs fell under this term. Strictly, what came to them from their father or their own labors was **peculium profectitium**. Categories of **peculium castrense** and **quasi castrense** were devised to account for what a son earned in the military or in civil service or clerical positions, respectively. **Peculium adventitium** was a catchall category for property from any other sources, mainly from the mother or her kin.

Praeterire To pass over a **suus haeres** in silence. This was not allowed and generally voided a testament, leaving the estate to pass in intestacy, by which the **suus haeres** was first in line.

Propinqui/proximiores Nearest relatives or neighbors.

Pupillus Minor child **sui iuris**, so subject to guardianship, until turning the age of majority, which was twenty-five in Roman law but could be variously set by different local laws.

Raptus Abduction of a woman contrary to the will of her parents.

Repudiatio The opposite of **aditio**. The refusal of an inheritance, passing the right to inherit to the next in line by rules of intestacy or by substitutions in a will.

Res extra dotem A third category of women's property during marriage, which included assets not brought to the marital home or come to her after marriage. Her rights of ownership and control were more extensive here than in relation to dowry or **parapherna**.

Societas omnium bonorum A contractual arrangement (overt or tacit), generally among brothers, regarding common ownership and management of assets, working from common residence and occupation. Distinct from mere **fraterna** by which brothers lived together but kept at least some assets distinct to each.

Spurius (filius) Illegitimate child born from an illicit sexual relationship (as adultery or incest), said to be of an "unknown" father. Few or no inheritance rights. Could be legitimated only by distinct act of legitimation, as subsequent marriage of the parents was generally out of the question.

Stuprum Illicit intercourse with an unmarried woman, including a widow, thus distinct from adultery. Presumption of consent on her part unless the use of violence was proven.

Substitutio Device by which a testator, worried about the failure of his will for lack of heirs (by their decease, incapacity, or unwillingness), could name substitutes (**substitutio vulgaris**). Substitute for a child below the age of puberty, who by law could not make a will, was **pupillaris**. A third form was the substitution in trust (**fideicommissum**).

Trebellianica By a law of 56 the heir under a trust did not face actions on the estate, which went instead against the beneficiary under the trust. Another act of 73 extended the **Falcidian** quarter to the heir, exempt from the conditions of the trust in favor of the beneficiary.

Tutela Guardianship of minors whose father had died to protect them and their property. The **tutor/tutrix** was required to make an accounting of all actions at the point the heir came of age, but was otherwise empowered to manage property, even to sell it, in order to support the minor.

Ususfructus Right to use and take **fructus** (fruits) from another's property without diminishing its value or condition. Strictly personal right that was not transferable, though the owner could not transfer it to the detriment of the usufructary. Frequently arose in the terms of a will, giving someone the practical rights of ownership without title.

Velleianum (senatus consultum) Law of 46 forbidding women to obligate themselves for another. The transaction was not null ipso facto, but were the woman sued to fulfill her commitment she could raise this disability, as could those who were potentially obligated through her. Renunciation of this right had to be public and repeated according to Justinian.

Bibliographical Essay

INTRODUCTION

Mary Ann Glendon, *The Transformation of Family Law: State, Law, and Family in the United States and Western Europe* (Chicago: University of Chicago Press, 1989) provides a contemporary context to the sorts of changes and continuities in family law that we consider. Essential for domestic life of Italian families are Renata Ago, *Economia barocca: mercato e istituzioni nella Roma del Seicento* (Rome: Donzelli, 1998) and Cesarina Casanova, *La famiglia italiana in età moderna: ricerche e modelli* (Rome: Carocci, 1997). An overview of economic activity and developments in the period, though focused specifically on Florence, is Richard A. Goldthwaite, *The Economy of Renaissance Florence* (Baltimore and London: Johns Hopkins University Press, 2009).

A defining position on the historical study of gender is Joan Wallach Scott, "Gender: A Useful Category of Historical Analysis," *American Historical Review* 91 (1986): 1053–75. Joan Kelly's, "Did Women Have a Renaissance?" in *Becoming Visible: Women in European History*, ed. Renate Bridenthal and Claudia Koonz (Boston: Houghton Mifflin, 1977), 137–64, set the stage for the study of women and gender in our period. For earlier, see Jennifer Ward, *Women in Medieval Europe 1200–1500* (London and New York: Pearson, 2002). A paradigmatic approach is that of Merry E. Wiesner, *Gender, Church and State in Early Modern Germany* (London and New York: Longman, 1998).

Romeo De Maio, *Donna e Rinascimento* (Milan: Mondadori, 1987) is an example of an analysis that relies chiefly on literary sources, not legal. Even Laura Lee Downs, *Writing Gender History* (London: Hodder Arnold, 2004), as a more methodological statement, neglects law. One of the few that approaches law directly is Christine Meek, "Women between the Law and Social Reality in Early Renaissance Lucca," in *Women in Italian Renaissance Culture and Society*, ed. Letizia Panizza (Oxford: European Humanities Research Centre, 2000), 182–93. Also Thomas Kuehn, *Law, Family, and Women: Toward a Legal Anthropology of Renaissance Italy* (Chicago: University of Chicago

Press, 1991). Lloyd Bonfield, "Developments in European Family Law," in *Family Life in Early Modern Times, 1500–1789,* ed. David I. Kertzer and Marzio Barbagli (New Haven: Yale University Press, 2001), 87–124, raises the related issue of the neglect of law in studies of family.

Studies of law in relation to marriage begin with the four volumes edited by Silvana Seidel Menchi and Diego Quaglioni *I processi matrimoniali degli archivi ecclesiastici italiani* for Il Mulino of Bologna: *Coniugi nemici: la separazione in Italia dal xii al xviii secolo* (2000); *Matrimoni in dubbio: unioni controverse e nozze clandestine in Italia dal xiv al xviii secolo* (2001); *Trasgressioni: seduzione, concubinato, adulterio, bigamia (xiv-xviii secolo)* (2004); *I tribunali del matrimonio (secoli xv-xviii)* (2006). But also important is Charles Donahue, Jr., *Law, Marriage, and Society in the Later Middle Ages* (Cambridge: Cambridge University Press, 2007).

Useful for a more theoretical take on law are Fernanda Pirie, *The Anthropology of Law* (Oxford: Oxford University Press, 2013), especially her notion of legalism; Christopher Tomlins and John Comaroff, "'Law As . . .': Theory and Practice in Legal History," *UC Irvine Law Review* 1, no. 3 (Sept. 2011) [Symposium Issue: "Law As . . .": Theory and Method in Legal History]: 1039–79; and David M. Engel, "How Does Law Matter in the Constitution of Legal Consciousness?" in *How Does Law Matter,* ed. Bryant G. Garth and Austin Sarat (Evansville: Northwestern University Press, 1998), 109–44. Pierre Bourdieu, an influential French sociologist, offered a provocative sense of law in "The Force of Law: Toward a Sociology of the Juridical Field," *Hastings Law Journal* 38 (1987): 814–53. A balanced critique of Bourdieu is Robert Boyer, "L'anthropologie économique de Pierre Bourdieu," *Actes de la recherche en sciences sociales* 5 (2003): 65–78 and Jacques Caillose, "Pierre Bourdieu, jurislector: anti-juridisme et science du droit," *Droit et société* 56–57 (2004): 17–39. Also interesting is Bruno Latour, *The Making of Law: An Ethnography of the Conseil d"etat,* trans. Marina Brilman and Alain Pottage (Cambridge: Polity Press, 2010).

On the education and professional lives of jurists, see Paul Grendler, *The Universities of the Italian Renaissance* (Baltimore and London: Johns Hopkins University Press, 2002); Manlio Bellomo, *Saggio sull'università nell'età del diritto comune* (Catania: Giannotta, 1979); James A. Brundage, *The Medieval Origins of the Legal Profession: Canonists, Civilians, and Courts* (Chicago and London: University of Chicago Press, 2008). On forms and methods of legal thought, see James Gordley, "Ius Quaerens Intellectum: The Method of the Medieval Civilians," in *The Creation of the Ius Commune: From Casus to Regula,* ed. John W. Cairns and Paul J. Du Plessis (Edinburgh: Edinburgh University Press, 2010), 77–101, and Kees Bezemer, "The Infrastructure of the Early Ius Commune: The Formation of Regulae, or Its Failure," in *The Creation of Ius Commune,* 57–75; Italo Birocchi, *Alla ricerca dell'ordine: fonti e cultura giuridica nell'età moderna* (Turin: Giappichelli, 2002); Maria Gigliola di Renzo Villata, "Tra consilia, decisiones e tractatus . . . le vie della conoscenza giuridica nell'età moderna," *Rivista di storia del diritto italiano* 81 (2008): 15–72; Mario Ascheri, *Tribunali, giuristi e istituzioni dal medioevo all'età moderna* (Bologna: Il Mulino, 1989); Antonio Manuel Hispanha, *Introduzione alla storia del diritto europeo* (Bologna: Il Mulino, 1999); Manlio Bellomo, *The Common Legal Past of Europe, 1000–1800*, trans. from 2nd ed. Lydia Cochrane (Washington: Catholic University of America Press, 1995).

An important study of the legislative power of cities and the statutes they created is Giorgio Chittolini, "Statuti e autonomie urbane: Introduzione," in *Statuti, città, territori in Italia e Germania tra Medioevo ed Età moderna*, ed. Giorgio Chittolini and Dietmar Willoweit (Bologna: Il Mulino, 1991), 7–45, which may best be read in conjunction with an examination of the political institutional history of Italian communes, such as Lauro Martines, *Power and Imagination: City-States in Renaissance Italy* (New York: Knopf, 1979). Studies of juristic intervention in cases and their modes of statute interpretation include: Massimo Vallerani, "The Generation of the Moderni at Work: Jurists between School and Politics in Medieval Bologna (1270–1305)," in *Europa und seine Regionen: 2000 Jahre Rechtsgeschichte*, ed. Andreas Bauer and Karl H. L. Welker (Cologne: Böhlau, 2007), 139–56; Mario Ascheri, "Il 'dottore' e lo statuto: una difesa interessata?" *Rivista di storia del diritto italiano* 69 (1996): 95–113; Claudia Storti Storchi, "Giudici e giuristi nelle riforme viscontee del processo civile per Milano (1330–1386)," in *Ius mediolani: studi di storia del diritto milanese offerti dagli allievi a Giulio Vismara* (Milan: Giuffrè, 1996), 47–187; Andrea Romano, *"Legum doctores" e cultura giuridica nella Sicilia Aragonese* (Milan: Giuffrè, 1984). The pathbreaking work in this area was Lauro Martines, *Lawyers and Statecraft in Renaissance Florence* (Princeton: Princeton University Press, 1968); on which see Julius Kirshner, "A Critical Appreciation of Lauro Martines's *Lawyers and Statecraft in Renaissance Florence*," in *The Politics of Law in Late Medieval and Renaissance Italy: Essays in Honor of Lauro Martines*, ed. Lawrin Armstrong and Julius Kirshner (Toronto: University of Toronto Press, 2011), 7–39. Manlio Bellomo, *I fatti e il diritto: tra le certezze e i dubbi dei giuristi medievali (secoli xii-xiv)* (Rome: Il Cigno Galileo Galilei, 2000), 465–70, 654–60, insists on the parallel between academic and forensic arguments and the fundamental place of *ius commune* in each, to the point of minimizing, if not denying, any distinction between theory and practice.

Incisive and discerning analyses of *consilia* are: Sara Menzinger, "Consilium Sapientium: Lawmen and the Italian Popular Commune," in *Politics of Law*, 40–54, and her *Giuristi e politica nei comuni di popolo: Siena, Perugia e Bologna, tre governi a confronto* (Rome: Viella, 2006); Julius Kirshner, "Consilia as Authority in Late Medieval Italy: The Case of Florence," in *Legal Consulting in the Civil Law Tradition*, ed. Mario Ascheri, Ingrid Baumgärtner, and Julius Kirshner (Berkeley: Robbins Collection, 1999), 107–40; Mario Ascheri, "Le fonti e la flessibilità del diritto comune: il paradosso del *consilium sapientis*," in ibid., 11–53; Massimo Vallerani, "Consilia iudicialia: Sapienza giuridica e processo nelle città comunali italiane," *Mélanges de l'École française de Rome: Moyen Âge* 123 (2011): 129–49.

Mario Ascheri, "Il consilium dei giuristi medievali," in *Consilium: Teorie e pratiche del consigliare nella cultura medievale*, ed. Carla Casagrande, Chiara Crisciani, Silvana Vecchio (Florence: SISMEL-Edizioni del Galluzzo, 2004), 243–58. A valuable older study is Luigi Lombardi, *Saggio sul diritto giurisprudenziale* (Milan: Giuffrè, 1967). He concludes that the *consilium pro parte* was an intermediate form between the decisory *consilium sapientis* and the unalloyed advocacy of one party's claims in an *allegatio*. Giovanni Rossi, "La forza del diritto: la communis opinio doctorum come argine all'arbitrium iudicis nel processo della prima età moderna," in *Il diritto come forze, la forza del diritto: le fonti in azione del diritto europeo tra medioevo ed età contemporanea*, ed. Alberto SciumⅡ (Turin: Giappichelli, 2012), 33–61.

On forensic process, useful are: Massimo Vallerani, *La giustizia pubblica medievale* (Bologna: Il Mulino, 2005), English translation by Sarah Rubin Blanshei, *Medieval Pulbic Justice* (Washington: Catholic University of America Press, 2012); Mario Ascheri, "Il processo civile tra diritto comune e diritto locale: Da questioni preliminari al caso della giustizia estense," *Quaderni storici* 101 (Aug. 1999): 355–87; on criminal procedure, Trevor Dean, *Crime and Justice in Late Medieval Italy* (Cambridge: Cambridge University Press, 2007). A more particular study of procedures in one sort of case is François-Joseph Ruggiu, "Pour préserver la paix des familles … : Les querelles successorales et leurs règlements au xviiiᵉ siècle," in *La justice des familles: Autour de la transmission des biens, des savoirs et des pouvoirs (Europe, Nouveau Monde, xiiᵉ-xixᵉ siècles*, ed. Anna Bellavitis and Isabelle Chabot (Rome: École Française, 2011), 137–63.

For those interested in historical studies of nuns, there are some excellent works: Anne Jacobson Schutte, *By Force and Fear: Taking and Breaking Monastic Vows in Early Modern Europe* (Ithaca: Cornell University Press, 2011); Jutta Gisela Sperling, *Convents and the Body Politic in Late Renaissance Venice* (Chicago: University of Chicago Press, 1999); P. Renée Baernstein, *A Convent Tale: A Century of Sisterhood in Spanish Milan* (New York and London: Routledge, 2002); Sharon T. Strocchia, *Nuns and Nunneries in Renaissance Florence* (Baltimore: Johns Hopkins University Press, 2009). On prostitutes, Maria Serena Mazzi, *Prostitute e lenoni nella Firenze del Quattrocento* (Milan: Il Saggiatore, 1991).

CHAPTER 1

On the utility of such sources for studying the history of family, see Ingrid Baumgärtner, "Consilia–Quellen zur Familie in Krise und Kontinuität," in *Die Familie als sozialer und historischer Verband: Untersuchungen zum Spätmittelalter und zur frühen Neuzeit*, ed. Peter-Johannes Schuler (Sigmaringen: Jan Thorbecke, 1987), 43–66; while Mario Sbriccoli, *L'Interpretazione dello statuto: Contributo allo studio della funzione dei giuristi nell'età comunale* (Milan: Giuffrè, 1969) addresses the patterns and tropes of statute interpretation.

Manlio Bellomo, *Problemi di diritto familiare nell'età dei comuni: Beni paterni e "pars filii"* (Milan: Giuffrè, 1968) discusses the general issues of property relations between father and son while Thomas Kuehn, *Emancipation in Late Medieval Florence* (New Brunswick: Rutgers University Press, 1982), takes on the narrower issue of liability. Also useful is Thomas Kuehn, "Debt and Bankruptcy in Florence: Statutes and Cases," *Quaderni storici* 137 (Aug. 2011):

355–90. On the use and liability of sureties, Julius Kirshner, "A Question of Trust: Suretyship in Trecento Florence," in *Renaissance Studies in Honor of Craig Hugh Smyth* (Florence: Giunti Barbera, 1985), 129–45. Fascinating on the process of debt collection is Daniel Lord Smail, *Legal Plunder: Households and Debt Collection in Late Medieval Europe* (Cambridge, MA and London: Harvard University Press, 2016).

A penetrating essay on law and family is Renata Ago, "Ruoli familiari e statuto giuridico," *Quaderni storici* 88 (April 1995): 111–33; followed closely by Maria Carla Zorzoli, "Una incursione nella pratica giurisprudenziale milanese del Seicento e qualche riflessione su temi che riguardano la famiglia," in *Ius mediolani*, 617–57. They contrast with Giulio Vismara, "L'unità della famiglia nella storia del diritto in Italia," *Studia et documenta historiae et iuris* 22 (1956): 228–65. Useful, though from a different context, is Laura Edwards, "The Peace: The Meaning and Production of Law in the Post-Revolutionary United States," *UC Irvine Law Review* 1 (2011): 565–85.

For family history: Nino Tamassia, *La famiglia italiana nei secoli decimoquinto e decimosesto* (Milan: Sandron, 1910); Philippe Ariès, *Centuries of Childhood: A Social History of Family Life*, trans. Robert Baldick (New York: Random House, 1962); Peter Laslett, *The World We Have Lost*, 2nd ed. (Cambridge: Cambridge University Press, 1971) and idem, ed., *Household and Family in Past Time* (Cambridge: Cambridge University Press, 1972) are representative of a household-centered line of research. David Reher, "Family Ties in Western Europe: Persistent Contrasts," *Population and Development Review* 24 (1998): 203–34, offers the contrast between north and south in terms of weak and strong kinship ties; for which also see Igor Mineo, "Stati e lignaggi in Italia nel tardo medioevo: Qualche spunto comparativo," *Storica* 2 (1995): 55–82; and directly from a legal point of view Andrea Romano, *Famiglia, successioni e patrimonio familiare nell'Italia medievale e moderna* (Turin: Giappichelli, 1994). See also Jack Goody, *The European Family: An Historico-Anthropological Essay* (Oxford: Blackwell, 2000), for a functionalist anthropological perspective; and Mary Hartman, *The Household and the Making of History: A Subversive View of the Western Past* (Cambridge: Cambridge University Press, 2004).

John Hajnal, "European Marriage Patterns in Perspective," in *Population in History*, ed. D. V. Glass and D. E. C. Eversley (London: Arnold, 1965), 101–43, importantly offers the contrast of different marital patterns of northern and southern Europeans.

Michael Mitterauer and Reinhard Sieder, *The European Family: Patriarchy to Partnership from the Middle Ages to the Present*, trans. Karla Oosterveen and Manfred Hörziner (Chicago: University of Chicago Press, 1982); Jean-Louis Flandrin, *Families in Former Times*, trans. Richard Southern (Cambridge: Cambridge University Press, 1979); Raffaella Sarti, *Europe at Home: Family and Material Culture 1500–1800*, trans. Allan Cameron (New Haven and London: Yale University Press, 2002); Lawrence Stone, *The Family, Sex and Marriage in England, 1500–1800*, abridged ed. (New York: Harper & Row, 1979). Also Beatrice Gottlieb, *The Family in the Western World from the Black Death to the Industrial Age* (Oxford and New York: Oxford University Press,

1993); Eviatar Zerubavel, *Ancestors and Relatives: Genealogy, Identity, and Community* (Oxford and New York: Oxford University Press, 2012).

James Casey, *The History of the Family* (Oxford and New York: Blackwell, 1989) vitally distinguishes family as moral or conceptual entity from lived experiences, as does John R. Gillis, *A World of Their Own Making: Myth, Ritual, and the Quest for Family Values* (New York: Basic Books, 1996). A fine general evocation of Italian family history is Franca Leverotti, *Famiglie e istituzioni nel medioevo italiano: dal tardo antico al rinascimento* (Rome: Carocci, 2005). Gianna Pomata, "Family and Gender," in *Early Modern Italy*, ed. John A. Marino (New York and Oxford: Oxford University Press, 2002), 69–86. Her concern with the relative balance between the two coexisting modes of thinking about family, as vertical lineage or horizontal cognate group, stands in interesting contrast to that of the corresponding essay in the chronologically previous volume in the Short Oxford History of Italy, namely, Julius Kirshner, "Family and Marriage: A Socio-Legal Perspective," in *Italy in the Age of the Renaissance*, ed. John M. Najemy (New York and Oxford: Oxford University Press, 2004), 82–102. Also David Herlihy, "Family," in his *Women, Family and Society in Medieval Europe* (Providence and Oxford: Barghahn, 1995), 113–34.

Anthropological works, beyond that of Goody, include Robert C. Ellickson, *The Household: Informal Order around the Hearth* (Princeton: Princeton University Press, 2008); Marshall Sahlins, *What Kinship Is and Is Not* (Chicago: University of Chicago Press, 2013); James Leach, "Knowledge as Kinship: Mutable Essence and the Significance of Transmission on the Rai Coast of Papua, New Guinea," in *Kinship and Beyond: The Genealogical Model Reconsidered*, ed. Sandra Bamford and James Leach (New York and Oxford: Berghahn, 2009), 175–92; Tim Ingold, "Stories against Classification: Transport, Wayfaring and the Integration of Knowledge," in ibid., 193–213; Janet Carsten, *After Kinship* (Cambridge: Cambridge University Press, 2004).

The classic study of Florentine households is David Herlihy and Christiane Klapisch-Zuber, *Tuscans and Their Families: A Study of the Florentine Catasto of 1427* (New Haven and London: Yale University Press, 1985). See also a review of their book by R. M. Smith, "The People of Tuscany and Their Families in the Fifteenth Century: Medieval or Mediterranean?" *Journal of Family History* 6 (1981): 107–28.

For Florence otherwise, Richard Goldthwaite, *Private Wealth in Renaissance Florence* (Princeton: Princeton University Press, 1968); F. W. Kent, *Household and Lineage in Renaissance Florence: The Family Life of the Capponi, Ginori, and Rucellai* (Princeton: Princeton University Press, 1977); Christiane Klapisch-Zuber, "'A uno pane e uno vino': The Rural Tuscan Family at the Beginning of the Fifteenth Century," in her *Women, Family, and Ritual in Renaissance Italy*, trans. Lydia G. Cochrane (Chicago: University of Chicago Press, 1985), 36–67; Sergio Tognetti, *Da Figline a Firenze: Ascesa economica e politica della famiglia Serristori (secoli xiv-xvi)* (Florence: Opus Libri, 2003); Alessandro Valori, "Famiglia e memoria: Luca di Panzano dal suo 'Libro di Ricordi': uno studio sulle relazioni familiari nello specchio della scrittura," *Archivio storico italiano* 152 (1994): 261–97.

On families in other places, James S. Grubb, "House and Household: Evidence from Family Memoirs," in *Edilizia privata nella Verona rinascimentale*, ed. Paola Lanaro, Paola Marini, and Gian Maria Varanini (Milan: Electa, 2000), 118–33, and his *Provincial Families of the Renaissance: Private and Public Life in the Veneto* (Baltimore and London: Johns Hopkins University Press, 1996); Cristina Cenedella, "Proprietà ed imprenditorialità a Milano nel secondo Quattrocento: la famiglia del patrizio Ambrogio Alciati," *Studi di storia medioevale e di diplomatica* 11 (1990); 199–255; Franca Leverotti, "Strutture familiari nel tardo medioevo italiano," *Revista d'historia medieval* 10 (1999): 233–68; Anna Bellavitis, *Famille, genre, transmission à Venise au xvie siècle* (Rome: École Française de Rome, 2008); Chiara Porqueddu, *Il patriziato pavese in età spagnola: Ruoli familiari, stile di vita, economia* (Milan: Unicopli, 2012); David Rheubottom, *Age, Marriage, and Politics in Fifteenth-Century Ragusa* (Oxford: Oxford University Press, 2000), makes important points about the dynamics of a lineage in contrast to the fixity of name, coat of arms, and so forth.

On the law in Venice, Gaetano Cozzi, "Authority and the Law in Renaissance Venice," in *Renaissance Venice*, ed. J. R. Hale (London: Faber & Faber, 1973), 293–345; James E. Shaw, *The Justice of Venice: Authorities and Liberties in the Urban Economy, 1550–1700* (Oxford: British Academy, 2006); Umberto Santarelli, "La riflessione sugli statuti di Bartolomeo Cipolla," in *Bartolomeo Cipolla: Un giurista veronese del Quattrocento tra cattedra, foro e luoghi del potere*, ed. Giovanni Rossi (Padua: CEDAM, 2009), 161–74.

On the relative difference in the legal and social situation of women in Florence and Venice, Samuel K. Cohn, Jr., "Donne in piazza e donne in tribunale a Firenze nel Rinascimento," *Studi storici* 22 (1981): 515–33, reprinted in his *Women in the Streets: Essays on Sex and Power in Renaissance Italy* (Baltimore: Johns Hopkins University Press, 1996), 16–38; Stanley Chojnacki, *Women and Men in Renaissance Venice: Twelve Essays on Patrician Society* (Baltimore: Johns Hopkins University Press, 2000), 27–52; but see also Isabelle Chabot and Anna Bellavitis, "A proposito di 'Men and Women in Renaissance Venice' di Stanley Chojnacki," *Quaderni storici* 118 (April 2005): 203–38.

Concerning genealogical trees and related diagrammatic conceptions of kinship: Christiane Klapisch-Zuber, "The Genesis of the Family Tree," *I Tatti Studies in the Italian Renaissance* 4 (1991): 105–29; eadem, "Family Trees and the Construction of Kinship in Renaissance Italy," in *Gender, Kinship, Power: A Comparative and Interdisciplinary History*, ed. Mary Jo Maynes, Ann Waltner, Brigitte Soland, and Ulrike Strasser (London and New York: Routledge, 1996), 101–13 (reprint of a 1994 article from *Quaderni storici* 86, 405–20), and the more thorough and handsomely illustrated *L'Arbre des familles* (Paris: La Martinière, 2003). See also Simon Teuscher, "Flesh and Blood in the Treatises on the Arbor Consanguinitatis (Thirteenth to Sixteenth Centuries)," in *Blood and Kinship: Matter for Metaphor from Ancient Rome to the Present*, ed. Christopher H. Johnson, Bernhard Jussen, David Warren Sabean, and Simon Teuscher (New York and Oxford: Berghahn, 2013), 83–104; Anthony Molho, Roberto Barducci, Gabriella Battista, and Francesco Donnini, "Genealogy and Marriage Alliance: Memories of Power in Late Medieval Florence," in *Portraits of Medieval and Renaissance Living: Essays in Honor of David*

Herlihy, ed. Samuel K. Cohn, Jr., and Steven A. Epstein (Ann Arbor: University of Michigan Press, 1996), 39–70.

Sandra Cavallo's works include, "L'importanza della 'famiglia orizzontale' nella storia della famiglia italiana," in *Generazioni: Legami di parentela tra passato e presente*, ed. Ida Fazio and Daniela Lombardi (Rome: Viella, 2006), her "Family Relationships," in *A Cultural History of Childhood and Family in the Early Modern Age*, ed. Sandra Cavallo and Silvia Evangelisti (Oxford and New York: Berg, 2010), 15–32 and her *Artisans of the Body in Early Modern Italy: Identities, Families and Masculinities* (Manchester and New York: Manchester University Press, 2007),

For readings of Alberti, see John M. Najemy, "Giannozzo and His Elders: Alberti's Critique of Renaissance Patriarchy," in *Society and Individual in Renaissance Florence*, ed. William J. Connell (Berkeley: University of California Press, 2002), 51–78; Thomas Kuehn, "Leon Battista Alberti come illegitimo fiorentino," in *La vita e il mondo di Leon Battista Alberti: Atti di convegni internazionali del Comitato Nazionale VI centenario della nascita di Leon Battista Alberti, Genova, 19–21 febbraio 2004*, 2 vols. (Florence: Olschki, 2008), 1: 147–71.

Julie Hardwick, "The State," in *A Cultural History of Childhood and Family in the Early Modern Age*, ed. Sandra Cavallo and Silvia Evangelisti (Oxford and New York: Oxford University Press, 2010), 135–51, notes the importance of political connections for family. Daniela Frigo, *Il padre di famiglia: Governo della casa e governo civile nella tradizione dell'"economica" tra cinque e seicento* (Rome: Bulzoni, 1985) surveys the advice literature of the sixteenth century. Elizabeth W. Mellyn, *Mad Tuscans and Their Families: A History of Mental Disorder in Early Modern Italy* (Philadelphia: University of Pennsylvania Press, 2014) has noted the presumption of patrimonial competence as a mark of sanity.

Discussion of the Ciuranni relies on Isabelle Chabot, *Ricostruzione di una famiglia: i Ciurianni di Firenze tra xii e xv secolo* (Florence: Le Lettere, 2012). Maria Pia Contessa, "La costruzione di un'identità familiare e sociale: un immigrato cipriota nella Firenze del secondo Quattrocento," *Annali di storia di Firenze* 4 (2009): 151–92, is our source for Giorgio di Baliano. Tim Carter and Richard A. Goldthwaite, *Orpheus in the Marketplace: Jacopo Peri and the Economy of Late Renaissance Florence* (Cambridge, MA: Harvard University Press, 2013).

For discussion of the precedents left in Roman law, Laurent L. J. M. Waelkens, "Medieval Family and Marriage Law: From Actions of Status to Legal Doctrine," in *The Creation of the "Ius Commune"*, 103–25; Yan Thomas, "Il padre, la famiglia e le città: Figli e figlie davanti alla giurisdizione domestica a Roma," in *Pater familias*, ed. Angiolina Arru (Rome: Biblink, 2002), 23–57; Peter Birks, "The Roman Law Concept of Dominium and the Idea of Absolute Ownership," *Acta juridica* (1985): 1–37; Alain Pottage, "Introduction: The Fabrication of Persons and Things," in *Law, Anthropology, and the Constitution of the Social: Making Persons and Things*, ed. Alain Pottage and Martha Mundy (Cambridge: Cambridge University Press, 2004), 1–39; Philippe Moreau, "The Bilineal Transmission of Blood in Ancient Rome," in *Blood and Kinship: Matter for Metaphor from Ancient Rome to the Present*, ed.

Christopher H. Johnson, Bernhard Jussen, David Warren Sabean, and Simon Teuscher (New York and Oxford: Berghahn, 2013), 40–60 and Anita Guerreau-Jalabert, "Flesh and Blood in Medieval Language about Kinship," in *Blood and Kinship*, 61–82; Carlos Amunátegui Perelló, "Problems Concerning *Familia* in Early Rome," *Roman Legal Tradition* 4 (2008): 37–45.

On paternal power for later periods, see Marco Cavina, *Il padre spodestato: l'autorità paterna dall'antichità a oggi* (Bari: Laterza, 2007); Manlio Bellomo, "La struttura patrimoniale della famiglia italiana nel tardo medioevo," in *Marriage, Property, and Succession*, ed. Lloyd Bonfield (Berlin: Dunckler and Humblot, 1992), 53–69.

Bartolo's views of nobility are discussed by Guido Castelnuovo, "Revisiter un classique: noblesse, hérédité et vertu d'Aristote à Dante et à Bartole (Italie communale, début xiiie-milieu xive siècle)," in *L'hérédité entre Moyen Âge et Époque moderne: perspectives historiques*, ed. Maaike ver der Lugt and Charles de Miramon (Florence: SISMEL-Edizioni del Galluzzo, 2008), 105–55. For a discussion of the legal features of his argument in a different context, see my "Bartolus's Definition of Family: An Aspect of Juridical Thought in Petrarch's Time," in *Studi petrarcheschi*, forthcoming.

The final quotation is from Massimo della Misericordia, "Founding a Social Cosmos: Perspectives for a Historical Anthropology of Early Modern Lombardy," in *A Companion to Late Medieval and Early Modern Milan*, ed. Andrea Gamberini (Leiden and Boston: Brill, 2015), 356–79.

CHAPTER 2

On Cipolla, *Bartolomeo Cipolla: un giurista veronese del Quattrocento tra cattedra, foro e luoghi del potere*, ed. Giovanni Rossi (Padua: CEDAM, 2009).

On women in the Renaissance, Joan Kelly, "Did Women Have a Renaissance?" in *Becoming Visible: Women in European History*, ed. Renate Bridenthal and Claudia Koonz (Boston: Houghton Mifflin, 1977), 137–64; Margaret L. King, *Women of the Renaissance* (Chicago: University of Chicago Press, 1991); Ian Maclean, *The Renaissance Notion of Women: A Study in the Fortunes of Scholastic and Medical Science in European Intellectual Life* (Cambridge: Cambridge University Press, 1980). On the *querelle des femmes* and related issues, see Gisela Bock, *Women in European History*, trans. Allison Brown (Oxford: Blackwell, 2002); Constance Jordan, *Renaissance Feminism: Literary Texts and Political Models* (Ithaca: Cornell University Press, 1990); Merry E. Wiesner, *Women and Gender in Early Modern Europe* (Cambridge: Cambridge University Press, 1993).

For the earlier period, Patricia Skinner, *Women in Medieval Italian Society, 500–1200* (Edinburgh: Pearson, 2001), 190–95; Maria Teresa Guerra Medici, *I dirirtti delle donne nella società alto-medievale* (Naples: ESI, 1986).

Anthropological studies of women and honor include Julian Pitt-Rivers, *The Fate of Shechem of the Politics of Sex: Essays in the Anthropology of the Mediterranean* (Cambridge: Cambridge University Press, 1977); Pierre Bourdieu, *Outline of a Theory of Practice*, trans. Richard Nice (Cambridge: Cambridge University

Press, 1977); and in general, Frank Henderson Stewart, *Honor* (Chicago: University of Chicago Press, 1994). See also Martine Segalen, *Love and Power in the Peasant Family*, trans. Sarah Matthews (Oxford: Blackwell and Chicago: University of Chicago Press, 1983).

For Strozzi and Datini, Ann Crabb, *The Strozzi of Florence: Widowhood and Family Solidarity in the Renaissance* (Ann Arbor: University of Michigan Press, 2000); eadem, *The Merchant of Prato's Wife: Margherita Datini and Her World, 1360–1423* (Ann Arbor: University of Michigan Press, 2015); Iris Origo, *The Merchant of Prato* (New York: Octagon, 1979).

The legal situation of women in southern Italian communities is nicely laid out by Elena Papagna, "Le dame napoletane tra Quattro e Cinquecento: Modelli culturali e pratiche comportamentali," in *Con animo virile: Donne e potere nel Mezzogiorno medievale (secoli xi-xv)*, ed. Patrizia Mainoni (Rome: Viella, 2010), 485–526; and Patrizia Mainoni, "Il potere di decidere: Testamenti femminili pugliesi nei secoli xiii-xiv," in *Con animo virile*, 197–261; Maria Teresa Guerra Medici, "Donne, famiglia e potere," in *Con animo virile*, 31–51.

On women in law, Elisabeth Koch, *Maior dignitas est in sexu virili: Das weibliche Geschlecht im Normensystem des 16. Jahrhunderts* (Frankfurt am Main: Klostermann, 1991); Annalisa Belloni, "Die Rolle der Frau in der Jurisprudenz der Renaissance," in *Die Frau in der Renaissance*, ed. Paul Gerhard Schmidt (Wiesbaden: Harrassowitz, 1994), 55–80; Marie A. Kelleher, *The Measure of Woman: Law and Female Identity in the Crown of Aragon* (Philadelphia: University of Pennsylvania Press, 2010); Thomas Kuehn, *Law, Family, and Women: Toward a Legal Anthropology of Renaissance Italy* (Chicago: University of Chicago Press, 1991) and "Person and Gender in the Laws," in *Gender and Society in Renaissance Italy*, ed. Judith A. Brown and Robert C. Davis (New York: Longman, 1998), 87–106; and most importantly Simona Feci, *Pesci fuor d'acqua: donne a Roma in età moderna: diritti e patrimoni* (Rome: Viella, 2004).

For the Roman law on women, useful are Yan Thomas, "The Division of the Sexes in Roman Law," in *A History of Women in the West*, ed. Georges Duby and Michelle Perot, 5 vols., vol. 1: *From Ancient Goddesses to Christian Saints*, ed. Pauline Schmitt Pantel (Cambridge, MA: Harvard University Press, 1992), 83–137; Suzanne Dixon, "Infirmitas Sexus: Womanly Weakness in Roman Law," *Tijdschrift voor Rechtsgeschiedenis* 52 (1984): 343–71; Antti Arjava, *Women and Law in Late Antiquity* (Oxford: Clarendon Press, 1996); Nikolaus Benke, "Why Should the Law Protect Roman Women? Some Remarks on the *Senatus Consultum Velleianum* (ca. 50AD)," in *Gender and Religion: European Studies*, ed. Kari Elisabeth Berrisen, Sara Cabibbo, Edith Specht (Rome: Carocci, 2001), 41–56.

On women in markets, see Ann Matchette, "Women, Objects, and Exchange in Early Modern Florence," *Early Modern Women* 3 (2008): 245–51; Laurence Fontaine, "Il posto delle donne nella piccola economia finanziaria in Europe in età moderna," *Quaderni storici* 137 (Aug. 2011): 513–32; Martha Howell, *Commerce before Capitalism in Europe, 1300–1600* (Cambridge: Cambridge University Press, 2010); Laurence Fontaine, *L'économie morale: pauvreté, crédit et confiance dans l'Europe préindustrielle* (Paris: Gallimard, 2008); Claire Crowston, "Family Affairs: Wives, Credit, Consumption, and the Law in Old Regime France," in *Family, Gender, and Law in Early Modern France*, ed. Suzanne Desan and Jeffrey Merrick (Philadelphia: University of Pennsylvania Press, 2009), 62–100.

CHAPTER 3

Some interesting perspectives on fathers and paternal power are Julie Hardwick, *Practice of Patriarchy: Gender and Politics of Household Authority in Early Modern France* (Philadelphia: Penn State University Press, 1998); Manlio Bellomo, *Problemi di diritto familiare nell'età dei comuni: Beni paterni e "pars filii"* (Milan: Giuffrè, 1968) and "Famiglia (diritto intermedio), *Enciclopedia del diritto* 16: 744–79 (1967); Thomas Kuehn, *Emancipation in Late Medieval Florence* (New Brunswick: Rutgers University Press, 1982); and Marco Cavina, *Il padre spodestato: l'autorità paterna dall'antichità a oggi* (Bari: Laterza, 2007).

Thomas Kuehn, "L'adoption à Florence à la fin du Moyen Âge," *Médiévales* 35 (1998): 69–81; Lucia Sandri, "Formulari e contratti di adozione nell'ospedale degli Innocenti di Firenze tra tardo Medioevo ed età moderna," *Mélanges de l'Ecole Française de Rome: Italie et Méditerranée modernes et contemporaines* 124 (2012), online, https://mefrim.revues.org/281 consulted 19 December 2012; Philip Gavitt, *Charity and Children in Renaissance Florence: The Ospedale degli Innocenti, 1410–1536* (Ann Arbor: University of Michigan Press, 1990) and *Gender, Honor, and Charity in Late Renaissance Florence* (Cambridge and New York: Cambridge University Press, 2011); Nicholas Terpstra, *Abandoned Children of the Italian Renaissance: Orphan Care in Florence and Bologna* (Baltimore and London: Johns Hopkins University Press, 2005).

Also of note for themes in this chapter: Thomas Kuehn, *Illegitimacy in Renaissance Florence* (Ann Arbor: University of Michigan Press, 2002); Julius Kirshner, "Baldus de Ubaldis on Disinheritance: Contexts, Controversies, *Consilia*," *Ius Commune: Zeitschrift für Europäische Rechtsgeschichte* 27 (2000): 119–214; Antonio Marongiu, *Beni paterni e acquisti nella storia del diritto italiano* (Bologna: Zanichelli, 1937).

In general on the *giovani*, see Elisabeth Crouzet-Pavan, "A Flower of Evil: Young Men in Medieval Italy," in *A History of Young People in the West*, ed. Giovanni Levi and Jean-Claude Schmidt, trans. Camille Naish, 2 vols., vol. 1: *Ancient and Medieval Rites of Passage* (Cambridge, MA and London: Belknap Press of Harvard University Press, 1997), 173–221; Renata Ago, "Young Nobles in the Age of Absolutism: Paternal Authority and Freedom of Choice in Seventeenth-Century Italy," in *History of Young People*, 1: 283–322; Sandra Cavallo, "O padre o figlio? Ruoli familiari maschili e legami tra uomini nel mondo artigiano in età moderna," in *Paterfamilias*, ed. Angiolina Arru (Rome: Biblink, 2002), 59–100.

Elvira Contini, "*Societas* e famiglia nel pensiero di Baldo degli Ubaldi," *Rivista di storia del diritto italiano* 82 (2009): 19–92.

CHAPTER 4

From the vast literature on marriage, useful have been Daniela Lombardi, *Matrimoni di antico regime* (Bologna: Il Mulino, 2001); James A. Brundage, *Law, Sex, and Christian Society* (Chicago and London: University of Chicago Press, 1987); Ruth Mazo Karras, *Unmarriages: Women, Men, and Sexual Unions in the Middle Ages* (Philadelphia: University of Pennsylvania Press, 2012). For the debates at the Council of Trent, Gabriella Zarri, "Il matrimonio tridentino," in *Il concilio di Trento e il moderno*, ed. Paolo Prodi and Wolfgang Reinhard (Bologna: Il Mulino, 1996), 437–83; Charlotte Christensen-Nugues, "Parental Authority and Freedom of Choice: The Debate on Clandestinity and Parental Consent at the Council of Trent (1545–63)," *Sixteenth Century Journal* 45 (2014): 51–72; Chiara Valsecchi, "'Causa matrimonialis est gravis et ardua': consiliatores e matrimonio fino al Concilio di Trento," *Studi di storia del diritto* 2 (1999): 407–580.

On aspects of the process of marriage, see Osvaldo Cavallar and Julius Kirshner, "Making and Breaking Betrothal Contracts (Sponsalia) in Late Trecento Florence," in *"Panta rei": studi dedicati a Manlio Bellomo*, ed. Orazio Condorelli, 3 vols. (Rome: Il Cigno Galileo Galilei, 2004), 1: 395–452; now in Kirshner, *Marriage, Dowry, and Citizenship in Late Medieval and Renaissance Italy* (Toronto: University of Toronto Press, 2015), 20–54. Philip L. Reynolds and John Witte, Jr., eds, *To Have and To Hold: Marrying and Its Documentation in Western Christendom, 400–1600* (Cambridge: Cambridge University Press, 2007) contains a number of useful essays, including Judith Evans-Grubbs, "Marrying and Its Documentation in Later Roman Law," in *To Have and To Hold*, 43–94, and Thomas Kuehn, "Contracting Marriage in Renaissance Florence," 390–420.

Studies utilizing court records are Charles Donahue, Jr., *Law, Marriage, and Society in the Later Middle Ages* (Cambridge: Cambridge University Press, 2007); Silvana Seidel Menchi and Diego Quaglioni, eds, *Matrimoni in dubbio: unioni controverse e nozze clandestine in Italia dal xiv al xviii secolo* (Bologna: Il Mulino, 2001); Silvana Seidel Menchi and Diego Quaglioni, eds, *Coniugi nemici: la separazione in Italia dal xii al xviii secolo* (Bologna: Il Mulino, 2008); Chiara La Rocca, *Tra moglie e marito: Matrimoni e separazioni a Livorno nel Settecento* (Bologna: Il Mulino, 2009); Cecilia Cristellon, *La carità e l'eros: il matrimonio, la Chiesa, i suoi giudici nella Venezia del Rinascimento (1420–1545)* (Bologna: Il Mulino, 2010).

On marriage and household, Peter Laslett, ed., *Household and Family in Past Time* (Cambridge: Cambridge University Press, 1972); David Herlihy, *Medieval Households* (Cambridge, MA: Harvard University Press, 1985); Wally Secombe, *A Millennium of Family Change: Feudalism to Capitalism in Northwestern Europe* (London and New York: Verso, 1992).

Cases of forced consent or rape include Silvana Seidel Menchi and Diego Quaglioni, eds, *Trasgressioni: seduzione, concubinato, adulterio, bigamia (xiv-xviii secolo)* (Bologna: Il Mulino, 2004); Joanne M. Ferraro, *Marriage Wars in Late Renaissance Venice* (Oxford and New York: Oxford University Press, 2001); Daniela Hacke, "'Non lo volevo per marito in modo alcuno':

Forced Marriages, Generational Conflicts, and the Limits of Patriarchal Power in Early Modern Venice, c. 1580–1680," in *Time, Space, and Women's Lives in Early Modern Europe*, ed. Anne Jacobson Schutte, Thomas Kuehn, Silvana Siedel Menchi (Kirksville: Truman State University Press, 2001), 203–21; Anne Jacobson Schutte, *By Force and Fear: Taking and Breaking Monastic Vows in Early Modern Europe* (Ithaca and London: Cornell University Press, 2011); Giovanni Cazzetta, *Praesumitur seducta: onestà e consenso femminile nella cultura giuridica moderna* 53 (Milan: Giuffrè, 1999); Caroline Dunn, *Stolen Women in Medieval England: Rape, Abduction, and Adultery, 1100–1500* (Cambridge: Cambridge University Press, 2013); Joanne M. Ferraro, *Nefarious Crimes, Contested Justice: Illicit Sex and Infanticide in the Republic of Venice, 1557–1789* (Baltimore: Johns Hopkins University Press, 2008).

Valuable studies of marriages in particular communities are Mauro Carboni, "Marriage Strategies and Oligarchy in Early Modern Bologna," in *Marriage in Premodern Europe: Italy and Beyond*, ed. Jacqueline Murray (Toronto: Centre for Reformation and Renaissance Studies, 2012), 239–56; Lucia Ferrante, "Marriage and Women's Subjectivity in a Patrilineal System: The Case of Early Modern Bologna," in *Gender, Kinship, Power: A Comparative Interdisciplinary History*, ed. Mary Jo Maynes, Ann Walther, Brigitte Soland, and Ulrike Strasser (London and New York: Routledge, 1996), 115–29; James S. Grubb, *Provincial Families of the Renaissance: Private and Public Life in the Veneto* (Baltimore: Johns Hopkins University Press, 1996).

On England, Barbara Hanawalt, *The Wealth of Wives: Women, Law, and Economy in Late Medieval London* (Oxford: Oxford University Press, 2007); J. H. Baker, *An Introduction to English Legal History*, 4th ed. (Oxford: Oxford University Press, 2007).

Jane F. Gardner, *Women in Roman Law and Society* (London: Croom Helm, 1986) discusses women's legal agency.

On marital relations, Giuliano Marchetto, "Diritto sul corpo e 'servitù coniugale' nella dottrina canonistica pretridentina," *Annali dell'Istituto storico italo-germanico in Trento* 34 (2008): 89–112. On marital property relations, the classic study is Manlio Bellomo, *Ricerche sui rapporti patrimoniali tra coniugi: contributo alla storia della famiglia medievale* (Milan: Giuffrè, 1961); to which should be added Laurent Mayali, *Droit savant et coutumes: l'exlusion des filles dotées xiième-xvème siècles* (Frankfurt am Main: Klostermann, 1987). Essential are the numerous studies of Julius Kirshner: idem and Jacques Pluss, "Two Fourteenth-Century Opinions on Dowries, Paraphernalia and Non-Dotal Goods," *Bulletin of Medieval Canon law*, n.s. 9 (1978): 65–77; Julius Kirshner, "Li Emergenti Bisogni Matrimoniali in Renaissance Florence," *Society and Individual in Renaissance Florence*, ed. William J. Connell (Berkeley and London: University of California Press, 2002), 79–109, now in *Marriage, Dowry, and Citizenship*, 55–73; Julius Kirshner, "Materials for a Gilded Cage: Non-Dotal Assets in Florence, 1300–1500," in *The Family in Italy from Antiquity to the Present*, ed. David I. Kertzer and Richard P. Saller (New Haven: Yale University Press, 1991), 184–207; Julius Kirshner, "Pursuing Honor While Avoiding Sin: The Monte delle Doti of Florence," *Studi senesi*

89 (1977): 177–258; Julius Kirshner, "Family and Marriage: A Socio-legal Perspective," in *Italy in the Age of the Renaissance*, ed. John M. Najemy (Oxford and New York: Oxford University Press, 2004), 82–102. Also informative is Jane Fair Bestor, "The Groom's Prestations for the Ductio in Late Medieval Italy: A Study in the Disciplining Power of Liberalitas," *Rivista internazionale di diritto comune* 8 (1997): 129–77. Absolutely vital on dowries and women's rights to and control of property is Isabelle Chabot, *La dette des familles: Femmes, lignage et patrimoine à Florence aux xive-xve siècles* (Rome: École Française de Rome, 2011).

Maristella Botticini and Aloysius Siow, "Why Dowries?" *American Economic Review* 93 (2003): 1385–98, pose the vital question in functional terms and raise doubts as to the size of dowry in relation of patrimony as a whole, as does Gregory Hanlon, *Human Nature in Rural Tuscany: An Early Modern History* (New York: Palgrave Macmillan, 2007). Allan A. Tulchin, "Low Dowries, Absent Parents: Marrying for Love in an Early Modern French Town," *Sixteenth Century Journal* 44 (2013): 713–38, takes a similar perspective for France.

On fear and lack of consent for religious vocations, in addition to Schutte (above), Sharon T. Strocchia, "Taken into Custody: Girls and Convent Guardianship in Renaissance Florence," *Renaissance Studies* 17 (2003): 177–200; Saundra Weddle, "Identity and Alliance: Urban Presence, Spatial Privilege, and Florentine Renaissance Convents," in *Renaissance Florence: A Social History*, ed. Roger J. Crum and John T. Paoletti (Cambridge: Cambridge University Press, 2006), 394–412.

Julius Kirhsner, "Women Married Elsewhere: Gender and Citizenship in Italy," in *Time, Space, and Women's Lives in Early Modern Europe*, ed. Anne Jacobson Schutte, Thomas Kuehn, Silvana Siedel Menchi (Kirksville: Truman State University Press, 2001), 117–49; now in *Marriage, Dowry, and Citizenship*, 161–88, is one of few examinations of the issue. Stefanie B. Siegmund, "Division of the Dowry on the Death of the Daughter: An Instance in the Negotiation of Laws and Jewish Customs in Early Modern Tuscany," *Jewish History* 16 (2002): 73–106. Siegmund suggests that Jewish practices may give the lie to the idea that lower nuptiality among Christians was the consequence solely of dowry inflation.

The now classic study of guardianship is Gigliola Villata di Renzo, *La tutela: indagini sulla scuola dei glossatori* (Milan: Giuffrè, 1975); to which can be added Francesca Morandini, ed., "Statuti e ordinamenti dell'Ufficio dei pupilli et adulti nel periodo della Repubblica fiorentina (1388–1534)," *Archivio storico italiano* 113 (1955): 522–51, 114 (1956): 92–117, 115 (1957): 87–104; Giulia Calvi, "Widows, the State and the Guardianship of Children in Early Modern Tuscany," in *Widowhood in Medieval and Early Modern Europe*, 209–19; Giulia Calvi, "Dal margine al centro: soggettività femminile, famiglia, Stato moderno in Toscana (xvi-xviii secc.)," in *Discutendo di storia: soggettività, ricerca, biografia* (Turin: Rosenberg & Sellier, 1990), 103–18; eadem, "'Cruel' and 'Nurturing' Mothers: The Construction of Motherhood in Tuscany (1500–1800)," *L'Homme* 17 (2006): 75–92; B. A. Holderness, "Widows in Pre-Industrial Society: An Essay upon Their Economic Functions," in *Land,*

Kinship and Life-Cycle, ed. Richard M. Smith (Cambridge: Cambridge University Press, 1984), 423–42; and Caroline M. Fisher, "Guardianship and the Rise of the Florentine State, 1368–93," in *Famiglia e poteri in Italia tra Medioevo ed età moderna*, ed. Anna Bellavitis and Isabelle Chabot (Rome: École Française de Rome, 2009), 265–82.

A famous example of a social misalliance denied in court is Gene Brucker, *Giovanni and Lusanna: Love and Marriage in Renaissance Florence* (Berkeley and London: University of California Press, 1986).

On retrieval of a dowry from a financially strapped husband, Julius Kirshner, "Wives' Claims against Insolvent Husbands in Late Medieval Italy," in *Women of the Medieval World*, ed. Julius Kirshner and Suzanne F. Wemple (Oxford: Blackwell, 1985), 256–303; now in *Marriage, Dowry, and Citizenship*, 131–60; Thomas Kuehn, "Protecting Dowries in Law in Renaissance Florence," in *Studies on Florence and the Italian Renaissance in Honour of F. W. Kent*, ed. Peter Howard and Cecilia Hewlett (Tournhout: Brepols, 2016), 199–216.

On the marital obligations of spouses in southern Italy, see Serena Ferente, "Women and the State," in *The Italian Renaissance State*, ed. Andrea Gamberini and Isabella Lazzarini (Cambridge: Cambridge University Press, 2012), 345–67. Thomas Kuehn, "Family Solidarity in Exile and in Law: Alberti Lawsuits of the Early Quattrocento," *Speculum* 78 (2003): 421–39, is an example of women and dowries in the political distress of exile. See also Elena Brizio, "In the Shadow of the Campo: Sienese Women and Their Families (c. 1400–1600)," in *Across the Religious Divide: Women, Property, and Law in the Wider Mediterranean (ca. 1300–1800)*, ed. Jutta Gisela Sperling and Shona Kelly Wray (New York and London: Routledge, 2010), 122–36; Megan Moran, "Brother-Sister Correspondence in the Spinelli Family and the Forming of Family Networks in Sixteenth-Century Italy," *Sixteenth Century Journal* 44 (2013): 47–71, at 71; Serena Giuliodori, "¿Qué fuentes?, ¿Qué cuestiones? Los estudios sobre la capacidad patrimonial de la mujer en Italia durante la baja edad media," *Studia historica, Ha. Medieval* 26 (2008): 91–109.

On the different situation regarding women's legal agency in Venice, see Linda Guzzetti, "Women in Court in Early Fourteenth-Century Venice," in *Across the Religious Divide*, 51–66. Pathbreaking here has been the work of Stanley Chojnacki, notably the essays in *Women and Men in Renaissance Venice: Twelve Essays on Patrician Society* (Baltimore: Johns Hopkins University Press, 2000); but see also the careful critiques of Anna Bellavitis, "Genere e potere politico fra Medioevo ed età moderna," *Quaderni storici* 118 (2005): 230–38, and Isabelle Chabot, "Ricchezze femminili e parentela nel Rinascimento: Riflessioni intorno ai contesti veneziani e fiorentini," *Quaderni storivi* 118 (2005): 203–29.

The "cruel" mother emerged from Christiane Klapisch-Zuber, "La 'mère cruelle': maternité, veuvage et dot dans la Florence des xive et xve siècles," *Annales ESC* 38 (1983): 1097–1109; see also Isabelle Chabot, "Seconde nozze e identità materna nella Firenze del tardo Medioevo," in *Tempi e spaze della vita femminile nella prima età moderna*, ed. Silvana Seidel Menchi, Anne Jacobson Schutte, and Thomas Kuehn (Bologna: Il Mulino, 1999), 493–523.

On widows, Sandra Cavallo and Lyndan Warner, eds, *Widowhood in Medieval and Early Modern Europe* (New York and London: Longman, 1999); Isabelle

Chabot, "Lineage Strategies and the Control of Widows in Renaissance Florence," in *Widowhood in Medieval and Early Modern Europe*, 127–44; "Widowhood and Poverty in Late Medieval Florence," *Continuity and Change* 3 (1988): 291–311; "'La sposa in nero': la ritualizzazione del lutto delle vedove fiorentine (secoli xiv-xv)," *Quaderni storici* 86 (Aug. 1994): 421–62.

Martha Howell, "The Properties of Marriage in Late Medieval Europe: Commercial Wealth and the Creation of Modern Marriage," in *Love, Marriage, and Family Ties in the Later Middle Ages*, ed. Isabel Davis, Miriam Müller, and Sarah Rees Jones (Turnhout: Brepols, 2003), 17–61, suggests that reliance on moveable property encouraged more companionate marriages.

CHAPTER 5

On plague mortality and preparing for death, Philippe Ariès, *The Hour of Our Death*, trans. Helen Weaver (New York: Vintage, 1982); Alberto Tenenti, *Il senso della morte e l'amore della vita nel Rinascimento* (Turin: Einaudi, 1957); Sharon Strocchia, *Death and Ritual in Renaissance Florence* (Baltimore and London: Johns Hopkins University Press, 1992). More broadly on death and inheritance, Jacques Chiffoleau, *La comptabilité de l'au-delà: les hommes, la mort et la religion dans la région d'Avignon à la fin du Moyen Âge, vers 1320-vers 1480* (Rome: École Française de Rome, 1980); Samuel K. Cohn, Jr., *Death and Property in Siena, 1205–1800: Strategies for the Afterlife* (Baltimore and London: Johns Hopkins University Press, 1988); and his *The Cult of Remembrance and the Black Death: Six Renaissance Cities in Central Italy* (Baltimore and London: Johns Hopkins University Press, 1992); Thomas Kuehn, *Heirs, Kin, and Creditors in Renaissance Florence* (Cambridge: Cambridge University Press, 2008).

Important, but succinct, for the Roman law basis of inheritance is Borkowski and du Plessis, *Textbook on Roman Law*, 210–30. Clearly central to my understanding of the medieval period is Andrea Romano, *Famiglia, successioni e patrimonio familiare nell'Italia medievale e moderna* (Turin: Giappichelli, 1994). On the feudal law, see Harry Dondorp and Eltjo J. H. Schrage, "The Sources of Medieval Learned Law," 7–56, and Magnus Ryan, "Succession to Fiefs: A Ius Commune Feudorum?" 143–57, in *The Creation of the Ius Commune: From Casus to Regula*, ed. John W. Cairns and Paul J. Du Plessis (Edinburgh: Edinburgh University Press, 2010). On the acceptance into law of primogeniture, see Bartolomé Clavero, "Dictum beati: a proposito della cultura del lignaggio," *Quaderni storici* 86 (Aug. 1994): 335–63. Paolo Grossi, *Il dominio e le cose: percezioni medievali e moderne dei diritti reali* (Milan: Giuffrè, 1992), is the most thorough and readable account of property law.

The best overview of inheritance statutes remains the workmanlike survey of Franco Niccolai, *La formazione del diritto successorio negli statuti comunali del territorio lombardo-tosco* (Milan: Giuffrè, 1940). See also Laurent Mayali, *Droit savant et coutumes: l'exclusion des filles dotées xiième-xvème siècle* (Frankfurt am Main: Klostermann, 1987); and for a parallel development that, however, had little resonance in case literature, Roberta Braccia, "'Uxor gaudet de morte mariti': la donatio propter nuptias tra diritto comune e diritti locali," *Annali della Facoltà di Giurisprudenza di Genova* 30 (2000–2001): 76–128. On inheritance in Venice, see Anna Bellavitis, *Famille, genre, transmission à Venise au xvie siècle* (Rome: École Française de Rome, 2008) and her "Patrimoni e matrimoni a Venezia nel Cinquecento," in *Le ricchezze delle donne*, 149–60. Also of interest is Laura Turchi, "L'eredità della madre: un conflitto giuridico nello stato estense alla fine del Cinquecento," in *Le ricchezze delle donne*, 161–85. For Milan, see Thomas Kuehn, "Gender and Law in Milan," in *A Companion to Late Medieval and Early Modern Milan*, ed. Andrea Gamberini (Leiden and Boston: Brill, 2015), 406–31.

Jewish law is nicely covered by Vittore Colorni, *Legge ebraica e leggi locali: ricerche sull'ambito d'applicazione del diritto ebraico in Italia dall epoca romana al secolo xix* (Milan: Giuffrè, 1945). Useful on statute interpretation is Laurent Mayali, "La notion de '*statutum odiosum*' dans la doctrine romaniste au Moyen Âge: Remarques sur la fonction du docteur," *Ius Commune* 12 (1984): 57–69.

Important on various features of dowry law are, Julius Kirshner, "Maritus Lucretur Dotem *Uxoris Sue Premortue* in Late Medieval Florence," *Zeitschrift der Savigny-Stiftung für Rechtsgeschichte, Kanonistische Abteilung* 77 (1991): 111–55; Gian Paolo Massetto, "Il lucro dotale nella dottrina e nella legislazione statutaria lombarda dei secoli xiv-xvi," in *Ius mediolani*, 189–364. For examples of security for dowry and delays in repayment, see Julius Kirshner, "Encumbering Private Claims to Public Debt in Renaissance Florence," in *The Growth of the Bank as an Institution and the Development of Money-Business Law*, ed. Vito Piergiovanni (Berlin: Dunckler and Humblot, 1993), 19–75.

CHAPTER 6

For the Roman law basics of testaments, see Borkowski and du Plessis, 217–40. On the jurisprudential interpretation of testaments, see Andrea Padovani, *Studi storici sulla dottrina delle sostituzioni* (Milan: Giuffrè, 1983); Ferdinando Treggiari, *Minister ultimae voluntatis* (Naples: Edizioni Scientifiche Italiane, 2002); Giovanni Chiodi, *L'interpretazione del testamento nel pensiero dei Glossatori* (Milan: Giuffrè, 1997). For analysis and an edition of Arsendi, Andrea Romano, *Le sostituzioni ereditarie nell'inedita "Repetitio de substitutionibus" di Raniero Arsendi* (Catania: Giannotta, 1977); Giovanni Rossi, "Il testamento nel medioevo fra dottrina giuridica e prassi," in *Margini di libertà: testamenti femminili nel medioevo*, ed. Maria Clara Rossi (Verona: Cierre, 2010), 45–70.

On the prevalence of *fideicommissa* in practice, see in general, Gregory Hanlon, *Early Modern Italy, 1550–1800* (New York: St. Martin's, 2000); Renata Ago, *Gusto for Things: A History of Objects in Seventeenth-Century Rome*, trans. Bradford Bonley and Corey Tazzara, with Paula Findlen (Chicago: University of Chicago Press, 2013). She builds on the anthropological insights of Annette B. Weiner, *Inalienable Possessions: The Paradox of Keeping-While-Giving* (Berkeley and Los Angeles: University of California Press, 1992). An interesting case for which there is abundant documentation is found in Tim Carter and

Richard A. Goldthwaite, *Orpheus in the Marketplace: Jacopo Peri and the Economy of Late Renaissance Florence* (Cambridge, MA, and London: Harvard University Press, 2013). Another example can be found in Thomas Kuehn, "Fideicommissum and Family: The Orsini di Bracciano," *Viator* 39 no. 2 (2008): 323–42. An example of inventories of different sorts in the hands of one noble is Barbara Furlotti, *A Renaissance Baron and His Possessions: Paolo Giordano I Orsini, Duke of Bracciano (1541–1585)* (Turnhout: Brepols, 2012).
On the essential features of *fideicommissa* in law, Mario Caravale, s.v. "Fedecommesso (diritto intermedio)," *Enciclopedia del diritto*, vol. 17 (Milan: Giuffrè, 1968), 103–14; Luigi Tria, *Il fedecommesso nella legislazione e nella dottrina dal secolo xvi ai nostri giorni* (Milan: Giuffrè, 1945); Mario Bernardo Angelo Comneno and Filippo Angotti, *La sostituzione fedecommissaria* (Rome: Imperium, 1959).
Excellent studies of *fedecommessi* in different communities include Stefano Calonaci, *Dietro lo scudo incantato: I fedecommessi di famiglia e il trionfo della borghesia fiorentina (1400 ca–1750)* (Florence: Le Monnier, 2005); Maura Piccialuti, *L'immortalità dei beni: Fedecommessi e primogeniture a Roma nei secoli xvii e xviii* (Rome: Viella, 1999); Maria Carla Zorzoli, "Della famiglia e del suo patrimonio: Riflessioni sull'uso del fedecommesso in Lombardia tra Cinque e Seicento," *Archivio storico lombardo* 115 (1989): 91–148, also in *Marriage, Property, and Succession*, ed. Lloyd Bonfield (Berlin: Duncker & Humblot, 1992), 155–213; Letizia Arcangeli, *Gentiluomini di Lombardia: Ricerche sull'aristocrazia padana mel Rinascimento* (Milan: UNICOPLI, 2003); Gerard Delille, *Famille et propriété dans le Royaume de Naples xv-xix siècle* (Rome: École Française, 1985).
On *censi*, Lorenzo Polizzotto, "I censi consegnativi bollari nella Firenze granducale: Storia di uno strumento di credito transcurato," *Archivio storico italiano* 168 (2010): 263–323.
On women's wills and other matters of testamentary practices, useful are Shona Kelly Wray, "Women, Testaments, and Notarial Culture in Bologna's Contado (1348)," in *Across the Religious Divide*, 81–94; Paolo Lanaro, "'Familia est substantia': la trasmissione dei beni nella famiglia patrizia," in *Edilizia privata nella Verona rinascimentale*, ed. Paolo Lanaro, Paolo Marini, Gian Maria Varanini (Milan: Electa, 2000), 98–117; Simona Ricci, *"De hac vita transire": la pratica testamentaria nel Valdarno superiore all'indomani della Peste Nera* (Florence: Opus Libri, 1998); Gianna Lumia, "Mariti e mogli nei testamenti senesi di età moderna," in *Le ricchezze delle donne*, 43–63; Linda Guzzetti, "Dowries in Fourteenth-Century Venice," *Renaissance Studies* 16 (2002): 430–73; Giovanna Petti Balbi, "Donna et domina: pratiche testamentarie e condizione femminile a Genova nel secolo xiv," in *Margini di libertà: testamenti femminili nel medioevo*, ed. Maria Clara Rossi (Caselle di Sommacampagna: Cierre, 2010), 153–82; Paolo Paterni, "Le leggi della città, le leggi della famiglia (Lucca, xvi-xviii secc.)," in *Le ricchezze delle donne*, 65–78; Gianna Lumia, "'Ut cippus magis conservetur': La successione a Siena tra statuti e testamenti (secoli xii-xvii)," *Archivio storico italiano* 161 (2003): 3–51; Linda Guzzetti, "Le donne a Venezia nel secolo xiv: Uno studio sulla loro presenza nella società e nella famiglia," *Studi veneziani*, n. s. 35 (1988): 15–88.

In addition to her *Famille, genre, transmission à Venise*, Anna Bellavitis, *Identité, mariage, mobilité sociale: Citoyennes et citoyens à Venise au xvie siècle* (Rome: École Française, 2001); eadem, "Il testamento a Venezia nel xvi secolo: diritto, dovere e spazio di libertà," in *Famiglie: circolazione di beni, circuiti di affetti in età moderna*, ed. Renata Ago and Benedetta Borello (Rome: Viella, 2008), 23–45 and her "Women, Family, and Property in Early Modern Venice," in *Across the Religious Divide*, 175–90. On the south, Patrizia Mainoni, "Il potere di decidere: testamenti femminili pugliesi nei secoli xiii-xiv," in *"Con animo virile": Donne e potere nel Mezzogiorno medievale (secoli xi-xv)*, ed. Patrizia Mainoni (Rome: Viella, 2010), 195–261. Also Giovanna Petti Balbi, "Donna et domina: pratiche testamentarie e condizione femminile a Genova nel secolo xiv," in *Margini di libertà*, 153–82; Isabelle Chabot, "'Io vo' fare testamento': le ultime volontà di mogli e di mariti, tra controllo e soggettività (secoli xiv-xv)," in ibid., 205–38.

Further information on the Viviani case can be found in Thomas Kuehn, "'Nemo mortalis cognitus vivit in evo': Moral and Legal Conflicts in a Florentine Inheritance Case of 1442," in *The Moral World of the Law*, ed. Peter Coss (Cambridge: Cambridge University Press, 2000), 113–33.

CHAPTER 7

A succinct treatment of the themes of this chapter is John M. Najemy, "Governments and Governance," in *Italy in the Age of the Renaissance*, ed. John M. Najemy (Oxford: Oxford University Press, 2004), 184–207, which expands his treatment in John M. Najemy, *A History of Florence, 1200–1575* (Oxford: Blackwell, 2006), esp. 215–16; also Isabelle Chabot,"Le gouvernement des pères: l'État florentin et la famille (xivᵉ-xvᵉ siècles), in *Florence et la Toscane, xivᵉ-xvᵉ siècles: les dynamiques d'un État italien*, ed. Jean Bouttier, Sandro Landi, and Olivier Rouchon (Rennes: Presses Universitaires de Rennes, 2004), 241–63.

On paternalism, see Constance Jordan, "The Household and the State: Transformations in the Representation of an Analogy from Aristotle to James I," *Modern Language Quarterly* 54 (1993): 307–26; Cesarina Casanova, *Regine per caso: Donne al governo in età moderna* (Bologna: Il Mulino, 2014); Julia Adams, *The Familial State: Ruling Families and Merchant Capitalism in Early Modern Europe* (Ithaca: Cornell University Press, 2005); Igor Mineo, "Stati e lignaggi in Italia nel tardo medioevo: qualche spunto comparativo," *Storica* 2 (1995): 55–82.

The conditions of political exile are explored by Randolph Starn, *Contrary Commonwealth: The Theme of Exile in Medieval and Renaissance Italy* (Berkeley: University of California Press, 1982); Christine Shaw, *The Politics of Exile in Renaissance Italy* (Cambridge: Cambridge University Press, 2000); Thomas Kuehn, "Family Solidarity in Exile and in Law: Alberti Lawsuits of the Early Quattrocento," *Speculum* 78 (2003): 421–39. Reintegration of magnates has been masterfully studied for Florence by Christiane Klapisch-Zuber, *Retour à la cité: les magnats de Florence, 1340–1440* (Paris: École des hautes etudes en sciences sociales, 2006). On the reintegration of political exiles and the example of the Pazzi of Florence, Osvaldo Cavallar, "I consulenti e il caso dei Pazzi: Consilia ai margini della in integrum restitutio," in *Legal Consulting in the Civil Law Tradition*, ed. Mario Ascheri, Ingrid Baumgärtner, and Julius Kirshner (Berkeley: Robbins Collection, 1999), 319–62, and his "Il tiranno, i dubia del giudice, e i consilia dei giuristi," *Archivio storico italiano* 155 (1979): 265–345.

Essential on the problems of citizenship and *origo* for women marrying to men of other communities is Julius Kirshner, "Women Married Elsewhere: Gender and Citizenship in Italy," in *Time, Space, and Women's Lives in Early Modern Europe*, ed. Anne Jacobson Schutte, Thomas Kuehn, and Silvana Seidel menchi (Kirksville: Truman State University Press, 2001), 117–49.

The legal situation of the Mezzogiorno is best laid out (again) by Andrea Romano, *Famiglia, successione e patrimonio familiare nell'Italia medievale e moderna* (Turin: Giappichelli, 1994), along with his "Successioni mortis causa e patrimonio familiare nel Regno di Sicilia (secoli xiii-xvi)," in *La transmission du patrimoine: Byzance et l'aire méditerranée*, ed. Joelle Beaucamp and Gilbert Dagron (Paris: De Boccard, 1998), 211–45. Also E. Igor Mineo, *Nobiltà di stato: Famiglie e identità aristocratiche nel tardo medioevo, La Sicilia* (Rome: Donzelli, 2001). Important on succession in feudal law is Cristina Danusso, "La donna e i feudi: uno sguardo alla prassi successoria dell'Italia centro-settentrionale fra Tre e Quattrocento," *Rivista di storia del diritto italiano* 65 (1992): 181–239. For Naples Giuliana Vitale, *Élite burocratica e famiglia: dinamiche nobiliari e processi di costruzione statale nella Napoli angioino-aragonese* (Naples: Liguori, 2003), and Gérard Delille, *Famille et propriété dans le Royaume de Naples, xve-xixe siècles* (Rome: École Française de Rome, 1985); Maria Antonietta Visceglia, *Il bisogno di eternità: i comportamenti aristocratici a Napoli in età moderna* (Naples: Guida, 1988).

For Jewish family life and law, see Robert Bonfil, *Jewish Life in Renaissance Italy*, trans. Anthony Oldcorn (Berkeley and London: University of California Press, 1994); Roni Weinstein, *Marriage Rituals Italian Style: A Historical Anthropological Perspective on Early Modern Italian Jews* (Leiden and Boston: Brill, 2004); Karen Frank, "Jewish Women and Property in Fifteenth-Century Umbria," in *Across the Religious Divide*, 95–108; Osvaldo Cavallar and Julius Kirshner, "Jews as Citizens in Late Medieval and Renaissance italy: The Case of Isacco da Pisa," *Jewish History* 25 (2011): 269–318; Diego Quaglioni, "Gli ebrei nei consilia del Quattrocento veneto," in *Consilia im späten Mittelalter*, ed. Ingrid Baumgärtner (Sigmaringen: Jan Thorbecke, 1995), 189–204; Daniel Bornstein, "Law, Religion, and Economics: Jewish Moneylenders in Christian Cortona," in *A Renaissance of Conflicts: Visions and Revisions of Law and Society in Italy and Spain*, ed. John A. Marino and Thomas Kuehn (Toronto: Centre for Reformation and Renaissance Studies, 2004), 241–56.

Particularly useful for understanding sumptuary laws and their enforcement are: most importantly, Catherine Kovesi Killerby, *Sumptuary Lw in Italy, 1200–1500* (Oxford: Clarendon Press, 2002); also Ariel Toaff, "La prammatica degli ebrei e per gli ebrei," in *Disciplinare il lusso: la legislazione suntuaria in Italia e in Europe tra Medioevo ed età moderna*, ed. Maria Giuseppina Muzzarelli (Rome: Carocci, 2003), 91–105; Franco Franceschi, "La normativa suntuaria nella storia economica," in *Disciplinare il lusso*, 163–78; Mario Ascheri, "Tra storia giuridica e storia 'costituzionale': funzioni della legislazione suntuaria," in *Disciplinare il lusso*, 199–211; Carole Collier Frick, "Picture Perfect: Female Performance and Social Liminality in the Florentine Renaissance City," in *Structures and Subjectivities: Attending to Early Modern Women*, ed. Joan E. Hartman and Adele Seeff (Newark: University of Delaware Press, 2007), 253–78, and her larger study, *Dressing Renaissance Florence: Families, Fortunes and Fine Clothing* (Baltimore: Johns Hopkins University Press, 2002); Diane Owen Hughes, "Sumptuary Law and Social Relations in Renaissance Italy," in *Disputes and Settlements: Law and Human Relations in the West*, ed. John Bossy (Cambridge: Cambridge University Press, 1983), 69–99.

CHAPTER 8

An enlightening presentation of *fideicommissa* and the general state of legal doctrine is Giovanni Rossi, "I fedecommessi nella dottrina e nella prassi giuridica di ius commune tra xvi e xvii secolo," in *La famiglia nell'economia europea secc. xiii-xviii*, atti della "Quarantesima settimana di studi," 6–10 aprile 2008, ed. Simonetta Cavaciocchi (Florence: Firenze University Press, 2009), 175–202. More broadly Luigi Lombardi, *Saggio sul diritto giurisprudenziale* (Milan: Giuffrè, 1967).

On insanity and patrimonial rationality, Elizabeth W. Mellyn, *Mad Tuscans and Their Families: A History of Mental Disorder in Early Modern Italy* (Philadelphia: University of Pennsylvania Press, 2014).

Mauro Carboni, "Marriage Strategies and Oligarchy in Early Modern Bologna," in *Marriage in Premodern Europe: Italy and Beyond*, ed. Jacqueline Murray (Toronto" Centre for Reformation and Renaissance Studies, 2012), 239–56, gives an account of paternal management of children for one community; for which also see also Alessandro Pastore, "Rapporti familiari e pratica testamentaria nella Bologna del Seicento," *Studi storici* 25 (1984): 153–68.

The notion of alienable possessions comes from anthropologist Annette B. Weiner, *Inalienable Possessions: The Paradox of Keeping – While Giving* (Berkeley: University of California Press, 1992). A sparkling study of a succession of inventories and the various uses of a noble's property in our period is Barbara Furlotti, *A Renaissance Baron and His Possessions: Paolo Giordano I Orsini, Duke of Bracciano (1541–1585)* (Turnhout: Brepols, 2012).

On parallel problems with entails in the Anglo-American common law tradition, a recent and illuminating take is Claire Priest, "The End of Entail: Information, Institutions, and Slavery in the American Revolutionary Period," *Law and History Review* 33 (2015): 277–319. On the writings of *illuministi* on inheritance, Roberto Bonini, "Ancora sui fedecommessi nel Settecento illuminista," *Rivista di storia del diritto italiano* 71 (1998): 147–56. Also Marco Cavina, "Padre umanisti," in *Il Rinascimento giuridico in Francia: Diritti, politica e storia*, ed. Giovanni Rossi (Rome: Viella, 2008), 313–22.

The notion of an inheritance crisis is set forth by Philip Gavitt, *Gender, Honor, and Charity in Late Renaissance Florence* (Cambridge: Cambridge University

Press, 2011); R. Burr Litchfield, *Emergence of a Bureaucracy: The Florentine Patricians, 1530-1790* (Princeton: Princeton University Press, 1986). The role of women is traced by Maura Palazzi, "Work and Residence of Women Alone in the Context of a Patrilineal System (Eighteenth- and Nineteenth-Century Northern Italy)," in *Gender, Kinship, Power: A Comparative and Interdisciplinary History*, ed. Mary Jo Maynes, Ann Waltner, Brigitte Soland, and Ulrike Strasser (London and New York: Routledge, 1996), 215–30. In general, Giovanna Benadusi, "Social Relations," in *The Cambridge Companion to the Italian Renaissance*, ed. Michael Wyatt (Cambridge: Cambridge University Press, 2014), 338–63.

Caroline Castiglione's contributions are: "Accounting for Affection: Battles between Aristocratic Mothers and Sons in Eighteenth-Century Rome," *Journal of Family History* 25 (2000): 405–31; "Mater Litigans: Mothering Resistance in Early Eighteenth-Century Rome," *Historical Reflections* 35 (2009): 6–27; "When a Women Takes Charge: Marie-Anne de la Trémoille and the End of the Patrimony of the Dukes of Bracciano," *Viator* 39, no. 2 (2008): 363–80. These and other essays can now be found in her *Accounting for Affection: Mothering and Politics in Early Modern Rome* (New York and London: Palgrave Macmillan, 2015).

Roberto Bizzochi, "La dissoluzione di un clan familiare: i Buondelmonte di Firenze nei secoli xv e xvi," *Archivio storico italiano* 140 (9182): 3–45, discusses the decline of one Florentine lineage.

The position taken by Edward C. Banfield, *The Moral Basis of a Backward Society* (Glenoce: Free Press, 1958), has to be read against the criticisms of Frank Cancian, "The Southern Italian Peasant: World View and Political Behavior," *Anthropological Quarterly* 34 (1961): 1–18; Sydel Silverman, "Agricultural Organization, Social Structure, and Values in Italy: Amoral Familism Reconsidered," *American Anthropologist* 70 (1968): 1–20. Less inclined to accept the notion of amoral familism are J. Davis, "Morals and Backwardness," *Comparative Studies in Society and History* 12 (1970): 340–53; also William Muraskin, "The Moral Basis of a Backward Sociologist: Edward Banfield, the Italians, and the Italian Americans," *American Journal of Sociology* 79 (1974): 1484–96. Banfield's ideas were picked up by Robert D. Putnam, *Making Democracy Work: Civic Traditions in Modern Italy* (Princeton: Princeton University Press, 1993); but see also the essays in Nicholas A. Eckstein and Nicholas Terpstra, eds, *Sociability and Its Discontents: Civil Society, Social Capital, and their Alternatives in Late Medieval and Early Modern Europe* (Turnhout: Brepols, 2009). John Hooper, *The Italians* (New York: Viking Penguin, 2015), 182–85, also refers to Banfield. On the condoning of deceit in transactions, mainly by Guicciardini, see Thomas Kuehn, "Multorum Fraudibus Occurrere: Legislation and Jurisprudential Interpretation Concerning Fraud and Liability in Quattrocento Florence," *Studi senesi* 93 (1981): 309–50. The concluding comments about personhood rely on Janet Carsten, *After Kinship* (Cambridge: Cambridge University Press, 2004).

Index